Tipping Point

To Will,

Best wishes for the
New Year...

Helen
Michael

Tipping Point

Britain, Brexit and Security in the 2020s

**Michael Clarke and
Helen Ramscar**

I.B. TAURIS
LONDON • NEW YORK • OXFORD • NEW DELHI • SYDNEY

I.B. TAURIS
Bloomsbury Publishing Plc
50 Bedford Square, London, WC1B 3DP, UK
1385 Broadway, New York, NY 10018, USA

BLOOMSBURY, I.B. TAURIS and the I.B. Tauris logo are trademarks of
Bloomsbury Publishing Plc

First published in Great Britain 2020

Cover design by Adriana Brioso
Cover image © Hi-Story / Alamy Stock Photo

A catalogue record for this book is available from the British Library.

A catalogue record for this book is available from the Library of Congress.

ISBN: HB: 978-1-7883-1918-8
PB: 978-1-7883-1919-5
ePDF: 978-1-7883-1921-8
eBook: 978-1-7883-1920-1

Typeset by Deanta Global Publishing Services, Chennai
Printed and bound in Great Britain

To find out more about our authors and books visit www.bloomsbury.com and
sign up for our newsletters.

Contents

Illustrations

Figures

Tables

Introduction: The tipping point

Britain is living through troubled times both at home and abroad. The upbeat atmosphere of 2012 around the triumphantly successful London Olympics, Paralympics and the Queen's Diamond Jubilee reflected a core of pride in British society, how it welcomed visitors and presented itself to the rest of the world. There was an afterglow of optimism for Britain's commercially inventive, high-tech future. The country seemed fashionable and self-confident as it faced new challenges.[1] But the reality was that all this was little more than a brief upturn, a welcome blip, amid a series of trends that were actually moving in the opposite direction. Both the country itself and its international neighbourhood became objectively less confident and secure over the decade from 2010 to 2020. As it embarks on a new decade, few things look as if they will get much better.

Of course, the turn of a decade is always a time for reflection, even though the coincidence of years ending in round numbers and a sense of old and new trends is just that – a coincidence. But in the case of the 2020s there really does seem to be a coincidence of decades and trends. A number of international political trends are either coming to an end or rapidly being overlaid by more powerful forces – which amounts to much the same thing – and politics around the world displays more discontinuity than consistency. Political observers have lost their power to be surprised by the turn of events: the rise of autocracy in formerly democratic societies; the election of populist leaders who intend to break up domestic and international organizations; more than one who are openly committed to the street murder of criminals and opponents; the growing political power of the massive internet companies; and the election of President Trump in 2016 which presaged an attempt to make fundamental changes in the global role of the United States. In Britain, 2016 saw the Brexit vote, which represented the greatest strategic and economic change in the status of the country for well over half a century.

Indeed, shifts of this character have come to represent a 'new normal' in a way that often blinds us to the degree they actually change the political landscape.

Their sheer novelty entrances observers and it is often difficult to foresee how the deeper implications of sudden and dramatic changes will play out.

To rise above the novelty value of events and see them in strategic perspective, this book tries to examine Britain's security prospects for the coming decade by linking the legacies of the immediate past with the emerging trends of the future. They are not a naturally good fit. This suggests that some uncomfortably new thinking will be required if Britain's leaders are to navigate the country to a reasonably secure status in a decade that shows all the signs of being unpredictable and extremely turbulent. But the news is not all bad. It is our contention that Britain could come through the 2020s with renewed vigour and better prospects than for many a decade if it is able to analyse its security challenges clearly and mobilize all its diverse, hard and soft, obvious and less obvious, national resources effectively. Britain has some natural advantages and real strengths to confront its security challenges, but they must be mobilized consciously and incisively. And soon.

A tipping point is upon us in the coming three or four years. The Brexit process that comes to a head in that time certainly increases all the stakes and dramatizes some of the choices, but it did not create the tipping point. It has been increasingly clear over the last decade that the 2020s would, in any case, pose some completely new challenges to a country such as Britain; challenges that could not be addressed by mere continuity. Our contention is that the early 2020s will be a decisive test of political vision and leadership. The convergence of a number of longer-term trends will turn British security into something of a high wire act; but the Brexit process, in effect, whips away the safety net.

Legacies of the past decade

Notwithstanding the glorious summer of 2012, or Britain's inexhaustible fund of humour and irony, the country has suffered the political equivalent of a nervous breakdown in the decade just ending. There was a steadily growing sense of domestic political hiatus after 2008 and the onset of the global economic crisis. Thirteen years of Labour government came to a shuddering end in 2010 as the international banking crisis subsequently turned into a full-scale domestic recession. The country was becoming polarized and angry and after an indecisive election result it required a unique Conservative/Liberal Democratic coalition to form a working government. This Coalition took power as Western economies seemed to be teetering on the precipice of complete collapse. To their credit, the tail end of the Labour government and the beginning of the Coalition fended off the worst of the economic crisis though they could not much mitigate the long-term consequences of the recession that it created.

But the economic crisis had the effect of highlighting some deep-seated social and economic tensions that were not far below the surface of British politics.

In 2014, in the midst of the deepening recession, the country was threatened with the constitutional break-up of the United Kingdom. The General Election of 2010 had given the Scottish Nationalist Party (SNP) an almost clean sweep of Scotland's seats at Westminster. Prime Minister David Cameron tried to diffuse the nationalist tension with a Scottish independence referendum that came close (45 per cent to 55 per cent in the event) to giving the SNP a popular majority within Scotland for outright secession from the Union. Whichever way they go, secession referendums anywhere in the world have a record of leaving a legacy of bitterness and frequently also a sense of unfinished business. This one proved to be no exception. The General Election of 2015 unexpectedly gave David Cameron a slim but workable overall majority of twelve seats at Westminster. But the stabilizing effects of this were immediately negated in 2016 when Cameron again attempted to use a referendum to settle an insoluble issue – this time within his own party – with a national vote on Britain's continuing membership of the European Union (EU). On 23 June 2016 Britain took the historic decision, by a popular majority of 52 per cent to 48 per cent, to leave the EU after forty-six years of membership.

It was inevitable that such a momentous decision would create political turmoil, though few observers foresaw the extent to which predictable 'turmoil' would turn into an outright constitutional crisis and then a political nightmare by the turn of the decade. The turmoil began immediately. Having been defeated in his own referendum, David Cameron immediately resigned. In a chaotic scramble among senior Conservatives to replace him, Theresa May eventually emerged as prime minister, being the last one standing in a political cage-fight of notable acrimony. She became prime minister without a popular vote by her Conservative Party, still less by the wider British electorate.[2] Lacking normal electoral legitimacy, Theresa May had to navigate uncharted waters – no country of this size had ever left a trading bloc of the EU's size[3] – while also trying to hold together an increasingly divided cabinet and parliamentary party. In June 2017 she dashed into a snap election to try to give herself the personal legitimacy to carry the divisive Brexit policy through. It became known as 'the election that everybody lost' and the prime minister's gamble threw away even the small Conservative majority she had inherited. Now heading a minority Conservative government, Mrs May could only carry on by entering into an informal coalition with Northern Ireland's small Democratic Unionist Party (DUP). The critical process of negotiating Britain's exit from the EU increasingly became an exercise in internal party and parliamentary management.

Less than eighteen months later the turmoil had become a constitutional crisis. It was clear by the end of 2018 that the withdrawal deal the prime minister had negotiated with the EU was unacceptable, for different reasons, to all shades of parliamentary opinion. The European Union (Withdrawal) Act 2018 stated that Parliament must approve two documents negotiated between the government and the European Union; the Withdrawal Agreement and the Political Declaration setting out the framework for the future relationship between the EU and UK. Three issues became insoluble sticking points – the Northern Ireland border with Ireland, immigration into Britain from the EU, and the future relationship with the European customs union and the single European market. Mrs May leant towards a hard Brexit on all these issues, apparently to appease the small, intransigent Tory faction that had pressured Prime Minister Cameron into offering the referendum. But they withheld their support for her deal, largely on the Northern Ireland border question, while 'soft Brexiteers' withheld their support largely over the customs union and single market access. To her European counterparts Mrs May had become a lame duck prime minister; a leader who could not deliver on the deal she had negotiated and whose time in Downing Street was therefore running out. From the autumn of 2018 she was simply incapable of governing in the ways that genuinely mattered. In a three-year administration, Mrs May lost no fewer than forty-four ministers and members of her government – thirty-two of them in Brexit disagreements. Her deal was rejected three times in Parliament, deadlines for leaving the EU were missed; as a result, the country was required to hold European Parliamentary Elections she had said would never happen, and Conservatives – the party of government – came fifth with less than 9 per cent of the popular vote. In June 2019 Theresa May finally resigned the premiership and was replaced by Boris Johnson, who won a decisive majority among the 140,000 members of the Conservative Party who chose the next leader and therefore, in this case, also the prime minister.

The Johnson government immediately injected a sense of purpose into what had become a sclerotic Brexit process. To the many supporters of Boris Johnson in the country this seemed very welcome. But it did not change the underlying realities. He was leading a minority government, none of the three underlying issues were any nearer to resolution and the third deadline for leaving the EU – that Prime Minister Johnson had repeatedly pledged to respect, 'do or die' – was rapidly approaching. In reality, Prime Minister Johnson constituted his government to push through a 'no-deal Brexit' in the face of the EU's refusal to reopen the Withdrawal Agreement that it had already negotiated with the previous government. It was also constituted to fight a simultaneous, or else a very early, general election. In both respects, the Johnson government was locked into Britain's own domestic political hiatus more than in managing an inherently weak negotiating hand in relation to the EU. Committed to weathering a 'no-deal Brexit', in defiance of a parliamentary majority, the new government, in effect, embraced a full-scale constitutional crisis over 2019–20 whatever course of action Britain subsequently took. The stark fact was that in the three and a half years since the referendum decision, the Brexit conundrum had not only failed to produce *any* successful outcomes; it had also acted as the anvil on which the constitution and the British party system were taking a real hammering.

By the end of 2019, therefore, Brexit had become a political nightmare. As we will discuss in Chapter 8, it has turned into a new English civil war, in the sense that Brexit is *the* defining issue, especially among the English, of Britain's current politics. In June 2019 over 70 per cent of the British electorate judged Brexit to be the most important issue facing the country, going far beyond the economic or legal arguments made about it in political debate. It had come to represent something more visceral throughout British society. The country had gone through two bitter general elections, with another looming, and two equally bitter referendums in four years. The public was more angry, polarised and dangerously uncivil than at the onset of the 2008 economic crisis. And by 2019 it was abundantly clear that the Brexit majority of the 2016 referendum had been a vote simultaneously against both Brussels and Westminster. In the midst of a constitutional crisis neither of the two main parties knew how to react to this, or calm inflamed passions they themselves had helped stoke.

While the Conservative Party was characterized as having fallen prey to narrow English nationalism and succumbed to abusive bloodletting on Brexit issues, the Labour Party was engaged in a different civil war. Shifting dramatically leftwards after its defeat in 2010, and reacting against a decade of 'Blairism', the Labour Party began a struggle for the soul of twenty-first-century socialism after its defeat in 2015. All across Europe, the left seemed to lack any realistic answers to the stresses of globalization. New leadership in the Labour Party and a radical mass movement resurrected the Trotskyite 'New Left' that had been largely expelled from the party in the 1980s and now put it in full control of the Labour movement. Labour's defeat in the 2017 election – its third electoral defeat in a row – had a galvanizing effect on its internal battles. It was felt that this highly traditional, but now rebranded, Labour Party was tantalisingly near to electoral victory, given the collapse of unity within the Conservative government. Labour was just as deeply split on Brexit – 61 per cent of its MPs after the 2017 election found themselves representing constituencies that had voted to leave the EU. But its New Left leaders didn't regard Brexit as their main concern. They privately did not want to become the government before 2020 and were determined to saddle the Conservatives with all the blame for the Brexit mess. Then, they calculated, Labour might subsequently be elected with a thumping majority that would see them through maybe three terms of government over the 2020s when they could build their socialist response to globalization. For Labour's new leaders, Brexit was the means to a different end.

Both main parties, for different reasons, were split from top to bottom and demonstrated that they could neither handle the Brexit issue in itself, nor together drag the country out of a constitutional crisis that had hobbled the process of competent government. The attention of an exasperated electorate shifted to the other, minor parties of British politics. But Brexit had polarized them too. The Liberal Democratic Party had always and consistently opposed Brexit and though they were severely punished by the electorate in 2015 for their role in David Cameron's coalition government (as is usually the way for minor coalition partners in British politics) there were signs in 2019 of some resurgence in LibDem support on the basis of their consistency on this single issue. Other breakaway centrist groupings who opposed Brexit made no headway.

For both main parties, however, the truly disruptive political phenomenon of the decade was the United Kingdom Independence Party (UKIP). UKIP had successfully provoked the 2016 referendum by seriously threatening the unity of the Conservative Party and then taking votes away from Labour. But there seemed little future for it once the referendum had gone its way. It rapidly fell into ultra-right factionalism and became irrelevant to mainstream British politics. But the failure of the major parties to 'deliver Brexit' swung UKIP's original supporters – and now many others – behind a completely new Brexit Party created by Nigel Farage, a populist politician infinitely more suited to one-man-band politics than national consensus. His Brexit Party was launched just one month before the 2019 European Parliamentary Elections calling for a 'democratic revolution in British politics' in the face of a 'broken' two-party system. Capturing the febrile mood, his new party took first place in those elections with 35 per cent of the popular vote, pressing Britain to leave the EU at the end of October 2019 with or without an agreed deal.

Britain ended the decade facing another chaotic election and seriously divided over Brexit. Its main political parties had manifestly failed to rise to the challenge and were at war within themselves. Brexit and the Corbyn leadership of Labour had become intertwined national political logjams. The political centre ground was confused, and among the special interest parties, the DUP looked to preserve its own Northern Ireland interests as it helped keep the Conservative government ship afloat just long enough to limp towards the next election, and the SNP waited warily for the best opportunity to demand a second independence referendum that would break up the UK. Not surprisingly the Boris Johnson government suffered seven straight defeats in parliament that left his government effectively boxed in until there could be another election.

Britain's external security environment was scarcely better. Aside from the instabilities directly caused by the economic crisis itself, the decade from 2008 was marked by several contradictory security trends. In London, there was a determination to relinquish military commitments in the Middle East and South Asia. Both Labour and the Coalition government worked hard to withdraw from counter-insurgency wars in Iraq and Afghanistan – two operations that had started well enough but which had both descended into civil wars in which the allies' presence had become part of the problem. British leaders were resolved not to cut and run from these wars, but from 2007 they were certainly looking for opportunities to cut and walk from them, albeit in step with Washington. British combat forces withdrew from Iraq at the end of 2009 and from Afghanistan at the end of 2014.

But the desire to end foreign entanglements – domestically unpopular as they had become – was difficult to maintain and Britain flip-flopped in and out of a subsequent series of indecisive operations that left the public frankly confused over what Britain was trying to achieve. In 2011 Britain and France found themselves unexpectedly taking the lead in an air campaign over Libya to remove the regime of Colonel Gaddafi following his brutal behaviour against opposition forces. But in 2013 the government could not convince Parliament that it needed to join the United States in military intervention to deter the Assad regime in Syria from using chemical weapons just as brutally against *his* opposition forces. In 2014 the forces of the terror group 'Islamic State' (IS) thrust from their bases in Syria and moved deep into Iraq, even threatening Baghdad. In 2015 Britain joined a US-led coalition to bomb IS forces in Iraq, though not in Syria. In 2016 it belatedly extended this air war to Syria. In 2018 it joined the United States in launching deterrent air attacks into Syria following yet more uses of chemical weapons – on exactly the same rationale Parliament had rejected five years earlier. But by then Russian forces and Iranian intervention were actively propping up the Assad regime and Western military action was very tentative, given the risk of serious escalation. Western governments were effectively elbowed out of the politics of the Levant by a novel coalition between Russia, Iran and Turkey, who preferred to see the Assad regime survive, even at a brutal price.

British policy in South Asia and the Middle East was caught in cycles of inconsistency during the decade. Working through 'proxy forces' on the ground had become fashionable among Western powers, but they rapidly lost control over their clients. Britain had to keep, and then increase, a training mission in Afghanistan as US forces were drawn back towards the country. British air power was drawn into the sideshow of eliminating the IS 'Caliphate' in Iraq and Syria but was unable to stay out of the Syrian civil war proper; goaded by Assad's brutality against his own people into periodic military strikes, but not enough to reverse his grip over the country. Britain backed 'moderate Syrian opposition groups' who were actually not very 'moderate' and progressively losing to an Assad regime viciously revitalized with strong Russian air support. And over the border in Iraq it was helping train new Iraqi forces who subsequently turned against their Kurdish allies – who were also being trained by Britain. The reality of working through 'proxy forces' on the ground that had seemed so attractive after 2001, and then again after 2014, showed that it was frequently Western countries who were the proxies and leaders on the ground who were actually calling the shots.

In essence, clear strategic commitments made in 2001 and 2003 to wage expeditionary warfare alongside the United States had turned a decade later into little more than tactical military dabbling as US leadership faltered, the Levant began to melt down under the pressures of the 'Arab Uprising' and Afghanistan renewed its thirty-year civil war. The Western allies had never committed themselves deeply enough to cope with the underlying trends driving events in Afghanistan or Iraq. The result was that the real strategic beneficiaries from the

Afghan war of 2001–14 were India and China; and the real strategic beneficiary from the Iraq War of 2003–09 was the West's erstwhile adversary, Iran.

Over the twelve years following Tony Blair's retirement as prime minister in 2007, British leaders tried to put their Middle East and South Asia operations behind them. They looked, instead, for some retrenchment in foreign and security policy as the heaviest of their military involvements in Iraq and Afghanistan were wound up. But even as they tried to shake off the shadow of those two strategic failures and look forward, they were confronted by the prospect that the immediate neighbourhood in Europe and the Mediterranean was significantly more unsettled and could become potentially dangerous in the years ahead.

Far from retrenchment and a break from expensive and unpopular expeditionary warfare from which they could refocus their security thinking, British leaders at the end of the decade were faced with new security challenges nearer to home for which they were not well-prepared. Political consensus on common defence among the European democracies progressively weakened even as the security pressures from more aggressive Russian actions and the remorseless process of uncontrolled migration increased. Above all, the United States seemed to be undergoing a long-term political reorientation away from its traditional transatlantic roots – less instinctive in its support for European security and far more transactional, and conditional, in its approach towards its Western allies under successive Bush, Obama and Trump administrations.

If Britain was suffering a domestic nervous breakdown in 2019, the European Union, the Western military alliance and the wider 'transatlantic community' were scarcely better off in either economic or security spheres. Our subsequent analysis looks at this collective loss of confidence and political vitality in Britain's own neighbourhood as one of the key determinants of its security in the decade to come.

Such domestic and geopolitical problems are daunting enough. They may be regarded as the empirical challenges; those that are factually based and easy enough to identify, even if their solutions are not. Strong leadership in Western countries will evidently be required to navigate through such empirical challenges in the decade of the 2020s. But in a truly globalized world the security challenges go deeper than merely the geopolitical headlines.

Modern security challenges are also uniquely conceptual. What constitutes 'national security' for a country such as Britain in the era of globalization? More specifically, what is to be defended, and why? From the beginning of the twentieth century it was not difficult to appreciate what threatened British national security, in the wars and challenges of great power competition – fascism and bolshevism – and in the internal challenges to the British Empire. The twentieth-century world was certainly highly 'international', but it was not genuinely 'globalized' in the way it is now. That is a phenomenon only of the last thirty years, when production, distribution, communication and social cohesion has become so intensely networked across the world as to penetrate deeply into the highly advanced economies.

During the first two decades of this century the networked global economy put foreign owners in charge of most of Britain's water, energy and communications networks. London boomed under the pressure of foreign ownership of commercial and private property, as well as many iconic British trading names. The World Wide Web, which revolutionized the primitive internet, was invented in 1989 by a British scientist working at CERN in Geneva, but globalization put Chinese components and American software into most of the computers in use across the country, and algorithms originally devised in California drove the explosion in social media that the World Wide Web created. If the prospects of using military forces to fight outright war for the defence of Britain and its interests were obviously only a small part of the whole security picture – as seemed to be the case in the years immediately following the collapse of the Soviet Union – then what was vulnerable and what was to be defended in such a complex society?

The best answer the government offered during the 1990s was that Britain needed to protect something more abstract. It was defined as its 'way of life'; its ability to maintain personal freedom and national prosperity in a globalized world. In 2008 this was officially codified in a neat phrase that British security policy was designed to enable 'its people to go about their daily lives freely and with confidence'.[4] This was a perfectly good intellectual conception and it captured what Britain most wanted for its naturally inventive and commercial people. But it was not very helpful in defining just what national security was all about or where government money should best be spent; and it certainly looked strained in the darkening international climate after the 9/11 terror attacks on the United States.

It derived from the government's work to produce a formal 'National Risk Assessment' as the basis of a coherent, holistic approach to national security (of which 'defence' was only one part, albeit the most expensive) and it pursued this approach consistently across the next decade. It categorized three tiers of national security threat according to the likelihood and potential impact of different events and trends. It was a contentious list that went in and out of fashion among officials, but it highlighted how wide the spectrum of 'insecurity' can be for a modern European society in a globalized world. In this holistic conception, maintaining security runs from dealing with natural hazards, such as severe weather events, accidental disasters, or health pandemics, to protecting the critical national infrastructure from shortages or deliberate attack, dealing with the effects of international criminality and terrorism, confronting the dizzying prospects of cyberattacks on Britain, through fighting 'hybrid warfare', right across the spectrum to outright international conflict in defence of British interests or of the British homeland itself.[5] The government's new approach also defined a 'prosperity agenda' alongside the National Security Strategy, which was the more optimistic flipside of an essential truth that 'national security' also involves protecting and promoting the country's core economic interests. For all the flood of official documents over the last decade that have tried to spell out these various threats to national security, the essential conceptual challenge remains largely unresolved. Which aspects of our society are most important to us? In what ways might they be genuinely insecure, and how to defend them?

Britain is a more self-consciously globalized state than many of its partners. Its leaders promote a self-image that Britain embraces both the opportunities and the risks of operating in the fast-moving, ever-more networked world. Britain has shown itself to be good at playing the globalization game. With 0.8 per cent of the world's population, it nevertheless remains the fifth (by some calculations, sixth) largest economy in the world and constitutes almost 4 per cent of global GDP. It is overwhelmingly a service economy with high-end manufacturing centres. It is the tenth largest exporter of goods in the world and the third largest exporter of services. It accounts for around 3 to 4 per cent of all world trade. It hosts the biggest financial centre in the world; accounts for around 12 to 15 per cent of the world's creative industries and still publishes around 8 per cent of all the scientific papers in the world (and over 14 per cent of the most 'highly cited', according to the Royal Society). It attracts more inward investment within the OECD than any country other than the United States, and has almost 6 million of its citizens living and working abroad. Britain prides itself on being a successful multicultural society. Such favourable snapshots, however, pose two immediate questions. Do these snapshot statistics reveal robust and consistent trends or are they actually sliding downwards from higher levels that used to prevail? And if they do indicate a genuine and consistent picture, how secure can Britain be as such an open trading and investing nation? Potential vulnerabilities do not begin at the national border. For globalized world players like Britain vulnerabilities are deeply woven into the fabric of their economy and society.

This, in brief outline, is the political legacy that Britain takes into the 2020s; a mixture of empirical and conceptual national security challenges. The empirical challenges are all becoming more severe, and while recent governments have accepted the logic of the conceptual challenges, there is scant evidence that they are being vigorously addressed. Britain's political nervous breakdown has drained a great deal of confidence from the country as it faces whatever the 2020s will bring.

Facing the next decade

It is one of the great clichés of government reports and statements that the future is full of uncertainties. But the future is always uncertain, and political decisions normally appear fraught with imponderables until they are made. Why should the

2020s be more uncertain or fraught than previous decades appeared to those confronting them at the time?

In fact, there are very good reasons to believe that the 2020s will be uniquely unpredictable and difficult years for British security. The political nervous breakdown we have sketched, culminating first in the turmoil and then the nightmare of Brexit, is a huge impediment to clear strategic policy-making. Despite some optimistic political statements about the 'global Britain' that will arise from the Brexit process, remarkably little of any substance emerged from the policy machine to give real form to the slogan. The country cannot focus on the challenges of the 2020s until it knows what 'the Brexit outcome' will be – and that goes somewhere beyond the benighted withdrawal process itself.

In one sense, everything waits on the near-term outcomes of 2020. In the midst of a political and constitutional crisis, at the time of writing, an immediate tipping point is already upon us. Brexit created an increasingly serious political paralysis within Britain between 2016 and 2020, and both governance and the inner confidence in British democracy suffered as a result. Nevertheless, the sun still rises the day after the Brexit deadline, and life continues. The early weeks and months of 2020, however, are critical to the public's perception of Britain's future in the decade to come, with a national mood either of continuing crisis or of new directions. Whichever ways the mood tips, it will have more to do with key symbols of future relationships, such as the Irish border, traffic flows across the Channel or employment trends in high-profile economic sectors, than the long-term, underlying realities. And it was clear by the end of 2019 that all sides of the domestic argument, no less than EU leaders and officials, were out of genuinely new ideas to break the immediate deadlock and were already playing to history, to avoid the blame for what happened next, or the charge that they did nothing while events played out.

One strategic perspective is already a reality, however. Britain crossed a Rubicon in 2016, and it will not have the same relationship with its European partners in the coming decade however the Brexit process eventually ends. Even if Britain remained in the EU, it would not remain in the organization as the same sort of actor it was prior to 2016. It is impossible to believe that Britain would be anything other than politically semi-detached and still struggling with its own visceral identity crisis, even if it reversed its decision to leave the EU. And while the other twenty-seven members of the EU would certainly welcome such a reversal, European politics have moved on a long way since the organization was compelled to envision a future without one of Europe's 'big three' states. In short, Brexit has already imprinted itself on Britain's strategic future, even in the event that the process itself is interrupted or somehow reversed.

The Brexit legacy increases all the strategic stakes for Britain. It promises a white-knuckle ride that could oscillate between buccaneering diplomatic élan in a globalized, networked world and straight national isolation – caught between disinterested, preoccupied European partners and a Trumpist, disengaged United States. Britain is not currently in a good position to manage such a ride successfully. It does not have a well-balanced economic base to utilize all its resources and instruments of global influence effectively, and it seems to have lost the political consensus necessary to harness them to a settled vision of Britain in the world of the 2020s.

Not least, the Brexit legacy comes at the end of a decade where British policy-makers have been slow to appreciate how much the circumstances of the immediate post-Cold War world actually disguised underlying weaknesses in Britain's foreign and security position. The Cold War had played to Britain's natural strengths. It emphasized its long-standing closeness to the United States, and it demonstrated military prowess, intelligence capacities and Britain's well-respected diplomatic networks that had a tangible effect in reinforcing the Western consensus against the powers of Soviet communism. This was followed by a period of almost thirty years after the collapse of the Soviet Union when the Western world enjoyed high levels of absolute security and economic dominance. Western leaders could choose when and where, and how determinedly, to fight for what they regarded as essential security. This period – more than a generation – increasingly appears as an interregnum between the great alliance competitions of the Cold War and the great power competitions that are emerging for the 2020s. The bipolarity of the Cold War gave way, it has been said, to the 'unipolar moment' of US dominance.[6] The more relaxed circumstances of this historical moment allowed Britain, and other European partners, to exercise some discretion in security affairs and it almost certainly exaggerated their relative international power and influence. But the 'unipolar moment' was indeed no more than a moment in history and it has clearly passed. The world is faced instead with a multi-polar future that is being formed, as we write, from political, economic and social fragmentation, decentralized power and decision-making and all amid the intense pressures of globalization. There will be no return to the old multilateralism. Whatever emerges from this period may turn out to be multilateral, but if so, it will be a new multilateralism based on different international actors probably playing by somewhat different rules.

For the more immediate future, the 2020s looks set to demonstrate the renewed importance of absolute power, as exercised by those states that can claim it. The fact is that significant second rank players in the world, like Britain, now struggle to exercise their strategic choices in the diminishing space between the new great power competitions.

The 'Big Four' great powers of the twenty-first century are the United States, China, Russia and India; defined by size, economy, political importance, influence abroad and their potential to shape the world in ways that suit them. Other big powers are undoubtedly important; Saudi Arabia and Iran in the Middle East, Japan in East Asia, Turkey in the Middle East and Central Asia,

Nigeria in West Africa, Brazil in Latin America, and the significant European powers across their own region and the Mediterranean. But none of those powers have the global significance of the Big Four. The broad economics are compelling, such as the trajectories of their relative shares of global GDP. In 1990 as the 'unipolar moment' began, the Big Four accounted for 35 per cent of global GDP; by 2023 – even as the proportions readjust between them – they look set to account for 48 per cent, while the EU proportion of global GDP will almost have halved (Table 1).

The four great powers – the cooperation and conflict between them, and their ability to enlist allies and friends – create the geopolitical weather patterns that other countries and organizations have to live within. That is not surprising. In the last decade all four powers have striven to change their world power status relative to each other. The great geopolitical wheels of world politics have been turning faster and more remorselessly since 2010 and the lesser powers, for all their prosperity, technology and natural influence, have to adjust their own strategic outlook accordingly.

This analysis begins from the proposition that, after a difficult political decade that has ended in domestic chaos, British politics have been so focused on the domestic and institutional consequences of Brexit that they have obscured more important strategic issues. The Brexit vote has telescoped what would anyway have been a new decade of challenge to Britain's foreign and defence policies during the 2020s – where international affairs are not moving in their favour – into an immediate point of strategic inflexion for the future.

Table 1 Share of global GDP

	1990 (%)	2023 (%)
United States	22	13
China	4	21
Russia	5	4
India	4	10
European Union	27	15
*Britain**	*4*	*3*
Total of global GDP	62	63

Source: IMF Datamapper / Financial Times, 29 May 2018, using World Bank figures.
*Britain's figure is included in the EU figure but it is also listed separately here for comparison.

This is the tipping point: a moment of strategic choice that is on a par with the great free trade debates of the 1840s, attempts at the creation of new world orders in 1919 and 1945 or even with the stark and desperate choices faced by Britain in 1940.

Somewhere between now and 2023 or 2024 the main lines of Britain's security future for a long time to come will be determined, either by a series of conscious choices and shifts in national resources or else by the march of events, where political leaders will be slaves to new domestic and external pressures they barely understand, let alone influence. This book is accordingly structured around three essential questions: How should we interpret the structural and more immediate challenges to British security? How do the challenges of Brexit figure in that assessment? How do we judge the strengths and weaknesses in Britain's hand as it confronts the complex security demands of the next decade? Only by providing some answers to these questions will it be possible for British leaders to manage the tipping point that is almost upon us, and from which there can be no hiding and no turning back.

Britain's long-term challenges

Chapter 1
The geopolitical wheels

There is a curious phenomenon in current attitudes to world politics. By most empirical measures the world as a whole is becoming a better place; with dramatically less absolute poverty, better health care, higher life expectancy, more social mobility, diminishing deaths in war, lower financial inequality globally and so on.[1] But few observers see it this way and popular attitudes in Western societies assume that the world is becoming ever more dangerous; characterized by vicious wars and political fragmentation, human misery among victims and refugees, environmental stress and food insecurity, and threats that range from international criminality and terrorism to the possibility of major wars featuring the proliferation of more and terrible weapons.

In fact, both views are simultaneously true. As a whole, the human population, all 7.6 billion of us, live in far more favourable material circumstances than was the case in the twentieth century. Not least, since there are almost four times as many of us in 2020 as there were in 1920, the statistical chances of being among those unlucky enough to be caught up in wars, famine, disease or inescapable poverty are less than they were a century ago. Population has increased far more quickly than have casualties in war, for example. And in that time, there have also been dramatic advances in global technology, health and welfare. On the other hand, the world is far more disordered than it appeared to be in the latter half of the twentieth century. The constellation of political forces is undoubtedly changing. Individuals are more affected by things well beyond their own control or even that of their own governments. The conventional 'rules among the powerful' and the principles of international law that seemed to control the global system in the last century are under great pressure; new rising powers claim the rights to make new rules and international institutions are struggling to remain relevant. Violent conflict and war remain ever present and, most alarmingly, the prospects of future conflicts that might even rival some of those in the twentieth century, seem to be growing. The twenty-first-century world may be a better one than the twentieth in almost every material respect, but it is also more disordered, volatile and confusing.

More than most other powers in the world, Britain finds itself located at the centre of this paradox. It lives in a home that is prosperous within a peaceful continent. But the neighbourhood is going down and the wider world is changing. The paradox of two apparently contradictory trends that are simultaneously true is one that exercises the Western powers, and the Europeans, most of all. In the last ten years explicitly revisionist great powers have not only asserted themselves in Europe, the Middle East and East Asia, but also demonstrated that they are prepared to use, or threaten, major military force to pursue their objectives. The US response has been ambiguous and not reassuring in any of these regions.[2] It is Europe's conception of the global order, its existing prosperity and security, and European international rules which have organized it in the past that are under most pressure. That power of the European countries exercised over three centuries to shape the international rules, and passed to North America after 1945, is increasingly challenged by the growing disorder of the twenty-first century.

Turning geopolitical wheels among the four great powers

In defining the major geopolitical trends, it is important not to be seduced by short-term crises and the vacillations in policy within and between the great powers. Domestic instability, economic difficulties, elite power struggles and electoral earthquakes can all change the atmosphere of great power international relations. And history has a habit of demonstrating how small and immediate political events can suddenly become a trigger for much greater political change, for both good and bad. In reality, all countries zigzag their way through immediate challenges and in response to what they perceive in front of them. They nevertheless zigzag along some longer-term trend lines. Analysts can normally discern such underlying trend lines fairly clearly. But they normally struggle over the speed with which the powers will progress along those trend lines; given how much political leaders shift their policy positions as short-term surprises emerge; and the possibility that other longer-term trends might emerge more strongly or more quickly than expected.

Insofar as the four great powers and the relationships between them create the political weather for significant smaller countries such as Britain, the underlying trends are reasonably clear. The challenge for British policy-makers is therefore not so much to discern these trends but rather to anticipate how they might play out in the short to medium term (around five to fifteen years) and decide what they mean for Britain in the world.

The mega-trend for the 2020s that matters most to Britain is that US power is challenged more seriously than at any time since it emerged onto the global stage at the end of the First World War.[3] In particular, the single most important geopolitical mega-trend for the coming century will be the way the relationship between the United States and China plays out. There is a large element of truth in the glib observation that 'China goes global while the US goes home'. There may be some doubt as to whether the US is really in the process of 'going home', or how US policy for the 2020s can best be interpreted; however, there is no doubt that China is 'going global'. China's current 'rise to globalism' (in historical perspective, actually a 'return to globalism') is bigger, faster and more deliberate than that attributed to the United States after the 1940s.[4] In 2017 President Xi Jinping made it abundantly clear that China was thereafter ready to assume its (rightful) 'global role' and that it would project power accordingly.[5] Washington and Beijing both sent out contradictory signals about their intentions towards each other. The key geopolitical question is whether the direction of their bilateral relationship will tend towards a new accommodation – resetting a relationship that has become antagonistic on many fronts including trade, technology, espionage and military operations in the Pacific – or else emerge as a determined effort on Washington's part to limit or block the rise of China on the world stage. Certainly, President Donald Trump's intention was to reset the relationship in terms of a new strategic deal more favourable to the United States.[6]

Graham Allison has raised the spectre that US–China relations could be the subject of a twenty-first-century 'Thucydides trap'; whereby a rising and a declining global power are predetermined towards military conflict.[7] A new US–China Cold War could be starting that would not favour the United States in the way of the old US-Soviet Cold War.[8] Henry Kissinger did not necessarily disagree with this but posited that Washington and Beijing needed to explore a move beyond mere balance of power politics – the active coexistence he himself had facilitated with China in the 1970s – to a genuine twenty-first-century partnership; not just an accommodation of different interests, but a close identity of key interests.[9] If Washington and Beijing genuinely agreed on how global politics should best be organized, that compact would surely shape the world for everyone else. Robert Kaplan defined their bilateral competition within a 'new medievalism'; taking place in a more fluid and less organized world that mirrors many of the conditions of medieval Europe, but which is nonetheless intensely competitive.[10] As Europe declines in relative terms, argues Kaplan, 'Eurasia' will cohere as a region and a renewed arena of great power competition. The United States, already rethinking its commitments in Pacific Asia, may or may not take up the challenge of competing with China for influence across Eurasia.[11] Either way, European middle-rank powers will struggle to maintain their own freedom of action within a new US–China nexus. Whatever form it takes, there is little disagreement that Washington's relations with Beijing constitute the most critical bilateral relationship in world politics over the coming decades.

This key bilateral relationship is part of a network of relations that also involves Russia and India, not in an explicit 'four power system' but more as a constellation of 'intensive bilateralism' between them that cuts across all their relations. Russia has important strategic relationships with both China and India, and for the last decade it has also pursued a deepening antagonism with the United States and most of the European powers.

Russia is a big, important and special power in global politics; but it is weakening in a strategic sense.[12] With plentiful natural resources, a population of 144 million, continental space across Europe, Asia and the Arctic, a powerful culture and great social cohesion, Russia's economy is nevertheless considerably smaller than that of Britain.[13] It is cash rich, at least when oil and gas prices are high, but investment-poor in general, since global companies don't trust its commercial environment or its rule of law. Its nuclear forces, some of its air forces and its submarine forces are highly capable, but most of its naval power is patchy, at best, and its million-strong army is repeatedly being restructured and modernized from its moribund state in the 1990s. Corruption at all levels and the economic autocracy around President Putin, and the oligarchs who control Russia, systematically frustrate all attempts at reform in most sectors of Russian society.

The world of the 2020s seems not to be moving in Russia's favour. China progressively displaces the influence it formerly had in central Asia when the Soviet Union included so many of these territories. Western powers did not welcome it into a new society of post-communist nations and its soft power influence in the rest of the world is low. For all its intrinsic strengths, Russia is relatively isolated in world politics. From its pre-eminence as the heart of the communist Soviet Union that so influenced the twentieth century, Russia faces being the least significant of the four great powers, eventually to be overtaken by India as a source of global influence. In Michael Burleigh's words, Russia is a 'decayed, resentful nation' though its challenge to Western powers should be handled no less carefully for all that.[14]

Perhaps because of the very fact that time is not on Russia's side, President Putin's leadership became increasingly autocratic in domestic politics and assertive in international relations. If it is weakening in the long term, Russia has nevertheless shown itself prepared to act aggressively and to take risks in the short term where it sees key interests at stake. The atmosphere changed dramatically after the short war between Russia and Georgia in 2008; and the Ukraine crisis of 2013–14 became a turning point. As he justified the annexation of Crimea in 2014, President Putin made it very clear that the dissolution of the old Soviet Union had been 'an outrageous historical injustice' at a time when it was 'incapable of protecting its interests'.[15] Russia would henceforth try to recover its power and influence over the territories it formerly controlled and push back against the Western powers that he believed were determined to keep Russia weak. He adopted an unambiguous revisionist position in relation to Europe and the Western world.

So, while Russia loses power both to China and India in the coming decade, its antagonism towards the United States and the West is likely to continue; assertive in Middle East politics, seeking also to displace Western influence in the Mediterranean and parts of Africa. Most significantly, Russia aims to create a permissive political environment in Western Europe and within the US political establishment so that its long-term recovery of some power and influence in Eastern and Central Europe cannot effectively be opposed. It is an opportunistic policy that seeks to exploit the growing fissures in Western consensus wherever possible and create new ones where it can – though this is based on real strategic weakness as much as President Putin's own tactical cunning.[16]

Russia can try to imitate US military power, as the old Soviet Union did, and match it in some limited respects. And Russia can work with some of the erstwhile adversaries of the United States in the Middle East, Asia and Africa to frustrate US policy in many ways. But the Washington–Moscow relationship no longer sets the tone for other relations between the Big Four. The United States explicitly scales its strategy and its military plans against what it thinks China will achieve in the 2020s.[17] For US leaders, Russia's revisionist challenge is not trivial but nor is it central to their strategic thinking. If they can deal with China's re-emergence as a global power, they reason, they will also have the capacity to contain Russian revisionism. This is not so comforting to the Europeans, however, who are unsure how US strategic priorities would operate in practice and who are not in good shape to resist short-term Russian pressures on their own.[18]

India, meanwhile, became a more proactive global power after 2014 than for many previous years under the assertive leadership of Narendra Modi leading the nationalist Bharatiya Janata Party (BJP).[19] In May 2019 Modi led his BJP to a landslide election victory that he claimed would create a 'new India'; it had 'stunned the world' he said, and the 2022 celebration of India's 75th anniversary would be 'a golden opportunity to take India to new heights'.[20] India will have the biggest national population in the world – with 1.3 billion in 2017 it will soon overtake China's 1.4 billion – and from a low base, it is the fastest growing large economy in the world; around 7 per cent annually. This is larger than China's official growth figure, which is probably overestimated. This does not make it a rich country, of course. India struggles to realize the full economic and political potential it undoubtedly possesses.[21] Its GDP per head of population is only about 40 per cent of China's level and 12 per cent of that in the United States. Its natural 'emergence' seems always to be just on the next horizon, always undermined by its aged infrastructure, a corrupt governmental grip on the economy, patchy globalization, and a lack of social and political cohesion to make the most of its economic and strategic opportunities. Nevertheless, India is on course to reach GDP per head levels that are comparable with China's by 2030. Its size makes India a paradox in terms of political power. In a decade, it is said, 'India would still be a relatively poor country, as China is now. But it would be a superpower'.[22]

India is emerging from two leadership generations where it opposed most of the mechanisms of the existing international system on the grounds that they were inherently pro-Western and discriminatory and where it had tried hard to lead the developing world along alternative paths. This worked more at the rhetorical than the practical level, however, and India's effective role in world politics was smaller than its size might have warranted. Attitudes towards new forms of global governance changed as the impacts of globalization began to be felt and the Western world suffered a loss of confidence and power with the 2008 economic crisis. Indian leaders became more proactive and interested in shaping global trends by cooperating more closely with traditional mechanisms and power structures.[23]

More than that, however, the rapid emergence of China to an explicitly global role has had the effect of galvanizing strategic thinking within New Delhi. China has, in effect, provoked this large, potentially wealthy and under-performing country to become a more significant global player.[24] China and India both fear that the other is intent on surrounding them to limit their freedom of action. China particularly fears Indian influence around its troubled north western lands that include Xinjiang and Tibet, in addition to its borders with Nepal, Bhutan and Burma. India fears China's naval and port facilities across the Indian Ocean – its 'string of pearls' bases – that include a growing presence in Sri Lanka and also in East Africa.

One of the most game-changing developments in great power politics over the last decade is the creation of China's 'Belt and Road Initiative' (BRI). Launched in 2013 with close on $1 trillion in a first round of foreign loans and investment, the BRI is set to become a geopolitical force across most of Asia and significant parts of Africa, if it is even partially successful.[25] Some $6 trillion is expected to be spent on BRI infrastructure projects between 2020 and 2040. It sweeps up many existing schemes and initiatives and re-packages them with renewed drive and cash. The BRI represents nothing less than a 'Eurasian pivot' for China, aiming to create multiple infrastructure and connectivity projects to facilitate trade and commercial cooperation. In practical terms, it covers oil and gas projects to help secure China's energy needs; connectivity, in creating rail, road and seaport links going west and south west; trade and business stimulation, through the creation of 'special economic zones'; and joint ventures in manufacturing and production in high growth sectors.[26]

For many observers, the BRI is a debt for equity trap. A tiny country such as Djibouti owes China the equivalent of 80 per cent of its GDP. A major country such as Pakistan owes it over $10 billion – around 4 per cent of its GDP. Sri

Lanka defaulted on its Chinese debts and as a consequence, the strategic port of Hambantota is Chinese-owned. In Greece, the port of Piraeus is owned by the Chinese state company COSCO, and Hungary, Poland, Portugal and Italy have all entered into debt or investment relations with the BRI. Nevertheless, the BRI grandly expresses China's historic view of the world. Its domestic economy needs to expand, and it has an Asiatic destiny that is quite distinct from its future in the Pacific. In Beijing's view, there is a bigger and longer game to play than mere economic competition with the United States. As envisaged in 2019, the BRI involves some sixty-eight countries, accounting for 65 per cent of global population and 40 per cent of global GDP. In this conception, three economic hubs are particularly significant for Beijing. Kazakhstan becomes a key Chinese gateway to Europe; Pakistan the key gateway to the Indian Ocean; and Djibouti, the gateway into eastern and central Africa.[27]

By 2018 a pushback against some of these grand ambitions had already begun along parts of the six land corridors of the BRI. Trade by Asiatic land routes is much more expensive (as well as more bureaucratic and corrupted) than trade by sea. The new silk road will not be a one-way or inevitable process and pushing on too hastily creates some real opposition. The November 2018 bombing of the Chinese Consulate in Karachi and the May 2019 bombing of the Zaver Pearl-Continental Hotel at Gwadar are cases in point. The Balochistan Liberation Army that claimed responsibility for both attacks considers Chinese and foreign investment in the areas as a form of colonization.[28] But it will be a feature of the geopolitical landscape well into the 2020s and beyond. For India, in particular, the BRI creates the prospect of Pakistan, Afghanistan and Sri Lanka becoming deeply connected to, and dependent on, China; of Chinese military presence as far west as Gwadar, in Djibouti at the entrance to the Gulf, and of a network of Chinese trading relationships that could adversely affect India's traditional markets as it seeks to reach the next horizon in its emergence as a twenty-first-century global power.[29]

India and China have been military adversaries since their war in 1962 and border fighting in 1967. They have always watched each other warily across the Himalayan borders. But China's growing navy and the BRI has made their military competition genuinely geopolitical – in the sense that it covers all other aspects of the Sino-Indian relationship and turns it into an outright competition for influence across the Asian region, the Indian Ocean and within the institutions of world politics that enshrine the rules of the system.

These are the main outlines of the megatrends between the great powers – the turning geopolitical wheels – within which Britain's international security future will lie. All four of the great powers have different agendas and are all 'emergent' in their own way; a new attitude in the US to global institutions and emerging bellicosity over what it now most fears after the Cold War; a new assertiveness from a weakened Russia as it pushes against unfavourable global conditions; the quicker emergence of India as a global player as it feels provoked by its giant neighbour; and the undoubted story for the 2020s – the first full and explicit phase of China's return to great power status in world politics and economics.

The last decade has witnessed the evident growth of more intense geopolitical competition between these four great powers. That is not surprising. But all four have also shown that they prefer to deal with each other, and with the rest of the world, bilaterally rather than collectively.[30] The world has evidently entered a period of great power bilateralism that seems almost certain to intensify in the years ahead. And that matters greatly to everyone else in the world, and not least to Britain.

New trends in military confrontation and warfare

In pursuing their bilateral, geopolitical competitions, the four great powers compete in many different ways, using economic, diplomatic, and institutional means to try to shape their world in ways most favourable to them. These means shade into the military and security spheres at many points. It is possible to discern both traditional and non-traditional ways in which military security is developing apace between them and how far the conditions of modern globalization blur all the boundaries between one area of national policy and another.

The great powers certainly compete in traditional military ways by building up extensive military forces that effectively dwarf those of the second rank powers. Patterns of military expenditure tell part of the story. But the relative sizes of their respective military establishments also reveal other differences in scale. In essence, there has been a return to the big battalions in great power military affairs after the era that was characterized mainly by peace-keeping and stabilization operations, some successful and others turning into altogether bigger military commitments.

Preparations to fight traditional all-out wars became more prevalent after 2010, as all the Big Four invested heavily in new military assets they felt most relevant to their future strategies – nuclear and air power in the case of Russia; land power in India, air and naval power in China, and across the board investments in the US military. And while military expenditures have risen sharply in Russia, across Asia and in the US, they have either fallen or risen very little in Europe.

Their preparations for traditional wars do not mean that the Big Four necessarily expect to fight them. Their military postures take more subtle forms. China and Russia cannot compete across the board with the US. But they can compete in some areas, such as nuclear and air power. More importantly, they pursue

Table 2 Proportions of global military expenditure of the Big Four and the next six biggest military spenders

United States	35%	Saudi Arabia	4%
China	13%	France	3.3%
Russia	4%	Britain	2.7%
India	4%	Japan	2.6%
		Germany	2.5%
		South Korea	2.3%
Total	56%	Total	17.4%

Source: Stockholm International Peace Research Institute, Yearbook, Stockholm, SIPRI/ Oxford University Press, 2017.

Table 3 Number of active military personnel in the Big Four and the next six biggest military spenders

United States	1,347,000	Saudi Arabia	227,000
China	2,183,000	France	203,000
Russia	1,013,000	Britain	152,000
India	1,395,000	Japan	247,000
		Germany	177,000
		South Korea	630,000
Total	5,938,000	Total	1,636,000

Source: International Institute of Strategic Studies, The Military Balance, London, IISS, 2017.

'anti access/area denial' (A2AD) strategies to neutralize US military dominance by making certain areas such as Northwest Europe, northern Syria, the Black Sea, or the East and South China Seas too dangerous for US forces to operate easily. They use their best war-fighting capabilities to compete directly with the US for lesser geopolitical objects than victory in war. The US is correspondingly determined to prevent such constraints becoming a norm for the 2020s. India, meanwhile, focuses its military preparations on A2AD in relation to China but also on the possibility of outright war – even nuclear war – with its erstwhile adversary Pakistan. It is in the nature of active geopolitical competition that powers must scale their military capabilities for general war, not simply to try to deter it, but actually to achieve many lesser political objectives by demonstrating their military prowess.

The second rank military powers of Europe try to keep up with this return to major war-fighting capabilities by maintaining world-class forces with some of the best equipment available. But their personnel and equipment numbers are low in absolute terms, they are less able to operate a virtual monopoly of the best equipment in the world as sophisticated military technologies become more diffused, and most of them have less than full-spectrum forces – able to do a little of everything. Their small forces are, at best, unbalanced, even though they generally anticipate acting collectively.

More to the point, Russia and China, along with some of their smaller allies in Asia, south Eastern Europe and the Middle East, effectively weaponized a range of other instruments of influence in their geopolitical competition. Western analysts described the growth of 'hybrid warfare' as a means of military and pseudo-military competition that could be used in surprisingly impactful ways. Hybrid warfare campaigns might simultaneously use a wide range of instruments, including full-blooded campaigns of distorted information, social media offensives to sow discord in a targeted society, cyberattacks to create confusion, the use of terrorist groups, local militias or irregular troops as proxy fighters, and sometimes also regular troops in formed units but operating clandestinely and out of uniform (an illegal practice in international law). Other than the use of social media and cyberattack, there is nothing conceptually new in such hybrid warfare.[31] In the past it was simply called 'subversion'. But Western powers have not had to deal with it since the height of the Cold War and the astonishing power of cyberspace and social media has added real punch to these renewed techniques of subversion. Western powers saw them emerging even in the Balkans and the Baltic states during the 1990s, but then saw more coordinated hybrid campaigns of military/civil subversion in the Russian war with Georgia in 2008, throughout the Ukraine crisis that began in 2013, and then in the civil war in Syria after Russian intervention in 2015. China and its ally, North Korea, used the general techniques more subtly both in pursuing big intelligence offensives and in disruptive cyberattacks. In response, the United States and its allies feel compelled to both counter and compete with the growth of hybrid warfare. The West, after all, can do everything their adversaries can do, but as liberal democracies they struggle to coordinate – legally – so many disparate political and social responses.

The weaponization of so much human information and new civil technologies that were not previously regarded as matters of national security has taken modern warfare in new directions. Most discussed are the prospects of cyber capabilities being used decisively in future conflicts. An all-out 'cyber-war' is difficult to imagine – where cyberattacks make living intolerable to the point where a society capitulates to the pressure.[32] Nevertheless, Western defence planners became alarmed at how vulnerable their own critical national infrastructures (CNIs) had become with the intrinsic digitization of all industrial control systems.[33] Public utilities, transport, communication links, health provision and government data in most countries have been protected by obsolete cyber security for many years and they became networked in ways their own designers no longer understood. Attacks on a country's CNI, if not an explicit act of war, could nevertheless be a very effective component of a broader war-fighting campaign happening elsewhere or in another domain.

If 'cyber wars' as such seem unlikely, high levels of 'cyber insecurity' are well-accepted in all modern societies.[34] North Korea is widely believed to have sponsored criminal hackers using the 'WannaCry' virus. And in 2018 the British government named Russia as the country behind the crippling 'NotPetya' cyberattack. Western intelligence forces are widely believed to have successfully cyber attacked Iran's nuclear centrifuge programme over a number of years using the two versions of the 'Stuxnet' virus, slowing Iran's nuclear programme very considerably.

More unpredictable than all this, however, are the prospects of radical new innovations in many existing technologies changing the whole balance of effectiveness between modern military forces. The big military powers have invested a great deal of research in robotics, the application of artificial intelligence, and in supercomputers to give them new military capabilities. All of these elements will begin to mature as they are applied during the 2020s.[35] But current research already goes a great deal further. Novel technologies might create new forms of warfare that could conceivably invalidate many traditional forms of battle; the raw destructive power of big weapons, the pervasive influence of troops to occupy territory, the battle-winning powers of control of the air or low earth orbits, or the advantages of good intelligence, command and control.

The weaponization of such technologies may not be far away – certainly within the lifespan of many major weapons platforms now entering service among the second rank powers. The prospect that current generations of troops could be massively augmented by robotics, artificial intelligence and nanotechnologies is impressive enough; but it is overshadowed by the thought that future generations of troops might be augmented as individuals by physical and cognitive prosthetics, or even be genetically engineered to have particular intellectual or war-fighting advantages bred into them.[36] The prospect that current weapons could be made far more accurate to reduce collateral death and damage is overshadowed by the thought that future weapons might be programmed to create new pathogenic characteristics to affect certain genetic groups in a population, or to change the genetic makeup of agriculture or livestock.[37] The prospect that the 'computing' element in modern battlefield management puts great power in the hands of sophisticated military establishments is overshadowed by the thought that if and when quantum computing really arrives it may smash all the secure encryption that existing computers can devise and open up every existing computing system.[38] Super-computing, let alone quantum computing, raises the spectre of binding together combinations of novel technologies that could link genetics, biotechnology, artificial intelligence, or nanotechnologies to create types of warfare that are largely beyond our imaginings.

The only near-certainty is that to the extent that such novel technologies are capable of being weaponized, it will take place in the US and China, probably in Russia too, and perhaps in some specialized sectors also in India. If the essential characteristics of warfare are on the cusp of major change, they will be driven by at least three of the Big Four military powers. And the second rank powers, such as those in Europe, have come to realize that in future they may have to compete on all fronts simultaneously. They already have to be prepared to back up any use of their military capabilities with cyber security, domestic security against crime, subversion or terrorism and a complex information campaign to maintain political coherence. The 'security spectrum' is so much wider than it was even a decade ago. But within the coming decade they will probably also have to add protection against the aggressive application of artificial intelligence and robotic devices, the proactive protection of critical national infrastructure, guarding against social media campaigns which might suddenly undermine the psychological will of the population, or even their physical ability to carry on against genetically-targeted micro-biological attack. The permutations are endless and the necessary preparations can be no more than sketchy.

In a world where the geopolitical wheels between the Big Four powers are again turning so relentlessly, the second rank military powers all face daunting national security challenges. In the fifteen- to twenty-year interregnum after the end of the Cold War the second rank military powers assumed they had ample time to restructure and modernize their military forces. They assumed they could still compete for military influence among the security interests of the Big Four. Modernizing their military forces would be a process of twenty or more years as sophisticated new equipment was brought on stream. But the suspicion grows that the fourth industrial revolution may have begun to undermine such equipment cycles with new, disruptive technologies. In the 2020s, even the modernized forces of the second rank powers face the danger of progressive marginalization – because their national security tasks are now so much wider, because they are so much smaller than the big players, and because they are increasingly left behind in another revolution that rapidly weaponizes new technologies and new applications of old technologies.

The European security consensus

Set against these global trends, the security consensus across Europe has changed drastically since the 1990s and is not well placed to confront the likely challenges we have outlined above. There were transatlantic rows aplenty during the Cold War and many differences and disagreements between the European allies who naturally saw security challenges through their own national lens. But rows were usually followed by reconciliations as countries accepted the greater imperatives of their common defence. The basic security consensus was largely self-correcting. Over the last two decades, however, a weakening security consensus has worked in more cumulative ways; one disagreement feeds another and repeated efforts to re-establish strong political consensus have not matched the momentum of more divergent underlying trends.[39]

In that time, NATO enlarged itself from sixteen members to twenty-nine, adding responsibilities and extending its essential 'Article 5' security guarantee to others, while few of the new members provided meaningful additional military strength.[40] NATO's core military power is much less than when it was half its present size. And over the same years the European Union made a number of efforts to take on greater security roles. These were not necessarily unsuccessful but proved to be limited to military constabulary roles and peace support operations; useful but not capable of being strategically decisive – and all pitched, even at their absolute maximum, at least one military level below that required for effective war fighting.[41]

With its central organization and vital Atlantic link that unites the US, Canada, Iceland and Greenland with European nations as far south and east as Turkey, NATO still remains the world's most impressive standing military alliance. Meanwhile the EU demonstrates a consistent ambition to become a more effective focus for security cooperation among its own members.[42] These may be regarded as inherent security strengths. But NATO and the EU are multinational organizations, so their national members can together only provide one set of European armed forces, only one layer of physical infrastructure to support them and move them around a heavily populated continent, only one complex of industry, research and development to keep them up to date. And the simple fact is that for all the modernity of European armed forces, they have become predominantly 'hollow' in the last two decades – there on paper but at very low readiness, not operating together enough, lacking sufficient transport and in a continent where even moving military forces around NATO's home territories is significantly more difficult than it was 20 years ago.

This represents the sharp end of a perfect storm that has been brewing for European security since the economic crisis of 2008. Russian objectives since the 2008 war with Georgia have explicitly been to neutralize Western influence over ex-Soviet states and friends, to lessen the reality of US defence commitments to Europe and to create a passive political climate in Europe in the face of security challenges.[43] NATO states are openly divided about how seriously to take this challenge. After 2013 NATO's internal cohesion was severely strained by a different security agenda among its northern members who worry more about Russian bellicosity, as opposed to those members in the south, whose preoccupation was increasing flows of refugees across the Mediterranean and south Eastern Europe. Meanwhile, NATO faced the near defection of Turkey from the alliance, as Ankara worked with Russia and Iran against Western policy in the Middle East.[44] Important NATO summits in 2014, 2016 and 2018 made renewed commitments to collective and effective action in all three domains, but the underlying trajectory remained one of allied disharmony.[45]

During the same years the European Union apparently passed the high-watermark of its integration and political convergence marked by the Lisbon Treaty of December 2007. The decade of economic crisis that began immediately afterwards exposed big structural problems in the Eurozone, which were mitigated but not rectified in the following decade and helped stimulate waves of populist discontent that took both ultra-left- and ultra-right-wing forms, creating crises of governance in many EU countries.[46] In 2018 six EU states featured populist 'ultra' parties already in government. Across the EU there were eleven such parties who had achieved upwards of 20 per cent in popular support and who were therefore set to be long-term features of their national politics.[47] Their popularity will rise and fall with successive elections, but there is little doubt that extremist parties have become part of the European political fabric for the foreseeable future.

The European migration crisis turned from being driven by the immediate effects of wars in Afghanistan and the Middle East to something more evidently structural. Population growth in Africa finally began to increase significantly above the global average, in a continent characterized by instability and under-development.[48] Long-term pressures of uncontrolled migration northwards are likely to increase, while Europe's Mediterranean borders cannot be policed in the way that land borders can. The population of continental Europe is ageing and shrinking and European labour markets, hungry for workers, have a poor record in integrating unskilled migrant labour. For many observers, the challenge of migration (and integration) has rapidly become the political acid test for the EU as a whole. If the EU cannot create a viable process to deal with such pressures, they believe, its members will retreat into national solutions, driven by extremist politics, that will fatally undermine free labour movement, the single market, and hence the grand aspirations of the Lisbon Treaty. The political attractions of the EU's 'empire of virtue' seem to be diminishing.[49] This increasingly presents the organization with a sharp long-term geopolitical choice; re-consolidate and further integrate around a new Franco-German axis, possibly in a 'variable geometry' model; or else accept that the EU would dilute itself across twenty-seven or more economies that were no longer naturally converging.[50] Britain's 2016 Brexit referendum vote to leave the EU occurred in the middle of this hiatus, and partly as a result of it.

Not least, the reassessment within the United States of its role in the world, a reassessment that had been going on consistently from the 1990s, became more urgent after the multiple crises of the years around 2008 – notwithstanding President Barack Obama's attempts to 'reset' many relationships. The 'America First' slogan of President Trump was not so much a break with the past as a spike in a longer-term trend that can be traced back at least to the early Clinton Administration in 1993. Even after the stunning victory to liberate Kuwait in 1991 the US immediately backed away from the commitments that would be required if the lazy rhetoric that then emerged of a 'new world order' were to be honoured. It would not tolerate US casualties in battle and wanted others to do much more. The 9/11 attacks ended the sensitivity to casualties, but the US was thereafter in a different mood. It was clear during the Iraq crisis of 2002 that the US certainly welcomed allies to its side but did not need them. Secretary of Defence Donald Rumsfeld was happy with 'workarounds' if public opposition in Britain prevented it joining the US.

President Obama's attempt to re-orientate US security policy towards Asia and the Pacific after 2008 was largely unsuccessful as the US was dragged back to Middle East conflicts and Russian actions in Europe, but the underlying intention was clear. President Trump exploited a mood that was sceptical of the Europeans and increasingly worried about China, but he did not create it. In 2018 the Pentagon spoke frequently about the role of alliances in the Trump administration's security policy, but its essential orientation was towards unilateral power and action.[51] President Trump crystallized something that had been happening for a long time. There is a world of difference between a superpower who convenes and leads a group of liberal democracies, and one that invites them to join in courses of action it will take regardless – 'America First' as 'America alone'.

The perfect storm of European security is therefore both institutional and national. NATO is faced with a critical dichotomy between its northern and southern security agendas and struggles to upgrade its military capacity to provide some reassurance against growing Russian bellicosity and pressure on its eastern members. The EU finds its integrationist progress stalled by the global economic crisis, the unreformed Eurozone, and the structural challenge posed by uncontrolled migration into and within the EU area. Meanwhile, national politics within European countries are increasingly polarized as ultra parties and movements drive wedges into mainstream national politics. The economic recovery from the 2008 crisis was tepid and patchy across Europe and arrived too late to prevent fragmentation and social resentment arising in most societies. Authoritarian governments in Eastern Europe strengthened while more democratic governments in Western Europe weakened in the face of fractured and polarized electorates. As the political power of Germany's Angela Merkel declined, so the focus for any significant European political leadership diminished with it. Healthy European security has normally depended on a combination of two or three leaders from the big four European countries – German, France, Britain and Italy – being strong personalities, politically strong at home, who agreed with each other on future security policy. By the end of the decade none of these circumstances existed and European security would have to await a new generation of national leaders who might fulfil such conditions.

The United States took full note of this lack of collective leadership. And whatever short-term responses the US offers to immediate crises and problems around Europe and the Middle East, it is difficult to avoid the conclusion that its long-term commitment to European security interests is now strictly conditional.

For many years after the Second World War European politicians and their publics could face the problems of a continent liberated from the spectre of fascism and then from the dead hand of communism with a sense that Europe was now somehow irreversibly prosperous and essentially secure. However difficult immediate challenges were, they could be addressed in the confidence that prosperity and security would always be increasing, even if sometimes only slowly. That confidence is less well-founded these days. Instead of being a simple fact of modern European life, its growing prosperity and security begins to look like the result of an untypically favourable period where the early growth of globalization coincided with the lack of external challenges to European and Western policy.[52] What seemed like the 'new normal' may have been a lucky and temporary break after the 1980s. Certainly, Europe is living in a far more dangerous and volatile neighbourhood, it is less consensual in its view either of what it represents or what it should try to safeguard. It has become a troubled neighbourhood and neither continuous prosperity nor essential stability can be taken for granted.

Chapter 2

The global economic turmoil

The security of any society is intimately linked to its economic health. That is no less true of Britain than any other country. If it lives in a troubled neighbourhood, where the geopolitical wheels are remorselessly turning, it is also having to make its way in a wider economic environment that is in a state of structural transition. These two dimensions of global change are closely connected and they will make the 2020s a tricky decade through which Britain must negotiate a path. We will consider some of the domestic effects of this economic transition in the next chapter, but it is important first to describe just how profoundly the global economic environment has changed from the days when Britain felt well protected and intrinsically part of a well-functioning and prosperous economic system. The news is not all bad for Britain. The economic underpinnings of its security are not necessarily diminishing, but they are most assuredly changing.

The last decade has been characterized by an ongoing global economic crisis. What has become known as 'the global financial crisis' of 2008–11, was followed immediately by the resulting 'great recession' which lasted, one way or another, for seven more years. The decade of crisis certainly inflicted some lasting damage on global growth prospects and there is good reason to believe that it may not be over. What emerged by way of economic recovery after 2017 – slow, tepid and patchy as it was – may turn out to be a lull between two similar and related storms, since so many of the underlying conditions that produced the 2008 crisis are substantially unchanged.[1]

As analysts are now able to bring some historical perspective to bear on the tumultuous economic crises of the last ten years, it is probably more accurate to see it not so much as a great dislocation of the global economic system (though it was certainly destabilizing) but rather as a vicious symptom of other transformational trends in globalization.[2] Placed in context, the 2008–18 decade of economic crisis was at the centre of two other long-term – very disruptive –

trends already at work. One was the unrestrained growth of globalization and its economic and social networks, and the other was the powerful shift in the economic centre of gravity towards Asia. The first trend profoundly affected the onset of the crisis; the other, the way it played out.

Globalization and networks

There are many ways to understand the phenomenon that has been loosely referred to as 'globalization'. For most analysts, it became an economic phenomenon when the 'globalization of markets' was first – controversially – noted in 1983.[3] For many, it constitutes a manifestation of the 'third industrial revolution' and a transition into the fourth.[4] Like previous industrial revolutions, the third and fourth are only effective where they involve harnessing new technologies at the moment when some important societies are open to their economic potential and prepared to embrace the social and human changes they involve.[5] Certainly, the computing, communications and transport revolutions coincided with strong motives in Western economies to revolutionize manufacturing methods and create new forms of value from services of all kinds, arts and human creativity. Another perspective is to understand the surprisingly recent nature of the phenomenon, where international marketing coincided only in the late 1980s with the exponential development of the internet and the World Wide Web, financial deregulation, and the end of the Cold War which allowed for much greater human and economic mobility around the world. What exploded only thirty years ago went far beyond the transnationalism that had long existed in global economics and world politics, or even the extensive interdependence that had been noted in the 1970s. By the turn of this century many societies across the world – not all, but certainly all of the key geopolitical ones – were not just highly connected but had become economically enmeshed together. And if not socially so deeply entwined, they were nevertheless mutually affected by each other's economic performance and also by their demographic trends and prevailing ideas to a degree unprecedented in history.

This very recent globalization revolution is based predominantly on the contemporary power of networks. Not since the technology of the printing press in the sixteenth century has the general public experienced such a leap in its ability to share information and ideas as created by the arrival of the internet. With unprecedented swiftness, the ability of citizens to tap into this knowledge network has vastly increased in both scope and depth through search engines and an array of devices capable of diving into the fund of knowledge and information with a simple click. It also facilitates the darker sides of human nature; the circulation of fake news, conspiracy theories, criminal behaviour of all kinds, and mob behaviour, such as the 'Indian WhatsApp lynchings' of 2017–18 that killed forty-six people and critically injured another forty-three, all on the basis of completely untrue cyber rumours. We live, it is said, in 'the Age of Network Power', with 'game-changing' implications for politics everywhere.[6] This is not to say that the wild, networked power of the individual somehow triumphs over the hierarchical power of governments and institutions; but rather that the endless games of political power between people and government are played out in a new, third dimension of cyberspace where the rules are being rapidly rewritten.[7] It means, too, that the inherent tendency of networks to be more innovative than established hierarchies speeds up the power of political change as new patterns of behaviour frequently take such rapid effect.[8]

The speed with which cyberspace has emerged as a key political domain has been historically unprecedented. By 2018, around 4.2 billion of the 7.6 billion people in the world were online. At the turn of this century that proportion was around 3 per cent; by 2010 it was 30 per cent and now stands at over 55 per cent. The graph projection of internet connectivity among the global population has so far proved to be a straight line. On average, internet users have 5.5 social media accounts each and operate on more than one device.

Table 4 shows how those gross figures are distributed across the major regions of the world and also indicates what is likely to happen next. The 16 per cent of global population represented by Europe and North America currently account for just over 25 per cent of people online across the world, but that figure will reach full capacity quite soon. The 72 per cent of global population in Asia

Table 4 Internet usage by region, December 2017

	Population (in billions)	Percentage of world population total	Percentage of whom are online	Percentage of global online total
Asia	4.2	55	48	49
Africa	1.2	17	35	11
Middle East	0.3	3	64	4
Europe	0.8	11	85	17
North Atlantic	0.4	5	95	8.1
Latin Am/Caribbean	0.7	8.4	67	10
Australia/Oceania	0.04	0.6	69	0.9
Total	7.64	100		100

Source: Miniwatts Marketing Group 2018.

Table 5 Internet coverage of the major service providers

	Global users (in billions)	Launched in	Owned by
Facebook	2.3	2004	Facebook
YouTube	1.5	2005	Google (Alphabet)
WhatsApp	1.5	2009	Facebook
Facebook Messenger	1.3	2011	Facebook
WeChat	1.0 (90% in China)	2011	Tencent
Instagram	0.7	2010	Facebook
Twitter	0.3	2006	Twitter

Source: Extracted from Niall Ferguson, The Square and the Tower, London, Allen Lane, 2017, pp. 353–6, and author's own calculations.

and Africa, however, only make up 60 per cent of the world's online population and considerable expansion across both these continents is inevitable before full capacity is reached.

For the time being, a small number of predominantly Western-based companies are still the major providers of this ever-globalizing demand. At the end of 2017 the biggest internet service providers were ranked as illustrated in Table 5. This indicates that there has been consolidation among a few giant companies. This is to be expected when a major technology is still new and national regulatory frameworks are inherently weak.[9] Nor is there much prospect of an effective international regulatory framework in the near future. But this picture may become more diverse quite quickly, as Asian demand burgeons and individual governments begin to hit back against over-mighty monopolies.

This is clearly not a flash in the technological pan. It is a revolution as profound as that created by printing. 'Cyberspace' is a new domain of human activity that simply did not exist before 1984 when the internet was created, followed, as it was, by the World Wide Web in 1989.[10] Cyberspace has no spatial or temporal limits. Even global population is not a finite limit for cyberspace. If everyone on the planet is eventually connected via the internet, it is evident that people still want to be connected through multiple devices for a greater range of activities. And organizations constantly evolve, transforming themselves to new purposes. This expanding range of human activity is currently facilitated by the development of multiple apps. In 2000 apps using internet services barely existed: the earliest performing recognizably internet-based app functions can be dated to around 1997.[11] But by March 2017 the five market leaders were responsible for supplying more than 6.5 million different apps. And since apps for mobile devices – smart-phones, tablet computers and wearables – are generally easier and cheaper to produce than for static computers, their current growth is exponential. Apple estimated that by the end of 2016 its 2.2 million apps had been cumulatively downloaded around 140 billion times.[12] In addition to the downloading of vast amounts of data through app technologies, social networks distribute and proliferate material – text, images, interactive functions – of all kinds to an unprecedented degree. Facebook's 2.3 billion users are estimated by the company to distribute written material or images via their system around 10 million times every day – that is more than 3.6 billion 'likes' or 'shared' items every year, and the number is growing at an annual rate of around 11 per cent worldwide.[13] In 2016 Mark Zuckerberg claimed that the Messenger and WhatsApp systems, owned by Facebook as separate services, were handling around 60 billion encrypted messages every day.[14]

There is no end to the range of human activities that are facilitated – or themselves generated – by individuals and organizations using internet connectivity. The tangible reality of the internet is no more than a large series of submarine cables, a small number of satellite links, ubiquitous fibre optic wiring and massive warehouses (in only a few places) stuffed with servers. But no one knows how big the internet really is. Its likely size can only be estimated. Cisco calculated that by 2019 annual internet traffic would have reached two zettabytes; and Gartner Inc estimates that over four zettabytes of content is already stored across the internet.[15]

As far as the global economic system is concerned, the central role of the internet, the resulting knowledge revolution, and the rapid commercialization of these developments, has changed global business models in ways that governments are still struggling to grasp. For one thing the internet's intrinsic links to massive computing power make it possible to operate traditional business models far more efficiently – cutting logistics costs, creating manufacturing robotics, reducing labour levels, creating more efficient information systems and so on. Companies such as Amazon use the power of the internet to operate an essentially traditional retail model built on lowering fixed costs and operating very efficient logistics (albeit alongside advertising innovations such as marketing 'home assistants' such as 'Siri' or 'Alexa'). Likewise, Microsoft supplies software through an essentially traditional business model. But companies such as Facebook, Alphabet (Google) or Twitter have business models that turn the normal relationship between retailer and customer on its head. In these cases, the account holders – the users of the service – have become the product. The real customers are the advertisers who pay for ever more intimate access to the product – in Facebook's case the 2.3 billion people around the world who use its free services. In 2019 every individual Facebook user in North America generated $112 in advertising revenue. In Asia, comparable revenue was only $11 per person, but this market is about to burgeon.[16] In 2018 and 2019 Facebook (owners also of WhatsApp, Messenger and Instagram networks) suffered a number of commercial and political setbacks that seemed to make it unpopular with many of its users, but it was still worth over $422 billion and growing.[17] The cheapness and capacity of modern data analytics, even before the imminent arrival of new breakthroughs in artificial intelligence, make this a very lucrative business model, built almost entirely on the money that aggressive advertising is prepared to invest in reaching into the lives of account holders.

New business models based on novel forms of arbitrage – in effect, micro-brokerage – have also arisen. In 2019, the world's largest taxi firm, Uber Technologies, owned no cars. The world's most popular media company, Facebook, created no content. The world's most valuable retailer, Alibaba, carried no stock. And the world's largest accommodation provider, Airbnb, owned no property. Such burgeoning companies became the tip of an iceberg, where available broadband space, concert seats, travel tickets or home delivery could be brokered by companies that don't provide the goods, but engage in peer to peer selling at prices that are adjusted by the minute according to market conditions. Such companies created disruptive business models based on their power to harness global information and act as highly sensitive brokers, between a potential provider of under-used capital (such as private cars, spare bedrooms, craftsmen in-between jobs) and an immediate customer. The speed and sensitivity of markets that previously only existed in the global financial sector now operate in more mundane sectors that have real day-to-day impacts on the population at large.

Mega-companies either with new business models (like Alphabet or Facebook) or essentially traditional business models with global internet-based processes (like Amazon or Alibaba) have become the new big beasts in the global economy. In 2001 Microsoft was the only internet technology company to feature in the world's top five companies, measured by market capitalization. By 2015 Exxon was the only non-internet company still left in the top five, and by 2017 all five top slots were occupied by Apple, Alphabet, Microsoft, Amazon and Facebook.[18] These companies play across the global economic system, more nimbly than even Pfizer or Exxon ever could, operating largely in between national jurisdictions, minimizing their tax liabilities and disrupting or undermining their competitors. The biggest of them can consolidate and buy up new enterprises rather than face their competition; and anti-trust actions on the part of Western governments are far more tentative and less impactful than was the case before the globalization revolution.[19]

Nevertheless, there is growing evidence of some political pushback against the apparently unrestrained nature of all this. What has been termed 'globalization 2.0' may be upon us, and for some, even a 'globalization 3.0' during the 2020s. The political pushback has begun to happen on a number of different and uncoordinated fronts but is no less significant for that.

The most evident form of political pushback has come in the waves of political populism that have swept across the democratic world during the last decade.

From economically stressed societies in Southern Europe to disruptive or extreme political parties in Western and Northern Europe; from Trumpism in the United States to populist authoritarian leaders in Brazil, Venezuela, Turkey or the Philippines, there are symptoms of popular discontent across the world where electorates feel that globalization trends have long gone beyond their control.[20] Of course, 'populism' is a hold-all term for a series of political developments that all have their own particular causes. The phenomenon is such a knee-jerk reaction that it may not last long and populism does not, in any case, provide a coherent anti-globalization philosophy.[21] It draws strength from disparate things; the outrage caused by the explosion in offshoring private funds and the apparent inability of governments to prevent it – 'the dark side of globalization', it is said.[22] Or else it is provoked by the declining growth in real incomes among middle-class Western workers, or the effects of global population migration reaching 3.4 per cent in 2017 and heading for over 4 per cent by 2025.[23] But whatever else drove this political pushback in different societies it was united by the rapid economic disruption – inequality to many – created by the global economy and a yearning search for 'identity' that many felt had been lost.[24] 'Globalization 2.0' will not be able to ignore the claims to authority of the nation state or the reactions of discontented populations where fear and a sense of powerlessness are created by the influence of economic juggernauts.

Another form of reaction to globalization has been a degree of regulatory pushback, mainly from Western governments, as they have tried to rein in some of the more egregious, monopolistic tendencies of the bigger internet players and the disruptive social implications of some of the emerging business models. The market leaders in the 'social media revolution', such as Facebook or Twitter, have been locked in disputes with national and Europe-wide policing services and civil liberties legislators over their potential to host criminal and terrorist content, and are accused of being insufficiently responsive to legitimate national security requirements in countries where they operate so extensively. The leaders of the 'Uber-revolution' and the 'Amazon revolution' have similarly been unable to avoid successive battles with national regulators and competition authorities around the world in disputes over whether the competition they create to existing industries is legitimate.[25] And all are under pressure to pay more than legally minimal levels of national taxation on the massive turnovers they generate in countries where they market themselves so extensively.[26] After a decade of buccaneering growth by the tech giants, Western states, albeit individually so far, are beginning to push back against their raw economic power, if not their actual business models.[27] In 2019 the British government published a series of proposals for a new raft of regulations that might be applied to the internet giants under domestic law.[28]

Whereas Western liberal governments try to regulate more closely these manifestations of economic globalization, a number of less liberal governments have moved from trying to impose even heavier regulation towards outright co-option of internet technologies for their own illiberal purposes. This constitutes a third type of traditional state-based pushback against the first flush of economic globalization. Internet message encryption was created initially by mathematicians within the US military, in order to communicate secretly with defectors living in fear in their own home countries or for US intelligence organizations operating abroad. End-to-end encryption technology such as TOR – The Onion Router – has become a normal feature of day-to-day internet life. It is not surprising that some regimes considered this hard-to-crack network a challenge to their political hierarchies. Authoritarian states such as Belarus, Iran, Uzbekistan or North Korea have quickly learnt how to manipulate internet access to their own advantage.[29] And they have banned many Western internet companies from operating within their territories and developed their own services. Over a dozen other significant states have interfered with popular access to some of the big internet service providers. In response, the service providers have frequently trimmed their commitments to openness to preserve their market access in more repressive societies. Even as internet penetration has been relentlessly advancing, 'internet freedom' has been in political retreat since 2010. Just over half of the countries of the world allow internet operations that are partially or totally free; over a third of countries operate internet access in ways that are judged to be overtly 'not free'.[30]

Even more dramatically, two of the Big Four states – Russia and China – have moved from heavy regulation of the internet to a conception of 'internet sovereignty' that makes no apology for severe regulation and promotes the internet specifically as a national ideological asset – an overt expression of national power. The 2013 revelations of Edward Snowden regarding the cyber activities of the US National Security Agency seem to have confirmed the Kremlin's view that the internet was being used directly as a US foreign policy tool. Russian policy moved decisively from internet regulation – often characterized as 'dictatorship of the law' – to the national co-option of the whole cyber domain in order to fragment information-sharing, monitor internal opposition forces, manipulate trends of content and to invest a great deal of money and personnel to project its cyber power outwards on the world in support of Russian foreign policy.[31]

China, against all previous expectations, has gone even further down the road of internet sovereignty by using the raw power of its developing market, something that Russia simply lacks. The 'great firewall of China' has given way to a government-dominated internet market of over 750 million users (54 per cent of the population).[32] It has become a world leader in e-commerce and accounts for over 40 per cent of it. Three of its biggest companies, Alibaba, Tencent and Baidu are among the world's top ten internet companies by market capitalization. The Chinese government has moved from fearing the power of the internet to seeing it as a positive economic and political asset, and it promotes to its own population a 'sovereign' and 'Chinese' internet as a national virtue. It allows only approved companies to operate within it. Like Russia, it uses the internet to detect internal dissent, and it can live with balkanized, fragmented access to it once there is enough economic momentum behind it.[33] It does not matter if some of the Chinese elite have full access to the global internet nor even that the majority of the population know that there is a bigger cyber world out there they cannot access. As long as it delivers economic development and Chinese national values, Beijing's leaders regard the approach as a sustainable way to live in the new global economy without undermining their political control.[34] In Xinjiang province the Chinese government is accused of using very extensive cyber power in all its aspects to repress and control the indigenous Uighur Muslim peoples of the region.[35] Most significantly, China's 'sovereign internet' is set to exert increasing influence over the cyber domains of many of the sixty-eight countries its Belt and Road Initiative may eventually encompass – some 65 per cent of the global population. The United States has already characterized China's 'sovereign internet' as an illegitimate trade barrier.[36] As Eric Schmidt, the ex-chief of Google expressed it, the next decade would likely see the US-led global internet competing with a Chinese-led and 'Chinese-rules' internet (alongside all the cyber products and services that Chinese companies are developing) that would operate across some regions and in many different countries.[37] Whereas democratic powers understand the cyber world as a domain of politics in which they have to make their case, Chinese and Russian leaders aim to control the domain internally and manipulate it as far as possible externally.

The fact is that networked globalization in 'phase 1.0' has driven the world economy very fast and prosperously, if not particularly equitably. But 'globalization 2.0' will see more networked fragmentation and new distributions of power and influence within it. The fragmentation of globalized networks that were mainly the preserve of Western societies for their first thirty years will have some significant geopolitical consequences.

The economic shift to Asia

The potential of China in the world's markets and its manufacturing and cyber power can sometimes distort the broader picture. The economic shift in the economic centre of gravity towards Asia is not in any sense unexpected. In the year 1500 Asian economies are estimated to have accounted for around 63 per cent of global GDP. In 1820 the figure was still 60 per cent. Only between 1820 and 1870 did European colonialism have a major impact. It turned out to be a relatively brief – though very intensive – period of Western economic predominance. Indeed, from the 1970s something of the historical norm has been in process of being reasserted. Asian economies have moved once more to account for over 50 per cent of global GDP and will reassert, and probably exceed, the 63 per cent level of the sixteenth century. This is hardly surprising since more than half of the world's current population (over 3.8 billion people) live within a circle that could be drawn to encompass China, India, Pakistan, Japan and the countries of South East Asia.

Nor is the story all about China. It made up less than half the total of Asia's GDP in the sixteenth century and does so still. The Chinese economy is the second biggest in the world and is set to become the biggest in the foreseeable future.[38] It has the advantage of expanding from a low base thanks to the pragmatism of Deng Xiaoping during the 1980s in turning its back on some of the self-defeating economic fiascos of the past. But its products and companies are generally not yet world beaters, one-party governmental corruption is still a major drag on its development, its population is ageing, and average GDP per head in China is still much less than half that even of crisis-hit Greece. The key geopolitical point for the future, however, is that China is probably best placed among all the Asian powers to make the most of its economic size and growth *potential* in both economic and political terms.

If this picture presents a very predictable long-term trend, there is nevertheless an abrupt jolt when the speed of the tail is considered. In an extensive analysis in 2012 the McKinsey Global Institute used work from the University of Groningen to track the world's 'economic centre of gravity' since the beginning of the Christian era until a projected date of 2025. The analysis is startling. Until the year 1000 the centre of gravity was located firmly in East Asia and it barely moved at all; it was still mainly in Asia in 1500. But by 1820 it was beginning to move to the European imperial powers. By 1950 it was in North America. So it was in 1990. But by 2025 – less than forty years over a period of two millennia – the 'economic centre of gravity' will be almost back where it began.[39]

Quite simply, the world is now witnessing the most *rapid* shift in economic power in human history. The rapidity of this shift in economic gravity challenges institutions, states and leaders in all parts of the world to adjust to it in an orderly fashion. It does not mean that prosperity is necessarily transferring from Western economies to the emergent economies of Asia. In any case, 'Asia' is an imprecise term that encompasses very different societies across a huge land area. But Asian economics, for good and bad, rich and poor, will be the drivers of the global economy in this century, and Western societies will only remain so developed and prosperous insofar as they are able to integrate themselves into Asian (and in time, African) economic growth.

Not least, this rapid shift makes it clear that the Asian-driven world economy will be a straight fact for the 2020s, not merely an approaching trend. It may take longer for the prevailing rules of the global economic system to become distinctly Chinese or more influenced by Asian economic interests than those derived from the US-European tradition, but the sheer magnetic pull of Asian markets is already being felt.

The phenomenon is also driven by the relative decline of the European economies. This is not just a matter of recent economic performance among the Europeans, poor as that has been, but more a perspective of scale and management. The European Union is the world's single biggest (and most deeply integrated) international market of over 500 million people. With or without Britain in it, the European market will only be around a third the size of the integrated national market of China at almost 1.4 billion, and growing. The EU accounted for 27 per cent of global GDP in 1990 and, despite two decades of strong growth until 2007–08, will comprise merely 15 per cent, or even less, by 2023. Over the ten years 2012–22 the average growth rate in China, based on past performance and future projections, is estimated at 6.7 per cent, in India it is 7.3 per cent, in Vietnam 6.2 per cent and in Indonesia 5.3 per cent. By contrast, the average GDP growth over the same period for the EU is estimated at 1.6 per cent and for the broader European Area at 1.4 per cent.[40] For the United States over the same period the average figure is estimated at 2.1 per cent.[41]

But Europe's relative decline is also evident in the management of the global economy. As the traditional international institutions – like the IMF, the World Bank or the WTO[42] – struggle to cope with the pressures of globalization, the new Asian Infrastructure Investment Bank, or China's BRI are seen by many as attempts to re-write the international economic rules.[43] There is some debate about this, but everything to play for, since the biggest influencers in the world economy have, in reality, become a few thousand big corporations, their interlocking shareholdings and a very small number of successful asset managers. Only twenty or thirty major banks really matter at the global level, and there are perhaps a hundred internationally significant financial firms.[44] European institutions and managers can certainly be players in these competitive constellations, and Europe is an attractive home for Asian investment. Between 2015 and 2016 Chinese investment in Europe almost doubled, mainly from Beijing's state-backed firms and investment funds. And China tries to operate bilaterally when it invests abroad, dealing with individual governments rather than organizations like the EU.[45] All of which emphasizes the fact that European countries as a whole – even the EU – can no longer act as a central pillar of the global economic system. As Adam Tooze puts it, 'Rather than an autonomous actor, Europe risks becoming the object of other people's capitalist corporatism. . . . Europe is out of the race. The future will be decided between the survivors of the crisis in the United States and the newcomers of Asia'.[46]

The continuing economic crisis

This emergence of a more bipolar economic world, balanced between the natural power of the liberal, decentralized US economy and the growing influence in Asia of the centrally planned Chinese system, has emerged most clearly from the global economic crisis of the last decade. More importantly, it is not clear that this crisis can be assumed to be over. And as the original crisis highlighted growing economic bipolarity between the United States and China, so its potential continuance will move to reinforce that geopolitical trend.

In 2007–08 the crisis began from small symptoms to become a structural crisis for the whole world economy. It began with an unsustainable bubble in home ownership in the United States, an overheating to which the US Federal Reserve turned a blind eye. This coincided with inadequate capitalization among almost all Western banks, at a time when packages of short-term loans had become contaminated with toxic (i.e. unrepayable) debt and an explosion in 'derivatives' – inventive new ways of making profits out of banking that had the effect of making the system simply opaque. And it all happened at a time when the US/China trade relationship was spectacularly unbalanced.[47] This created a set of systemic problems, in which there was an equally systemic failure on the part of *all* regulatory authorities – the US Federal Reserve, central banks, the major accountancy firms, national regulators, not to mention national legislators – to understand what was really happening.[48]

The economic reckoning could not be deferred indefinitely. In 2008–09 a severe banking crisis rapidly turned into a sovereign debt crisis as some governments themselves faced bankruptcy. The Eurozone crisis followed as a direct result, though for different reasons, and was at first completely mishandled by the EU. By then, the crisis had flowed into the real economies of the Western world, creating 'the great recession' – in fact the longest in modern economic history[49] – and impacting on trade and investment in the more vibrant economies of Asia. Mishandling the Euro crisis and the extra regulations introduced in the United States acted as powerful brakes on the cyclical recovery that might otherwise have been expected. In the end, no region of the world and no sector of the global economy were immune from the effects of the financial crisis and 'the great recession'. By the end of 2009 Western government had pumped $13 trillion into their failing banks to prop them up.[50] The political response among world leaders was unified in intention through a rejuvenated G20 process (partly through British initiative) but was less than consensual in its subsequent actions.[51] The experience of the G20 as a global forum was helpful but ultimately sobering. There would be no grand bargain approach to saving the world economy.

Instead, the global economy was eventually rescued from complete disaster by the decisions of three separate actors; the US Federal Reserve, the European Central Bank and the Chinese Government. Once banks, big and small, were collapsing under the pressure, the Fed kept the financial system alive by creating liquidity – 'quantitative easing' – in effect printing dollars to prevent more bankruptcies while they worked out tighter rules for the international banking sector to restore its creditworthiness. Under new management, the European Central Bank's chief, Mario Draghi, used three simple words that the ECB would do 'whatever it takes' to preserve the Euro. 'And believe me', he said, 'it will be enough'.[52] The comment was unplanned and controversial. Germany hated the idea of letting Greece and other recalcitrant economies off the hook by printing money. But the effect was exactly that. Against all its own rules, the ECB became a banker of last resort. The debtor nations of Southern Europe (and Ireland) were still bullied into draconian public sector reductions, but the ECB had created enough faith in the future of the Euro to prevent its imminent collapse.

Most important of all, the government in Beijing, facing a dramatic drop in export revenues as the crisis bit into Western economies and fearing domestic unrest as unemployment inside China surged, embarked on a massive and thoroughly Keynesian stimulus programme worth over 12 per cent of its GDP.[53] It shifted the Chinese economy in unplanned directions and increased its interdependence in the Western-style global economy. It added even more debt to China's already growing stock and made the country – like the United States – one of the world's biggest debtor countries. Nevertheless, the stimulus worked, for China and for large parts of the trading world. If the ECB had saved the Euro, it was the Fed and the Chinese government who together saved the world economy; the Fed rescued the banking system and China saved the trading system. Not surprising, then, that at the Davos World Economic Forum in January 2017 it would be Chinese President Xi Jinping who claimed to be the leader of the open, free-trading world, while President Trump's America would be cast – even among many of its allies – as a protectionist wrecker acting against the common good.[54] This was unfair given what the rest of the world owed to the Fed during the Obama presidency; but it set the prevailing tone for the years to come.

The recovery from the great recession was underway by 2017. It was fortunately characterized by synchronous economic cycles, so the recovery proved more uniform across the world and its economic sectors than has often been the case after previous recessions. On the other hand, the recovery was slow and tepid and the global economy is certainly vulnerable to any new downturns that might come along within the next five years. There is certainly some hope that the next few years will witness strengthening global growth, led by the key economies in Asia and in the United States.

Nevertheless, a sense of fragility surrounds the global economic system for a number of more structural reasons, whatever happens up to 2025. First, governments across the world, banks, industries and citizens are still carrying historically unprecedented amounts of debt. As Figures 1 and 2 illustrate, total global debt is less than it might have been if the trends up to 2008 had not been checked during the crisis. But it is no less than it was then and is still close to a staggering 400 per cent of total GDP among the mature economies.[55] Figures 1 and 2 also show that the main trend shift is that government debt has taken the place of banking debt – the 'financial corporates' – as equally or more exposed to future shocks.

Mature economies (debt as a % of GDP)

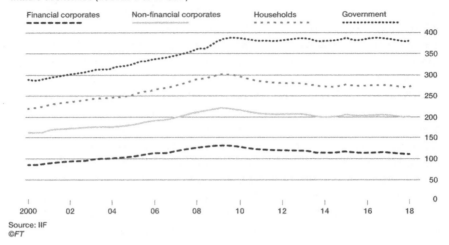

Source: IIF
©FT

Figure 1 Aggregate debt soared pre-crisis, then stabilized post-crisis.

Mature economies (debt as a % of GDP)

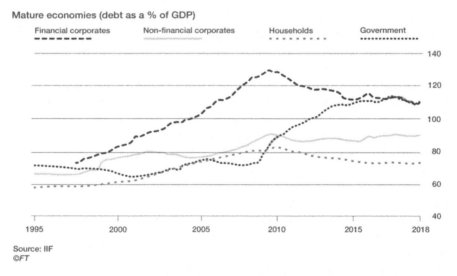

Source: IIF
©FT

Figure 2 Private deleveraging is offset by government leveraging.

Whereas the 2008 shock began as a banking crisis and became a sovereign debt crisis in its second phase, any future debt crisis will likely begin as a sovereign debt crisis. The emerging market economies, already over-leveraged (increasingly on the basis of expensive Chinese loans), are particularly vulnerable to a new debt crisis. Secondly, even in the face of this debt mountain, very little else has changed in the global economic system beyond a raft of greater restrictions on the banking sector. The simple fact is that governments, citizens and major companies are still addicted to debt, across a dollar-based financial system where the geopolitics underlying economic performance are rapidly shifting. It is not clear that in a future crisis there would be anything more to save the system than the ad hoc responses of a decade ago by the Fed, the ECB, the Chinese government or even the G20.

If anything, the actors that averted a bigger disaster last time would have even less room for manoeuvre next time. After a decade of low or negative interest rates, where governments still struggle to attract lenders, central banks have less ability to stimulate their economies to fend off a new recession. In present circumstances there are few fiscal and monetary tools left unused in their armouries that would pack a sufficient economic punch at the global level. Governments also have less political slack to use. The crises of the last decade left extremist and protectionist parties close to power, or even in office. Mainstream parties in most Western states have moved towards some of their own extremes in response. Incoming autocratic governments around the world make international cooperation in some sort of Keynesian response to a future crisis less likely; and ratcheting up current political upheavals with even more economic pain is more than most liberal Western governments can contemplate. A drift towards global protectionism makes it unlikely that the G20 could again act even as an effective forum for consensus.

Individual leaders and managers may have learnt from the global financial crisis and the great recession. There is no shortage of thinking about how to stabilize the global economy in the event of a renewed crisis. But global debt is still mountainous, management structures are largely unreformed, economic and political room for manoeuvre is more constrained. Above all, the centre of economic gravity moves all the quicker towards the Asian societies as a result of the last crisis. The economic bipolarity between Washington and Beijing will ultimately determine the outcome of the next crisis, and that bipolar relationship has moved in a far more competitive than cooperative direction in recent years.

Chapter 3
The social revolution

We have seen that, in geopolitical terms, a new and more stark world security order is emerging quickly in front of us. Economic power is also evidently in transition and may still be undergoing a prolonged structural crisis as that transition takes place. Within a society like that of Britain, open to global economic and social forces and one that sees itself as naturally internationalist, many of these pressures are all too evident. Change within Britain has been so rapid in the last twenty years that it may come to seem like a new social revolution – in the globalization of the economy, in demography, in Britain's view of itself. Of course, it shares these symptoms with many of its European partners. But it does so on the basis of a different historical experience and, as we discuss in the next chapter, with more to win and lose in the wider world as liberal democracy is put under pressure. In contrast to any of the grim struggles for survival during the twentieth century, Britain's own social cohesion has emerged as one of the significant challenges to a successful security future.

Historical legacies

Britons have traditionally perceived their country through the powerful self-image of a long-settled and essentially peaceful society which has therefore enjoyed great advantages over many other countries in the world. All societies need attractive stories to tell themselves about themselves; it is a core part of the psychological cement that holds them together. Like most national self-images, what Winston Churchill habitually called Britain's 'island story' of long-standing security and settlement will not bear too much historical examination. These islands have been invaded numerous times, both successfully and unsuccessfully, since 1066.[1] Since the fourteenth century Britain has been involved in two different 'Hundred Years' Wars' with France covering over 230 years, three bitter civil wars totalling 50 years, and two world wars that covered

10 tumultuous years which seemed to threaten its effective extinction.[2] As Linda Colley remarks, 'The UK, as it exists now, is substantially the result of luck, accident and, above all, multiple wars.'[3] Its hundred years' wars and its civil wars built a political consciousness; invasions, wars and threats of wars united the four kingdoms of the British Isles; and the two world wars increased the cohesion and organization of its centralized government. Even leaving wars aside, Britain has been far more socially conflicted during its modern history than most of its citizens traditionally like to think.[4] But somehow it has also evolved and endured with a pragmatic and tolerant, politically liberal mainstream and a predominant national psyche that eventually came to see 'Britishness' more as a strong commitment to citizenship than to noisy patriotism – an essentially civic, rather than an ethnic perception of nationhood.[5]

Being created and sustained substantially throughout conflict, contemporary Britain now faces the 2020s with a historical legacy shaped by two major trends. One evident trend is that after 1945 Britain lived through a prolonged period of 'peace in a time of war'.[6] It faced the existential threat of a completely devastating, probably nuclear, third world war between the West and the communist world. This threat waxed and waned over the period but did not effectively disappear until the mid-1980s and finally became 'residual' after the collapse of the Soviet Union in 1991. The Cold War drove high levels of military mobilization, where extensive forces were kept on a permanent war footing for almost fifty years. Nevertheless, Britain also enjoyed the economic benefits of a prolonged peace throughout the Cold War, which coincided with a long period of historically exceptional economic growth across the Western world. As we saw in Chapter 2, that period of habitually high growth may now be at an end. And in a disordered world where even European wars remain possible and where nuclear weapons continue to proliferate, the threat to Britain's very existence has not completely disappeared, though it is regarded as highly unlikely, at least in the way it was feared during the Cold War. In reality, the natural expectations of three generations of Britons are now shaped by seventy years of prosperity, alongside the comfort of hindsight that victory in two world wars was then followed by a deeper ideological victory in the Cold War. Only writers of fiction choose to dwell on how different Britain's recent history might have been; the political and social establishments do not.[7] A sense that the country's very existence is now historically 'safe' has shaped the national consciousness since the Cold War ended in 1991; and that it has a right and an expectation to ever-growing prosperity has seemed axiomatic since 1945. These twin assumptions appear to be a natural part of the British psyche with which it faces the 2020s. A strong national consensus, therefore – the 'island story' we want to tell ourselves, the social cement that binds British society together, and so much more – now derives from the experience and expectations of three generations that have lived through historically untypical times in modern British history.

A second trend is that from the late 1980s, just around the time when the end of twentieth-century epochal wars, the burdens of empire, and the retreat from great power status played themselves out of the British national story, so the domestic impacts of globalization began to have tangible impacts on society. Indeed, many of them have been felt more quickly and strongly than in other Western countries. In the space of thirty years globalization has redrawn the international and domestic maps of politics. In this time British society has gone through a number of significant changes as it responds to the inducements and pressures of globalization. An opaque but rapid social revolution is taking place within Britain; driven by new social trends that have naturally replaced older ones, through responses to unsolved and long-standing political and economic pressures, and because globalization, for good and bad, works well in a country with an economy like Britain's.

The general nature of globalization, as discussed in Chapter 2, is open to dispute. Some argue that its high-water mark has already passed, others that it is an overblown concept, still others that the state – particularly among the authoritarian great powers – is reasserting its authority against globalization's subversive influences. There is little argument, however, that economic globalization has already been a transformative force and is likely to move continuously forward in the coming decade.[8] This matters to Britain in many ways that now go deep into the fabric of its society.

Britain's globalization revolution

The United States and Britain did much in the 1980s to promote and strengthen the 'neoliberal' model of free-trading liberal capitalism.[9] It was an approach that accepted the power of international market forces and looked for ways to accommodate, rather than to change, them. This general model did much to shape the way economic globalization took off in its first phase, so it is not surprising that the economies of the United States and Britain have been most affected by it.

By the mid-1980s the structure of the British economy already made it the most receptive in Europe to the phenomenon of globalization. It idealized the free market, was moving towards a deregulated banking sector, and embraced globalized production and trade. Not least, the transformation of the British economy into a predominantly service economy was faster and more profound than was ever anticipated. Britain's manufacturing sector made up 30 per cent of its GDP in the 1980s, but is less than 10 per cent today. It is buoyed up with some powerful niches of high-end manufacturing, as in aerospace or pharmaceuticals, but manufacturing still accounts for only 8 per cent of the workforce. Britain has opened itself as much as possible to foreign investment and ownership.

Certainly, until the Brexit vote, it prided itself as the commercial 'aircraft carrier' of Europe, hosting around 500 major multinational headquarters operating across the continent and serving them through the financial powers of the City, the respected institutions of UK law, and all the social advantages of British cities as corporate bases for foreign companies. There are more start-up businesses (and therefore more failures) than in other European countries and greater labour flexibility in almost all sectors. Around a third of all British manufacturing jobs are in foreign owned companies. The giant digital companies such as Amazon, Facebook, Uber or Google operate with few restrictions and low tax liabilities. Their activities lower costs dramatically and transform market conditions in ways the government – actively promoting the development of a fully digitized economy – is reluctant to regulate heavily (and perhaps unable in any case to do so effectively). Some of the major utilities and essential networks in Britain; water, energy, parts of the transport system, the internet (which must now be counted as a utility), parts of the postal services and sectors of the cash and payments systems, are now largely foreign owned – indeed in some cases by foreign government funds. In the globalized free market, as James Meek points out, some of Britain's major public utilities have actually been re-nationalized into government ownership, just not that of the British government.[10]

As the second phase of globalization kicks in during the 2020s, 'globalization 2.0' will not be so evidently driven by the Western economies. There are many arguments over how the neoliberal economic model will stand up to the pressures and opportunities that will then arise. There can be little doubt, however, that the first phase of globalization has already contributed greatly to rapid social change in Britain within the last thirty years.

Key aspects of the economy have become hourglass shaped. There is unmet demand for more skilled labour at the top of the hourglass and a glut of low-skilled jobs at the bottom. Depending on how they are defined, somewhere between 25 per cent and 40 per cent of all British jobs are now low skilled.[11] Meanwhile, skilled manufacturing or clerical jobs in the middle are heavily squeezed, the more so as automation and artificial intelligence take effect. Britain has a few big, successful companies and a great many small ones; some five million people (15 per cent of British workers) are now self-employed, more than twice as many since the 1980s.[12] There are comparatively few middle-sized enterprises, so the components and services those enterprises would otherwise have produced for the big companies are mainly imported. The typical effects of such a heavily top and bottom employment model are that Britain's service industries are ever dependent on importing skilled labour, while its manufacturing firms face supply chains that have to import far more components, say, than their German counterparts.

The employment hourglass is superimposed on a very obvious geographic pyramid in the way jobs and wealth are distributed, where they gravitate so strongly towards the south east of the country. Many midland and northern areas, including 'coastal Britain', are caught between some city-based bright spots and wide areas that have clearly been left behind by globalization.[13] Economic divisions in Britain have tended to be politicized by the devolution debates affecting the other kingdoms of the Union, but the most acute north/ south population, employment, growth and welfare divisions are undoubtedly within England.

The economy generally performed well from the mid-1990s until the economic crisis that began in 2008, but its success in seizing many of the opportunities thrown up by the first stage of economic globalization also added to these demographic and social imbalances. Economic stability and the impressive growth that seemed to exist before 2008 rested heavily on deregulation and free capital movements, low taxation and vigorous consumer spending – driven by extensive credit and a buoyant housing market. Being so open to market forces incurred obvious structural costs, and successive government policies were unable to mitigate their more malign impacts or address the fundamental imbalances they reinforced.[14] Thus, while employment levels remained consistently high, both productivity and wage growth were dangerously low and national economic growth – more than a decade after the 2008 crisis when other economies regained some momentum – was expected to be well below 2 per cent as Britain entered the 2020s.

These downsides of globalization reinforced other demographic pressures that were already evident by the time of the millennium. Just as England's workers have gravitated towards the south east, so the predominance of the population living within England, as opposed to the other kingdoms that make up the United Kingdom, has continued to grow. Modern British politics have long been tormented with problems arising from the constitutional position of Northern Ireland and in more recent years with Scottish and Welsh devolution, but almost 85 per cent of Britain's population already live in England (a historical high point). And from 2016 to 2026 population growth in England is expected to be almost twice the level in either Scotland or Wales.[15] The population of England is expected to reach 60 million by 2029, with London touching 10 million.[16] The resident community in England drives deeper demographic change within Britain as a whole; in its age, structure, ethnicity, religious observance and political identity. The England-heavy nature of population distribution also affects patterns of foreign investment, demand and public spending that creates growing political tension not just between the component kingdoms but more generally between Britain's 'north' and 'south', broadly defined[17] (Table 6).

In fact, England may be said to have developed its own devolution problem since the 1980s in the role that London plays within both the economy and the national psyche. The UK now comprises a union that offers effective devolved powers to Scotland, Northern Ireland, Wales and London, with a resulting

Table 6 UK population distribution since 2017

	Population (in millions)	% of overall population
England	55.6	84.2
Wales	3.1	4.7
Scotland	5.4	8.2
NI	1.9	2.9
UK Total	66	100

Source: Office of National Statistics.

economic and democratic deficit in the non-devolved parts of northern, midland, south western and coastal England.[18]

In effect, England outside London has become Britain's 'fifth kingdom'. London is Europe's only truly global city, but its undoubted success as a city distorts the British economy elsewhere. Greater London is one of Europe's most prosperous regions. The per capita GDP in West London is over six times the EU average. More to the point, average incomes in London were already 63 per cent higher than the British average in 1998 and 77 per cent higher by 2016. At the other end of the scale, average incomes in North East England were just 41 per cent of the London average.[19] London's 8.7 million inhabitants relate to the wider world more naturally than to the rest of Britain. On average, 34 per cent of non-British nationals live in the five London boroughs with the highest proportions of migrant residents, whereas across the rest of the country the average is 9.3 per cent.[20] London's inhabitants comprise 13 per cent of the national population, produce over 20 per cent of the national output, absorb some 35 per cent of national infrastructure expenditure and almost 54 per cent of all spending on transport infrastructure.[21] A great deal of London's success has actually been stimulated by government-backed investment in infrastructure and development – levels of state intervention that have dwarfed those in any other part of the country. The hourglass shape of employment is particularly acute in the capital and it has a churn of residents that saw an inflow of 7.3 million and an outflow of 6.8 million in less than a decade up to 2011.[22] By any international standards London's wealth, culture, financial, legal and educational services make it one of the jewels in Britain's crown, and it continues to enjoy historically large degrees of executive autonomy – within the financial City and latterly also across Greater London. But it is increasingly divorced from the rest of the country both economically and socially. In the nineteenth century the great midland and northern cities were their own economic and political 'powerhouses';

more revenue was raised locally than nationally. But London is now eight times bigger than the next biggest British city. In the devolved Britain of the twenty-first century, an increasingly centralized England sees the government in London control around twice as much public spending as that of France, Japan or Italy and over three times as much as that of Germany.[23] This was all exacerbated after the 2008 economic crisis, when local government suffered expenditure cuts that eventually amounted to about 40 per cent. Local government bore the overwhelming brunt of the austerity agenda that Conservative-led administrations felt the need to impose.[24]

In short, however, the national economy performs from one period to the next, its altered structure makes it appear increasingly unbalanced; patchily but not effectively devolved, over-centralized but subject to quixotic foreign ownership, dynamic but not sustained by its own workforce. It is prone to uneven and inequitable success, overheating during the good times and exaggerating the pain for too many during the bad.

Into this troubling picture the spectre of uncontrolled migration into Britain and involuntary social change – the growing suspicion that multiculturalism is failing – has assumed new potency. In the mid-1990s some 4 million British residents (7 per cent of the total population) were born abroad and constituted a relatively settled minority population within a country that officially defined itself as 'multicultural'. That did not change very much until the turn of the millennium. But then, drawn largely by the need to fill vacancies in the hourglass employment picture, 3 million more migrants settled in Britain, as recorded in census data between 2001 and 2011. By 2018 the figure was 12 million (over 18 per cent of the total population) – and significantly, closer to 25 per cent in England.[25] Over a million people are believed to be in the country illegally, the majority in south and east England.[26] Successive governments had been making it easier for migrants to come to British jobs during the 1990s, and in 2004 the Tony Blair government opened its doors without restriction to workers from the new East European members of the EU. Official estimates were that about 50,000 migrants might come from these countries over four years. The government was taken aback when the number turned into more than 1 million; followed in 2012 by another spike as young Italian, Spanish and Portuguese migrants tried to escape the effects of the Eurozone crisis.

A political backlash was all but inevitable, but still the hourglass shape of the job market and the pyramid shape of job distribution demanded more foreign labour to keep an unbalanced economy moving in the teeth of its biggest recession since the 1930s and its slowest ever recovery following the 2008 crisis. London crossed the 'majority-minority' threshold in the 2011 census where the 58 per cent 'white British' population of 2001 had fallen to 45 per cent (having stood at 86 per cent in 1971), with Manchester and Birmingham not far behind.[27] This changing demographic picture, particularly in the case of Muslim minorities in the cities, played into the hands of jihadist terror groups who offered a sense of identity to alienated young Muslims and contributed to a wider sense of unease that somehow British society was simply changing ad hoc and certainly too rapidly for comfort. The extreme right in Britain – far less influential than in many other European countries, but feeding off the same fears and incipient xenophobia – repeatedly made the link between the generality of immigration and the particular problem of jihadist terrorism. Mainstream politicians rejected such links but the general perception of it seeped into the public consciousness. By 2011 European leaders in Germany, France, Spain and including Prime Minister Cameron had all said that they thought multiculturalism, at least as it had been assumed to work, was simply not up to these levels of stress. In Britain, foreign-born individuals among the total population had jumped from less than 6 per cent in 1980 to over 13 per cent in 2015. In Ireland it was from 6.5 per cent to 17 per cent over the same period; in the Netherlands from 3 per cent to 12 per cent, in Italy from 2 per cent to about 10 per cent. Less dramatic in France and Germany – from around 10 per cent to over 12 per cent and 13 per cent over the same period – the figures were still politically disruptive. Neither the social democratic Left nor the mainstream Right in Europe had any good answers to the unease these changes caused.[28] The Europe-wide immigration crisis of 2015 and then serious terror attacks in Paris, Brussels, Berlin, London and Manchester in 2016 and 2017 melded the separate and distinct concepts of immigration, multiculturalism, citizenship and public safety into a toxic political argument about Britain's willingness and ability to maintain its tolerant and pragmatic approach to demographic change.[29]

In truth, there had never in Britain been a meaningful policy of integration, other than to hope and assume that assimilation would happen naturally over a long enough period of time. The assumption was based on a laissez-faire multiculturalism and in that sense was characteristically British. But the most critical stress on British multiculturalism was the *rapidity* of change after the turn of the century.[30] Globalization speeded everything up and the British public, while more open than most of their European neighbours to the economic benefits of immigration, nevertheless consistently believe by about three to one that immigration into Britain is too high and out of control.[31] The issue has become toxic, it hovers near the top of every national political agenda and it pulls against the country's immediate economic interests.

The long-term political and social effects of these economic and demographic trends are uncertain. After 2010 there were three general elections whose results were indecisive, two crucial referendums that left questions about Britain's national identity more open than resolved, and two changes of government under new Prime Ministers – Theresa May and Boris Johnson – without any nationwide vote. Some analysts have noted the return of antagonistic class consciousness to Britain, but with substantially different views of what class and identity now mean. The 'Great British Class Survey' of 2013 posited that new types of social status and inequality have arisen, more deep-seated than those that were previously based largely on occupation and income.[32] David Goodhart sees something more critical than social class. He notes that even in 'global Britain' around 60 per cent of the population live within twenty miles of where they were at the age of fourteen (and 42 per cent within 5 miles). He defines a critical fault line in British society between the minority of 'anywheres' who dominate the policy elites and can live and function wherever they are and the majority of 'somewheres' who have a strong sense of place and resist the idea that globalization is somehow unstoppable. At the very least, they don't see why they should be paying a disproportionate price for Britain to enjoy the lopsided benefits of globalization.[33] Still others claim that the country is now uniquely segregated in ways that social class, employment or regional attachment cannot properly explain – accepting that the dynamics behind the Brexit vote are still not well understood.[34] There is common ground among the analysts, however, on two critical issues; firstly, that Britain's globalized prosperity certainly leaves regions and large groups of people behind; and secondly, that there is a corresponding democratic deficit which leaves too many with a feeling of powerlessness over their future prospects and a deepening disenchantment with Britain's leaders and elites and those national political institutions they have long dominated.

Loss of political control may be the necessary price that modern societies pay to absorb the benefits of economic globalization, but Britain (like some other states, not least the United States) has now witnessed some powerful social and political forces pushing back against that logic. The rage may be unfocused; it may be directed at creating upsets rather than clear alternatives, but it is no less sincere, or potent, for all that.

The springs of disunity

Hovering over these social and demographic shifts are the two great historic, institutional issues of the last decade; Britain's decision of 2016 to leave the European Union and the possibility that the UK might break up with self-declared Scottish independence – a prospect that seemed very real in 2014 at the time of the Scottish referendum. The pressures on British social cohesion of the Scottish independence question and the Brexit vote are symptoms of deeper social tensions as much as causes in themselves. They happen for their own particular reasons but they also feed off other pressures that have remained largely unaddressed for long periods. They are both cause and effect of a challenge – if not a crisis – in the way Britain sees itself in the future and what Britons assume they should stand for.

Unlike the union with Wales, England's formal unions with Scotland, Ireland and latterly Northern Ireland were always more in the nature of waypoints in a protracted series of conflicts and compromises that have never been fully resolved. Modern devolution in Scotland, Wales and Northern Ireland was driven by short-term compromises to meet immediate needs. Each devolution is quite different from the others, leaving much 'unfinished business' around the British constitution.[35] Britain and Ireland, for example, have always been joined at the hip. On one side of the Irish Sea, almost 10 per cent of Britain's current population claim Irish ancestry.[36] On the other side, the Belfast ('Good Friday') Agreement of 1998 to end 'the troubles' in Northern Ireland could not prevent the political and geographical paradoxes of Northern Ireland's historic 1922 border with the Irish Republic arising as a major stumbling block in Britain's Brexit negotiations. Britain outside the EU, and Ireland within it, will never have an uncomplicated relationship. Or in the case of Scotland, the Union of 1707 was far more a mutual compromise than a diktat and only ever partial, which, as Colley says, 'helps explain why it has endured for so long'.[37] Over a century ago in 1911 the Liberal government discussed transforming the UK into a federation to address some of its erstwhile constitutional problems. But the wars and challenges of the twentieth century bound the UK together more closely to create an image of permanence around these constitutional compromises. The current experience of Britain's prolonged peace has not made the case so convincingly. For some observers the UK now stands merely a couple of steps from the brink of dissolution, delayed only by the constitutional hiatus surrounding Brexit, before being subject to a second (possibly successful) referendum on Scottish independence and a more rapid change in the status of Northern Ireland vis-à-vis the Republic, as Britain redefines its relationship with the EU and its single market.

The dissolution scenario represents the confluence of a number of factors. De-industrialization in the 1980s affected the devolved regions severely. The devolution that was later enacted for Scotland and Wales certainly had effects thereafter in diversifying domestic policy and it stimulated, as much as it assuaged, forces of economic and cultural separation. Across England, by contrast, very little changed and attempts to create English devolved assemblies simply failed, mainly because voters didn't want 'more politics' from a system in which they had already lost much faith. The collapse of both Conservative and then Labour Party support in Scotland created an unstoppable momentum for an independence referendum (narrowly lost by the nationalists in 2014) and decisive victories for the Scottish National Party in both Scottish Parliamentary and British General Elections. The SNP, with its ambition to dissolve the UK, became the political voice of Scotland, notwithstanding some electoral reverses in 2017.

The dissolution of the UK also remains on the agenda because pressures for Scottish independence now also coincides with the possibility that Brexit will harm – and is already harming – the economy of Northern Ireland unless its links with mainland Britain are loosened significantly. Squaring the circle that Northern Ireland must remain constitutionally within the UK while also maintaining a soft customs border with the European Union – the Irish Republic – suggests that whatever the final outcome of Brexit, politicians in Belfast may eventually have to make a choice between economic and political priorities. And dissolution also remains on the agenda through the progressive disenchantment in England with Westminster politics, the effects of the 2008 crisis and the apparent inability of the system to produce more decisive government after the long period of Labour administrations between 1997 and 2010. English resentment at more demands for devolution in Wales and for independence referendums in Scotland; and exasperation at the collapse of power sharing among the communities of Northern Ireland has all contributed to a fear that the essential institutions of British government have been misfiring for well over a decade.

The Brexit vote of 2016 reflected a multidimensional political crisis. It was certainly a revolt against the federal ambitions of the EU. But it was also a revolt against Westminster on several other grounds; the low competence of the political establishment, the pro-EU stance of the SNP, the privileged devolution of London, the economic dominance of the south east, and so many unpopular policies that seemed to have been foisted on a population that felt it had too small a voice.[38] As we discuss in Chapter 8, the Brexit vote seemed to wrap up, in one decisive act of will, both a general push back against the domestic effects of globalization and a series of specific grievances that had been festering within the body politic for too long.

None of this is politically healthy and it suggests that Britain will still embark on the early 2020s in a state of manifest political and constitutional crisis. It will be far removed from Britain as it was in 2000 or even in 2010. Of course, Britain has shown itself good at weathering political storms and at maintaining its essential institutions even under the greatest of pressure. Somehow, Britain's political moderation has always preserved its essentially liberal and entrepreneurial character. And it has been noted that, as fierce as the Brexit debate became right across Britain, it was still conducted largely within Parliament and in noisy, but peaceful, public demonstrations and media arenas. But a darker explanation is also plausible. It has been observed that Britain is actually as much a country of extremes as of median trends.[39] The extremes normally check each other and create an illusion of general stability – until something like Brexit or Scottish independence highlights the divisive nature of these extremes.

The division between 'somewheres' and the 'anywheres' certainly fed deep social and political polarization over Brexit issues after the 2016 referendum. So did the increasing north/south division of the economy as one ameliorating policy after another ran out of steam in the austerity climate. Britain's social fabric is characterized not merely by rapid change but seemingly also by growing extremes. For all the educational sophistication among middle-class Britons, for example, the country displays the lowest literacy and numeracy rates of any comparable Western European country. Britain's financial sector, with all its attendant legal and management services, is the most lucrative in the world, but it sits within a broader low-wage, low-productivity economy that persistently lacks sufficient capital investment. As one foreign observer noted, 'The more tense are the pent up springs of opposite extremes forced together, the more disruptive is the snap when it ultimately comes.'[40] Balancing out extreme trends in a changing society is not the same as managing them. Stability may be more fragile than politicians normally assume. For the immediate future, political volatility should be taken as the norm. A ten-country study in 2019 into populism found very convincing statistical evidence for the rapid emergence of two growing political tribes in Britain; the 'economically angry' and the 'culturally traditional'. Both of them cut across the major political parties in ways they could not accommodate, and with which they would struggle for the next decade.[41]

British citizens, in all their variety and vigour, may have positive views about their own lives and futures, but it does not follow that the British state is a confident collective person, or one that enjoys a settled or mature view of its own character. At most, it relies on a faith born of its own history; that if its political longevity depended on 'luck, accident and above all, multiple wars', then it will somehow come through this historically untypical, very different, period with its identity intact. That faith will be tested severely in the 2020s.

Chapter 4
The crisis of liberal democracy

Britain's own struggles with its sense of identity may be seen as part of a broader global phenomenon. Modern liberal democracy is under pressure and in retreat. And if Britain is to face its future with confidence, it would be as well if it were on an upswing in liberal democratic influence in the world rather than the reverse. But the internal cohesion of the liberal democracies and their global influence cannot be taken for granted. The health of the liberal democracies has become a structural security challenge in itself.

In 1991 when the Soviet Union collapsed, liberal democracy was popularly assumed to be triumphant. The liberal democracies had beaten the fascists in 1945, then they had out-performed the communists on every front, the new Russia had adopted 'wild West capitalism' and Chinese communist leaders were desperately trying to accommodate the free market without losing power. Liberal democratic capitalism seemed to have emerged as the default political and economic system when all other systems failed. It was even regarded as an inevitable fact of life in the 'end of history' thesis. The key question was no longer about who opposed it and whether it had to be fought for, but rather how well everyone was adapting to its existential truth.[1]

Within twenty years of those halcyon assumptions, however, liberal democracy and the ways it regulated modern capitalism was in retreat; and since the economic crisis of 2008 it has appeared to be in a state of manifest crisis. Whether this will turn out to be a temporary loss of confidence or a long-term ideological failure of political commitment is one of the underlying security conditions of the 2020s. That matters greatly to the 'Western world' in general but it matters even more particularly to Britain.

In history, Britain gave more to modern concepts of liberal democracy than most other societies, even if it did not always honour their implementation as early or as fully as others did.[2] The mythology surrounding the principles behind

Magna Carta and the effects of the 'glorious revolution' and the Bill of Rights in 1688–89 had a seminal influence on modern international politics. Notions of popular, democratic sovereignty and the American and French revolutions were driven by ideas from across Europe. But the prevailing rules of the international system that have held for over 300 years are based on the presumption that it is (or should be) a system of open and free societies, respecting each other's legitimacy and sovereignty, derived very specifically from the historical experience of three maritime trading powers – first the United Provinces of the Netherlands, then Britain and its empire and then the United States and its own 'empire of liberty'.[3] The international system with which we embarked on the twenty-first century was still governed by the rules derived essentially through the three acronymic powers – the UP, the UK and the USA. But its legitimacy and applicability is undoubtedly being questioned in the conditions of current world politics.

There are three overlapping trends that account for the pressure that the current international order is under as we enter the 2020s: the retreat of mainstream liberalism and democratic confidence within most Western societies; the growth of populist movements around the world; and a rise in overtly authoritarian governments who show diminishing regard for domestic or international conventions and law. Such trends threaten what the British government always calls 'the rules-based international order', even in the short term. They also have to be seen in context of the views of the coming political generation of Britons who will inherit liberal capitalist ideas that may seem less implicitly obvious than they were assumed to be among their immediate predecessors.

The retreat of Western liberalism

The dramatic nature of the 2008 economic crisis was a severe knock to the confidence of liberal democracies. Governments and finance ministries had failed to foresee it and struggled to contain its globalized and interdependent effects throughout Western societies. Demand fell everywhere, unemployment rose and public spending was either slashed or heavily restrained in most Western countries. The political classes and mainstream political parties appeared to be powerless in the face of cruel market forces, a shift in economic power away from the West, and yet the conspicuous ultra-wealth of a large global elite seemed to have escaped either responsibility or fair taxation. The decade of the global economic crisis and the great recession between 2008 and 2018 was characterized as a time of 'political insurgencies' in Western politics where new movements, extremist parties and perverse patterns of voting overturned many prevailing assumptions and created more political volatility than Europe or the United States had seen since the 1930s.

In reality, the shocks of the economic crisis were reverberating against shaky liberal political foundations well before the end of the last century. For some analysts, Western countries had become 'managerial states', 'market states', 'technocratic states' – little more than bureaucratic frameworks to mediate global market forces for their citizens; standing for little either morally or ideologically and breeding popular cynicism about the democratic process.[4] For others, the problem was that the delicate compromises necessary for the functioning of representative democracy had broken down. Democratic representation, that implicit covenant which empowered an electorate without sliding into the tyranny of the majority or even into mob rule, had been steadily undermined by failing institutions, poor politicians and casual electorates. The 'permissive consensus' that supported all the delicate compromises of representative democracy was strained and, in some countries, simply broken.[5] Still others saw the problem deriving from a model of relentless market economics – neoliberal capitalism – that has failed to create proper 'stakeholder capitalism' where citizens feel politically connected to their society and perceive their personal worth as something more than being merely one of the 'factors of production'.[6] Globalized economic growth is all very well, the argument goes, but if it undermines national institutions, it exposes a hollowed out society when growth shudders to a halt, as it periodically will.

Such explanations are all entirely plausible. Whatever the causes of such democratic disenchantment, however, the immediate political symptoms are readily apparent.

Support for mainstream parties throughout Europe has been in structural decline for some time. National voting patterns vary from election to election but there is an underlying trend of 'de-alignment' from mainstream political parties in key European states. West European politics for over a generation had been dominated by the agendas of social democratic parties – whether in or out of government. But their share of the popular vote collapsed by almost 30 per cent between 1980 and 2015 – and precipitously so after 2008.[7] In the 2017 British general election, the two main parties soaked up over 80 per cent of the vote in what might have seemed like a return to the old mainstream; but closer analysis showed 'vote switching' at historically high levels, mainly over Brexit issues.[8] Neither of the two main parties could rely on their core votes for the 2020s, and some major political realignments are expected in the immediate years to come. The Jeremy Corbyn leadership of the Labour Party had the effect of largely unravelling it as a social democratic party of the left as the 'momentum' movement behind him drove the party to more entrenched positions. By the end of 2018 social democratic parties were in government in only seven of the twenty-eight EU states, and the 'collapse' of social democracy or its 're-invention' had become the pervasive political question across the continent.[9]

Meanwhile, extremist parties, single-issue or ultra-nationalist parties, attracted growing support throughout Europe, not merely in the new-born liberal democracies such as Poland, Hungary, Serbia or Croatia but most noticeably in the old and established democracies of Europe: Germany, France, Italy, the Netherlands, Denmark, Sweden, Austria, even Switzerland. Long-standing but fringe extremist parties suddenly made big electoral gains and had visible impacts on national political debates within many countries. The primary reasons for their success were always different.[10] In Greece and Italy both ultra-left and ultra-right parties were elected mainly to oppose the imposition of economic austerity on their societies. In Sweden, the Netherlands, Germany and Austria extremist parties of the ultra-right won support chiefly on fears of uncontrolled immigration. In Denmark, the ultra-right party was explicitly anti-Islamist; in the Netherlands the same issue lurked behind a range of other grievances. In Spain and Belgium both austerity and separatist pressures drove extremist and nationalist movements. And in Britain a complex mixture of anti-EU frustrations (as well as some optimism) and economic and anti-immigration fears were increasingly wrapped into the divisive Brexit issue.

Britain's nervous breakdown over Brexit and the possible dismembering of the kingdom itself have been characterized by the tensions between popular referendums and the institutions of representative democracy.[11] There have been no fewer than eleven official referendums in Britain since 1973, mostly concerning devolution.[12] Referendums and general elections are not happy partners in Britain's representative democracy. National referendums 'undermine political pluralism', says Philip Stephens; they occur when 'parliamentary democracies seek to shrug off responsibility'. They were, said Margaret Thatcher, 'a favourite device of demagogues and dictators'.[13] Certainly, earlier British referendums proved to be difficult exercises, and the later referendums on Scottish independence and then Brexit severely compromised the way representative democracy had normally worked and left bitter legacies that cast doubt on the ability of the main political institutions to cope with a society divided in so many different ways.

The Brexit vote was Britain's version of a more general political phenomenon among its neighbours. For the last decade, successive governments across Europe struggled to assert their traditional authority as the mainstream political support they relied on was chipped away by extremist, separatist or single-issue movements. Quite apart from growing political volatility across Europe, and though mainstream politics in most countries can still be identified after the buffeting of recent years, there is nevertheless strong empirical evidence dating back to the 1980s to show that mainstream politics moved distinctly to the right and became significantly more authoritarian in the policy positions major parties adopted – especially between 1990 and 2000.[14] As always, in the globalized world, it is the unprecedented speed of social and economic change that most disconcerts European electorates.[15] And the effect is that proximity to power has not 'domesticated' nationalist, separatist or extremist parties over the last thirty years; those parties have generally become even more committed and extreme while mainstream parties have given up some of their centre ground to take up positions they would previously have regarded as extreme. In some cases during 2017 and 2018, where support for populist parties appeared to have stalled in national elections, as in France, the Netherlands and for a while also in Britain, it is notable that mainstream parties only overshadowed them precisely by adopting some of their key policy stances.

Such trends are symptomatic of something more long term. The political culture that underpins democratic institutions is evidently changing.[16] In Britain, as in other European societies, rates of active civic participation in charities, churches, unions, environmental groups, professional groups, even sports or educational groups have fallen steadily since 1997 and average less than one in six of the population.[17]

In a Western climate that reasserts nationalism in most countries and separatism in some of them, 'identity politics' increasingly takes precedence over mere economic advantage. If governments in Western Europe have seemed ineffective, even passive, in the face of the economic and political challenges they have recently faced, political debates among their populations have become all the more fierce. Social media creates echo chambers of anger for the heavily committed. Conventional respect for other political viewpoints has visibly declined. Domestic politics in the United States, Britain and most other European states has been characterized as 'uncouth', sometimes even at the very top. In popular discourse, the obscure concept of 'authenticity' takes precedence over political 'rationality' as it would have been understood in a previous generation.[18]

The growth of populism

The growth of populism represents a dramatic symptom in the crisis of confidence that liberal democracy continues to experience.

Populism is a difficult concept to define precisely though most observers think they know it when they see it. It was noted as a growing trend in modern world politics even in the 1960s, dominated as it then was with colonialism and the ideological struggles of the Cold War.[19] But the term has taken on a more distinct connotation in the present century as a generalized revolt against some of the consequences of globalization and the impacts of the world economy on different national societies. Some writers contend that populism is devoid of real political content; it is a means, not an end – just a technique for getting and holding power. It is probably more accurate, however, to acknowledge that populism does contain the elements of what has been called 'a thin ideology'.[20]

Certainly, it is a way of looking at politics in mass society and expresses deeply held instincts of some sort of 'natural community', in contrast to the 'otherness' of those who do not, or never can, share in it. Populism tends to be cyclical and is often driven by short-term pressures. But its appearances are always a symptom that existing political institutions are somehow inadequate.

Populist leaders articulate issues that resonate with ordinary citizens. In some cases they express quite accurately what worries people; in others they put wholly different perspectives on key concerns and create a sense that there is some kind of national crisis over them. And in some cases, populist leaders simply confront more assertively real political problems that established government has not been able to solve. What unites populist leaders around the world is the claim that they represent 'the real people' of a society – those whose voices are not heard, those who are not represented by the elites and the technocrats who necessarily run the affairs of state. In addition, populist leaders frequently claim legitimacy from some ingrained sense of a society's essential nature or its history as the nation. To be potent, populism must create, or reinforce, a strong perception that representative democracy is failing, or that national political institutions simply cannot address the problems that motivate people.

Populist leaders therefore claim to be more directly democratic than the political mainstream they oppose. They often try to create 'movements' that are broader than even mass political parties and through such movements mobilize mass participation in favour of their policies and solutions. Populist leaders always seek to appeal over the heads of their political opponents to the 'real' citizens beyond. They believe in being 'directly democratic' and not necessarily 'liberal' in the broadest sense of the term. When in government, populist leaders in Turkey, Hungary, the Philippines and the United States have argued in different ways that they represent 'illiberal democracies' or 'conservative' or 'Christian' democracies. They don't have to be 'liberal', they argue, to be truly democratic or legitimate.[21]

Liberal critics of populist leaders and their movements are vehemently unconvinced by the argument that all this can be a dramatic exercise in direct democracy. Such movements, they maintain, are actually unsubtle attacks on essential democracy. This is based on the view, firstly, that 'direct democracy' is a myth in any meaningful sense. Regular national referendums and popular votes are simply impossible to conduct in large modern societies – notwithstanding the successful experience of Switzerland or California at local levels. Populist 'movements' may be large but they are used by leaders to create greater division, rather than inclusion, within their societies. And they are no device to express detailed political thinking. They intimidate popular debate as much as they express it. Secondly, it is said, populist leaders use the arguments of direct democracy to achieve political power and then resort to all the elitism, clientism, corruption and state capture they previously opposed; though this time with fewer safeguards on governmental behaviour. Indeed, with an instinct for 'one person, one vote, once only', populist leaders in power have a persistent record of tampering with electoral rules to ensure they stay there.[22]

The expression of populism differs from one part of the world to another and is significantly different in the multiparty systems of Europe as compared to the two-party system in the United States. In Europe, the picture is complex but the underlying trends are still clear enough. In the last twenty years overtly populist parties more than doubled their vote in national elections. In 1980, 10.6 per cent of Europeans voted for populist parties; by 2016 it was 20 per cent and by 2019 it was 25 per cent. Populist parties were in government, singly or in coalition, in eleven European countries.[23] Of course, it took different forms according to local political conditions. In Northern Europe, successful populist parties tended to be radically right-wing; in Southern Europe, primarily because of economic conditions, populist parties tended to be mainly ultra-left-wing; and Western Europe, as in Britain and Ireland, was more dominated by single-issue populist parties.[24] In central and Eastern Europe parties that were previously in the political mainstream have become effectively populist movements under autocratic leadership.[25]

There have been some spectacular national performances where populist parties have cut deeply into the established 'voting intentions' of certain countries. In Hungary, the Fidesz party commanded around 55 per cent of future voting intentions in 2018, the Freedom Party of Austria (FPO) around 26 per cent, the Five Star Movement in Italy some 28 per cent, the Alternative for Germany (AfD) over 13 per cent, or Podemos in Spain at least 15 per cent. If translated into votes at national elections, these proportions allow populist parties to become either effective at blocking minorities or to have the right to participation in coalitions. And in other cases it either gets or keeps them fully in government. Thus, Hungary's Fidesz party has been in a clear governing majority since 2010; the Five Star Movement entered a coalition government in Italy during 2017; and the AfD put itself into the position of a blocking minority in German politics after 2015.

Paradoxically, the exception to this populist wave was Britain's UKIP. It commanded at its peak in 2014 only around 15 per cent of popular support and by 2018, after a precipitate collapse, barely registered on the scale of voting intentions, struggling to survive as a national political entity. But as it grew towards it electoral peak, it cut into support for the major parties, fundamentally affected their policy stances, and arguably had the greatest single effect of any populist party on the national politics of its country.[26] It focused a demand that spanned all sections of society for withdrawal from the EU and campaigned successfully for a national referendum on it. And as UKIP disappeared from the political map, its nemesis, the Brexit Party, suddenly sprang to life like a phoenix in 2019 as another single issue, populist expression of dismay at the failure of the mainstream political establishment to 'deliver Brexit'. The new party claimed to be more than a single-issue group, as UKIP had been and promised to shake up British political life in a fundamental way. It is not clear how realistic this aspiration will turn out to be.

Throughout much of the Americas, populism has swept a broad path in recent years. Anti-establishment politicians such as Evo Morales in Bolivia, Cristina Fernandez de Kirchner in Argentina, Luiz Inácio Lula da Silva and then Dilma Rousseff in Brazil, or Hugo Chávez in Venezuela seemed to mark the beginning of a new cycle of populism in Latin American politics both ultra-left and ultra-right. In subsequent years, outright radical populists came to power, such as Jair Bolsonaro in Brazil and Andrés Manuel López Obrador in Mexico, while Nicolas Maduro continued to pursue the dictatorial populism that he inherited from Hugo Chávez in 2013. There is good polling evidence that faith in democracy within Latin America is lower than in any other region of the world and there is a growing sympathy among unhappy populations (paradoxically) both for anti-establishment movements as well as military rule.[27] As in years past, populations in many Latin American countries have turned to a generation of self-proclaimed 'saviours' rather than rely on their political institutions to represent them.

In the United States the presidency of Donald Trump represented a different variation of populism. He came as an outsider candidate into a Republican Party that was already deeply split by a populist subgroup in the 'Tea Party' movement. Against a great deal of mainstream opposition within party ranks he rode a tide of populist support, first to take the Republican nomination for president and then, to the astonishment of the world and by a narrow and controversial majority, the presidency itself. President Trump represents a phenomenon in US politics as much as he represents his own ebullient character and his style of leadership and statesmanship.[28] His ability to win through says much about the polarization of US politics dating back to the Bill Clinton presidency of the mid-1990s; the fragmentation of both traditional parties and a notable loss of confidence in the institutions of government and in law and the constitution itself that was traditionally so esteemed.[29] The United States has had populist presidents in the past; however, in this case, though populism certainly takes its own distinctive US form, it results from a number of antecedents that are all too familiar in other parts of the world.[30] As an overtly populist leader, at war with parts of his own government, the press and swathes of US society, President Trump found many other international populist authoritarians with whom to make common cause.

Authoritarian governments around the world

It is hardly coincidental that trends noted above should also be manifested in a notable growth of authoritarian-minded governments around the world. The new assertiveness of great power leaderships in China and Russia and the decade of economic crisis after 2008 ushered in a series of leaders and parties with increasingly autocratic instincts. Liberal democracy, social democratic parties and an optimistic sense that the 'world of globalization' was somehow immutable were all challenged by leaders who took a much narrower view of their national interests and were prepared to pursue them aggressively.

'Autocracy' is often used as a hold-all term for governments that might otherwise be described as 'despotic', 'totalitarian', 'chieftain', 'kleptocratic' or simply 'dictatorial'. There are no watertight categories and for our purposes that is not important.[31] The significance of growing autocracy in governments around the world is the effect it may have on characteristic behaviour within the international system, the attitudes of different governments to international law and institutions, and not least to prevailing political values – in particular the distinctive Western values that have so shaped the international system until recently.[32]

Judged, as such, from a Western and liberal democratic perspective, the respected analyses of Freedom House are illuminating.[33] According to its annual indexes, Freedom House chronicles a significant recent decline in politically free countries across all regions in the world. From 2006 to 2017, despite spikes in the trend lines (inevitable in proportions among the small absolute number of fewer than 200 countries in the world), underlying trends showed a dramatic fall in the number of countries where political freedom was evidently improving and a steady, slightly less dramatic, rise in the countries where standards of freedom declined. There is no evidence that these trends are yet beginning to swing back in favour of political freedom and open government.[34] Countries where political freedom was judged to have been severely or significantly reduced from even recent previous levels spanned a spectrum to include governments in Turkey, Russia, the Central African Republic, Burundi, Hungary, Bahrain, Mexico, Ukraine, Azerbaijan, Kenya, Mali and Tajikistan, among others.[35] In 2018 it was judged that, in contrast to the situation not long after the end of the Cold War, only 45 per cent of countries could now be judged as essentially 'free'; some 30 per cent were only 'partly free' and 24 per cent of countries were self-evidently 'not free' by any Western standards. In terms of global population this suggests a situation in which 61 per cent of the global population live in states where their political freedom is significantly, or wholly, curtailed, judged by liberal democratic standards. Only 39 per cent of the global population enjoy most of those privileges.[36] No more than about 15 per cent of the global population have ready access to genuinely free media sources.

The implications for British security

Britain has long been characterized as a pragmatic power in global politics – liberal democratic to be sure but not overtly ideological in its approach to the world. During the Cold War it took up a confrontational position against the

Soviet Union insofar as it directly threatened British interests but actively looked for opportunities to promote cooperation and dialogue with Moscow. At times when the United States locked horns more ideologically with the Soviet Union, Britain promoted, with some success, a 'dialogue wherever possible' approach in the mid-1950s, the late-1960s and again in the mid-1980s. Similarly, in relation to most of the powers of the Middle East, Latin America and many parts of Africa and Asia after British decolonization, the country took overtly pragmatic approaches to governments that were by turns populist and highly autocratic in many cases. Why, therefore, should current trends described above be any more of a challenge for Britain in the 2020s than they were thirty or forty years ago, when Britain was not seriously disadvantaged by them?

The difference between the twentieth and the twenty-first centuries lies in the retreat of Western liberalism as the predominant force shaping the organization of world politics. To put it simply, the rules of international politics that were developed and policed – insofar as they were inconsistently enforced – by the Western powers are regarded as less morally binding and less enforceable by an increasing number of governments around the world – and in some cases even within the West. In the 1990s and the early 2000s when Western countries could act largely unopposed by other major powers, they themselves played fast and loose with their own international rules. They often behaved inconsistently, struggled to remain within accepted international legal frameworks and justified themselves with arguments that have subsequently been played back at them by adversaries they now accuse of acting unlawfully. The approach to dealing with jihadist terrorism in the early years after the 9/11 attacks on the United States, the whole concept of a 'war on terror' and then the Iraq War of 2003 and its bitter aftermath had a particularly toxic effect on the reputation of the United States as leader of the free world, which extended to many of its allies and friends, and particularly Britain. The long-term strategic effects of the 9/11 attacks on the United States have been all that their instigator, Osama bin Laden, must have hoped.

If the Western powers are partly responsible for a moral decline in their own rules of coexistence, there are also many examples of ways in which international order has, in any case, deteriorated in recent years, as we examine more fully in Chapter 7.

Autocratic and populist leaders have shown themselves to be indifferent or hostile to international institutions and often to the basic principles of international law. There is diminishing faith across the system in 'international regime' approaches to the management of energy, nuclear proliferation, climate change, migration, organized international crime, international monetary policy, international health or cyber security.[37] An international system that was characterized by very high degrees of institutionalization and acknowledged interdependence between the states within the system some twenty years ago has tipped markedly towards one that is orientated towards the direct exercise of national power. The Big Four powers – China, the United States, India and Russia – under assertive, nationalist leaders, all behave in ways that are less constrained by system rules and conventions than two decades ago. Russia annexed Crimea from Ukraine through the use of force in 2014; China militarized several coral atolls in the South China Sea and asserted sovereignty through force majeure even against UN legal rulings in 2017; and in 2018 the United States reneged on its 2015 eight power nuclear deal with Iran, having already withdrawn from multilateral Pacific and European trade pacts. Such actions set the political weather for the rest of the international system. Not surprisingly, important regional powers like Iran, Egypt, Nigeria, Brazil, Kazakhstan or Indonesia place little faith in international regimes that are not underpinned by some minimum level of consensus among the Big Four.

It is unclear whether the traditional rules of the international system are breaking down, or instead being steadily replaced by new rules, based more representatively on the emerging constellation of great powers and regional powers during the decades to come. Or, a steady decline into predominantly jungle rules may be underway, as we discuss in Chapter 7. Whichever way the system is heading, there is much at stake for British security in this hiatus about the power of established international rules and their legitimacy.

Through history and political conviction Britain has a lot invested in what it refers to as the 'rules-based international order'. The fact that it is even accorded such a title is evidence that it is under threat. Until recent years it seemed so obvious it did not need to be named. For in naming a 'rules-based international order' there is an implicit assumption that alternatives are available. The 'rules' are understood to be the existing – Western – rules based on principles derived from capitalist, liberal democratic thinking. Any alternatives would revolve around new rules or perhaps merely jungle rules. Throughout the twentieth century, Britain enjoyed both hard power and diplomatic heft in being one of the cradles of modern liberal democracy and even more as one of the rule setters of international relations. Any threats of an identity crisis for liberal democracy, both within Western societies and across the wider international society of states – threats that seemed to have been banished for a brief period after 1991 – put Britain's wider interests in some jeopardy.

Generational change is also relevant. Challenges to Britain's traditional political and moral persona must be addressed by the upcoming generation of British citizens. Whether or not the influence of Western democratic liberalism can be restored in the conduct of world politics, or simply be overshadowed by different ideas as new centres of power emerge and project their own values, it is Britain's 'millennial' and 'centennial' generations who will live with the security consequences.

The millennial generation, born between 1980 and 2000, have long been part of the British electorate and the centennial generation, born after 2000, will soon join them. Millennials make up 14 per cent of the total population. About 30 per cent of the population is younger than them, and 56 per cent is older – not surprising as a relatively ageing population pushes towards 70 million by 2030.[38] But there are discontinuities compared even to the recent past. As against the European average, Britain's population is growing healthily, but 54 per cent of its growth in the coming decade is expected to arise from net inward migration.[39] More than a quarter of millennials were born abroad and, as younger people, the highest concentration live in London. They are more ethnically and racially diverse than previous generations,[40] less religious,[41] the most formally educated, confident, connected and open to change.[42] They have been called the 'me-me-me generation' who 'want it all and want it now'[43] – except, it seems, when it comes to alcohol, cigarettes and sex.[44] They worry about home ownership, debt and job security in a service and gig economy,[45] and they care about environment, sustainability and global inequality.[46]

All this should make the millennials – and perhaps the centennials coming behind them, who have never known a world without a fully functioning internet – a good bet for a generation that will re-commit to liberal democratic and cosmopolitan values when Brexit Britain most needs them. But the older generation should not be too complacent about this. There is no evidence that millennials have a strong innate faith in Britain's current democratic institutions or the way they have been run since most of them were born. And the vast majority of their 2 billion millennial counterparts elsewhere in the world will not be entering positions of power in societies that have comparable liberal democratic traditions. There is so much for Britain to gain from the talent and cosmopolitan verve of the millennial generation if it really believes in the traditions of British liberal democracy, but so much to lose if it does not.

Britain's immediate challenges

Chapter 5
Dealing with the great powers

State-based security challenges have made a dramatic reappearance as key drivers of global geopolitics over the last decade. Towards the end of the last century it seemed that weakness and fragmentation within and between states had displaced the twentieth-century struggles between the most powerful as the driving force of international conflict. Even the peaceful end of the Cold War had the effect of replacing four European states with twenty-four new or reconstituted countries across Eurasia – many of them inclined to domestic conflict and instability.[1] And other long-standing and new states in Africa and Asia suffered fragmentation crises that also seemed to have become the stuff of international insecurity. The concept of 'new wars' and messy half-war-half-peace battle zones was prevalent.[2] Excessive political weakness rather than the excesses of political strength seemed to be the main cause of conflict, while expanding globalization seemed to have diminished the reality of military competition between the strong powers of the world. It was assumed they would certainly compete with each other but not in ways that were so resonant of the militarized, geopolitical struggles of the Cold War, and certainly not as in the era of the world wars.

The new reality, however, is that state-based military competition between the globally powerful, as well as regionally dominant powers, is now just as likely to occur as conflicts driven by fragmentation and state weakness. And though it may seem reassuring that state-based security threats exist in a far more constraining and complex global environment than at the end of the last century, the fact remains that state-based challenges are qualitatively different and more dangerous to Western powers than any of the challenges of political weakness and breakdown happening elsewhere, even those happening relatively close to home. The current preference of the Big Four powers for bilateral relationships rather than cooperative frameworks and multilateral arrangements to deal with peace and security, is a sobering reality that other states have no choice but to recognize.

The most immediate and important state-based challenges to Britain's security for the 2020s arise from the quite different, but clearly emerging, policies of Russia, China and the United States. Britain's relations with India are of a different character and order, which play into long-term perspectives of future security. But its security relations with the other three of the Big Four powers have to be characterized as near-term challenges.

Britain and the Russian challenge

Bilateral relations between Britain and Russia reached an unusual low point in 2019. It was unusual because Britain's traditional attitude towards Moscow always coupled Cold War toughness with a pragmatic desire to improve relations wherever it might be possible. And Moscow traditionally took Britain seriously as the European pillar of NATO and the country that most had the political ear of Washington. But while the attitude of Russian leaders was highly nuanced towards those European countries and leaderships where it felt a charm offensive was appropriate, such as Hungary, Bulgaria or Italy, who were unhappy maintaining European sanctions against Russia, Moscow saw no advantage in courting other countries, especially Britain, and no longer treated London as a useful conduit of influential thinking in Washington. There were many specific points of conflict. Russia's attempted novichok poisoning of Sergei Skripal in Salisbury during 2018 and Britain's orchestration of an international reaction to it were the most evident. It highlighted a Russian international assassination policy that had touched Britain and allied countries many times in recent years.[3] It was rapidly followed, thanks again largely to British intelligence work, with the exposure of clumsy Russian attempts to hack into the international chemical watchdog laboratories in the Hague investigating both the Skripal case and the Russian-backed use of chemical weapons in Syria. And then again, in successive Russian attempts to cyberattack the World Anti-Doping Agency records, as they sought to get the most important bans on Russian athletes lifted. Such activities represented, said the British government, 'indiscriminate and reckless cyber-attacks targeting political institutions, businesses, media and sport'.[4] In a broader context, President Putin explicitly supported the move towards Brexit, on the assumption, it seems, that it would weaken the EU and potentially create diplomatic isolation for Britain.[5]

Such thinking crystallized Russia's hardening attitude towards Britain over the previous decade; the country was not the useful diplomatic conduit it had once been, and if Britain had become a favoured home to traitors or rich Russian oligarchs whom the Kremlin wanted to assassinate, it was not deterred from cyberattacks or assassinations by any prospect of causing political outrage in Britain. And yet, Russian intelligence consistently underestimated Britain's criminal forensic abilities, the high reputation of its intelligence agencies and its ability to mobilize international opinion against egregious, state-sponsored assassination. Russian government and media paid Britain the back-handed compliment of undue attention as it tried to undermine every new revelation and statement made by London on these matters. Moscow mocked Britain for its domestic Brexit crisis and sought to needle it into diplomatic irrelevance even as it watched very carefully where Brexit might be taking it. And for their part, British political and military leaders became more unapologetic in pointing to 'increasingly aggressive Russian behaviour' and its 'hostile activities within our continent' and defined Russia as 'the most complex and capable security challenge we have faced since the Cold War' and 'far greater than the challenges that were presented as an insurgency in terms of Iraq and Afghanistan'.[6] Judged against the usual conventions of bilateral diplomacy, this was as low as Moscow-London relations ever got during the Cold War. It might be interpreted as an unfortunate cyclical blip that could be reversed in the coming years, as is in the nature of professional diplomacy. But there are good reasons to see the diplomatic chill between Britain and Russia as symptomatic of more structural changes rapidly affecting British security which will continue well into the next decade.

The leadership of President Putin is not likely to end until at least 2024 when his fourth presidential term expires. The government over which he presides shows no sign of wanting, or even being able, to change its general foreign policy. As outlined in Chapter 1, Putin's Russia is explicitly revisionist – dedicated, as he said in his 2014 Duma speech, to reversing as much as possible the 'catastrophe' of the Soviet Union's collapse in 1991. The short-term vision is to change the prevailing politics of much of Europe and the actual political geography of some of it, where it borders present-day Russia. The long-term vision is to re-establish Russia on a genuinely global scale, through a 'Eurasian mission' that effectively partners it with a rising China, and negates the natural power of the United States during the first half of the twenty-first century. This explicit revisionism is driven by motives that are both defensive and offensive.

They are defensive because Putin and his leadership group see the hand of Western powers in all the 'colour revolutions' of the post-Soviet states that would take them out of Russia's natural orbit.[7] They see the same hand in any significant civil dissent in Russia. They see that NATO goes on enlarging itself – eight times since 1949 – to encompass more of the states over which Moscow used to have either complete control or heavy influence.[8] Despite what NATO leaders say, Moscow argues, the Atlantic Alliance is structurally programmed to keep on growing; it simply cannot help itself. The idea that Georgia, still less Ukraine, might join NATO sometime in the future (as they have both requested) is viewed as a strategic nightmare by Russian leaders. And they remember a decade of weakness and near-chaos after 1991 which might have dismembered Russia itself and in which Western powers seemed content to ride a wave of 'wild-West capitalism' in Russia without ever trying to integrate it properly into the international system. Russia's special and great power status was simply ignored in these years and, for a variety of reasons, Moscow lost faith in the Western powers who seemed only to be able to cooperate with it strictly on their own terms.[9] A defensive mindset based on such preoccupations progressively became something close to a national paranoia, as Russians tried to explain to themselves why they were subject to so many types of international sanctions, why their government was vilified in many parts of the world and why Russia is perceived as being on the wrong side of history.

But this largely paranoid stance is also tactically offensive for equally compelling reasons. Presented with difficult policy choices the Putin leadership group characteristically opts for risky opportunism. They move in surprising and decisive ways that keep their adversaries off-balance. Russian autocrats can act quickly and without effective domestic opposition; and they have the political will to use military force whatever the humanitarian cost. Putin's leadership was established in 1999 through his willingness, as the new Russian prime minister, to destroy the Russian city of Grozny in order to crush the separatist rebellion in Chechnya. It was paralleled seventeen years later by Russian airpower helping the Syrian government to destroy its own city of Aleppo to drive out rebels and civilians alike. In 2019, as Syrian forces moved against the final rebel stronghold of Idlib, Syrian and Russian aircraft first bombed the hospitals – twenty-four facilities directly targeted – in advance of the offensive.[10] Russian leaders showed themselves prepared to use military force in brutal and decisive ways that Western leaders could never contemplate. And in between these events Russian leaders showed they were also prepared to use force in more informal ways. Faced with a 'colour revolution' and a new anti-Russian government in Ukraine during 2013, Russia sent irregular troops into the Crimea and then Eastern Ukraine to stimulate and support pro-Russian-separatist forces. The result was a unilateral annexation of Crimea in 2014 – the first European change of borders through military force since the Second World War – and the creation of another 'frozen conflict' within Ukraine's Donbass region – a zone of incipient conflict that could be manipulated sometime in the future – alongside those already existing in Transnistria, Abkhazia and South Ossetia.[11]

Russian military capabilities can be overstated. Though it increased the proportion of its GDP spent on defence by more than half in the decade after 2008 (hitting a peak of 5.8 per cent in 2016), its GDP was static or falling during these years as energy prices tumbled. Military reform was given high priority by the Kremlin, after a poor performance in the brief war with Georgia in 2008, though even then the results were patchy. Western observers always note clear improvements in some sectors of Russia's nuclear, air, rocket and submarine forces, as the implications are more evident to Western security. Trends among the troubled ground forces are, however, equally indicative. Here, there is a determination to move from fielding the old Red Army, of moderate quality but high numbers, to develop a new force designed primarily for offensive, very high-intensity, and short conflicts in and around Russia's 'near abroad'.[12]

If the world seemed to be moving against Russian interests in the years after the dissolution of the Soviet Union, Moscow reacted by showing it was prepared to use military force, both implicitly and explicitly, to create the conditions for some big territorial readjustments. In April 2014 President Putin deliberately spoke of the zones of frozen conflict around Ukraine as 'novorossiya' – the name of Imperial Russia's Black Sea territories that covered most of southern Ukraine, and he thereby created a storm of nationalist support for the notion in Russia. It was an interesting exercise in flying kites to gauge reactions.[13] Blocking Ukrainian shipping from the Kerch Strait in 2018 – an international waterway but claimed as Russian territory following the annexation of Crimea – was an internationally illegal attempt to strangle Ukraine's ports on the Sea of Azov, whose only access is via the Strait, and to create another Russian military pressure point in the Black Sea region.[14]

Russian assertiveness across the territories of the old Soviet Union extends to dark threats and hostile military gestures towards the former Soviet republics of the three Baltic states. In 2016 Russia introduced nuclear-capable *Iskandar-M* missiles into the Kaliningrad enclave bordering Lithuania and Poland in reaction to NATO's increased readiness levels. In 2017 the most sophisticated military exercises in recent Russian history were held along the borders of all three Baltic states and Poland – the forces clearly rehearsing offensive operations as well as defensive 'anti-access' strategies. Militarized hostility towards Georgia continued consistently after the conflict of 2008. Georgia's immediate neighbours, Azerbaijan and Armenia, have generally good, albeit tense, relations with Moscow, though it tries to mediate the long-standing conflict between them over separatism in Nagorno-Karabakh.

Meanwhile, Russian policy sought to weaken the collective strength of the Central and West European allies both in their NATO and EU forums, by wooing allies such as Hungary, Bulgaria, even Austria and Italy, that Moscow thinks susceptible to inducements. Moscow worked hard to create a new security relationship with Turkey (notwithstanding that Turkey remains a NATO ally), and it intervened at many levels in the politics of the Western Balkans – even being accused of promoting a plot by nationalist Russians to assassinate the Montenegrin prime minister and trigger an anti-Western coup. What is known as Russia's 'wedge strategy' is designed to create explicit military leverage in countries such as Bosnia, Georgia or Moldova and so diminish the security blanket and political influence of the Western powers across Europe. For

Moscow, there are some high-value diplomatic and strategic cards that can be played against the Western powers from north to south in Europe: a proactive military buildup that has left the West flat-footed in the Arctic, military pressure in north west Europe, inducements or energy blackmail in central and south Eastern Europe; and a robust military presence in the Eastern Mediterranean with the air and naval bases Russia established in Syria after 2015, new understandings with Israel, growing economic influence in Cyprus, and the deployment of significant numbers of Russian mercenaries to Eastern Libya in support of rebel militias.

From the perspective of most Western leaders this amounts to a catalogue of opportunities for Russia to undermine the already shaky strategic consensus between them. Even though the cards could never have been predicted to play out this way, their presence on the table suggested a form of Russian grand strategy that had been foreshadowed in President Putin's 2014 Duma speech; determined to recover as much influence – or even outright control – of the former Soviet space as possible, while working assiduously to create the permissive political environment among the NATO/EU powers who would be unable to counter any of this, and to keep them diplomatically off-balance and prevent them encouraging any more 'colour revolutions' inside or around Russia. Not least, it was a strategy designed to leverage the United States away from its European allies and seek out those in Europe who might become susceptible to Moscow's economic or military pressure. It represented a half-formed, but potent, version of the old Soviet Union's 'Finlandization' policy, but applied now to a number of possible countries nominally within the enlarged Western alliance.[15] *The Rossiyskaya Gazeta* of 2015 embodied a public version of Russia's most recent National Security Strategy and it made these intentions very clear.[16]

On the face of it this might suggest a return to the politics of the Cold War – where an essentially strong Western alliance resisted the tactical manoeuvres of an essentially weaker challenger who sought to disrupt it. It was a competition framed by the fearsome military forces of NATO and the Warsaw Pact. It may appear to be a cause of some relief that military competition between Russia and the West no longer exists in quite the same way. But new forms of military competition have arisen and the fact remains that great power politics of the last ten years have actually become more volatile than they were during the Cold War.

For one thing, Moscow was not explicitly revisionist during the Cold War. It was determined to hang on to its own sphere of influence from East Germany to Bulgaria, but it never seriously challenged the line of the 'iron curtain' that created its physical security zone.[17] Since the collapse of the Soviet Union, however, Moscow's sense of its physical security zone has moved 1,000 miles closer and leaves former Soviet republics like Ukraine, Georgia, Estonia, Latvia and Lithuania on the wrong side of it, *and* now as NATO allies or partners. President Putin's revisionist approach, however defensively minded from his perspective, therefore extends into the enlarged European family of capitalist democracies. The implicit Cold War rules that respected the stability of eastern and western spheres of influence and which tacitly agreed on which other regions were fair game for strategic competition cannot be observed, still less enforced, on the same terms. In contrast to the Cold War years, Moscow's strategic ambitions and the West's strategic responsibilities now overlap in several parts of Europe.

Secondly, Putin's Russia pursues a 'hybrid warfare approach' to strategic competition rather than one that relied so much on the heavy metal of military power years ago. 'Hybrid warfare' is an imprecise term but, as outlined in Chapter 2, refers to campaigns that simultaneously might use a wide range of instruments, including distorted information and social media offensives for 'the manufacture of doubt', to magnify civil unrest or to influence democratic elections. Cyberattacks now also form part of the technique, designed to create disruption or confusion. And at the sharp end, hybrid conflict seeks to use local fighters or irregular troops – even terrorist groups – as proxy fighters and sometimes to use regular troops in formed units but clandestinely and out of uniform ('little green men' as they were described in the Ukraine crisis). Other than the phenomenon of social media and cyberattack, there is nothing conceptually new in such hybrid warfare techniques. The Soviet Union regularly tried them all in earlier times and Western powers can be accused of trying some of them occasionally (and without much success).[18] But among those countries in the world that use such techniques as part of a well-conceived strategy, it is evident that Russia has adopted a hybrid approach with real sophistication and effect in recent years.[19] New military equipment and political tactics have been explicitly trialled across the Middle East since Russia intervened more proactively in 2015, and it has driven some real wedges into weakening Western influence in the region. As an authoritarian government it has the power to control most of the information flowing through the country and it can pull economic levers through its direct control of Russian companies that is not possible for democratic governments. The cyber domain of modern warfare and the impacts of internet hacking and artificial intelligence have reinvigorated the coordinated use of all available instruments of policy – the hybrid approach – to levels of sophistication that Moscow could not, and never did, achieve in the Cold War. For Western powers, defending a physical line along the boundaries of NATO territory was the predominant requirement for security during the Cold War – Soviet dabbling inside Western countries certainly existed during those years but was a relatively peripheral security concern. Now, however, the defence of physical borders is usually the peripheral requirement while security concerns centre on more intrusive developments. Border security is a necessary but hardly sufficient condition for defence against a revisionist power.

Thirdly, President Putin's economic and foreign policy futures are closely interconnected in ways that were never the case for the old Soviet Union.

Russia's economy is undoubtedly robust if only because so much of it is essentially unmodernized and, in the absence of much international investment, focused on its own domestic market. But it is highly dependent on income from its hydrocarbon exports and sensitive to changes in energy prices. Russia contains over a quarter of the world's proven reserves of natural gas and is the largest exporter of it. It is the third largest oil producer and the second largest oil exporter in the world, and also has a reserve of exportable coal that is good for over 400 years. It enjoys regional dominance in energy pipelines across Western and Southern Europe that limits development in the other energy-rich former Soviet states. It has attempted to manipulate existing pipelines routes and planned new ones for its own foreign policy purposes.[20] In three winters between 2006 and 2015 Russia was accused of naked attempts to use gas supply blackmail against Ukraine and hence also against European customers supplied via Ukrainian pipelines.

Nevertheless, Russia is also effectively hostage to its income from hydrocarbons. It exports 70 per cent of its oil, 30 per cent of its gas and 35 per cent of its coal. Indeed, its oil and gas exports alone make up 70 per cent of Russia's total annual exports. When prices were high at the turn of this century Russia was cash rich, but the longer-term trend of lower energy prices since the economic crisis of 2008 squeezed the economy severely over the following decade and pushed Russia into recession in 2015 with dramatic falls in average incomes and state spending.[21]

This matters for Russian foreign policy because the core of the productive economy still resides in a small number of massive extractive industry and technology companies that were easily captured by the new post-Soviet instant billionaires. And their capture had the effect of locking a small group of oligarchs around President Putin into a kleptocracy who control the heights of the Russian economy; making it inefficient and unable to escape a type of mafia capitalism that is immune to planned structural reform.[22] Unlike its ideological predecessor, the post-Soviet government in Russia stands for nothing other than its own survival and must make constant appeals to Russian nationalism and patriotism in the face of its poor economic performance during a prolonged period of lower energy prices.[23] The national paranoia therefore blames unjustified international sanctions and investor prejudice for the underperformance. But productivity is low, the quality of life is lower than Russians might have expected after 1991, population numbers are falling in absolute terms and ageing rapidly. A prolonged upturn in energy prices would certainly restore some cash and vigour to the economy, but would not give it the kick of structural reform it needs. Only a top leadership change to put the country under the control of people who do not personally own the commanding heights of the economy will be able to do that.

If, as is likely, Putin and the oligarchs come under growing domestic pressures with economic underperformance, there will be stronger incentives to play the great power card to bolster nationalist and patriotic themes among the Russian public. There is nothing new in autocrats doing that, but in modern world politics Western powers seek to punish adventurism with economic sanctions rather than outright military responses; and in the globalized world smart and targeted sanctions have proved to be far more effective than the blunt instruments they were during the Cold War. For Russian leaders, locked into a kleptocratic conspiracy, this prospect offers only a vicious circle; assertive foreign policy that attracts various forms of economic sanctions, at a time of prolonged low energy prices. Russian diplomacy works hard to have sanctions lifted and tries to split the Western allies over the issue, but sanctions undoubtedly still starve a weak economy of international investment. One way out of this bind is for Russian leaders somehow to change the terms of the geopolitical game decisively in favour of autocracies and authoritarian governments, working together with them to constrain the Western powers rather than vice versa. This is another reason why President Putin's revisionist vision poses a security challenge that is significantly different from that of the Cold War. The danger of diplomatic miscalculation – in Russia as well as the West – is greater in these circumstances than was the case then.

Understanding that the 2020s will not be a reversion to the conditions of the Cold War creates particular security challenges for Britain that go well beyond the diplomatic clashes of 2018–19. In the climate of the next decade Putin's Russia has a strong motive to single Britain out and try to isolate it in disputes that matter to London more than they matter to Britain's allies and friends. The international reaction to the botched GRU (Russia's military intelligence bureau) attempt to poison Sergei Skripal seemed to take the Kremlin aback. It was more an example of the GRU being out of full Kremlin control as it pursued a series of vendettas around the world. But the fiasco of it didn't obscure the fact that Britain was a target of Russian hostility and criminal interference – and regarded as a soft touch after the Litvinenko murder in 2006 – and not worth wooing in ways that even Germany, and certainly France and Italy, evidently are.

There is convincing evidence that Russian social media offensives tried to reinforce the referendum vote in favour of Brexit in 2016, and the Kremlin has publicly supported the Brexit process since then, seeming to see it as an opportunity to differentiate Britain on a number of important grounds from its close friends and allies elsewhere in Europe.[24] Britain has traditionally been the most important European player in creating and helping maintain political unity within NATO. It is also the European country that most assiduously implements agreed international sanctions against Russia. If Britain can be leveraged away from that role by the wider fallout from Brexit (or just nudged further along if it is happening anyway), then Russian strategy to achieve its newly assertive aims and get more sanctions lifted will be all the easier to achieve.

Then too, Russian military forces that are displayed to impress Western powers with their modernized capabilities are also designed to counter Western reinforcements coming into Europe from the United States. The Atlantic sea routes are critical. Particular attention has been given to creating a new generation of Russian submarines – the new *Belgorod* special mission submarine for one, to operate off British shores in the North Atlantic, to probing flights near to British airspace in the North Sea and renewed attempts to undermine the security of British nuclear submarines as they come and go into the mid-Atlantic on their three-monthly patrols. The 'Greenland-Iceland-UK Gap' (GIUK) has assumed a renewed military importance it has not known since the 1980s.

None of this would matter very much if the relationship between Europe and the United States – and in particular that between Washington and London – had remained reasonably stable over the last twenty years; but it has not. Whether the United States is seriously detaching itself from its previous levels of political commitment to European security is the single biggest determinant of Europe's future prospects in peace and war. If the Atlantic Alliance, in its broadest sense, continues to be based on proactive US leadership, then the strategic aspirations of Putin's Russia are unlikely to amount to more than a persistent nuisance to the core Western powers as they struggle with new security problems. But if US leadership is effectively absent, for whatever reasons, then President Putin's Russia will increasingly set the agendas surrounding new security problems, as well as the range of responses available to European leaders. And for Britain, given its erstwhile self-image as a political and military bridge across the Atlantic, responding to the presidency of Donald Trump looms as the greatest judgement call of all; how much should Britain rely on, and invest in, its close security relationship with the United States for the next decade or so?

Britain and the challenge of US strategy

Britain has a long history of dealing with differences between Washington and London. Even the Grand Alliance relationship during the Second World War, much romanticized in the years since, required constant British efforts and sacrifices to maintain it. And with each US presidency since that of Franklin D. Roosevelt British public and media opinion has (increasingly) obsessed over whether the United States and Britain have a 'special relationship'. In reality, every country has a relationship that is special – in some way sui generis – with a superpower like the United States. But British grand strategy since 1941 has continued to be largely predicated on the centrality of a close defence and security alliance with the United States, built upon genuinely shared democratic and liberal values and a willingness to defend them with hard military power if necessary. More than most countries in the world, Britain has tried to be a genuinely significant junior partner to the United States in global security matters. It has long been part of Britain's self-image and the country has expended a great deal of military, intelligence and diplomatic resource to manage the relationship over the years.

British media sensitivity over how 'special' is the Washington-London relationship normally concentrates on the personal chemistry between US presidents and British prime ministers. It has generally been good. With the exception of Presidents Johnson and Nixon between 1964 and 1974 all incumbents of the White House since Franklin D Roosevelt seem to have felt some personal affinity with British leaders. The presidency of George W. Bush and his friendship with British Prime Minister Tony Blair, however, came to seem like the last time there was an atmosphere of unforced friendly partnership between president and prime minister, and it came to an end in 2007 when Blair stepped down. Gordon Brown, as prime minister, took some pains to distance himself from a US president who seemed, by then, to be toxic in world opinion. Taking office in 2009, President Obama did not share any sentimental attachment to the bilateral relationship. His attitude to Britain was essentially transactional, even though he established some strong personal friendships among the British royal family and political elites.[25] After two Obama terms, President Trump was elected in 2016 and from the first, presided over evident chaos in the White House that made it impossible for British leaders to gauge where anyone's bilateral relations stood in the president's eyes, allies, friends or adversaries. President Trump stands for re-election in November 2020 and the most prudent working assumption among the allies of the United States is that he will serve until the end of 2024.

Too much is normally read, however, into the personal chemistry between Washington and London. Of course, personal relationships between leaders have an impact on the political atmosphere. But broader questions are at issue. The US/British relationship, skilfully handled for the most part by diplomats and officials on both sides, has shown itself well capable of managing personality differences at the top. It has also shown itself to be fairly robust in its ability to weather individual policy disagreements, even over issues as central to the United States as Britain's refusal to support the Vietnam War. The key structural question, instead, is whether the current relationship could really withstand a genuine divergence of *political values* and *strategic vision* for the future of the Western world.

In this respect, the challenge that US strategy really poses for Britain suggests some sobering realities that predate the Trump presidency by some years. Despite frequent avowals that the United States leads and defends common values among its democratic allies and maintains a shared vision of global order; and despite a strong British desire to help make this true, American security thinking since the 1990s shows a steady divergence in the way the United States and the Western allies interpret their respective visions of world order. There is even room for doubt as to how far core political values are genuinely shared.[26] The Trump presidency is not as eccentric or atypical as it often appears to non-Americans and it draws from some strong long-term domestic trends as well as the frustrations of dealing with a fast-changing global order.[27] If the Trump presidency turns out to be a genuine tipping point amid a growing transatlantic divergence, it will greatly diminish the strategic value of British commitments to a particular vision of global order and the British interpretation of the liberal values which underpin it.

President Trump's outlook on world politics appears to be grounded in a mixture of old and new forces arising from a complex historical background. For many years Donald Trump has believed in the inevitable competition between the United States and China and evidently wants his presidency to be noted for redefining that relationship, either through a grand bargain, or else through competition on terms more favourable to the United States.[28] As a natural 'two-front power' it was always inevitable that the United States will give relatively more weight to its Asia-Pacific front in the twenty-first century. The demographic trends of the United States lean that way and its geopolitical interests are more acute in the Asia-Pacific, as opposed to the transatlantic, region. Any president would see greater national challenges in Asia-Pacific than across Europe. Indeed, in this century the United States can be said also to have a third, more recent, natural front. The Arctic and the 'High North' present a high-value geopolitical interest as global warming opens up new Trans-Arctic trade routes and mineral riches inside the Arctic Circle.[29] This front can be expected to have an increasing pull on US strategic thinking in the 2020s.

Another element is that over the last thirty years the instinctive 'liberal internationalism' of twentieth-century US policy has been steadily eroded by both Democratic and Republican presidents as they responded to events. That liberal internationalism was a long-established product of Hamiltonian thinking that the United States should be responsible for creating a security and economic architecture for world politics, which then grafted onto it Wilsonian requirements that such architecture would only be stable if it housed democratic states committed to individual rights and international law. By the mid-twentieth-century liberal internationalism thus promoted itself as a mixture of political power and democratic ethics, led by the United States.[30] During the Cold War it did not seem to require much further justification.

When the Cold War ended and the 1991 Gulf War triumphed over an aggressive dictator, there was some early sloganizing around the United States leading a 'new world order', very much in the language of liberal internationalism. It was quickly evident, however, that successive Washington administrations were not inclined to continue making the singular sacrifices that the concept required. The United States got badly caught out trying to act as a humanitarian policeman in Somalia after 1991, followed by a messy intervention in Haiti during 1994. By this time, even Democratic President Bill Clinton – an instinctive internationalist – had become extremely sceptical of the ability of either the United Nations or the European allies of the United States to handle the progressive collapse of Yugoslavia. In 1995 the United States intervened in the war with an iron diplomatic fist and a NATO-based military enforcement plan that brooked no argument. In 1999 it led a NATO air campaign against Belgrade over Kosovo as that mis-managed territory of Serbia asserted its independence. Kosovo had always been the most dangerous piece in the disintegrating Yugoslav jigsaw. But there was no question of US ground troops being used in combat against Serbian forces under any circumstances. A Democrat president was still leading its allies, but the message to the Europeans had become loud and clear. US forces in Western Europe were drawing down to low numbers to reap a post-Cold War dividend, and the Yugoslavian wars of the 1990s marked the last time the United States would materially embroil itself in European security affairs, unless a significant crisis with Russia was underway. Within ten years even that caveat was not secure. It could be amended to mean 'unless US global interests were at stake' – which might or might not be triggered by a significant crisis with Russia.

In 2008 another instinctively liberal internationalist Democrat became president. Barack Obama was avowedly globalist in his outlook, believing the United States must play a vital role in world order. But he conceived the role differently.[31] As paraphrased in interviews with Jeffrey Goldberg, Obama believed that 'Asia represents the future. Africa and Latin America, in his view, deserve far more US attention than they receive. Europe, about which he is unromantic, is a source of global stability that requires, to his occasional annoyance, American hand-holding. And the Middle East is a region to be avoided – one that, thanks to America's energy revolution, will soon be of negligible relevance to the US economy'.[32] It was a new and different interpretation of liberal internationalism. Even so, the practice was disappointing. The Obama administration tried to 'reset' a series of relations after the conflictual Bush years, with Russia, Iran and China, but to no avail. The wars in Iraq and Afghanistan were difficult to terminate. Obama instinctively rebelled against what he termed the 'Washington playbook' that always reached for the military instruments of policy, and defence expenditure was sharply cut back. But more subtle policy instruments proved almost impossible to mobilize against a deteriorating global environment. The administration tried to 're-balance' its strategic attention towards Asia but did not get very far. It tried to drive Israel into a new deal with the Palestinians but was bitterly rebuffed. It tried to lead ambitious, new economic frameworks across Asia and with Europe but found them impossible to complete before the president left office. The central achievement of getting a nuclear deal with Iran was heavily criticized in the United States and then ostentatiously renounced by Obama's successor.[33] To observers in Europe, the Obama presidency, for all its sophisticated international reasoning, left American leadership more uncertain and ineffectual than before. If Democrat leaders – from Jimmy Carter, to Bill Clinton and Barack Obama – remained committed to some new version of liberal internationalism, they could not translate it convincingly into the globalized world that was daily diversifying before their eyes.

Meanwhile, different strands of Republican Party thinking assumed more mainstream status in US strategic approaches which had evolved rapidly after the era of President Ronald Reagan. Anti-interventionist republicans challenged hitherto conventional views that the United States should assume so many global responsibilities. This became a powerful undercurrent in modern republicanism. In 1999 President George W. Bush, however, represented a somewhat different strand that could be termed 'conservative internationalism' – and assertively so after the 9/11 terror attacks. His 'neo-con' philosophy was pushed along, needing to show results, by the pressures of the anti-interventionists. Sceptical about backsliding allies and weak international institutions, George W. Bush's republicanism in world affairs was built on a belief that as the 'sole remaining superpower' the United States could shape the changing world to its will if it was determined enough and prepared to act alone – across the Middle East, in Afghanistan, in Europe and with regard to a rising China. It expressed a potent mixture of new realism and sheer hubris that left US allies in some disarray after 2001. Everyone agreed that global institutions should work better than they did and that alliances were in need of redefinition. But a superpower behaving so unilaterally and high-handedly as during the Bush presidency weakened the global community in general and frayed the security consensus among the Western powers.

For Britain, this all became a roller-coaster ride in trying to share the strategic visions of the United States, from Clinton, to Bush and then Obama. Britain had made the most of its military and intelligence relationships with the United States during the Clinton years of the 1990s. After the 9/11 attacks Tony Blair got very close to President Bush and Britain embarked on far more difficult and controversial foreign interventions from 2001 to 2011 in Afghanistan, Iraq, Afghanistan again, and then – unintentionally as Obama tried to 'lead from behind' – also in Libya.[34] In truth, Britain was barely holding onto the strategic coat-tails of the United States during these years, contributing for most of the period to a right-wing, neo-con 'global-change agenda' in the United States while arguing in Europe that it was exerting influence on Washington to remain a liberal internationalist, status quo power. There is little evidence that it was.[35]

Nor was it only visions of the future that were becoming harder to reconcile. The expression of ethics and values in international relations were increasingly at issue. Britain, according to Tony Blair, stood 'shoulder to shoulder' with the United States over the 9/11 attacks, but it never signed up to the United States' 'global war on terror' that followed. Too many extraordinary measures were justified by the concept that the Western world was 'at war' with terrorists and those states who collaborated with them.[36] Britain's approach, as it had always been, was to remain focused on a criminal justice interpretation of terrorism and to avoid extrajudicial or extraordinary measures that diminished the rule of law, be it domestic or international. A 'war on terror' was conceptually imprecise and, by definition, endless. It was a dangerous and sloppy justification that led US policy-makers to argue that the laws of war, the Geneva Conventions and much of domestic law to guarantee the rights of one's own citizens were inadequate to the 'new circumstances' brought about by 9/11. Such thinking justified the existence of open-ended detention without trial at Guantanamo Bay, the use of 'enhanced interrogation techniques' that the UN had long defined as torture, the illegal 'rendition' of terror suspects from Western custody to friendly countries that were prepared to torture them. It justified the use of armed drones to assassinate terror suspects in countries outside a designated battle zone, and therefore outside the permissible limits created by the laws of war. It created a momentum for the invasion of Iraq in 2003 that was of questionable legality – legally defensible in international law but not convincing and certainly not universally accepted. The ambiguous arguments marshalled by the United States in 2002-3 for war against Iraq stood in stark contrast to the unarguable legal case for war against Iraq in 1991. And as America's wars progressed, both Republican and Democrat administrations made increasing use of special force 'black ops' – extrajudicial and often illegal – to try to prevail.

Britain worked hard after 2001 to maintain its criminal justice approach to the problem of international terrorism and its legality in acting against rogue state leaderships.[37] It formalized and tightened the legal processes by which its intelligence services operated and worked with partner services, and it tried to define the 'battlefield' carefully, where the rules of war applied over domestic legal constraints. But in the early years after 2001, some of the procedures were too rough and ready and there were certainly mistakes and misjudgements. Above all, however much it argued to the contrary, Britain could not escape the image of *complicity* with a US administration that seemed to treat international law in a cavalier fashion and was accused of losing its grip on some of the fundamental values of Western liberal behaviour. And when Britain tried to stand close to President Obama's brief reassertion of liberal values in world affairs, it seemed then to be complicit in his indecision and weakness over Afghanistan, Libya, Syria, Ukraine and more.

Whatever might be 'special' about Britain's relationship with the United States was out on a limb by 2016. The disappointments in Obama's internationalist-minded policy and the perception that the United States was effectively stymied by all the cross currents of the globalized world set the foreign policy scene for Donald Trump's populist victory, where the European powers were on the wrong end of many of candidate Trump's campaign promises.

The Donald Trump approach simply derided Obama's liberal internationalism for its weakness, took on the republican anti-interventionists and the neo-con assertive internationalists, and wrapped them into a third variation of American conservatism best understood as a reversion to 'Jacksonian nationalism'. It harked back strongly to a United States that believes principally in the power and legitimacy of the nation state over any international institutions and the futility of any foreign entanglements unless in direct defence of the US homeland.[38] As Walter Russell Mead put it,

> 'For Jacksonians – who formed the core of Trump's passionately supportive base – the United States is not a political entity created and defined by a set of intellectual propositions rooted in the Enlightenment and oriented toward the fulfilment of a universal mission. Rather, it is the nation-state of the American people, and its chief business lies at home. Jacksonians see American exceptionalism not as a function of the universal appeal of American ideas, or even as a function of a unique American vocation to transform the world, but rather as rooted in the country's singular commitment to the equality and dignity of individual American citizens.'[39]

Jacksonian nationalism is not isolationism. Americans understand that the United States must function across the globalized world. But it expresses 'nationalist, sovereigntist instincts' and a rejection of an 'international systems' approach to doing business.[40] In President Trump's interpretation, it relies primarily on bilateral approaches. There is real scepticism about multilateralism as a problem-solving device. The straightforward duty of US leaders is to battle for fellow Americans against evident threats to their security, trade and money. Jacksonian nationalists do not believe that international regimes to regulate trade, investment, even weapons proliferation or crime and terrorism, can ever be as effective as national action. In Trump's vision there is therefore intense scepticism about the benefits of globalization and international free trade. And he consciously rejects the steady accretion of international institutions, new rules and changing norms that have so rapidly accompanied the process of globalization.[41] Jacksonian nationalists don't see why the United States should expend resources maintaining an international system for the benefit of others and instead are comfortable with a minimalist 'balance of power' approach to world order. It is very suited to a conception of world politics based around the turning geopolitical wheels among the Big Four powers.

President Trump himself hardly articulates anything so consistent or philosophical but his instincts are clear; and he chose a portrait of President Andrew Jackson to hang in the Oval Office. His presidency demonstrates an innate populism that conforms closely to the image of 'Old Hickory'. Trump the man is less important than the phenomenon his presidency represents and the progression of republican international thinking that has reached this point. It is, of course, unclear how a future president, Democrat or Republican, might change this approach, but these conservative strands of international thinking have had a long gestation, beginning during the Clinton presidency in the 1990s, and notwithstanding President Obama's attempts to change direction. The United States led a thirty-year era that has been characterized as 'glorious liberalism', from 1945 to 1975. This was followed by thirty years of neoliberalism, set in train by the Reagan–Thatcher leaderships, from 1980 to 2010. As the 2008 economic crisis bit into the real economies and political systems of the Western powers, it is a plausible thought that President Trump may represent the most prominent crest of the first breaking wave of global, anti-establishment populism which may last for some years yet.[42]

This is the troubling light in which policy differences between London and Washington should be set. President Trump's chaotic remarks and tweets that seem to intervene in British domestic politics are no more than boorish breaches of protocol. More significant are real divergences between Washington and London on some key policies which go well beyond mere differences in diplomatic tone or emphasis. The most evident examples include withdrawal of the United States from the Iran nuclear deal, to which Britain remains committed; official renunciation of the 1987 Intermediate Nuclear Forces (INF) Treaty in Europe; withdrawal from the Paris Accord on climate change; the White House's unilateral decision to recognize Jerusalem as the capital of Israel and then to recognize the Israeli annexation by force of the Golan Heights in Syria; its vacillating policy in the Gulf; inconsistent US responses towards Russian policy in Europe; threatened trade war with China; and quixotic announcements of troop withdrawals from NATO, Iraq and Afghanistan taken without consultation (and subsequently modified or reduced to the status of conditional threats to allies).[43] All these issues show an American leadership that seems not only to have lost faith in cooperative approaches among allies but also to have become extremely sceptical about the utility of international society and the Western-based rules the United States itself largely shaped after the Second World War.

The wider implications of such disruptive and instinctive decisions were not lost on Moscow. Formally recognizing borders that had been changed by force, as in the case of the Golan Heights; or capital cities like Jerusalem, established in 'occupied territories' following a war, offered Russia a directly symmetrical argument for the annexation of Crimea by force and the occupation of the Donbass region in Ukraine. And President Trump's hostility to key arms control deals and his unreliability in sticking to commitments made it easy for the Kremlin to justify its increasing rearmament, especially in Europe. When the Trump administration casually extended its designation of terrorist groups to include the Iranian Republican Guard, it was, for the first time, officially classifying the arm of a foreign government as internationally terrorist, and opened the door to Iranian counter-claims against the CIA. It could prove to be a dangerous precedent. Most telling of all for Britain, President Trump reportedly mused on several occasions during

2018 about a total US withdrawal from the NATO alliance; a move that would undoubtedly kill the organization and fulfil one of President Putin's key strategic aims.[44] As Francois Heisbourg pointed out, 'Unconditional alliances are completely alien to his [Trump's] understanding of the world.'[45] Disagreements over specific issues will pass, but new strategic assumptions in Washington may not.

To set against these trends in leadership thinking, Britain and its allies could draw some comfort from Congressional resistance to them. President Trump's musings about NATO were sufficiently credible to provoke the promotion of bipartisan bills in both Houses of Congress to block such a move and a vigorous debate on its feasibility should the president return to the idea.[46] They could also believe in bureaucratic continuity. One of the genuine strengths of the relationship between the United States and Britain is the close working practices of the military and security services on both sides. If US presidents and party leaders view world politics in different ways these days, many within the military and civilian bureaucracies still share a consensus of more traditional thinking.

Under President Trump's first generation of key leaders, National Security Adviser General H. R. McMaster and Defence Secretary General Jim Mattis, ensured that the security establishment and the Pentagon pursued a noticeably more traditional role in relation to long-standing allies.[47] Official US national security statements in early 2018, from the National Security Council and the Pentagon, stressed the importance of allies to America's defence.[48] And while President Trump shocked his NATO allies with combative assertions at the Summit in Brussels, the fact remained that almost 65,000 US troops were still stationed across Europe – including Turkey; mostly in Germany, with others in Britain, Italy and Spain.[49] The United States accounted for 51 per cent of the Allies' combined GDP but over 71 per cent of NATO's combined defence expenditure (including 22 per cent of the common funding of the twenty-nine-member alliance) – a particular presidential bugbear.[50] Nevertheless, it was still contributing to seven different NATO missions.[51] In 2011 the US 2nd Fleet had been disbanded, but in 2018 it was reformed to be based at Norfolk Virginia for operations – largely anti-Russian – to operate across the Atlantic. While the White House seemed to have acquiesced in the Russian annexation of Crimea, the NSC (National Security Council) and the Pentagon ensured that US forces were leading the European Reassurance Initiative to bolster NATO defences in response to the Ukraine crisis. The Pentagon increased spending for this dramatically from 2015 and planned to have committed almost $100 billion to it by the end of 2018. US troops were placed in an overtly deterrent role, rotating in and out of NATO areas to make the point to the Kremlin. Some $2.2 billion was earmarked for more prepositioning of US military equipment in Europe and significant amounts were also devoted to partnering with NATO allies.[52] Not least, US troops led a multinational NATO force in Poland, and the USAF took its turn with other allies in 'air policing' over the Baltics and in south Eastern Europe.[53]

The president showed that he didn't care much for his European counterparts and could threaten a fundamental rupture in the NATO alliance on grounds of his instinctive Jacksonian nationalism, even as his security establishment were taking pragmatic steps to help NATO meet immediate military challenges. But by 2019 President Trump was involved in a third rotation of senior officials as resignations and sackings increased. And now the president had genuine ideological soulmates in all key positions. John Bolton became National Security Adviser, Mike Pompeo became Secretary of State, and first Patrick Shanahan and then Mark Esper were appointed to the Pentagon. It remained to be seen whether this would give more practical effect to presidential instincts and diminish the natural continuity that big organizations like the US military and its security services embodied. But no one lasted very long and John Bolton was replaced in September 2019. For his own reasons, President Trump is just as sceptical as President Obama about the way the 'Washington playbook' works when it comes to defence and security. President Trump's relationship with the whole National Security Council was reportedly very bad over the first years of his presidency.[54] If his instincts continue to develop in the same direction and the bureaucracy subsequently becomes more consistent with them, then Trump's Jacksonian nationalism may begin to have effects that go beyond the policy controversies themselves to the big assumptions that have underpinned US global diplomacy for over a century.

These prospects are alarming to London. Britain carved out its global role after 1945, and even more so at the end of the Cold War, as a 'significant second rank power' that was respected in the international community for its historic importance, its ability to act effectively, and the natural identity of its essential interests with those of the United States. It could argue simultaneously that it is both morally right and self-interestedly prudent to champion an America-led rules-based approach to international order. It works hard to maintain faith in multinational and regime arrangements to deal with global problems, particularly as most of them have been based on liberal internationalism – that blend of raw power and liberal democratic ethics – that Britain and the United States largely created themselves. The prospect that US leaders may, in effect, have fallen back on a simple bilateral power approach to international politics – the jungle rules to be examined in Chapter 7 – is both ethically and politically challenging for Britain.

British security and the rise of China

If the security challenges posed by Russian and US approaches to global politics seem to be reverting to traditional balance of power thinking, the essential challenges to British security posed by China could hardly be more different. China now behaves in traditional great power ways in the Asia-Pacific region, with its eyes on military bases, territorial control and access to resources. But Chinese policy raises rather different issues for security chiefs in Europe that challenge the way modern defence and security is conceived in a digital society. For Britain, any Chinese shadow over its future security is wrapped up in digital technology as much as in its growing geopolitical competition.

China's geopolitical re-emergence on the world stage has been the most commonplace observation in global analysis since the turn of this century. Deng Xiaoping, Jiang Zemin and then Hu Jintao were all pragmatic Chinese leaders between 1978 and 2012. Following Deng's lead, they concentrated policy on internal economic development in ways that readied the Chinese economy for the twenty-first century. Foreign policy from Deng Xiaoping onwards was watchful but only rhetorically assertive. But by 2017 Xi Jinping could stand at the 19th Communist Party Congress as the first Chinese leader to assert – convincingly – the country's historic right to its 'global role'; all the more so as the 2008 economic crisis and recent US policy seemed to create natural power vacuums that China would fill. The global role that Xi asserted could be seen in the systemic way China helped deal with the world economic crisis, as outlined in Chapter 2, and its potential to exacerbate, or even trigger, a re-run of it in the 2020s. It can be seen in the rapid development of the Chinese military and the way China chooses to use its military power to assert dominance, even sovereignty, in the East China Sea and the South China Sea. Coral atolls in highly disputed waters have been reclaimed and made into powerful military bases despite UN rulings that found against it. Over the last decade it has weaponized new technologies more quickly than expected and already has enough military capacity to deny easy (or safe) access for the military forces of other states – including the United States – to operate in what China defines as the 'first island chain' running from Japan to Malaysia; and in due course – it is believed – in a 'second island chain' running from Japan to Indonesia. It is an undisguised sphere of influence approach that threatens to impinge on the sovereignty of other Pacific countries. It is complemented by a renewed interest in seeking influence across Eurasia through the game-changing Belt and Road Initiative and the building of ports and facilities in central Asia and through to the Middle East, East Africa and Southern Europe.

All this should be seen in the light of China's emergence as the second biggest economy in the world, the biggest internal market, and the biggest single source of investment capital as Chinese sovereign wealth funds and private entrepreneurs look to invest their cash abroad. But China still remains relatively restricted to penetration from other economies and has obtained lots of trade benefits from the system without having to make painful adjustments itself, at least until the impact of the economic crisis really hit after 2010. In fact, Chinese leaders miscalculated the speed and strength of Western pushback against its economic policies. They believed they could reform economically at their own pace without taking much account of other powers and at a pace that suited a one-party state. But the reality of the globalized world economy has put Chinese leaders under real pressure to accept a world of reciprocal benefits.[55] Nevertheless, Chinese leaders are prepared to use the prospects of access to their internal market as an explicit bargaining chip, or a source of blackmail, in their political relations with other countries. As leaders of a communist party state they can make their demands stick much more effectively than leaders in Western capitalist countries. Such threats have become the first political weapon of choice for Chinese leaders who wish to exert pressure on another state.

President Xi Jinping made no secret of his wish to wield China's evident strengths in world politics and made it clear that he believes China is on the right side of history. At long last, and after much anticipation, China is almost ready to operate as a global superpower – and undeniably among the Big Four. Indeed, a 'G2 world' run effectively by the United States and China is not regarded as fanciful. Nevertheless, though China displays many of the symbols of an incipient superpower and has concentrated on developing some key military and technology sectors, there are some significant structural constraints facing leaders in Beijing, any one of which could derail a smooth move into superpower status.

One is the fact that it remains difficult to reconcile a burgeoning market economy with ever-tightening rule by the Chinese Communist Party. Throughout the twentieth century in countries across Asia, Africa, Europe and Latin America, effective market economies and one-party rule proved simply incompatible. Either one killed the other (as in Russia), or occasionally both co-existed at suboptimal levels (as in Yugoslavia). In the globalized world of the 2020s it is even more difficult to imagine how a growing market economy can function properly under tight political control. But China represents the greatest single human experiment in amalgamating a political and an economic philosophy that are, in theory, incompatible. If China creates something conceptually new from this amalgam and a socio-economic system that is demonstrably successful – a model of efficient 'authoritarian capitalism' more successful than anything in Russia – it will provide a huge example that many other countries and leaders may want to imitate.[56] It will be living proof that Western liberal capitalism is not some sort of default system – somehow natural and unavoidable when all alternatives have failed. That, in itself, would have a dramatic effect on world politics. But if China cannot make such a unique experiment work, in the face of its structural economic challenges, not to mention endemic corruption, then it is likely that government and economic imperatives will increasingly be at odds. Even some sort of uneasy and suboptimal coexistence between market economics and one-party rule is hard to imagine over the long run in the case of a country as big as China.

Secondly, China's impressive economic transformation and its technical achievements do not apply uniformly across the country or its economy. Current

Chinese leaders present their country to the world as stronger and more coherent than it really is and quote economic statistics that the rest of the world frankly doubt. Chinese annual growth was calculated officially as 6.5 per cent at the end of 2018, down from an average of 9.5 per cent over the previous 30 years, but thought by many Western economists to be nearer 4 per cent, or even lower, in reality.[57] Its high-tech sectors sit alongside unmodernized rural communities locked into inefficient agricultural production. Its 130,000 or so state-owned enterprises (SOEs) in old and heavy industries remain a brake on economic reform and a source of widespread corruption.[58] An ageing population is facing major pension and welfare gaps by 2030. Reform across all these sectors are top of Xi Jinping's agenda for the next decade, but economic interdependence with the rest of the world must also figure in that agenda. Reforming a massive economy in the globalized world of the 2020s, while also locked into the unique social experiment of authoritarian capitalism, is a herculean task that will involve many setbacks and missteps, even if it succeeds.

Thirdly, though Beijing speaks assertively about Chinese sovereignty and its numerous territorial claims, its leaders are deeply concerned at any hint of separatism. They are determined to prevent any 'colour revolutions' breaking out in China as they did in the former Soviet space and are increasingly neurotic about the Muslim Uighur peoples of Xinjiang province. The threat of terrorism and separatism in Xinjiang has led Beijing to mobilize all the attributes of digital technology: installing spyware in the only devices citizens are allowed to use, deploying intense surveillance for street-based facial recognition, QR Coding of homes, obligatory iris scanning and tissue typing, all to create 'personal citizenship scores' that are used to control employment and rights – alongside traditional 're-education camps' for more than a million people. It represents a total societal clampdown by the government with a mixture of old and very new methods.[59] For some, this represents an attempt to see whether digital government can monitor society through the 'internet of things' in its every detail across one troublesome province; a possible model for China's future.[60] For others, it is simply an old-fashioned authoritarian crackdown using the best of new technology. Either way, it should be understood that Xinjiang, not to mention Tibet, Taiwan and especially Hong Kong, are all deeply neuralgic issues for Chinese leaders and raise for them genuine fears that the People's Republic of China could be fractured, in effect, from within. A coincidence of internal political, and external security, crises for the Chinese leadership remains a major concern for them.

For European countries, the China of the 2020s is rich and powerful, but still trying to catapult itself from an undeveloped country of the twentieth century to a new type of post-modern economy in the twenty-first. It thinks of its security in largely traditional, territorially-based, ways but it also wants to create economic dependence in other parts of the world and enjoy the benefits of the global economy – and its new place in it – very much on its own political and economic terms.[61] China's foreign and security policy is no cleverer or more long-sighted than anyone else's. Its incipient power has been exercised crudely in many parts of the world and it has provoked some powerful resistance. But everyone understands that, unless the state somehow collapses, China's economic size and political power will only grow stronger in the coming decades and that Beijing can afford to make mistakes along the way.

The particular security challenges of this for Britain take different forms. China's geopolitical ambitions, both within the 'first island chain' and in the BRI across Eurasia pose some problems for Britain's allies and partners. The deepening British security partnership with Japan, for example, its traditional links with Brunei or Malaysia, or its new friendship with Vietnam, are all affected by Chinese sovereign claims in the East and South China Seas. Britain has to take a view on these claims based on international law and UN rulings, which normally provoke thinly veiled threats of economic retaliation from Beijing. More directly, Britain now deploys at least one major warship at all times to the Western Pacific in order to bolster the US naval presence in the area and demonstrate the freedom of international navigation through waters claimed by China. It is a purely symbolic political act to show support for a number of countries, and not least the United States, but there is a diplomatic price to be paid in the anger it generates from Beijing. In more general terms, China's global policy that builds infrastructure and lends money throughout Eurasia, Africa and parts of Latin America – without any Western democratic or governance conditions – challenges the general influence that significant Western countries customarily had in those regions. This may be regarded as fair political competition, but it has arisen quickly in some regions of natural interest to Britain; in Malaysia, Sri Lanka, Pakistan, the Horn of Africa or West Africa. In Britain's own continent, however, China can claim ownership in new and unsettling ways. Chinese companies have stakes in no less than sixteen shipping ports across Europe. In his annual State of the Union address in 2017, European Commission President Juncker proposed investment screening measures, saying it is 'a political responsibility to know what is going on in our own backyard so we can protect our collective security if needed'.[62]

China also poses another quite different form of security challenge for countries such as Britain. Its cyber capabilities threaten the integrity of the CNIs of key Western countries. Chinese leaders scoff at any such suggestion but analysts point out that the capability certainly exists and that China has a record of crude and manipulative behaviour under certain circumstances.

For years, China's industrial and political espionage efforts throughout the world have been legendary in their scale and intentions. The Chinese government have made massive efforts to gain as much political intelligence, particularly about Western countries, as possible. The approach has been broad and apparently unfocused. The Ministry of State Security (MSS, and the equivalent to Britain's MI6) is thought to employ over 100,000 people, half of them abroad.[63] It is said that Chinese intelligence gathers information on an industrial scale, not just through its MSS but also by employing unprecedented levels of cyber hacking, the extensive use of civilian hackers, civilians living abroad, tourists, university students abroad and employees in foreign companies. China has used significant segments of its civilian elite to create a different kind of state intelligence effort. Its commercial espionage and the blatant theft of intellectual property (hotly denied by Beijing) are credited with helping China achieve such rapid technological progress and are regarded as unpleasant facts of life by leaders and industrialists throughout the Western world.

It is impossible to tell whether these fears are exaggerated, though they are certainly believed by senior officials in many different countries. But China's reputation for espionage and widespread attempts at the technical penetration of industrial control systems in Western countries have created strong Western pressures pushing back. Its telecommunications sector, boasting successful global companies such as Huawei and ZTE, made itself intrinsic to the adoption of 2G, 3G and 4G networks in Britain and other countries, supplying critical hardware at competitive prices. But on the verge of the 5G network revolution, many Western countries decided that such commercial partnerships risk opening up their CNIs to the interference of the Beijing government. This fear was justified by China's draconian National Intelligence Law, enacted in 2017, that made it a legal requirement under Article 7 for Chinese 'individuals', 'citizens' and 'organizations' (therefore including companies) to 'support, cooperate and collaborate in national intelligence work'.[64] As a result, the United States, Australia, and New Zealand (all within the Five Eyes intelligence community) banned the use of Huawei components in their 5G systems, and the European Union decided to be very cautious in the use of their products. It hardly matters how much Huawei's directors protest that they operate purely on a commercial basis; the Chinese government has given itself the legal right to use Huawei and ZTE for espionage purposes if and when it chooses.

In Britain's case, the point at which these companies could be banned from critical 3G and 4G systems passed some years ago. British Telecom (BT), for example, began working intensively with Huawei in 2005. The resulting vulnerability exists and BT and the government tried to square the circle by keeping Chinese components out of 'core 5G' systems and having GCHQ (Government Communications Headquarters) and the NCSC (National Cyber Security Centre) work closely with the company itself to screen all new technology being installed.[65] But this did not end the matter or provide enough reassurance to allies. The issue represents a particular example of a more general phenomenon. Chinese entrepreneurs have invested heavily in Europe and the United States over the last decade, both in property and industry. In Britain, China is invested in three new nuclear power plants, its companies take shares in transport infrastructure, and its own giant suppliers operate right across the British retail sector.[66] China is already more deeply integrated into the fabric of the British economy than Russia ever was, and in sectors that are intrinsic to Britain's future as a digitized society. In the 'Asian century' and the 'globalized economy', in the 'cyber era' and the 'digital society', none of this is surprising. Nor does it need to be alarming to British policy-makers. But it indicates a different dimension to security; one that links the functioning of Britain's CNI and investment in British industry and society with the volatile geopolitical impact of a rising power on the other side of the world.

Finally, the rise of China is reaching a stage where it challenges something Britain always asserted as a core national interest – the rules-based international order. This is not to say that China behaves in ways that ignore conventional international rules and norms; it claims always to be very observant of them. There is vigorous debate over how true this is. It breaks the rules in spectacular ways within the 'first island chain' and in using espionage well beyond the accepted norms of state spying. Its human rights record diverges ever further from international norms. And Beijing's policy in Xinjiang stands as a growing affront to the universal concepts of human rights.[67] On the other hand, it entered the World Trade Organisation in 2001 and has done well by generally observing WTO trade rules. It tries in other ways to show how committed it is to UN peace-keeping operations and how sensitive to the sovereign rights of other nations.

The real argument is over whether China's growing role in world politics now has the effect of changing the prevailing rules and re-writing them, as all great powers tend to do, in its own interests. One school of thought believes that the United States, Britain and other key Western allies can pursue an effective 'lock-in' strategy that stresses the universal applicability and mutual advantages of the prevailing rules-based order.[68] More than a decade ago, however, others observed that China has operated 'both within and outside the existing international system while at the same time, in effect, sponsoring a new China-centric international system which will exist alongside the present system and probably slowly begin to usurp it'.[69] The truth is that a political and ethical vacuum has opened up within the international system that China naturally moves to fill. The vacuum has arisen because the Western world, since the end of the Cold War, has been less than punctilious in observing its own rules and under President Trump the Jacksonian nationalism of the United States has made dramatic efforts to reshape the network of international institutions and customary commitments.[70] The economic crisis beginning in 2008 emerges, yet again, as a key driver of broader trends. Its consequences deprived Western capitals of much moral authority.[71]

In institutional terms, China has moved quickly to fill the gap. The creation of the Asian Infrastructure Investment Bank (AIIB) in 2015, though depending more on the performance of China's national economy, was interpreted in the West as a direct challenge to the International Monetary Fund and the World Bank. It certainly reflected, in part, China's frustrations with the way the rules of those organizations were being interpreted. It quickly recruited ninety-three-member governments to the AIIB. The British government was an early participant, despite strong opposition in the United States. As former US Treasury Secretary, Larry Summers expressed it in 2015, London's decision to join the AIIB 'may be remembered as the moment the United States lost its role as the underwriter of the global economic system'.[72] The same can be said at least of the intention, if not yet the impact, of the New Development Bank for the BRICS countries, headquartered in Shanghai.[73] Similar trends are evident in the emerging financial and political arrangements being made along the six different routes of China's BRI – some sixty-eight countries covering 65 per cent of global population. When President Trump cancelled the Trans-Pacific Partnership (TPP) in 2017 China's less burdensome and simpler Regional Comprehensive Economic Partnership (RCEP) arose partly to fill the gap in regulating better trade within the region. RCEP includes all ten nations of the ASEAN grouping, plus Australia, New Zealand, India, Japan and South Korea (all potentially important partners for Britain).[74] In geopolitical terms, Washington had joined what became the TPP in 2008 as a way of developing a tighter framework of economic rules, without Beijing, that would have the effect of 'locking China in' to a broader system designed by the United States. Now RCEP is China's evolving framework of rules that, if anything, locks the United States out.

If countries like Britain now have to fit their national security strategies into the space between the turning geopolitical wheels of the big powers, it is clear that some genuinely new thinking will be required. Though it is now commonplace to refer to Putin's Russia as a revisionist power, it is fair to say that under recent leaderships, all three of these Big Four powers, from Britain's point of view, are now revisionist. Somehow, British policy-makers will have to reconcile different turns on each of these three geopolitical wheels. Russia, for all its weakness, is assertive under President Putin and prepared to explore hybrid warfare techniques while also employing traditional force (in cities such as Grozny, Aleppo or Idlib) more brutally and decisively than Western powers are prepared to do. The United States under President Trump, by contrast, is assertive in quite different ways that make it harder to be a loyal ally of the United States and threatens to undermine the key institutions, and even the principles, of the prevailing Western global order. And China poses both old and new types of challenge to the security interests of states such as Britain, not least in the possibility that China can begin, after its own fashion, to take up the slack in key global institutions and principles of behaviour if they are effectively relinquished by the United States.

Chapter 6
Securing from within

Modern societies not only face security challenges from the policies of other states. Sub-state challenges also loom increasingly large. Sometimes they are supported by, or originate in, the foreign policy of another state, as when a government sponsors foreign terrorism or private computer hackers to further its own ends. States sometimes take effective control over such activities. Nevertheless, the essence of the problem from the standpoint of states targeted in this way is to deal with a series of phenomenon that are, by their nature, sub-state in their style of operation. They emerge from the noisy cacophony of civilian society – the universe of organized and disorganized human behaviour that lies essentially outside the direct remit of democratic government.

The contemporary world poses sub-state challenges in many ways – in terrorism, political subversion or organized crime, for example. This has always been the case. What is most novel about the turn of the 2020s are the ways in which sub-state challenges originating elsewhere in the world have their greatest impacts at sub-state levels within Britain itself. The meshing of international society across so many borders and on a truly global scale leaves government, in many respects, as a bystander in the deepening fabric of international relationships. There are only certain things governments can control, though authoritarian regimes are pushing back against the trend. But open, Western governments are forced to rethink some of their fundamental purposes, and certainly their instruments of policy, in the globalized world.[1] In the ceaseless competition described by Ferguson between the marketplace of human dealings in the 'square' and the governmental powers of those who overlook it in 'the tower', the square is enjoying an ascendancy over the tower that may last for some time yet.[2]

Responding to sub-state challenges to national security, therefore, is just one of the ways in which governments have to face the broader problems of modern *governance*. In this respect, governments face situations where, in contrast to the mid-twentieth century, they are not leading technological revolutions but rather struggling to keep up with them. They are faced with technologies that are highly specialized, that are mixed and integrated in unpredictable ways, and which advance – at scale – across the world. They struggle to keep up with the state of the market and the drivers of its speed and directions. And they frequently struggle to maintain that greater part of the loyalty and commitment of their citizens that they had traditionally assumed was their right.

Governments have simultaneously to try to control digital communications, new technology applications or modern market forces while also seeking to gain advantages from them for their own societies and governance. The tradition of making governmental decisions in incremental steps was essentially risk averse and allowed for a good deal of trial and error. Making decisions in this way has long been regarded as inevitable and largely acceptable as 'top down', governmental policy.[3] But modern government is required to operate both vertically – top down – as well as horizontally across society to develop a more intimate relationship with the public that moves (more or less) as quickly as the public's own inclinations may shift from one preference to another. It must therefore distinguish between those policy areas that necessarily have to be regulated and controlled from the top, and those inherently more extensive areas where government can only act as convenors and influencers across society as a whole.[4] That is not an easy distinction to make in the practicality of real politics. In recent years a lot of effort has been put into thinking about these aspects of contemporary governance. In 2008 the Obama administration in the United States began to introduce serious behavioural insights into the implementation of public policy and from 2010 Whitehall took on a number of initiatives recommended by its new Behavioural Insights Team.[5] It was acknowledged that in many areas effective policy has to be horizontally structured and more dependent on the public 'nudge' rather than formal regulative or legislative processes.[6] Dealing with sub-state threats requires the government to demonstrate all these skills, working both vertically and horizontally.

Of course, the potential severity of state-based threats to Britain in the 2020s will normally overshadow most sub-state threats. But many sub-state threats are also manifestations of state-based animosity, and they are, in any case, proliferating. In the present environment, some non-state actors have the power to behave like states; and some states choose to behave like non-state actors. This range of different challenges was explicitly recognized in Britain in 2008 with the first publication of a National Risk Assessment that showed a spectrum of broadly defined security risks that ran from natural hazards, such as severe weather events, accidental disasters, or health pandemics; to protecting Britain's critical national infrastructure from shortages, failures, or deliberate attack; dealing with the effects of growing international crime; the threats posed by global terrorism; through to dealing with electronic attack or cyberattacks throughout British society.[7] Subsequent defence and security reviews used this framework as they extended the spectrum to include potential warfare of various kinds, whether 'hybrid' or in foreign conflicts in defence of British interests or even wars for the British homeland itself.[8] The approach also included a 'prosperity agenda' on the assumption that measures to defend Britain, and particularly those that made it more resilient from sub-state threats, would also create the conditions for domestic prosperity and make it a more attractive home to foreign investment and international commerce. At the time, this approach and the public discussion of it was something of a conceptual trend-setter across most Western governments and it was widely imitated.

Those state-based security challenges described in Chapter 5 were all derived from the geopolitical shifts in the status and behaviour of three of the four of the great powers of the 2020s, insofar as they had immediate impacts on British security. Though such challenges are easy to understand, it is evident that powers such as Britain can only do a limited amount about them. In the case of sub-state challenges, however, the logic is reversed. If only sub-state challenges can be properly understood, a globalized power like Britain has quite a lot of capacity to rise to them if it mobilizes all the skills of 'vertical' and 'horizontal' policy instruments – legislation, policing, regulations, nudges, the mobilization of constructive citizenship, public awareness and so on. Also something of a paradox, the sub-state threat that receives most public attention – international terrorism – is the one that has remained at a generally consistent level over the last quarter-century. It is likely to remain so into the 2020s and there is periodic debate over how much more attention this existential challenge is worth. Meanwhile, all the other sub-state challenges described here are increasing in both likelihood and potential severity.

International terrorism

Britain is no stranger to terrorism. It suffered frequent periods of anarchist and then Irish republican terrorism from the late nineteenth century onwards. This has involved prominent political assassinations and several attempted killings in patterns that persist to this day. Since the late nineteenth century, Fenian and then Irish republican terrorists successfully bombed Whitehall, Scotland Yard, Westminster Hall (twice), the House of Commons, Downing Street and many key facilities in Northern Ireland, in addition to fourteen other very prominent bomb and assassination attacks in various parts of mainland Britain.[9] It is a matter of some irony that in the very year the 1998 Belfast Agreement on Northern Ireland seemed to put an end to most (but in the event, not all) Irish republican terrorism in Britain, the spectrum of jihadist terror emerged as a new threat to British security.[10] And jihadist terror has remained as a 'generational challenge' to the country that is expected to stretch into the 2020s and beyond.

Not least, there has always been the likelihood of terrorist incidents in Britain directed at other countries or groups – an anti-Israeli hijacking of a British aircraft in 1970, Khuzestan Arab separatists holding the Iranian Embassy in London hostage in 1980, Libyan Embassy staff firing on Libyan protesters in St James's Square in 1984, and so on. By the end of the last century London had earned the contemptuous epithet 'Londonistan' in some foreign quarters because it seemed to provide a haven and meeting place for so many international terrorists conducting campaigns both within Britain and against other countries.[11] Being prepared to live with the threat of terrorism, and deal with it, has been the norm for Britain during much of the last 150 years.

As it revealed itself after 2001, however, the phenomenon of jihadist terror did represent something new and disturbing. It hit home for the Western world as an explicitly *international* phenomenon with the severity and novelty of the 9/11 attacks on the United States, but it hit home more specifically for Britain in the July 2005 London tube and bus bombings. The four London '7/7 bombers' of 2005 were the first ever suicide bombers in Europe, and all were British citizens from surprisingly settled backgrounds committing terror acts in the service of an international ideology. That event also highlighted the fact that there were troubling dynamics between Muslim and non-Muslim sections of British society; within different Muslim communities themselves; and small but significant elements of condonation – even complicity – with terrorist motivations. This highlighted deeper social problems that could not be handled merely by good policing and intelligence. Though jihadist terror is essentially driven by events abroad, it appeals to, and is able to manipulate, some significant fault lines within British domestic society.

Other potential terror threats still exist; Irish republican terrorism certainly remains a possibility and extremist right-wing terrorism in Britain, known as 'XRW' to the security services and driven partly by growing Islamophobia (exactly what jihadist terror intends to provoke) is a growing part of the threat picture for the future. In 2016 MI5 was specifically tasked to take on XRW responsibilities, as it was recognized then as a potentially organized terror phenomenon rather than only as a series of individual hate crimes. Since 2008 between ten and fifteen significant terror plots are normally intercepted or thwarted every year, of which XRW plots latterly have made up between a fifth and a quarter.[12]

Over the last twenty years, however, jihadist terrorism has been by far the most prevalent form of terror directed at, or within, Britain. Its appearance has had the effect of putting this particular strand of terrorism at the top of the country's domestic security agenda. It has dominated the headlines, partly because of its evident brutality – an apparent desire simply to kill and injure as many members of the public or security forces as possible – but also because its *terrorist* roots are derived from a barbaric medievalism which is intended specifically to reject the civic and democratic values of modern, secular society.[13]

Jihadist terrorism across Western countries is intended not just to hurt society by attacking individuals indiscriminately but also to shock it in a deeper sense, specifically to polarize the relationships between Muslims and non-Muslims. And in adopting some sophisticated methods, using cyber power or new bomb-making technologies, alongside very basic techniques, such as simple murder with knives or car-ramming, jihadist terrorism poses a type of terrorist threat to Britain and its partners that feels new and different.[14]

Jihadist terrorism is expected to represent a long-term threat to British security because it is essentially driven by structural forces largely outside the control, or even influence, of the British government. 'Jihadism' has emerged as an imprecise, but effective, term to describe something that has become an international movement in world politics. Jihadism draws inspiration both from eighteenth-century Wahhabi/Salafist thought and from the twentieth-century Muslim Brotherhood.[15] As a doctrine of fundamentalist action its contemporary history goes back to Egypt in the 1950s. The creation of the Al Qaeda movement itself can be dated to the war against Soviet forces in Afghanistan in the mid-1980s and thence to Osama bin Laden's organization in Sudan and back to Afghanistan around 1996, from where the 9/11 attacks were planned. As a religious ideology within the majority Sunni communities of the Muslim world, jihadism is driven by the strict Wahhabi/Salafi interpretation of Quranic teaching. Neither Wahhabism nor traditional jihadism, of course, are naturally or indiscriminately violent – in theological terms, quite the reverse. The *Takfiris*, however, following the most radicalized version of Wahhabi/Salafism to emerge from the 1980s, became the ideological and religious core of the terrorist movement now popularly labelled 'jihadism'.[16]

This movement pursues a violent fight, by all available means, against the 'apostates' and the 'unbelievers' (the *kuffar*) both within and outside the Muslim world. The concept of *Takfir* (effectively, ex-communication), in the hands of jihadists becomes a licence to kill all Muslim apostates who can be declared un-Muslim for their behaviour. Even more importantly, jihadists maintain that they have a duty to rebuild the caliphate – God's earthly government – and that Muslims everywhere live in a state of sin until this is achieved.[17] A modern Muslim theologian carefully defines the difference between 'mainstream Islam', 'Islamism' and 'Islamist extremism' and defines the strand of *violent* Islamist extremism as a belief in 'the requirement to establish an Islamic State following Sharia law exclusively and to repudiate and destroy all other religions and political ideologies and their adherents, including non-Muslims and "wrong" Muslims as an article of faith'.[18] From a purely political perspective, this makes it a movement for nothing less than international revolution. Though the assertions made by jihadist leaders across the world are often confused and contradictory, the underlying aims have emerged consistently over the thirty-five years that modern jihadism has been a global phenomenon. The targets of this movement, in rough priority order, are the 'apostate governments' of the Muslim world (the vast majority of them) who are not governing their Islamic peoples properly; the Shia Muslim peoples (around 10 per cent of the 1.7 billion Muslims in the world) who are, by definition, apostates; and the *kuffar* unbeliever peoples who can be ranked into Christians, Jews and Sabians – the 'peoples of the book' – who can be tolerated under strict circumstances; and Yezidis, Buddhists, Shinto, atheists and most others, who cannot under any circumstances.[19] Above all, modern jihadism stands for the creation of a new caliphate that will encompass a proper and holy Islamic State.

In practical terms this means that jihadism strives to convert or else attack the 'apostate governments' of the Muslim world and expel any Western presence and influence within them. It strives for the destruction of the state of Israel and genocide against Jews, notwithstanding their status as one of the 'people of the book'. It plans attacks in Western and other countries both to punish the *kuffar* for their decadence and their resistance, and also to help polarize opinion within Western societies to bring a Caliphatist revolution closer. It assumes that a new caliphate will exist in a state of perpetual war against the *kuffar* elsewhere in the world. Despite its extremism, this is also a coherent message. As Marc Sageman says, 'Its appeal lies in its apparent simplicity and elegance that resonates with concerned Muslims not well schooled in traditional Muslim teaching, which it rejects.'[20]

Such an ideology of world revolution might have remained marginal to international politics in a different era. But the fact is that since the 1980s a geographical 'arc of conflict' has emerged that extends from West Africa, through East Africa and the greater Middle East to South Asia. Indeed, in 2019 there were no major wars in other parts of the world, even if there was great insecurity in some of them. But over one billion people live within this arc (in a global population of over 7 billion) and jihadism has found fertile ground to promote itself amid the tension and disruption that accompanies it. It is both cause and effect of widespread instability. Thus, it is no coincidence that mainstream jihadist groups range from Boko Haram in West Africa, to Al Shabaab in East Africa, to Al Qaeda, now strong again in Yemen, Sinai and Libya, Islamic State (IS) dispersing across the region after its expulsion from the Levant to Jamaat-e-Islami and Hizbul Mujahideen in Pakistan and Kashmir. Other mainstream jihadist organizations also exist in lesser forms outside this arc in Russia's southern regions, in some Central Asian states, in the Jemaah Islamiyah organization in Indonesia or Abu Sayyaf in the Philippines. A long-standing ideology that rejects the mainstream political trends of world politics and the fertile ground of widespread instability across a swathe of regions that are important to Europe, constitute structural drivers of jihadism that are almost entirely out of Britain's hands.

A vigorous argument has gone on since the 9/11 attacks of 2001 as to how 'structural' these trends really are and how far the foreign policies of the

United States and its Western allies have contributed to, or even created, the jihadist challenge to the international order. This argument has been extremely vocal in Britain, particularly since the 2003 invasion of Iraq, which has been accused of stimulating terrorism in Britain, compounding the problem with a renewed campaign in Afghanistan in 2006 and simultaneously conducting a counterterrorism policy that has been accused of demonizing domestic Muslim communities and stoking Islamophobia. British security chiefs themselves acknowledged that Britain's military operations in Iraq and Afghanistan stimulated and focused jihadist terrorism in this country and provided a convenient narrative for jihadists to appeal for support among fellow Muslims. And mistakes in counterterrorism policies fed the image of victimization that jihadists want to promote – the polarization of a multicultural society.[21]

Nevertheless, the simple historical fact is that the jihadis' impact on Britain predates any of the foreign policy decisions cited as justification for their attacks. Indeed, when jihadism first emerged in Britain during the 1990s British troops were operating – and dying – to protect the Muslim communities of Bosnia and eventually Kosovo from attacks by the (Christian) forces of Serbia and Croatia.[22] Osama bin Laden's famous fatwa – his implacable declaration of war on Western societies – was issued in 1998. The most extensive terrorist plot in many years in Britain, foiled in 2004, had its origins in its leader, Omar Khyam, travelling to Pakistan for terrorist training in 2000.[23] Equally undeniable is the fact that the most recent expressions of jihadism in Britain have taken inspiration from events abroad, in most of which Britain had no involvement at all. None of the Western powers had any role in the so-called 'Arab Uprising' of 2011 and those Middle East countries that were turned on their heads by it were the ones in which Western powers had least direct involvement. As a result, the greatest driver of jihadism in recent years became the Syrian civil war beginning in 2013, which allowed the nascent 'Islamic State' movement to leap into existence, and by late 2014 to control territories across the Levant in which more than 8 million people lived, declaring it to be the new caliphate. It was only in response to the personal atrocities committed by IS against Yezidi peoples in Sinjar, and British and other civilians, together with its destabilizing effects on neighbouring states, that Britain entered into a military campaign to defeat IS after 2015.

Far more important than the sequence of events, however, is the very essence of the jihadist case. The modern jihadist challenge is that far fewer than half a million violent people, self-appointed to lead the whole Muslim world – which in itself is less than 23 per cent of global population – try to incite an international revolution that would overturn most of the existing system.[24] And this revolution would be carried out by means that violate every principle of established sovereignty and hard-won international and humanitarian law. In reality, jihadists attack Britain not for what it does in the world, but rather for what, in principle, it is.[25] Successive British governments have not been apologetic in claiming its rights enshrined both in the United Nations and in natural justice to oppose this movement, *not* on religious grounds but as an imperative defence of liberal democracy. There is ample room to debate the government's tactics by which this is best done and the balance of effectiveness in operating abroad as opposed to greater concentration on domestic matters. There is scope, and in Britain also the mechanisms, to analyse some severe misjudgements. But British governments have never weakened on the principle that they have a right and a duty to oppose jihadism outright.

Most movements that use terror tactics – separatists, nationalists, usurpers – are ultimately prepared to negotiate towards an end of their campaigns. Governments know this and frequently – eventually – explore the possibilities, though they are loath to admit it publicly.[26] But in the case of global jihadism, there is nothing that could be negotiated; no moral mainstream that both sides share as the basis of a political negotiation. So, for Britain, jihadism can only be treated as a particular type of criminality. The government will not accord jihadists the dignity of being soldiers, still less warriors, in a 'war on terror' and it therefore accepts the limitations and some of the frustrations of applying a criminal justice approach to this particular terrorist challenge.

For Britain in the 2020s, then, this threat can be expected to wax and wane with developments mainly within the 'arc of conflict'. The actions of the British government whether in the domestic environment or abroad can only have marginal effects on this truth. In reality, whatever political leaders say in the aftermath of terror attacks, British policy for dealing with jihadism has been one that accepts its 'generational' nature. It will be a fact of life for some time to come. It therefore pursues a containment approach, to keep the number and impact of successful attacks down to tolerable levels that do not prevent British society from evolving peacefully in its own characteristic ways.[27] In enacting this policy, it has been largely successful for over two decades.

The number of credible jihadist terror plots against Britain that have been devised in the last twenty years is a matter of definition – when does inherent intention become a definable plot? Analysts count them by different rules; however, as an order of magnitude, there is general agreement that the number is somewhere between 160 and 300.[28] In the twenty years since 1998 only six jihadist terror plots inside Britain were successful, four of them all in 2017. This indicates a success rate of somewhere between 96 per cent and 98 per cent for the police and security forces in thwarting jihadist terror. On the other hand, at least ten additional home-made bombs were planted during this period that would have exploded if they had been built properly, in attacks covering London, Glasgow and Exeter. The police and security forces have therefore undoubtedly been effective, but also lucky. And they will have to continue to be effective and lucky in the future. Success rates can never be so perfect as to offer complete protection from terrorist attacks within an open society. The public instinctively understand this fact and there is a high degree of societal resilience that works in the government's favour.

Whatever the incidence of terror attacks on Britain over the next ten years, however, there are two aspects in which their impacts may be more troubling. Britain's own social divisions, economic, demographic, multicultural, and now, Brexit-related, are all part of the fabric of modern British society that jihadist terrorism seeks to exploit. Of the 264 convictions for jihadist related crimes in Britain between 1998 and 2015, it is significant that 16 per cent of the offenders were converts, 76 per cent were known to the authorities prior to their terrorist offences and 26 per cent had prior criminal convictions.[29] Terrorists in Britain do not come out of the blue. And social divisions do not create terrorism but they go some way to account for the fact that an international movement can inspire a 'home-grown' terrorist phenomenon by offering a sense of identity to some who might have rejected it from their previous life experiences. As in other European states, divisions continue to provide those niches of support and tacit condonation that allow a tiny minority of jihadist activists to present themselves as part of a global movement and to challenge all Britain's Sunni Muslims to support it.[30] In Chapter 3 we established that the major fault lines in British society appear to be growing rather than diminishing. Despite loud assertions to the contrary, there is no evidence that some of the obvious structural inequalities in British society – socio-economic disadvantage and lack of political voice – are the causes of home-grown terrorism. But where terrorist motivations derive from external sources, these fault lines nevertheless define concentrations of empathy – 'significant precursors' – among jihadi activists and it would be perverse to deny their growing importance.[31] International research indicates that throughout Europe neighbourhoods matter greatly in jihadist recruitment. 'It is a small-world phenomenon that is best understood as a real world process of *networked social contagion*', as Jytte Klausen expresses it.[32] And the fact is that while Britain's counterterrorist policies enshrined in the CONTEST strategy, have been largely successful in the three policing and intelligence strands of it, they have been consistently troubled and only partially successful in the fourth 'prevent' strand that tries to address the dynamics of jihadi radicalization.[33] Countering radicalization within communities from a top-down governmental perspective is not only the most ambitious aspect of the overall strategy but also the least well-resourced in relation to its wide objectives. In truth, British governments made the policing and intelligence aspects of the CONTEST strategy work well after 2005, but there was little political appetite to venture too deeply into its anti-radicalization dimensions. All the indications are that countering domestic radicalization towards jihadism, driven by external events but reflected in the fault lines of British society, will become more difficult in future years.

The other troubling aspect of the terror threat in the coming decade, in this case not exclusive to jihadism but potentially shared by all groups who choose to use terror as a weapon, is the spectre of 'cyber terrorism'. On the face of it, this is an obvious evolution of any security threat in the globalized world but in the case of terrorism, it is a difficult concept to define.[34] Sophisticated cyber power offers all terrorist groups the prospect of using the World Wide Web both as a vast underground network – of unknown and growing size – where they can conceal information, material and identities that is also a burgeoning city on the surface where they can hide in plain sight while appealing for support, extorting money, creating their own version of reality, or cajoling and threatening likely recruits. The potential to operate simultaneously and cheaply both underground and over ground has changed the established nature of nineteenth- and twentieth-century terrorism. As long as they remain nimble across the ground-level city of the open net and the underground vastness of the dark web, terror groups can use their cyber power to perform both traditional, as well as new functions in terrorist planning and development. The old terrorist model of cell structures – where a small cell of three or four people had only a tenuous contact with any other cell in the organization – can be turned on its head in the case of a mass terror movement. Such groups openly connect themselves; they franchise their operations and issue broad campaign calls in ways that cannot be blocked or censored quickly enough. From 2004, Anwar al-Awlaki, working mainly from Yemen, inspired a number of terror plots inside Britain, including pipe-bomb attack planning on Westminster, the actual stabbing of an MP and at least two plots against the London Olympics.[35] From 2012 Islamic State's Mohammad al-Adnani regularly called on jihadists everywhere to use rocks, knives, cars, poisons, choking and any methods they could find to kill Westerners at random – a call that was mirrored in the act of Michael Adebolajo and Michael Adebowale to murder Fusilier Lee Rigby in the street in 2013 and then in a further plot that would have done the same to soldiers at the Remembrance Day service in 2014.[36] A vehicle lorry attack killed eighty-six people in Nice in July 2016 and in December Anis Amri drove a lorry into shoppers in Berlin's Christmas market. Three similar attacks followed in and around London in 2017, alongside two home-made bomb attacks in Manchester and London with devices and planning directed from the dark web. Modern terrorists had effectively weaponized both the open and secret parts of the web in ways that could scarcely have been anticipated twenty years ago.

On the other hand, the web *itself* has not so far been directly weaponized. There have been no successful 'cyber-bombs', 'cyber-poisons' or 'city stoppers'. In Nagorno-Karabakh during 1999 there was a reported terror attempt to alter blood group records in hospitals to endanger all blood transfusions, and in 2006-7 an apparent Al Qaeda attempt to attack telecommunications networks across financial services located in London's Docklands.[37] These both rate as minor attempts and nothing comparable has been confirmed since. Creating cyber-bomb programmes is a great deal more difficult than the glib labels suggest, but they may be coming. And the advent of more sophisticated 3D printing technologies – 'additive manufacturing' – suggests some truly worrying possibilities.[38] Alongside innovations in materials science, the possibilities of amateurs being able to obtain basic materials of sufficient quality and remotely access a manufacturing process they need know nothing about to create firearms, explosive or chemical devices would constitute a new dimension in networked terror.

The question remains, however, that with so much technology operating in their favour, why don't terrorists launch outright cyber wars against Western societies? Some British security chiefs warn of exactly this possibility.[39] The answer seems to be both perceptual and operational. Most terror groups, and certainly jihadist terrorists, are not interested in causing merely 'inconvenience' or 'disruption' through a cyberattack – they already have that at airport security around the world. Terrorists aim to create real destruction: death, flames, human tragedy and all the pornography of violence. They aim to shock peaceful peoples in democratic societies not just annoy them. Al Qaeda, in particular, remains focused on attacking transport, in the belief that this is one of Western society's weak spots, where public panic could have debilitating effects on a national economy.

The idea of using the web itself for cyberattacks on other societies, therefore, is only really attractive to modern terror groups if they can use it to create real violence and destruction – making trains crash, planes fall out of the sky, chemical plants blow up and so on. And, if successful, it has to be clear that it was they who caused it, *and that more will inevitably follow*. That is a tall order for even the most skilled terrorist groups. Claiming credit for occasional nasty accidents won't do. Terrorists can certainly claim that more home-made bombs, stabbings or vehicle attacks are inevitable for the foreseeable future. But they cannot easily mount a destructive 'cyber spectacular' and simultaneously promise that there will be many more. The 9/11 attacks on air transport were certainly spectacular – but to date they have not been successfully repeated or even matched. Not least, the cyber world works both ways and creates trails that counterterrorist agencies can also follow. Though the initiation of any act of terror always favours the perpetrators, the cyber or physical forensics created by it, in the long run, tends to favour the abilities of sophisticated policing to track it down.

The cyber domain offers terrorist groups many new possibilities in the way they organize, operate and eventually in the range of attacks that could be mounted. Limitations on how these possibilities might be employed lie more in the aims of the terrorists and their willingness to embrace new techniques, however, than in the ability of governments to prevent them in the first place. It will not be surprising if some of these perceptual barriers are breached in the next decade, even if the operational limitations remain severe.

International organized crime

If international terrorist groups have a strangely ambiguous relationship with cyberspace, there can be no doubt that international crime has turned itself into a major security concern for all states, largely because of ubiquitous cyber technologies. Criminal and terrorist groups are normally prepared to work together on regular occasions, though not normally over the long run. Their fundamental purposes are different. It may suit criminals and terrorists to use each other's networks where there are short-term mutual advantages, and in Western societies a large number of convicted terrorists have also spent some years as petty criminals or else have been part of criminal gangs before turning to terrorism. Nevertheless, criminal groups ultimately work for monetary profit and depend on essentially stable societies to provide it with more regularity; whereas most terrorist groups – and certainly jihadist groups – aim to destabilize normal society in the countries where they operate. The result is that terrorism and other criminalities tend to engage in a courtly dance involving figures of eight that alternately link and delink themselves, without entirely losing sight of each other as they pursue their own distinct objectives. For policing and intelligence authorities in Western states this presents obvious problems in the tendency of many investigations to burgeon into apparently unrelated areas. But all forms of networking are potential vulnerabilities for terrorist or criminal conspiracies, and there is little doubt that terrorist groups have made themselves vulnerable over the long term by their links to international crime.

The age of cyberspace, personal mobility and technology entrepreneurship has worked in favour of international criminality as completely as it has thrust the rest of society into the globalized world. No country, developed or otherwise, can consider its security without reference to the influence of international crime on the well-being of its citizens. Unlike Britain, most countries are only peripherally affected by international terrorism, but all are increasingly affected by international crime. It is Britain's fate to have to deal with them both. The prudent expectation is that while terror threats to Britain can be expected to spike upwards every so often, internationally driven criminal threats give every indication that they will increase steadily – even exponentially – in the coming years.

According to Europol figures, the number of Organised Criminal Groups (OCGs), operating on an international level, and under investigation within the 28 members of the European Union, increased by almost 40 per cent after 2013, from 3,600 to 5,000.[40] These OCGs involved 180 different nationalities. They have 'business models' that are close parallels of those used by legitimate companies to spread their risks and specialities across different fields of criminality. Such factors are thought to mark a trend towards a proliferation of smaller criminal networks whose business models have come to depend crucially on internet access and manipulation.[41] Groups focus their activities where the risks are perceived to be lower – in areas such as credit card fraud, trafficking and counterfeiting.[42] Europol also identifies a sharp increase since 2013 in what it called 'poly-criminality', whereby some 45 per cent of OCGs (over 2,200 of them) are engaged in, and in contrast to a decade ago, more than one type of illegal activity simultaneously. It is estimated that 70 per cent of them operate across three or more countries; 10 per cent of them in more than seven countries.[43]

Crime analysts describe four main 'engines' of organized crime which are intrinsic to everything else; namely, document fraud, which includes forgery, theft, impersonation and evasion; money laundering, either individually or via specialized syndicates; the online trade in illegal commodities both on the open and the dark web; and the illegal use of new (legal but not well-regulated) payment methods, including cryptocurrencies, online payments and internet vouchers. There are, for example, well over 1000 cryptocurrencies in the world and some of them are increasingly used for the payment of kidnap ransoms.[44] On the basis of these four 'engines' of organized criminality the most characteristic types of crime perpetrated in Europe by OCGs are currency counterfeiting; direct cybercrime, including ransomware and data theft; child sexual exploitation; environmental crime, including waste dumping; firearms trafficking; fraud, particularly in excise/VAT payments, payment card fraud, investment fraud and mass market fraud; intellectual property crime, particularly in pharmaceuticals, pesticides, food and beverages; narcotics, in production, distribution and trafficking, and in new psychoactive drugs; organized property crime, including vehicle theft and targeted property burglary; people trafficking, which encompasses illegal migration, prostitution, child trafficking and labour exploitation; sports corruption; and links to terrorist groups which normally involves trafficking, illegal migration, supplies and facilitation.[45]

For those who assumed that international criminal groups were still akin to the mafia or the Chinese triads, and who therefore inhabited essentially their own world of criminal exchange and violence that somehow excluded the rest of us, it is clear from this list that this is no longer the case. The list indicates, firstly, that across Europe all significant criminality is both organized and international. For the same reason, a great deal of it is also cyber-enabled. Secondly, OCGs self-evidently encompass a spectrum of crimes that bite deep into the day-to-day lives of ordinary citizens in any European country. The illegal market for narcotics is still the largest criminal market within the countries of the EU, worth over £20 billion a year.[46] Over a third of all OCGs operating in Europe deal in narcotics in one way or another, particularly since hundreds of new psychoactive drugs have been developed. And over two-thirds of those groups who deal in narcotics also engage in people trafficking and migrant smuggling, since narcotics are an accepted form of payment along smuggling routes and to other criminal networks.[47]

Within Britain there were over 115,000 narcotics convictions in 2018, with the majority of narcotics seizures, in order of volume, covering cannabis, cocaine, amphetamines and heroin. Psychoactive drugs will doubtless figure in the 'top four' in due course.[48] It is difficult to put a statistical value on these trends insofar as they affect local communities in Britain. One good independent study that sampled small communities in West Midland cities found that anything from 5 per cent to 17 per cent of recorded crime at even the neighbourhood level could be ascribed to organized crime, relating mainly to narcotics, violence and fraud. Over a quarter of theft and even shoplifting within one neighbourhood was traceable to OCG operations. There was, the research observed, relatively high degrees of OCG control in those neighbourhoods where they deliberately operated and inadequate police understanding of the international links to the incidence of local crime.[49]

Cyber insecurity

Both international terrorism and serious, organized international crime rely heavily for their current and future modus operandi on the cyber domain. The centrality of this domain is a hallmark of increasingly digitized societies, and in Britain it looms ever larger in the security equation. In 2012 the British government committed itself to a digital strategy for the delivery of services and explained why 'going digital' was vital for the British economy.[50] It emphasized, indeed embraced, the degree to which cyber security would therefore affect every aspect of national security, from the vital protection of key military command and control systems – including the cyber safety of the next generation of Britain's nuclear deterrent submarines[51] – to the ability of ordinary citizens to withdraw cash from their banks, register their vehicles or have a minor surgical procedure at a local hospital.

More than in most other areas of security policy, cyber security requires governments to act both in vertical, top-down, ways while simultaneously moving horizontally to nudge and cajole, as well as to regulate, vital areas of the economy and the social interactions they cannot control.[52] The government has a duty to safeguard from cyber interference of all kinds its own direct security domains such as defence and the police forces, the intelligence services, the diplomatic network and essential governmental machinery at both central and local levels. This it attempts to do in standard top-down fashion by requiring the relevant ministries to make their systems cyber secure and to coordinate the monitoring of such systems through central government. In these sectors government policy is backed by the considerable expertise available from GCHQ and some branches of the armed services but also by British companies led by 'primes' such as British Telecom and BAE Systems. It is a different story, however, for other governmental sectors such as the National Health Service, the legal or the benefits system, or in education, or core transport systems; and all the more so in the devolved administrations of Scotland, Wales and Northern Ireland who control some of these governmental services themselves. In these cases, both the lines of responsibility and the efficacy of existing cyber security measures are widely regarded as variable and have frequently been shown to be well below the standards that a secure 'digital society' might expect.[53] For the coming decade the government has no choice but to keep improving, standardizing and – most important – investing in cyber security for its central governmental functions.

It is in the sectors that require more horizontal government policy, however, that the greatest challenges for the future arise. By and large, the problems caused by casual nuisance hackers, or even politically-inspired groups, are no longer the key concern of government cyber security specialists. Most systems can deal with these intruders. But as the National Cyber Security Centre (NCSC) observed in 2018, the cyber challenge to British society was 'both growing and changing in nature as it grows'.[54] State actors, whether using a proxy group or acting directly, it said, 'constitute the most acute and direct cyber threat to our national security'.[55] In the previous two years there were over 1000 significant state-sponsored attacks directed at British government or related facilities.[56] More to the point, state-sponsored attacks, even on other countries, could be seen to have alarming effects on civil society outside the domains of government. Britain, among others, took to naming those countries it believed perpetrated the most evident attacks. Russia was named as the state perpetrator behind the 'NotPetya' and the 'BadRabbit' attacks on Ukraine in June and October 2017 which affected many major companies and transport networks across Europe and in Asia. The shipping company Maersk was put offline for ten days at a cost of over $300 million by the NotPetya attack. The WannaCry virus of May 2017 was an attempted ransomware attack affecting over 200,000 computers in 150 countries and caused some chaos in the National Health Service where many operating systems were carrying outdated security software. This attack was officially attributed by US and British intelligence to the Lazarus hacking group, sponsored by North Korea.[57] Indeed, North Korea was accused of using cyberattacks for more straightforward extortion than WannaCry, famously using the Lazarus group in 2016 to extract $81 million from the Bangladesh Bank via the SWIFT payments system.[58] Iran was widely blamed for cyberattacking British parliamentarians in June 2017. And successive incidents of 'cyber-enabled economic espionage' by China prompted the United States to establish a government task force to take it on while British, and other, governments named China in official documents as persistent and deliberate cyber-espionage offenders.[59]

As outlined in Chapter 5, the 'industrial levels' of espionage that China directs at Britain and its partners are difficult to fathom, since they appear to go well beyond the normal needs of a national intelligence service in pursuit of its own national security. There are questions over whether Beijing can interpret all the material its espionage sweeps up. It may simply overload its own policy system. Nevertheless, there is no credible doubt that China's industrial espionage has for many years been extensive and economically important to its development. It has ridden roughshod over the established rules governing intellectual property rights and has stolen key technologies in many industrial sectors throughout the Western world. At the end of 2018, after a series of private, unheeded warnings to the Chinese government and agreements within the G20 that appeared to have been ignored, the British government officially named China as a major source of cyber industrial espionage threatening British security. It specifically pinpointed the group 'APT 10', working for the Chinese Ministry of State Security from the city of Tianjin as one of the sources of extensive cyberattacks 'targeting intellectual property and sensitive commercial data in Europe, Asia and the US'.[60] It was, said the official statement, responsible for a 'sustained cyber campaign focused on large scale service providers'.[61] APT 10, also known as 'Red Apollo' or 'Stone Panda' had been operating since 2006 and is commonly regarded as the most extensive and sophisticated industrial espionage cyberattack mechanism in the world. It had previously accessed computers used in both the Pentagon and NASA and in 2017 in a massive 'Cloud Hopper' attack, got inside the networks of key companies in fifteen countries, including in Britain.[62]

Such activities and the angry reactions they then caused, however, do not invalidate the fact that the Chinese company Huawei – one of the biggest providers of telecoms hardware in the world – is also one of the most technically advanced and is intrinsically involved (along with China's ZTE and Finland's Nokia) with British Telecom in the construction of the 5G network. BT had a relationship with Huawei for its products that began in 2005 and chose to partner with it for the sake of its rapid innovation and sheer ambition to push technological boundaries forward. Security chiefs expressed detailed concerns about the original BT / Huawei partnership at the time and the extent to which Whitehall had been properly consulted.[63] From the beginning, BT aimed to safeguard the 'core' of the 5G network by working with Huawei and accepting its components only on the extensive non-core functions. It claims also to have strong procedures to deal with any security challenges posed by Chinese hardware, and, as Huawei points out, it has an imperative commercial interest at a key stage in the company's development to prove itself a reliable and safe supplier to foreign countries. Huawei equipment is extensively used in other popular British commercial networks such as Vodaphone, Sky or TalkTalk.

The Huawei 'security problem', as outlined in Chapter 5, is not just a matter of espionage – though that is certainly part of it – but rather a shadow of the whole '5G revolution' of which Britain is on the verge. The 5G network will power the first manifestation of the 'Internet of Things', of 'smart cities' and new revolutions in 'information and communications technologies' (ICT). There will be a step change in the use of data and the application of artificial intelligence (AI) to daily life. Installing any company's components only in the 'edge' and not the 'core' of the system will become irrelevant as the system matures and distinctions between 'core' and 'edge' become meaningless once so many parts outside the core are connected directly to each other, and not in a hub and spoke fashion. By 2030, what will really be at stake in a British '5G smart city' will not be the potential for Chinese espionage – which is present anyway and by many other means – but rather the dependence of critical infrastructure and day-to-day life on systems that might be capable of manipulation through a malign foreign power. It would be difficult and expensive for Britain to unpick completely its current relationship with Chinese suppliers to its next generation telecoms and cyber networks, and it would, in any case, have to work with foreign suppliers, via Nokia or Ericsson. So the government has a delicate path to tread, finally pushing back against outrageous levels of Chinese industrial espionage over many years, working to maintain high levels of cyber security across the economy and yet still allowing big commercial service providers to use Chinese components in a pragmatic approach to cost effectiveness and innovation to get the best from a digital economy.

Despite all the concerns over whether China does, or does not, pose a significant insider threat to Britain's cyber security, the most immediate and purposeful state-based cyber threats in the near future are still regarded as emanating from Russia. In 2018 the government alerted British banking, energy and water companies to Russian cyber threats and then later, along with US intelligence, issued a joint Technical Alert of malicious Russian cyber activity across several critical government and private sectors and within the internet service providers who supported them. 'Russian state-sponsored actors', it said, 'are using compromised routers to conduct spoofing 'man-in-the-middle' attacks to support espionage, extract intellectual property, maintain persistent access to victim networks, and potentially lay a foundation for future offensive operations'.[64] According to the CEO of the government's NCSC, the Russian 'appetite for attack on critical sectors' has increased steadily as bilateral relations have deteriorated and Russia is believed to have achieved some 'prepositioning for future disruptive attacks … a foothold [in the UK's internet infrastructure], an intrusion that you can use for ongoing espionage purposes or can develop as the potential for a hostile, disruptive and destructive act in the future'.[65] It remains a moot point whether knowledge of 'prepositioned' cyber viruses is largely generic or highly specific, and whether they can be eliminated before they are activated.

Though Britain was subjected to some successful attacks in health, energy, telecoms and central government sectors during 2018, it was nevertheless still the case that the country had not experienced the most severe form of cyberattack (defined officially as one leading to sustained loss of essential services, severe economic or social consequences, or loss of life). But security chiefs were clear that just such a severe attack was a matter of 'when, not if'.[66]

Meanwhile, as in all modern, digital economies, Britain's companies and its economic and social networks have to face a future in which cyberattacks are virtually certain to morph into more sophisticated, widespread and intrusive instruments of fraud, extortion or intimidation. There is only so much governments themselves can do across the private sector. They can act as a clearing house of information and alerts and they can create guidelines for business. They can support trade organizations such as ADS to promote good cyber security across key industries.[67] And they can support campaigns to promote better 'cyber hygiene' throughout civil society, which would, in itself, counter the vast majority of mid-range cyberattacks and nuisance hacking activities. In 2016 the British government initiated a five-year national cyber security strategy worth £1.9 billion to do all of these things, in addition to better protecting central government's own systems.

A key problem, however, is that good cyber security for all businesses and organizations is expensive. The very big companies at the apex of the British economy can afford the latest security systems; however, among the uniquely large number of small and medium enterprises further down the chain, many struggle to keep up with the demands of cyber security. They can afford systems that keep out malicious hackers and most fraudsters but not those that can stand up to state-based or state-sponsored attempts to lock up, or get inside, a series of information systems within one commercial sector. And police constabularies, health authorities, local government organizations and the like have faced severe budgetary cuts since 2010 and frequently limp on with cyber security they know to be inadequate but make a risk assessment that other spending priorities are more urgent.

There is some potential for the insurance industry to act as a powerful 'nudge' mechanism for government policy to find traction within the wider economy. Insuring against losses caused by cyberattack or cybercrime is an efficient way for common security requirements and standards to be introduced across economic sectors. If companies want insurance against cyber losses they have to prove, as with any insurance policy, that they are taking adequate precautions which meet national standards. The limitations of this approach, however, lie not with the concept but rather with the insurance industry itself, even though the business potential could be very lucrative. Though over 40 per cent of British companies report significant cyberattacks in any two-year period, and the insurance industry reports a doubling of its cyber insurance business in 2019, still only 9 per cent of British companies carry specific cyber insurance, and even in the financial sector the figure is only 25 per cent. It looks like a curious mismatch that is ripe for government 'nudging'.[68] In 1993 after the Baltic Exchange bombing the British government created a specific private sector company – Pool Reinsurance, now

Pool Re – to underwrite terrorist damage, and it later created Flood Re, to insure homes in flood-prone areas. But it cannot easily do the same in the case of cyber damage.[69] If state-sponsored cyberattacks can be interpreted as acts of (hybrid) war then insurance companies are not normally bound to pay out on claims.[70] More to the point, the insurance industry simply finds it impossible to price the risk of cyber losses accurately. There is too little reliable history on which to base actuarial judgements and no common understanding of how extensive the cyber damage, and consequent costs, could be in major incidents. So, the insurance industry moves very cautiously in this field and generally limits its exposure to losses of around $750 million for any cyber insurance policy – a moderate cover in light of potentially huge damages.[71]

The overall picture, then, is of government policy that has strategized for some of the cyber security challenges of the early 2020s. Boundaries have been established to decide what is vital to protect and what is not; some resources have been allocated, and government agencies try to promote common standards of cyber security. The fact remains, however, that the government regards a major, state-based, cyberattack on Britain's infrastructure as a matter of 'when, not if', and British public bodies and around 90 per cent of commercial enterprises are less cyber secure than would be required for state-based attacks and certainly under-insured for them. The 2020s might create a steep, and expensive, learning curve.

The critical national infrastructure

Intimately connected with cyber security is the question of also securing the CNI of the country. When open and market capitalist societies are so evidently vulnerable to foreign influences, both intended and unintended, the ability to protect the essential infrastructure of society is an important investment in modern security and also a way of maintaining the public's confidence in government during difficult times. Most modern states define their CNI in broadly similar ways. Britain's CNI is defined as the need to inject resilience into thirteen distinct sectors, officially listed as: chemicals, civil nuclear, communications, defence, emergency services, energy, finance, food, government, health, space, transport and water.[72] In addition, Britain's cyber security strategy adds that 'data holders' and 'media' sectors, among others, should also be regarded as important facilitators in defending these thirteen sectors since they would be pivotal in maintaining public confidence and support in the event of significant crises or outages.[73]

The most obvious threats to CNI in the 2020s arise from some combination of four main sources. The first of these is the possibility of terrorist attacks on the more dispersed and vulnerable of the CNI sectors. Transport remains a favourite target for international terrorist organizations since it presents so many easy opportunities to create deadly impacts on a civilian population. There has also been persistent interest among jihadist groups in targeting nuclear and chemical facilities and also in food distribution – as long as they could derive some attention-grabbing drama from it. This is technically difficult for any non-state group acting against Britain, but an enormous amount of harm could be done in all these areas if terrorists were, even once, successful. Secondly, CNI sectors are more obviously vulnerable to state-based actors, mainly through cyberattack, but also in some cases through deliberate sabotage (as in the case of British-owned or shared space satellites, civil nuclear plants or many parts of the defence sector) or possibly through market manipulation (as in the case of food or energy availability and distribution). In the event even of a distant conflict with a major adversarial power, such as Russia, Iran, North Korea, even China, British leaders must anticipate some 'hybrid' or 'asymmetric' techniques being used against some sectors of the domestic economy. In 1999 NATO forces operating against Serbia demonstrated exactly this thinking by showing that they could, at will, cut electrical power to Belgrade by non-lethal bombing of power stations that disabled their circuits. Thirdly, CNI is also at risk not necessarily from malign action but simply from networked effects either within Britain or abroad. In August 2019 large parts of Britain's national electricity grid went offline because of synchronous failures in two different power sources.[74] Britain's electricity grid actually operates independently as a 'wide area synchronous grid', but for the sake of resilience and backup it is connected by undersea cables to France, Belgium and Norway, with new connections to Ireland and the Netherlands. That links it to a massive twenty-four-nation European grid and another five-nation grid in Northern Europe. New undersea cables are under discussion to include Denmark and Iceland. The British grid may have plenty of scope to buy power from elsewhere if necessary, but it is also part of a complex grid system serving 425 million other people. Its backup may also be its vulnerability, and even the backup could not guard against the short-term outages of 2019.[75] The same applies to food distribution as one part of a highly transnational retail sector; even more so in telecommunications or air traffic control. The management of these sectors is very sophisticated and short-term disruptions can normally be handled without any noticeable impact on society (except in price variations). But simultaneous disruptions and shortages can create network failures that build their own momentum.[76] Finally, some CNI sectors have to be resilient against natural disasters to which they may be particularly vulnerable. Transport, emergency services, food distribution, health, water, even energy and chemical sectors can be severely, or even catastrophically, disrupted by severe weather events, accidental explosions, crashes, geological collapses and so on. The difference between poor countries that suffer so harshly from a natural disaster and rich countries that don't is usually the ability of the latter to prevent the cascading effects of the original event from triggering further crises.

Resilience planning in Britain's thirteen CNI sectors and the other 'facilitators' that underpin them are designed to allow for disruptions that could flow from any one, or more, of these four sources. The comprehensive nature of this list of sectors and the clear understanding of their importance, however, does not disguise the policy difficulties of creating genuine national resilience in them. For one thing, though the sectors can be neatly listed together they are very different from one another. 'Government' and 'defence' are clearly under very direct central control; 'health' and 'emergency services' somewhat less so. Sectors such as 'transport', 'water' or 'energy' are mainly privatized and connected to government policy only through the highly variable influence of regulatory bodies such as OFWAT, OFGEM, OFCOM or the ONR, and are sometimes surprisingly distant from government coordination.[77] But 'chemicals', 'food', or 'energy', not to mention 'communications' sectors, are all dispersed across dynamic and ever shifting markets that are largely outside any government influence, let alone direct control. The financial sector is unusual. Though it includes, through the Financial Conduct Authority (FCA), some 58,000 businesses in the sector that employs over 2.2 million people, it is by nature easier for a government to obtain institutional traction within it for something like resilience planning. The Treasury, the Bank of England and the scope of the FCA together provide a good way of corralling the financial sector into regulations and inducements to adopt national standards of resilience. This is not the case for, say, the food retail sector with its 3.7 million employees and its quarter million or so businesses that grow and contract very rapidly.[78]

Then, too, it has been pointed out by leaders in key industries that different CNI sectors are highly, and increasingly, interconnected. Systems failure in one can have rapid knock-on effects in another. In the coming years the sectoral approach that was adopted in Britain after 2008 needs to be augmented by more work to identify critical points of weakness and potential failure that are likely to straddle different sectors. Governments certainly understand that thinking about CNI has to include, in its own words, 'networks', 'processes' and 'systems' to account for the increasing reliance on digitally connected technologies across networks of previously isolated industrial control systems.[79] But this is much easier said in official documents than it is done in reality. Points of failure in computing and communications are the most obvious examples, but others in transport (particularly in air and bulk transport) and energy supply reliability are obvious points of potential failure across several sectors.[80] Indeed, the domestic energy sector moved to significantly more distributed, and also foreign owned, supply networks which make designed resilience in the National Grid a much greater challenge for the future. Thinking about resilience only as an afterthought in distributed energy supply, it is said by insiders, is a certain recipe for creating critical points of failure.[81]

In dealing with its own CNI agenda, therefore, governments are required to blend the top-down and the horizontal approach to policy in very sophisticated ways. For all the work that has gone into Whitehall planning since 2008, this is quite a challenge. No one really knows how wide all thirteen CNI sectors really are or can be sure where the critical points of failure might be, until they arise. By one 2011 estimate, around 80 per cent of Britain's CNI already resided in private ownership.[82] The stark fact is that government has the potential to exercise tight control over some areas but comparatively little influence over most of them. Its ability to inform, to induce or to nudge key commercial players into designed resilience (as opposed to afterthought resilience) is limited. Nor, in protecting Britain's CNI, can it rely so easily on incremental decision-making – characterized by risk avoidance and then trial and error. Major failures can be very destructive and possibly catastrophic on public confidence. On the other hand, no one can anticipate, or spend the money required, to cover all eventualities. By mid-2019 the government had spent at least £100 million on extensive planning for a 'no-deal Brexit', most of which remained classified, but which had to face exactly these challenges.[83] It will be a matter of great interest to policy analysts to see the details of these exercises as and when they are released; or even when they have to be put into effect.

The essence of the policy challenge is for government to have the ability to *move quickly* at the first signs of any system failure in the CNI domain, *contain* the problem and then *restore* capacity, simultaneously *communicating* accurately to the public to maintain confidence and national societal resilience. But it is very difficult for governments to be proactive in designing resilience into key systems they do not control so that they can do all this.

Silos and synergy

To be effective, modern governments have to understand the full spectrum of security threats they face and take a holistic view of how they can handle it – which instruments they can control, which they cannot, where they can 'nudge', where they can only watch and hope. All government bureaucracies have to be built on specialized, administrative silos, but true security requires a great deal of genuine synergy between them. Across the board, Britain has appreciated this better than many of its partners and has worked towards much greater synergy since the establishment of the National Security Council in 2010. But some areas are better served than others. In handling the challenges of governance outlined at the beginning of this chapter, it is evident that synergistic approaches have been adopted to deal with counterterrorism and, to a lesser extent, fighting organized international crime. Cyber security and safeguarding key CNI assets, however, are actually tougher propositions and government responses here present a more mixed picture. Government policy can only reach so far into those sectors and responsibility for overseeing them is divided between 'lead departments' in Whitehall with political responsibility divided between at least five different ministers.[84]

Security policies also require political will – some real synergy – to create more than the sum of the parts from separate policy silos. The collective political will to operate vigorous and proactive counterterrorism policies, for example, is hardly in doubt. But it is less so for other issues on the security spectrum, and there is every chance that some of the societal threats beyond the realm of jihadist terror are liable to grow and evolve more quickly than either government or British society may be able to handle adequately.

Chapter 7
Facing global institutions

In successive defence and security documents over the last decade, Britain has asserted its commitment to the preservation of 'the rules-based international order'. As noted in Chapter 4, the very act of naming such a concept shows that it is in trouble. A rules-based international order is not so ubiquitous that naming it is simply superfluous, even meaningless, and the phrase implies that there evidently are alternative forms of 'international order' on offer. More to the point, the 'rules-based' order to which British documents always refer are derived from largely Western rules, many of them developed, institutionalized, even drafted, specifically by Britain. As a perceptive analysis by Malcolm Chalmers indicates, the oft-used phrase is a somewhat lazy slogan that refers to a complex reality comprising 'four pillars'. They consist of three separate but overlapping sub-systems of rules and institutions – namely, a universal security system, a distinctly Western economic political and social system and a more universal economic system (though still based around Western thinking). And, most important, the working of all three sub-systems of the international order is based on a fourth pillar – the pattern of great power relationships that either underpins, or undermines, the other three.[1] This is a good characterization of the complex constellation to which Britain is irrevocably committed and which, by widespread agreement, is under severe and growing challenge.

There is a vigorous debate over the precise form the challenge to the rules-based international order takes.[2] It may be that evolving rules and international institutions will be dominated by non-Western powers in the future but will nevertheless remain faithful to the underlying liberal principles behind much of the existing order, such as universalism, concern for human rights or consensus decisions. This view is based on the idea that Western international values are not just ethical standards but also have a hard-nosed utility that is difficult to ignore, even if other powers design and operate the rules. Alternatively, it may be that non-Western powers will influence new rules and institutions according to distinctly illiberal and different cultural values than those that prevailed in the nineteenth and twentieth centuries when the current rules and institutions evolved. Or again, the current rules might simply transition to jungle rules. In effect, in this view, they would not be replaced by anything as ordered as we have taken for granted, but might simply lapse into a more rudimentary pattern of political coexistence. Jungle rules are not without their own logic (though it may be very harsh); they simply recognize the power realities of all actions as and when they come into contact with each other. But jungle rules contain no aspirations to improve or progress international society in any particular direction.

Whichever way the current rules and institutions might evolve matters a great deal to Britain's future security as well as to its self-image in world politics. The defence review of 2015 – generally acknowledged as a coherent strategic vision following the crisis-driven review in 2010 – set it out very clearly:

> We sit at the heart of the rules-based international order. The UK is the only nation to be a permanent member of the UN Security Council and in NATO, the EU, the Commonwealth, the G7 and G20, the Organization for Security and Cooperation in Europe, the OECD, the World Trade Organization, the International Monetary Fund and the World Bank.
>
> We use our membership of these organisations as an instrument to amplify our nation's power and prosperity. In all these organisations, we play a central role in strengthening international norms and promoting our values. We promote good governance, anti-corruption, the rule of law and open societies. We maintain and champion free trade, including through the EU, and we work with growing powers around the world to build a stronger and more resilient global economy.[3]

The government offered here an interesting list of eleven organizations that encapsulates its vision of how the rules-based international order manifests itself. Seven of these organizations were established in the 1940s and, with the exception of the European Union, Britain had a major – sometimes a determining – role in the creation of ten of them.[4] The statement goes on to say that Britain uses its membership of such organizations to 'play a central role' in strengthening and promoting British liberal values as a bedrock of international norms. This is an ambitious goal to assert and it is based on an institutional framework, the majority of which is over seventy years old. The same ambitious, albeit vague, goal was endorsed yet again in the two security reviews of 2018.[5]

Evolving international institutions

Traditional international institutions all struggle to adapt. They naturally resist the pressure to undergo comprehensive internal reform, since they are all so interlinked and could not be fundamentally reformed without also dismantling large swathes of the existing institutional fabric. That would involve many collective decisions to underwrite unprecedented political power shifts. And political power is not transferred so willingly, even where its ultimate destination may be in little doubt. Given the way the governing international institutions developed during the twentieth century, it is hardly surprising that Western countries are increasingly over-represented in their membership and management, and they would far rather ease their way to reform than undergo the shock of going back to the drawing board, or simply being displaced. So, they try to evolve incrementally, with due regard to new political realities, while the speed of underlying change in the last decade leaves them struggling to meet the challenges of new international problems.[6]

The most fundamental problem lies in the approach of the current great powers towards the traditional institutions of international society; the 'fourth pillar' of the Chalmers characterization. International institutions spring up and flourish most when the great powers have faith in them and see their own long-term national interests best served by expressing political power through their mechanisms. International regimes work predominantly through institutions and by codifying traditionally established norms of behaviour. When great powers lack this faith and demonstrate a sense of declining commitment to international institutions and regimes, the effect tends to be cumulative; if great powers think such institutions are dysfunctional for them, then they rapidly tend to become so for everyone else. The stark truth is that in any political system, rules and institutions are more important to the weaker than the stronger.

The central international institutions that most support the British version of the rules-based international order are the United Nations, NATO, the EU and the more ad hoc G7 and G20 frameworks. These particular institutions comprise a collection of responsibilities that, taken together, are universal, in that they operate globally; regional, in covering Europe and the transatlantic areas; and also highly functional, in that they are charged with managing swathes of security and economic policy. They are the institutions in which Britain's aspirations to be a proactive defender of the global order should be most evident. Even Brexit Britain, outside the European Union, would still look at the EU as one of the most important institutional forces for order and security and will want to cooperate with it as natural defender of Western political interests.

The United Nations is normally the first of the international institutions to be cited in British government documents. This is natural enough since though the UN is not the only repository of international rules and law, it is certainly the most important. The UN confers legitimacy on international accords, agreements, treaties, major statements of principle or intent. When something is enshrined in the UN it is customarily referred to as being part of international law (though that may also be hotly contested). Through the UN Security Council, the organization may also put real political power behind the law it creates. The reality that international action is, in fact, frequently prevented by the actual workings of the Security Council is quite intentional, since the UN can enshrine international law but only attempts to enforce it to the extent that there is political will and agreement among the Permanent Five members (P5) of the Security Council to do so. The effectiveness of the UN in its principal peace and security mission therefore waxes and wanes with shifts in global politics, and though it is much criticized there is no serious constituency for its abolition. If the whole UN system were dissolved tomorrow, the world would try to re-create something that looked much like it the day after. The question for the future is not, therefore, whether the UN will endure, but rather what influence it will exert for the future in enshrining, and occasionally enforcing, the international rules that are so much in Britain's national interests.

Britain's role as one of the original P5 members of the Security Council, increasingly anachronistic as that is, looms large in its aspiration to help maintain the rules-based international order, as well as being central to its image as a significant player in world politics. However inappropriate it may appear to have Britain, and France, among the current P5, the constitution of the Security Council is very unlikely to change in the foreseeable future, and Britain's P5 status is effectively locked into the most central part of the enduring United Nations Organisation and its wider family of agencies. Britain does not need to worry about its place in the organization, or the longevity of the UN, but the relevance of the UN to peace and security in the coming era is a critical consideration.

The uncomfortable fact is that the United Nations no longer commands enough commitment from the major powers, whatever platitudes their leaders utter every September at the opening of each General Assembly session. Russia and China were always sceptical about the work of the UN, because they felt – correctly – that it was politically stacked against them by its composition and by member state attitudes to the security issues that mattered most to them. But since the Reagan Administration of the 1980s, the United States has also become increasingly sceptical about the UN for precisely the same reasons – the sense that the membership is now stacked against the United States and unsympathetic to its preoccupations. Nor is this a zero-sum situation that has benefited Russia and China very much. The three great powers on the P5, using all the influence they have with groups of other states throughout the organization, have turned on the UN to berate it for its inefficiency, hypocrisy, and the ease with which its work can be captured by pressure groups and special interests.[7] Washington, Moscow and Beijing all have different charge sheets to present to the organization and in response, the UN has adopted a number of root and branch reform programmes (always on the assumption that it is facing its last chance) but they have never succeeded in making the UN more intrinsically central to maintaining twenty-first-century global order. Britain and

France, as P5 members, always put a good deal of effort into trying to broker political deals and to find routes towards progress across the spectrum of UN work. So do other influential states such as Germany, Sweden, Japan, South Korea, India or Brazil. Their efforts are frequently successful and help keep the UN moving forward on a number of fronts such as development, environment, world health or weapons proliferation. And the UN continues to be the most accepted legitimizer of the rules of the international system. Nevertheless, its ability to enforce those rules and attract genuine commitment from the great powers has been in steep decline for some years and this trough in political credibility is expected to last well into the coming decade, at least.

The other key institutions that are intrinsic to Britain's international aspirations are under similar pressure in their own particular ways, though largely for the same essential reasons – the attitudes of the great powers towards existing structures. As described in Chapter 1, NATO and the EU strive to adapt themselves to the diverging political concerns of their large, and enlarging, memberships, hoping to do so without undermining their own original purposes. Since they are both extensive and regionally based institutions, they are condemned to try to do this. Yet the macro trends of the twenty-first century put them under great external pressure. NATO's consensus and utility is questioned by the growing scepticism of the United States from within and the external pressures exerted on it by Russian revisionism from outside. The European Union is simultaneously pressured by the economic divergence within its own borders and the fear of another global economic crisis, constant upsets from uncontrolled migration and volatile populism in many of its member states. While autocratic leaders like President Putin and China's Xi Jinping look around Europe for strategic advantage, US leadership during the Trump administration is frankly eccentric and the cry goes up that Europe no longer has any strong (electorally strong as well as strong-minded) leaders in whom it can trust. From the perspective of the rules-based international order, the reality is that when major institutions like NATO and the EU are so preoccupied and internally focused, their ability to maintain or defend, let alone develop, the rules of the system become highly constrained. Their members begin to adopt national hedging strategies as faith in successful collective outcomes declines.

Meanwhile, the G7 and G20 meetings that feature prominently in British normative thinking about global politics are best understood as informal groupings that are precisely designed to reflect the state of relations among the great powers themselves and between the great powers and the rest of the members. They are, by definition, groups that bolster international institutions when institutions are strong and reflect their weakness when they are weak. And unlike a similar mirror that the UN holds up to the international system, the G7 and G20 groups are not themselves institutions, so they have no intrinsic stake in moving the political dial either one way or the other. The G20 was the most appropriate forum in which to address the global economic crisis of 2008 at the top political level and Britain worked hard, and successfully, to create as coordinated a response as possible through this forum.[8] But that was the last occasion on which the G20 moved global politics along to any appreciable extent. Both the G20 and the far more selective G7 groupings entered a phase after 2015 that largely reflected the national differences between their members rather than any deeply shared commitments to collective action.

Beyond these high-profile institutions, there are other very important international organizations, more functionally focused, that also play a big role in creating the framework of rules and order that are so easily taken for granted. They too are subject to some of the same transformational dynamics as those institutions with the highest political profiles. The IMF and the World Bank, to take the two most obvious, are still immensely important in the economic management of the developed world, but they increasingly struggle to navigate through the challenges posed by rising powers. Their pragmatic response has been to reinforce their operations in low- and middle-income countries, to try to keep the rising economic powers on board without altering the essential banking rules they enforce, and to try to bolster their authority through non-lending activities to strengthen the norms of behaviour among members. This is not generally judged as a successful multi-pronged approach to necessary change.[9] China's Asian Infrastructure Investment Bank (AIIB) poses a considerable challenge to the World Bank's portfolio and Beijing's own national lending to other countries impinges on the authority of the IMF, since much of it departs from IMF rules. The AIIB, however, does not really represent such a 'changing of the guard' challenge to international economic management.[10] The AIIB did not begin life as the IMF and World Bank did – as conscious attempts to create a global financial management structure. It is more a national instrument than a planned global management tool and its own future will be determined essentially by the outcome of China's internal institutional struggles as it transforms a society of provincial economies, state-owned enterprises, commercial banks and government ministries controlling their own loans. The growth of the AIIB may diminish the authority of the IMF and the World Bank without, in fact, substituting for it. Nor will the commercial development banks that sprang up after 2008 in the wake of the economic crisis. The New Development Bank of 2015 (the 'BRICS bank') based in Shanghai with modest terms of reference and resources is no more than a straw in the wind. Nor will much of the burden be taken up by the Japanese-led Asian Development Bank, which is more regionally focused and not a significant rule-maker. Indeed, its Japanese/US management structure has been heavily criticized over many years for the partiality of its investment policies and some of the harmful social effects of its sponsored projects. There is general agreement that the management power of transatlantic institutions over the international financial and banking system is diminishing and that Asian institutions are increasingly important, but it is not yet clear quite where and how international management functions will be performed as the authority of the IMF and the World Bank increasingly come into question.

In the same way, the World Trade Organisation, optimistic successor to the General Agreement on Tariffs and Trade, has considerably reduced its previous levels of ambition and nothing seems poised to compensate for that with any new and dynamic arrangements. The WTO's Doha Development Round, to liberalize and stimulate trade for the benefit of the developing world, began in 2001 and finally ran out of steam in 2008. In the event, the emerging economies showed their power against the rich world in killing proposals they did not see in their long-term interests.[11] Agricultural trade, in particular, has not been liberalized either in the rich or poor worlds. The WTO enshrines a great many global trading rules, but it cannot enforce its own trade law as the great powers impose illegal tariffs using entirely spurious 'national security' opt-out clauses. And the Trump administration in the United States publicly acknowledged that it was embarked on a policy to stymie the ability of the WTO to make binding trade judgements by refusing to agree replacement judges on the WTO's Appellate Panel.[12]

Other, less obvious, developments reinforce these economic institutional trends. The political pushback against globalization was accompanied by growing regionalization in patterns of trade. Principles of equality of treatment for international investors and companies were undermined everywhere as trade became more regionally focused amid a trend towards economic protectionism. 'As global rules decay', said *The Economist*, 'a fluid patchwork of regional deals and spheres of influence is asserting control over trade and investment', resulting in a tension between increasingly regional trading systems and a (still) global financial system.[13] The economic pushback against globalization took other contradictory forms after 2008. Air travel and air freight witnessed big increases and greater commercial integration. Similarly, data exchange rose exponentially (over sixtyfold) and human migration continued to increase as a result. At the same time, trade volumes remained lower than they were in 2008, the growth of multinational firms and foreign direct investment, cross-border bank loans and gross capital flows all reduced, some of them precipitously.[14] It was clear by 2015 that the world's major economies were no longer naturally converging, as they had seemed to be in the glory years of globalization after 1990.

Notwithstanding all its growing troubles, the European Union still represents the most successful international institution that has deepened economic integration among its members, despite all the countervailing pressures of natural economic cycles. The EU's success encouraged other organizations to try to imitate it but they have a poor record in developing anything so capable of creating effective transnational rules. Russia promoted a Eurasian Economic Union (EEU) in 2015 and a Eurasian Economic Commission (EEC) to manage internal trade and external tariffs.[15] But it does not live up to its integrationist objectives and Russia's own economy is too weak to drive it forward or invest heavily in its members. Instead, the Asian economies might have had more to gain from the Chinese-led Shanghai Cooperation Organisation (SCO), though this stalled over competing Chinese and Russian visions of its role and the SCO's influence was superseded by the practical, and more diffuse, effects of China's BRI.[16]

There are more international institutions in the world than ever before. Their influence, however, like that among the community of nation states, is more dispersed and less coherent than before. As the major economic powers carve out regional spheres of economic interests for themselves, the authority and efficacy of the global rules that were enshrined in the interlocking global institutions have been quietly diminishing.

International rules in functional sectors

Globalization may have stimulated markets and integration in a number of existing functional sectors and also opened up some emerging sectors to an unprecedented extent. But the forces of globalization do not necessarily create the international structures that seem to be required to manage vigorous sectors in a collective way. Too often, older international regime arrangements and the rules that accompany them have not been updated at the same pace. Instead, ad hoc and diffused national policies – sometime well coordinated, sometimes not – become the default for more coherent and enforceable rules.

Traditional functional sectors that are obviously part of the 'global commons' and for many years have been subject to attempts to manage them collectively include, for example, 'space', that dates back to the late 1960s, 'energy' that became an obvious part of the global commons after two oil crises in the 1970s, and 'climate change', that became the political touchstone of growing concern about environmental stress from the mid-1990s. In all cases the story is one of functional institutions struggling to compete with national policies or market-led behaviour based around national policies. Though a great deal is written about different levels of management in functional sectors such as these, the reality is that the international regimes around them are essentially declaratory. They express good intentions without enough structure or political will to make them stick.

Space law is built around five treaties concluded between the Outer Space Treaty of 1967 and the Moon Treaty of 1984, alongside the ongoing coordinating work done by the UN's International Telecommunications Union. This skeletal regime is faced with all the burgeoning problems of more crowded communications space, increasing amounts of orbital debris, new weapons developments in space – now reaching a real threshold of potential effectiveness – and the rights of burgeoning commercial enterprise in space as against the rights of those governments who have explored it so far. Some eleven states currently have a national ability to launch missiles into space and put up significant payloads, and over fifty states – more than a quarter of the countries in the world – operate equipment themselves in earth's orbit. Regular calls to update space law are lost in the growing scramble to use the new domain for both commercial and national security purposes.

In contrast to the recent commercialization of space, international energy markets are long established and economically sophisticated. Regulating them involves high volumes of trade in multiple types of product, large-scale investment, intellectual property protection and effective dispute resolution – all areas in which there are considerable bodies of national law and a strong motive for international governance arrangements to keep it all flowing and relevant for future challenges. Three international organizations represent the core of a global governance structure, such as it is; the Organisation of Petroleum Exporting Countries (OPEC), the International Energy Agency (IEA) and the International Energy Forum (IEF). The OPEC organization, representing the producers, has lost influence steadily as new producers and new energy sources joined the market in the 1980s and the IEF, uniting both the producers and consumers in the oil and gas markets, can only act as a liaison mechanism and clearing house of data and ideas. Tellingly, the IEA, predominantly Western-based, reaches out to countries such as China, India and Russia but cannot get them into the system as full members where their energy stocks would come under its remit.[17] The IEA is the nearest thing to a governing body in the energy sector. Its membership covers over 50 per cent of energy production and almost 75 per cent of global consumption, yet it still struggles to exert real influence over an ever-diversifying market, while regional bodies such as ASEAN and the European Union try to create their own versions of energy governance. Renewable energy markets, so long the poor relation of the sector, either rely on regional initiatives or self-appointed NGOs to try to create international forms of governance.[18]

'International energy governance', as one influential report pointed out in the midst of the economic crisis, 'has not kept pace with the emergence of major developing nations, with the changing relations between oil producers and consumers, with the emergence of climate mitigation as a central policy issue, and with the technological revolution that is required'.[19] Market forces continue to control the energy sector and impose on it what order and stability there is. In fact, energy prices have been relatively depressed in real terms for some years, even pre-dating the economic crisis, and are not expected to increase structurally for some time. The system has not been under sustained stress as a vital sector of the 'global commons'. But this cannot mask the fact that if energy supply, or the impact of energy on climate change, created international panic about shortages, or some other chaos in the markets, there would only be a weak international regime to try to impose some rules for the common good.

The third sector, climate change, is a functional global commons issue par excellence. The science behind it is very clear that climate change has the potential to harm every society in the world in ways none of them alone can prevent. It can only successfully be addressed at an international level. And yet the UN machinery has acted as little more than a repository of good intentions. The Kyoto Protocol on climate change in 1997 and then the Paris Accord in 2012 established international standards as entirely voluntary targets for states to take national action. These agreements can claim to have had some real success, however, not least in bringing the importance of the issue home to populations and governments across the world. On the other hand, the great power politics underpinning the approach could never be ignored. The US withdrawal from the Paris Accord in 2017 was a considerable blow to a developing international regime, and some big, polluting, states quickly began backsliding from their commitments. The world is better having the Paris accords than not, but progress continued to slip even from the modest levels that were agreed in 2015.[20] In fact, the history of the issue shows that the G8 framework (and then the G7 after Russia's expulsion) was the most dynamic driver for an international climate change agreement, and that was based on the personal political and coordinated drive of three leaders; US President Jimmy Carter, German Chancellor Helmut Schmidt, and the Canadian (briefly prime minister) Joe Clark. The G8 provided a useful on/off mechanism that became the vehicle for national political power among these three to create real momentum towards the climate change commitments of this century.[21] But such momentum was not sustained at the political level. The G20, significantly, has not proved itself to be a good management structure for this, most multilateral, of issues. It is too much a crisis management mechanism rather than a true international policy driver, and over recent years the G7 put more immediate concerns ahead of environmentalism. Climate change targets, vigorous civil society movements to promote them, and a new determination to take the science of climate change seriously, all help create some genuine coordinated action among a number, though not all, of the key national players working to meet the challenge. That is politically realistic. It has been observed that the effect of the Copenhagen Climate Change Summit in 2009 and then the Paris Accord in 2015 has been to shift the emphasis from intergovernmental policy towards national and sub-national policies on climate change. The Paris Accord, it has been said, moved the problem from one of creating a 'regulatory' regime to an attempt to create a 'catalytic' regime that encourages and cajoles individual governments to deal with the problem.[22] There is no certainty that this is working. It is also far short of the sort of institutionalization – the 'rule–making' – that a deepening sense of global order should require.

These are all well-established sectoral concerns for which regimes, of sorts, have existed for some time. It is instructive, however, also to think about sectors that have arisen comparatively recently to see if the relevant cooperative processes have proceeded any differently. Some of the new, and newly relevant, functional sectors might be taken as key indicators of the way the international order is now inclined to frame the management of global issues. An example, firstly, of a new functional sector without any long-standing international arrangements for its management, is that of cyberspace.

While cyberspace expands and deepens to the point where its actual size can only be estimated, it is far from developing as some sort of international free zone or a common information space available to all, as was widely assumed twenty years ago. Cyberspace is a new domain of politics so governments, once they perceive its possible relevance to society, naturally move to regulate, or even control, it. In this case, however, the technology that is intrinsic to the cyber domain moves faster than governments can interpret it. The normal bases for international governance arrangements, the three key requirements, hardly exist in this case. There is no agreement among governments about the real nature of the problems that cyber technologies pose; there is no agreement about the underlying principles that might guide efforts to solve those problems; and there is no mechanism for international coordination of anything that is agreed.[23]

In fact, the internet is becoming 'balkanized'; characterized by islands of freedom and intense surveillance, commercialization and protectionism, all coexisting in a complex and shifting tapestry, and operating at different levels of access. As such, it is less and less susceptible to any universal rules of governance. According to the analysis of O'Hara and Hall, there are now, in effect, four internets.[24] The original internet was the creation of 'Silicon Valley' and its early architects believed in it as a source of libertarian openness – something that would be world-changing at the human level. But a second version of the original is characterized as a 'bourgeois internet', very familiar in Europe, where state-level regulation curbs its libertarian character with restrictions in favour of legality, human rights, public decency or good taste. Governments seek to apply their powers to the internet exactly as they would to any technology that directly affected their citizens. A third variation is the 'authoritarian internet', under rapid development in Russia and China, whose governments not only believe that they can insulate their societies from the libertarian elements of the original, but also have learnt to use it proactively to create social cohesion (or maybe just fear) for authoritarian rule. In 2019, for example, Moscow introduced legislation to create a 'sovereign web' within Russia that would insulate it from any unapproved external inputs. At the same time, China was seen to extinguish 'the last vestiges of the global internet' when it shut out the only remaining general search engine in favour of its own Baidu system.[25] By mid-2019 both China and Russia were almost completely insulated from the global internet. Finally, a fourth internet has emerged, driven within the United States, which can be labelled the 'commercial internet', where the interests of the service providers are given priority above the sort of public protections that European states worry about. In this variation, as long as they are commercially viable, social networking sites can become 'walled gardens' for their users, not affected by external voices and certainly not interoperable, as the original internet architects had assumed. The commercial internet seeks new ways of maximizing profit by creating ever new forms of value for which someone is prepared to pay.

The four different internets are not without law and some of it tightened up considerably after 2018, but they are subject only to national law (or EU law) which is only partially, and inconsistently, harmonized. The possibility of defining meaningful international rules that cover the whole cyber domain, or even large parts of it, has now disappeared. NGOs have looked hard at the problem, the United Nations put its 'Group of Governmental Experts' onto it in 2010, so did NATO. The G20 has the issue on its standing agenda and in 2015 cyber governance and security was even subject to a non-binding bilateral agreement between the United States and China.[26] The reality, however, is that while the 'bourgeois internet' and the 'commercial internet' effectively compete for dominance within the Western world, the 'authoritarian internet' is poised to become the most dominant of the four variations – at least in terms of global usage. The reasons for this expectation are compelling. China's own economic size is a major factor and the 40 per cent of the Chinese population who are not connected to the internet constitute a considerable market for the future. Indeed, in rural China, and in India and Africa, some 3 billion potential new internet customers live under governments, many of whom may be more comfortable with an authoritarian internet than either a 'commercial' or a 'bourgeois' variation. Not least, China's BRI provides it with rule-setting influence in many authoritarian countries of central Asia, even if governments in those countries are not already followers of Russia's authoritarian cyber systems.[27]

A good example, secondly, of a newly relevant functional sector that has been recognized for many years but which is now lifted higher up the international agenda is the Arctic region. The Arctic is a region where the previous international regime now displays similar political and institutional fragmentation along the same lines of great power competition. The 'High North' and beyond that, the Arctic Circle, are areas where previously accepted rules existed with some stability for a long time but have been under increasing strain since the turn of the century as global warming has so affected the geostrategic importance of the region. The old rules are being undermined without any realistic prospect of them being meaningfully updated or replaced.

As the ice recedes and the Arctic becomes more accessible to navigation and mineral exploitation, a region that was known for low political tension and multilateral cooperation has seen rapid increases in military activity, led primarily by Russia. Moscow's military build-up has been far beyond what might be expected if its outlook were purely defensive. The Arctic High North is central to the security of Britain and its domination by a hostile power would put the security of the wider north Atlantic Ocean in some jeopardy.[28] A mixed array of legal governance regimes operates in the Arctic – treaties and agreements, understandings and calls to action that have stemmed from the Svalbard Treaty, UNCLOS III and UNCLCS processes, the International Maritime Organisation guidelines, and even through the World Wildlife Fund.[29] Since 1996 the leading intergovernmental forum has been the Arctic Council, which brings together the eight Arctic territorial powers (the 'A8').[30] This mixed and patchy international regime increasingly struggles to contain the political tensions created by a zone that is territorially split between the eight powers and is estimated to contain (soon to be recoverable) hydrocarbons that amount to over 1,600 trillion cubic feet of natural gas, 44 billion barrels of natural gas liquids and 90 billion barrels of oil.[31] New fisheries grounds are at stake, as are existing routes for vulnerable undersea cables. Not least, receding ice increasingly opens critical commercial sea routes into the North Atlantic with all the attendant security issues. The underlying truth is that while multilateral cooperation has proved more resilient than some had expected,[32] both Russia and the United States, and to a lesser extent, Canada, are moving steadily to carve out their own defensive and economic spheres across the High North in ways that leave Britain and other powers with security interests in the region struggling to make the old international regime effective against the press of an emerging geopolitical power struggle.[33] Parliamentarians in Britain have drawn attention to this on a number of occasions with little positive response from successive British governments.[34]

Finally, there is something to learn from the fate of one of the broadest and most important functional management regimes of all, which has been in sharp decline after reaching some dizzying heights of international cooperation that could not be maintained. Its fascination arises from the fact that its success was bolstered by so many other forces and because it seemed to have come close to creating that virtuous upward spiral where progress could be in fits and starts but nevertheless always in the same direction. Since the mid-1960s nuclear and conventional arms control has been a visible symbol of the growing codification of informal rules. Nuclear arms control between the United States and the Soviet Union, and more broadly reflected in agreements between NATO and the Warsaw Pact, sat at the apex of a movement towards ever-growing international cooperation that seemed genuinely to be an epochal game changer at the time. If Washington and Moscow could constrain more of their nuclear and conventional arms race in interlocking agreements, that was both an important symptom of better relations and had a multiplier effect in improving diplomacy across other spheres of security. Arms control, particularly nuclear arms control, was something of an intellectual driver of 'regime thinking', where a complex set of treaties, accords, agreements and understood patterns of behaviour could become progressively formalized in a circle of restraint that could be dignified as an 'international regime'.

This regime was characterized by a series of 'core treaties' that began with the Partial Nuclear Test Ban Treaty of 1963 and which then embraced three rounds of strategic arms limitation treaties up to 1994, with agreements on a fourth round successfully concluded in outline. An Anti-Ballistic Missile Treaty in 1972 was regarded as a cornerstone of the new approach. Progress was simultaneously translated to the wider world with the conclusion of the landmark Non-Proliferation Treaty (NPT) which refocused the power of the UN's International Atomic Energy Agency (IAEA). On the back of these foundations other treaties were also negotiated. The Comprehensive Nuclear Test Ban Treaty (CTBT) was signed in 1996 and there were preliminary negotiations to conclude a Fissile Material Cut-off Treaty (FMCT) to prohibit the production of weapons grade nuclear material. A Nuclear Suppliers' Group (NSG) of forty-six advanced states was formed to try to prevent nuclear technologies reaching states outside the NPT or non-compliant with IAEA commitments. And the Missile Technology Control Regime (MTCR) was created to keep missile technologies away from those states with illegal nuclear or other mass destruction capabilities. Quite separately, there were successful international measures to address the 'loose nukes' problem – to prevent nuclear weapons going missing after the old Soviet Union collapsed; and a number of UN sponsored and other joint initiatives to prevent nuclear and radiological material falling into terrorist hands. The momentum of this deepening regime was strengthened at very practical levels by an Intermediate Nuclear Forces Treaty (INF), primarily for Europe, that banned certain nuclear missiles from the whole continent; a Conventional Forces in Europe Treaty (CFE) that also applied to non-nuclear weapons in Europe, and a Chemical Weapons Convention (CWC) that banned a complete class of weapons across the whole world and a Biological Weapons Convention (BWC) that attempted to do the same. There were many other initiatives in these years – some successful, some stalled – affecting the development of other weapons and systems, from anti-personnel landmines to terrorist mass destruction devices.

It was altogether an impressive international regime; by some estimates the most effective and cohesive in any field since 1945.[35] But the history of arms control provides a salutary reminder that no international regime, however desirable for the sake of the world, however strong and deeply institutionalized, is bound to keep moving forward, to remain relevant or even to continue in existence.

The great power arms control regime has been in deepening trouble since the turn of the century.[36] The outline agreement for a fourth round of strategic arms reductions was abandoned and a US attempt under President Obama to replace the successful original treaties when they expired in December 2009 with a 'New Start Treaty' in 2010 (to expire in 2021) was repudiated by President Trump as, 'One of several bad deals negotiated by the Obama Administration'.[37] The Bush administration had already withdrawn from the landmark ABM Treaty in 2002, so killing it. A major blow was struck against the norms of non-proliferation and the NPT itself in 2018 when the United States withdrew from the Iran nuclear deal, which was designed to halt that country's nuclear programme for at least ten years and while it remained signed up to the NPT.[38] In 2019 the Trump administration withdrew the United States from the INF Treaty that had been part of European arms control since 1987. The NPT remained as an important treaty with some 190 members, but further progress effectively stopped after its 1995 Review Conference. The CTBT did not gain enough ratifications to enter into force, the FMCT was deadlocked after 2010, the MCTR and the NSG remain semi-effective, at best. Not least, the Conventional Forces Treaty in Europe could not adjust to the new political conditions after the Cold War. Discussions after 1999 on an 'adapted' version of the treaty failed, and in 2007 Russia 'suspended' its participation in it, followed in 2011 by a 'partial suspension' by the United States.[39] In 2015 Russia reported that it had 'completely' halted its participation in CFE commitments.

This is not all a story of United States and Russian bad faith. The more structural reasons that put pressure on the arms control regime are not difficult to understand. Treaties concluded in one era are always challenged by the technical innovations of another. The powers were content to conclude an Anti-Ballistic Missile Treaty when those technologies had little to offer, but kicked against it when the technologies began to look more viable. They were content to limit the number of nuclear missiles they held, but less willing to be tied to the number of warheads they could carry, once warhead miniaturization provided many new possibilities. Then, too, geopolitics changed everything. The end of the Cold War eventually put NATO's effective eastern borders a thousand miles nearer to Moscow. More important still, when the arms control regime began to move decisively forward in the 1970s, China was not a significant nuclear player, even though it had a nuclear bomb. But by the turn of the century, anti-ballistic missiles and intermediate nuclear weapons had become a feature in the US-China strategic equation, regardless of what Moscow might intend. China ducked for flimsy cover in finding endless reasons not to enter into any meaningful strategic arms control as it built up its forces. It joined some of the international arms control treaties and accords, though was conspicuously absent from others.[40] It was regularly accused of being a reckless nuclear technology and missile proliferator even as it tried to join the NSG and it would never reveal the extent of its strategic nuclear forces – the prerequisite for meaningful arms control. It was no surprise that there was no bilateral, strategic, arms control between Beijing and Washington. The impressive regime that had been built on, and had contributed to, détente between the United States and Russia in the latter part of the twentieth century simply failed to transfer to a third player in the great power strategic relationship. And the fourth of the great powers, India, exploded its first nuclear bomb in 1998 in a tit-for-tat exchange of nuclear tests with Pakistan that also rocked the whole NPT structure as two of the powers who had refused to sign the treaty indicated their practical contempt for it.[41]

There is some real justification for both Washington and Moscow to argue that the arms control regime was becoming both politically and technologically out of date and as long as Beijing remained unwilling to engage in meaningful arms control (while developing its weapons unfettered by treaty obligations). Washington, in particular, faced a classic two-front problem. The importance of this in the future of the rules-based international order is that Moscow and Washington reacted differently to the structural changes in their situation. Under President Putin's revisionist determination to rebuild Russia's international influence, Moscow maintained all its rhetorical commitment to the arms control regime but simply cheated, and worked around the letter and the spirit of a number of agreements. The United States could not cheat without being caught out by Congress and its own vigilant civil society groups. But US administrations publicly kicked against restrictions on emerging technologies when they saw China developing more strategic capacity and Russia more brazenly cheating.

In truth, and for different reasons, none of the four great powers really believed in the existing arms control regime by the turn of the twenty-first century; India because it never had, and always accused the regime of being an instrument of Western dominance; China because it did not want to be fettered while it was still building its military capacity; Russia because it could not now live with the technological restrictions that the old Soviet Union had once been able to embrace; and the United States because the neo-cons under Bush and then the Jacksonian nationalists under Trump were naturally suspicious of any international regime, and especially one that restricted the ability of their country to arm itself as it chose.

None of this is good news for European countries which cannot compete in military terms with the great powers, have run their own military forces down to very low levels and are faced with a volatile constellation of leaders in Washington, Moscow, New Delhi and Beijing. The Europeans relied on both nuclear and conventional arms control, in effect, to de-militarize their continent and so allow them henceforth to regard defence and security as less salient issues on their own national agendas. They put a great deal of faith in the depth and longevity of a broad and mutually reinforcing arms control regime that seemed to be a permanent and solid part of the diplomatic landscape they confronted. That regime is in serious trouble. It is certainly not dead, but it must be regarded as increasingly moribund and its permanence cannot be taken for granted.

International law

International law, as the more formal expression of the rules-based international order, has reflected many of these trends, for the same reasons. No less than domestic law, international law is always evolving according to cases as they arise. It is a matter of interpretation and the degree to which one interpretation may be widely shared, or not, by other governments in the system. Collective organizations such as NATO, the EU, the African Union or the Organisation of American States can make their own rulings that might not be made in the United Nations and still expect them to have some legal force. It was impossible, for example, to get agreement in the UN in 1999 for Western states to enforce decisions on Serbia to end its atrocities in Kosovo, but they relied on NATO resolutions to provide the legal framework for the military campaign that was then undertaken. In 2011, by contrast, the UN Security Council, including Russia and China, authorized military action to prevent government massacres in Libya – an authorization that President Putin felt was subsequently exceeded by NATO states and that he became resolved never to repeat. In addition, drawing on the Nuremberg precedents, an International Criminal Court was created in 2002, though the United States ostentatiously shunned it, to deal with genocide, crimes against humanity or war crimes.[42] Similarly, international tribunals were created, which like the ICC sat in the Hague, to deal specifically with crimes against humanity in the Former Yugoslavia and also in relation to war crimes in Rwanda and Sierra Leone.[43] The ICC was a permanent creation; the mandates of the others had all expired by 2017 and were in part replaced by UN 'residual mechanisms'.

It is evident that Western liberal thinking drove the practice of twentieth-century international law and progressively grafted onto the established legal recognition of sovereignty increasing concerns for human rights and civil liberties. All states, said the United Nations in 2005, had a 'responsibility to protect' (R2P) citizens in their own country and, by implication, in other countries wherever possible.[44] This had no legal force but it was a big declaration in principle that reflected a high-water mark in the evolution of international law towards humanitarian responsibilities. In a series of only half-conscious and pragmatic policy responses, Western states, in effect, had promoted human rights as politically neutral standards that would be binding as a matter of international law.[45] State sovereignty was assumed to have been transformed with additions of International Human Rights and Humanitarian Law to convert it into a doctrine that was largely about the state's responsibility towards individuals and its citizenry.[46]

But as political power became more widely distributed, the great powers, in particular, reasserted a more traditional – Westphalian – version of international legal sovereignty in both their behaviour and their justifications of it. The attraction of international courts was running out of steam by 2019 and major cases were increasingly diverted to national courts. The ICC had convicted fewer than ten suspects, all of them African. The overall effect was to diversify international law in practice after a long period when it had appeared to be moving fairly consistently along the R2P line. The result, as one legal scholar put it, was to create a 'multi-hub structure' for international law that reflects the growing multi-polarity between the great powers. Such multi-polarity puts pressure on legal processes to move from a global level to 'flexible, issue-specific subsystems'.[47] The rising powers take their cue from the leadership moods of the great powers. It is not that rising powers explicitly reject existing international law but rather seek changes in interpretation in response to specific issues.[48] Three particular points of tension, over the defence of 'sovereignty', the interpretation of 'legitimacy' and the role of the state in economic development, all mark the growing fault lines within the multi-polar legal world.[49] 'Rising powers', says Burke-White, 'are reasserting the pre-eminence of the state in international law, leading to a gradual turning away from the individualization of international law championed by the United States and Europe back toward the Westphalian origins of the international legal system'.[50]

In effect, then, international law is being reorganized around a number of national 'hubs' that express both resurgent political power and the legal justifications behind it. Many rising powers are attracted to the way China and Russia now interpret their international legal obligations while the United States provides an ambiguous model that is caught between its traditional universalist vision of (ever-growing) world order and the Jacksonian nationalist approach that puts a narrow interpretation of US national interests at the heart of its approach to law. It is not clear how this will develop in the coming decades, but the more state-centric approach continues to clash with erstwhile European interpretations of international law as it reaffirms the collective rights of a sovereign government above the individual rights of citizens, businesses and organizations everywhere.

The challenge of transformation

The evolution, growth and decline of institutions and behavioural norms are all entirely natural processes in a dynamic environment. Indeed, in any political system, domestic or international, the absence of institutional evolution is normally a clear symptom of sclerosis and decay. The challenges for Britain in the transformation of the current international order are more complex than the necessary adjustment to change that all states have to confront. One challenge for Britain is both political and conceptual. It has suited Britain to cast itself as an erstwhile defender of the rules-based international order and to show that it is prepared to use its military forces to back up that claim. This was a big part of the rationale for sending a task force to liberate the Falkland Islands in 1982 after an illegal invasion; it was intrinsic to the motives for undertaking the 1991 Gulf War as part of a big military coalition; it was argued vociferously again in the controversial case of the 2003 war against Iraq and it was sincerely maintained by successive governments in all twelve British military campaigns that followed the Cold War. And yet, the more precise meaning of such a broad commitment is never spelt out in much detail, certainly not in official documents or for public discussion.

Secondly, the reason for holding on to the characterization so instinctively indicates how intrinsic the existing order has been to British interests – a privileged role in the UN, key influence in NATO, a set of economic and financial rules that were based first on British Keynesian economic principles and then on US/British neoliberal market principles and a series of sectoral arrangements in which British diplomacy was seldom absent. Leaders did not have to think very hard in realizing that it was clearly in Britain's interests to maintain as much of this influence as possible. But as Chalmers points out, the three sub-systems of institutions and rules that make up the 'international order' are all different in scope and purpose. The need to prioritize British efforts between one and another as they change is likely to become more pressing. The relative political and financial costs of maintaining a rather simplistic, across the board, approach to international order are bound to increase significantly in the present climate. Britain runs the risk of being reduced to empty protestations in favour of the international order, in contrast to its previously proactive stance in promoting and defending important rules and institutions.

Thirdly, and most important, the great powers' backing, and often their preference, for 'regime approaches' to global problems that had been US-led and generally consensual is evidently changing. While it rode in the wake of US leadership, Britain could credibly claim to be an active upholder of the rules-based international order, in military, economic and diplomatic terms. US leadership created the political space for effective British policy. But this may not be the case in the future if the United States has lost so much faith in the current international order and is anyway reluctant to sustain the burdens of Western leadership. If the great powers have really begun to compete over the future of the international rules – or find themselves falling by default into jungle rules – then the influence of powers such as Britain to maintain a smooth transition towards a new order, may decline in two ways, as Hemingway said of bankruptcy, 'gradually, then suddenly'.[51]

The Brexit challenge

Chapter 8

The geopolitics of Brexit

Britain has long had an ambiguous relationship with the rest of mainland Europe. Popular views of British history stoutly maintain that the history of Britain is fundamentally an 'island story'. There are, after all, some 6,000 islands around Great Britain, including all the isles of Ireland, the Hebrides, Orkneys, Shetlands, the Isles of Man, Wight and so on. There would seem to be a good geographical case in arguing for some degree of British exceptionalism from the continent of Europe. History suggests a far more complicated relationship, however, where Britain has been alternately quite integrated, and by turns, apparently detached, from the European political mainstream.[1] For four centuries after the Norman conquest, England and continental Europe were united by dynastic links and the wars between them. From the mid-fifteenth century until the early eighteenth century, England did embody some genuine exceptionalism during the Tudor and Stuart periods – a fortress England and a civil war over the constitution that shocked the rest of Europe. But the Hanoverian succession in 1714 again put the country firmly into the European political mainstream – and played a big part in driving the creation of the United Kingdom itself. Thereafter, Britain pursued a full imperial role across the nineteenth century and in the twentieth attempted an 'Anglosphere' strategic role, as the mechanism for British influence. Across both centuries, as Britons habitually took for granted events in continental Europe, such global ambitions were largely dependent on basic stability in Britain's own neighbourhood. The country not only had a massive stake but also played vital roles in maintaining or restoring that stability at critical moments – intervening as 'the balancer'; however, reluctantly it accepted its 'continental commitment'.[2]

Where modern Britain sought to defend, or else separate, itself from continental power, particularly during the Tudor and Elizabethan periods, the French Revolution and Napoleonic wars, and again in both world wars, it was driven overwhelmingly by the desire to defend and preserve its own political system – its dynasty, then its protestant constitution, its early democracy, then its liberalism.[3] And though Britain has been invaded many times it has not suffered the traumas of defeat in any wars for the survival of its own form of governance. It has a self-conscious tradition in preserving successfully what it takes to be 'English', and latterly 'British'. Through its imperial role and its dominions, alongside heavy investments over the twentieth century in relations with the United States, it promoted an Anglosphere approach to its global security rather than a European one. In fact, the Anglosphere has been remarkably successful in warfare and defence. For over 330 years it is true to say that Britain and the United States, separately or together, prevailed in every strategically significant conflict they took on, from the War of the League of Augsburg in 1688 to the end of the Cold War in 1991.[4] It is hardly surprising that such a long record of strategic victory should feed a national psychology of exceptionalism but it also disguised the degree to which the success of the Anglosphere depended on the prevailing status quo across continental Europe.

This is the key to understanding the geopolitics of Britain's relationship with the European Union – and its leaving after almost fifty years. Britain supported some sort of European union immediately after the Second World War (as long as it could choose its own relationship with it) as one of the means to facilitate the ability of the Anglosphere to operate. But within twenty years it was the very failure of the Anglosphere approach to live up to the government's expectations that drove Britain to seek membership of the Common Market it had shunned, indeed tried to sabotage, at the time of its foundation.

In 1945, faced with post-war devastation and the growing hostility of Moscow, Britain strongly supported the evident geopolitical desirability of creating a united Europe. We are 'Europeans forging ahead', said Winston Churchill speaking in Strasbourg in 1949, 'laying the foundations of a United Europe … whose moral design will win the respect and acknowledgement of all humanity and whose physical strength will be such that no person will dare to disturb it'.[5] This vision of a united Europe was important to Britain for all the same reasons that had applied for the previous century and a half; to help create the conditions in continental Europe that would allow the Anglosphere to prosper in the wider world. The mechanism by which this should be done, whether it be the Council of Europe in 1949, the (failed) European Defence Community of 1954, the West European Union of 1955 or eventually the fledgling European Common Market of 1958 were all second-order institutional questions.[6] The geopolitical imperative for Britain in the 1940s was that Western Europe, at least, must be secure and recover its prosperity as soon as possible if Britain were to use the Anglosphere to address the wider problems of fighting global communism, withdrawing from empire and dealing with the pressures of decolonization. In the event, the founding of NATO in 1949 answered the most pressing European defence questions but not the wider security and prosperity concerns – not least the rehabilitation of defeated Germany inside a western camp that was becoming distinctly jittery.

Nevertheless, NATO proved to be a very good investment for Britain in the preservation of the Anglosphere approach to international relations. It linked the United States and Canada directly into European security and gave Britain a pivotal role in the defence aspects of transatlanticism. It also produced a split personality in the British approach to the international politics of Europe. In all military matters Britain was totally loyal to NATO and promoted its coordinating, even integrative, benefits among the members. NATO was, and is still, the heart of Europe's military security, thanks in large part to Britain's efforts over half a century. On the other hand, London was always inherently suspicious of the economic and social project that was embodied by the founders of the original Common Market, later the European Economic Community (EEC). NATO was certainly an organization for us; the EEC was not. But NATO was never enough to provide for the wider security needs of post-war Britain, and in 1961 the country was driven by a sense of decline abroad and economic underperformance at home into the decision to apply for membership of the EEC. After the fateful decision, it took more than a decade to see it through. There was continuing political and economic decline in the 1960s (albeit accompanied by impressive cultural renewal) as Britain strove to gain membership. It was finally agreed in 1971 and Britain was admitted in 1973 – in the very year the so-called 'golden age of economic growth' came to an abrupt end and the world economy entered a prolonged inflationary crisis and a decade of oil price hikes.[7] The early 1970s were difficult times for Britain. The Conservative government of 1970–4 had declared no fewer than five separate states of emergency before being turfed out in favour of a minority Labour government that, after another election, struggled on unconvincingly through a sterling crisis, an unsteady coalition, and then a failed devolution policy that triggered the election that ejected it from office.

The circumstances were very important. The original six members of the Common Market had entered into their novel arrangement with a sense of optimism and commitment; they were emerging strongly from the dislocations of the war and when the economic 'golden age' was in full swing. Britain, by contrast, entered the EEC as a refuge from the bracing winds of global politics, in a troubled national mood, just as the world economy took a dramatic turn for the worse. As a contemporary scholar expressed it in 1974, 'At the end of the story, when Britain entered the European communities in January 1973, it was as a European state with strictly European interests, no greater in power than France or Federal Germany and considerably weaker in economic strength'.[8] The Anglosphere seemed to be finished as a political force in world politics. The public was fatalistic and unenthusiastic about entering the EEC, and at the beginning membership seemed to make little practical difference as the Western world struggled to navigate the deepening economic crisis.

British political attitudes went through several different stages in reacting to the Common Market as it evolved to become the European Union of the 2020s.

As Peter Wilding puts it, Britain showed 'indifference' up to its application to join the EEC in 1961; real 'interest' in the frustrating application decade up to 1975 – driven as much by the fact that if France's President De Gaulle wanted to keep Britain out of the organization, there must be something worth joining. That was followed by fifteen years up to 1990 in which Britain was obviously 'interested' in the EEC and, under the leadership of Prime Minister Margaret Thatcher, constructive in trying to shape its future directions. But the next twenty years are defined as one of growing 'irritation', followed, after 2010 by 'a reckoning' which culminated in the Brexit referendum and the triggering of Article 50 of the Lisbon Treaty that put Britain on the road out of the EU.[9]

Despite later protestations to the contrary, the British policy elite and the public always knew that the European 'grand project' was designed from the first to move beyond deepening economic integration towards something more politically unified – in ways that might be historically novel. Three successive Thatcher governments worked to head off exactly those more visionary ambitions. Britain was keen to enlarge the membership of the organization to dilute progress towards deeper political integration and it was enthusiastic to build a single integrated market to make it more functionally grounded. Both ambitions were achieved to an extent that could scarcely have been imagined in the late 1970s. These years were the high-water mark of the battle of ideas between the European federalists and the British: Britain won the arguments on enlargement and on the single market; the federalists won a victory on creating the Euro, which turned out to be less than convincing under economic pressure, and on a single constitution, which was disastrously rejected across the EU.

But making progress in the British-preferred way actually encouraged the integrationists to try to take the grand project further forward, while they reinforced the British determination to interpret the benefits of EU membership in primarily economic terms. For the original and core EU members, particularly for France and Germany who knew what it was like to have their history overturned in war and revolution, there was no necessary contradiction between the economic and political ambitions of a grand project that could take Europe to a new political destination – something more than an integrated market but less than a European super-state. But for Britain, moving down the political road was always regarded primarily as the price it would have to pay for the economic advantages of membership. In addition to trying to dilute the progress of European integration, Britain was also successful in securing a number of important opt outs, on financial contributions, participation in the Schengen Agreement on borders, key elements of the social chapter[10] and most critically, on participation in the single currency that it had so vociferously opposed. It even ostentatiously opted out of the Lisbon Treaty obligation to commit itself to 'an ever closer union'. Nor was Britain's influence all about resistance to federalist instincts. Successive British governments over the years were prominent in reforming the common fisheries and common agriculture policies, in pushing a common foreign policy approach, creating better cross-border procedures for dealing with crime and terrorism, opening up new trade deals, creating new standards in environmental protection and not least in enforcing better standards in EU budgeting.[11]

But it was not enough. Growing Eurosceptic strands of opinion in Britain argued with increasing conviction that Britain's geopolitical status made the ultimate, albeit unknown, European destination unsuitable for such a country and that the EU, as it now was, had already exacted too high a political price for what economic advantages it offered. When the crunch came in the Brexit referendum of 2016 and the three and a half years of chaotic and bitter negotiations that followed, it was clear that the core EU nations could not be prized apart or picked off individually as many in Britain had assumed. France, Germany and the Benelux countries, Spain, Ireland and Sweden, at least, proved that there was something deterministic in the way they wanted to keep the EU moving forward, even if the future of the European grand project was becoming hazy. And the crunch also showed that Britain's '52/48 decision' to leave the EU was based fundamentally on a belief that Britain simply did not fit into this project. Britain's destiny was simply different, though even more hazy.

Since Britain had always interpreted its EU membership in essentially economic terms, it is curious that neither public nor elite opinion had ever been able to analyse the economic arguments for joining, staying or leaving very convincingly. In the late 1960s, the simple truth was that no one knew whether it would be economically advantageous for Britain to join the EEC. It was a matter of faith that it probably would be; though more certain that Britain would run out of economic options if it did not join. It was no clearer by the time of the 1975 referendum and remained a constant bone of contention as Eurosceptic opinion in Britain ramped up in the 1990s. Amid the 2016–19 political imbroglio the hard, empirical evidence all pointed towards the economic damage that leaving would do, but it was impossible to estimate the extent of any damage while the terms of leaving were unclear. More importantly, the Brexit arguments had reached a stage of such entrenched bitterness that the empiricism of such evidence was weighed equally in the public mind with the speculative and selective estimates of the committed Brexiteers. The truth this time round was that the country again assumed that no one knew what the balance of economic arguments really were, mainly because the political mainstream and the political classes either chose not to ask, or did not believe the answers when they did.

Britain voted narrowly to leave the EU, and the Theresa May government, and the controversial Johnson government that followed it, interpreted the mandate as an unstoppable commitment to deliver on that decision by whatever means necessary. Britain was leaving the EU not for clear reasons of economic advantage – just as in the 1960s, that was all more of a guess than a strategic calculation – but more fundamentally because of a growing new sense of British exceptionalism. But more than that, it was an English exceptionalism.

The English crisis of identity

Britain's Brexit decision was essentially an English Brexit, and the geopolitical challenge for the future is shaped by that. In the 2016 referendum, Scotland voted by a majority of 24 per cent to remain in the EU, Londoners by a majority of 20 per cent, in Northern Ireland by a majority of 12 per cent. Wales voted to leave by a majority of 5 per cent, and outside London, the English shires voted to leave by a majority of 11 per cent. Given the population distribution and levels of voter turnout across the country, the effect of voting in the English shires was to create a majority of over 2 ½ million people who voted to leave, as opposed to a majority of less than 1 ½ million across the other parts of the UK who voted to remain, all within a total of 33.6 million votes.[12]

Chapter 2 described how the unbalanced nature of the British economy – as both beneficiary and victim of rapid globalization – also indicated the growth of social and constitutional tensions across Britain. The Brexit process crystallized a more specific phenomenon, indeed, stimulated it, which also plays out as part of British exceptionalism. It is sometimes characterized as a rebirth of English nationalism but that isn't quite right. It connects in some ways to a keen sense of patriotism but the phenomenon is far more inchoate than a surge of self-conscious nationalism. It is more a sense of economic and social grievance that has created an evident crisis of identity within the English communities of the UK. The country began to experience a well-noted political nervous breakdown that steadily deepened after 2008, notwithstanding the triumph of a successful Olympics in 2012 and a (false) sense that it had put the economic crisis behind it.[13] In many respects, the growing disunity within the UK and the Brexit vote are two sides of the same coin and they both reflect a crisis of Englishness. It is a search for English identity in globalized Britain. English identity was hitherto taken completely for granted throughout modern British history; for generations 'English history' was synonymous in the public mind with 'British history' – it was the core of the national story. But it suffered a crisis of confidence and a sense of deepening unfairness during the last two or three decades.[14]

The 'hourglass' shape of the employment picture, the north-south economic divide, the social tensions created by an unbalanced British economy which sucks in foreign labour were all outlined in Chapter 2. By 2008 it was increasingly clear that Englishness had become politicized and not just by far-right activists and soccer hooligans. National government sitting in London self-consciously represented 'Britishness' and was driven all the harder to maintain the integrity of the UK in the face of secessionist parties in the other kingdoms who always wanted more, and Eurosceptic opinion throughout the country who saw the EU ever encroaching on that essential Britishness. Since Britain had, in practice, devolved political power to Scotland, Wales, Northern Ireland and, in effect, London, what has been called the 'England without London' segment – 47 million people, still some 71 per cent of the total UK population – increasingly saw themselves as English, and somehow under- or badly represented and comparatively disadvantaged economically. Only a decade after the 2001 national census that had recorded few structural changes, the 2011 census recorded that some 60 per cent of English citizens regarded themselves as solely 'English', even given the chance to choose a 'British' *and* an 'English' identity. This sole identification as 'English' was recorded at 70 per cent in the North East, 66 per cent in the North West, Yorkshire and the East Midlands.[15] Britishness and cosmopolitanism was very evident in London, but much less so elsewhere. As one detailed survey put it in 2012, time series data 'suggested that the stronger a person's sense of English identity, the more likely they were to be dissatisfied with the place of England within the post-devolution United Kingdom'.[16]

This was the psychological environment in which the Eurosceptics were able to ride a wave of growing sentiment for the country too many people felt they were losing; and anger for the way the economic crisis and austerity policies were eating into daily lives. Eurosceptic activists were eventually able to harness this into a national movement across three national political parties, counting UKIP, and then its Brexit Party successor. It created a bond between a London-based Eurosceptic political elite and a populist revolt in the shires that encompassed working, and middle-class, people in equal measure. It did, as they say, 'convert pain into meaning' – even if the outcome was likely to cause the English even more economic pain. At least it would mean something important to them and for reasons they understood.[17] At the time, the Eurosceptic campaigners could hardly have realized that they were tapping into something so essentially English. It was not clear until the Brexit referendum itself quite how national opinion across the UK would break down, but in the event, though the official British decision was marginal, the 'England without London' decision was overwhelming and proved decisive. Significant portions of the population in 'England without London' – in particular older workers, self-employed and pensioners – were in a mood to express their anger and frustration at a range of targets, but none that could be easily grasped.[18] They had seen Scottish nationalists, in particular, run a high-handed referendum campaign in 2014 that would have broken up the UK on the votes of less than 5 per cent of its total population. But the English could never leave their own union. 'Unable to exit Britain', as Anthony Barnett put it, 'the English did the next best thing and told the EU to fuck off'.[19]

In one sense, this was a sophisticated political and economic reaction. It had been evident across Europe and the United States for at least a decade that globalization put greatest pressure on unskilled, semi-skilled and clerical workers in rich countries; pressures considerably ramped up by austerity policies. They reacted by turning to both populism and protectionism.[20] In 2016, the 52 per cent who voted for Brexit were evidently voting against Westminster as well as Brussels. In the case of the 71 per cent of British citizens in the 'England without London' category, however, this was accompanied by all the popular imagery of Second World War Britain or the Britain of the pre-globalization age. As Fintan O'Toole saw it, the description of Britain's relationship with the EU as one of 'vassalage' was not just a parliamentary flourish. It ran deeply through the Brexiteers' campaigns both before and after the 2016 referendum and took some real hold on the imagination of core Brexit supporters in the country.[21] It extended to the (revealing) view that the EU had evolved to become a pseudo-imperialist mechanism based on a Paris–Berlin axis to promote mainly French political, and German economic, objectives; a sort of natural and unspoken alliance between French *grandeur* and German car workers. Even a prominent ex-diplomat mused that a new imperialism based around the EU might be desirable in the world of the 2020s.[22] Another scholar provided an imperial metaphor that became fashionable when he thought the EU akin to the old Holy Roman Empire, 'hapless and officious perhaps, but not malign'.[23] Whether malign or not, the EU was widely seen as preventing Britain making its own sovereign choices in certain important respects; though the practical impact of such restrictions was never specified at any strategically significant level.

The government held out the prospect that after exiting the EU a 'global Britain' would emerge in the 2020s as a different sort of actor in world affairs – a new type of player in the globalized world. But the vision never went beyond the slogan in any official government thinking in the years immediately following the Brexit vote. It remained a vacuous concept. The lack of any real interest in articulating a clearer path for the future could only be explained by the immediate distraction of dealing with the messy and divisive process of disentangling Britain from the EU. But the intellectual lacuna was very telling. In reality, Brexit supporters in the political elites, in government and among the general public were firmly fixed on what Britain had been, rather than what it might be in the future. The basis for British exceptionalism in continental Europe was not based either on economically or politically clear visions of any alternatives. If they had been, the negotiations between London and Brussels, and then within Westminster, would have been less traumatic. Instead, as the process went on throughout 2019, British exceptionalism was driven by an innate sense that the outcome would be either greater or lesser economic pain – it would certainly not be pain free – but that would still be a price worth paying for the recovery of some sort of historical exceptionalism.

Historical exceptionalism plays out badly within the Union of the UK, which, as we observed in Chapter 2, was created in a series of ad hoc responses to particular challenges. The Union is a pragmatic series of relatively recent arrangements built into an unwritten constitution and it has been durable, partly for that very reason and also because it has been strengthened by war. As William Hague had pointed out even in 2015 – in an argument that has been reflected increasingly often since – a Brexit vote under the political pressures that then existed in the country might 'end up destroying the United Kingdom'.[24] The status of Northern Ireland in the Union was a matter of intense conflict during 'the troubles' after 1969 but was then stabilized by the Belfast Agreement of 1998 (the 'Good Friday Agreement'). That of Scotland in the Union had been stable for most of the nineteenth and twentieth centuries but became troubled during the 1970s as the British economy suffered and North Sea oil offered some prospect of a viable, independent Scotland. In 2010, after some decades of political neglect by the major parties, Scottish independence roared back onto the national political agenda and remained there throughout the Brexit process.

English-led, historical exceptionalism is intimately connected with the Brexit decision and together they both make the dissolution of the UK in the 2020s considerably more likely than was previously the case: Brexit because the dynamics of the process may lead to greater demands to break away from the Union; and English exceptionalism, because the majority of the UK's population might not want to fight very hard to save it.

The tortured nature of the politics around the Brexit referendum and its three-year aftermath played fast and loose with all previous trends in Britain's devolution/dissolution arguments. The Scottish National Party agreed that their 2014 independence referendum, which they were quietly confident of winning, would settle the question 'for a generation' – *unless* other circumstances materially changed. Brexit was a massive material change. A majority of Scots had voted to stay in the Union in 2014 and assumed that they would thereby be staying in the European Union too.[25] But in 2016, while a clear majority of Scots voted to stay in the EU, the Union as a whole did not. The equation had changed completely and was no longer so binary a choice between Scottish nationalism and British Unionism. For on the one hand, an independent Scotland might expect to be welcomed into the EU as a new member, but would also find itself sharing its most important and lucrative border with a non-member country more than ten times its size; and moreover, where sterling would still be the currency rather than the Euro which Scotland would be obliged to adopt as a new EU member. This made independence an even more risky project. On the other hand, London visibly made a complete hash of the leaving process and risked ending up with an outcome that would leave the whole of the UK worse off, certainly for some years until stability returned. Some in Scotland pressed hard for the SNP to demand a second independence referendum to divorce themselves from what they saw as English madness.[26] SNP leaders were more cautious, waiting to see how the Brexit process would unfold before making a move on a second independence referendum. In effect, Brexit gave them the authority to demand a second referendum at any time. They could keep it in their pocket while they saw how the political land lay and how the reality of Brexit Britain played out in the minds of the Scottish public. After more than 300 years, the question of Scotland's union with England could wait another couple until the time was right to ask it again. But by June 2019 SNP leaders had put Westminster on notice that a second referendum on Scottish independence would be demanded before 2022.

Northern Ireland was complicated in its own characteristic ways over Brexit.[27] The province as a whole voted to remain in the EU, but the Democratic Unionist Party (DUP), on whose votes the minority British government had depended after the 2017 election, strongly represented the leave voters. Moreover, the DUP were, by definition, staunch *United Kingdom* unionists. This would only have been a matter of different degrees of loyalty to the concept of Britain were it not for the deeply inconvenient fact of geography that Northern Ireland represented the one part of the UK that shared a land border with the Irish Republic and therefore with the EU. By legal treaty – the Good Friday Agreement – the UK and Ireland were committed to preventing a hard border ever arising again between Northern Ireland and the Irish Republic, and by common consent, an invisible border was also a practical necessity to maintain the existing peace that the treaty had created. But if the two parts of the island of Ireland needed to ignore the border for the sake of peace, the EU and third countries – which is what Britain had voted to be – must have some enforceable border between them for trade, legal and security reasons, let alone the symbolism of sovereign jurisdictions. In over two years of negotiation between London and Brussels it was impossible to square this circle; the EU must have a recognizable border, but the island of Ireland must not. The terms of the Good Friday Agreement were not politically elastic; they had been enshrined into UK law alongside a change in Articles 2 and 3 of the Irish constitution.[28] The Irish government would not agree to anything that compromised the legal and constitutional commitments made in the Good Friday Agreement, and the EU was not prepared to undermine one of its most loyal members to accommodate a bad-tempered leaver; while the DUP, backed by strong 'UK unionists' in Westminster, would not countenance any other border arrangements (such as an international border operated between Northern Ireland and mainland Britain) that somehow set Northern Ireland apart from the rest of the United Kingdom. The issue stalled throughout the protracted negotiation of the Withdrawal Agreement.[29] Substantive negotiations on post-Brexit trade with the EU could not begin under the negotiating structure agreed by Theresa May's government. One Irish commentator at the time remarked that 'nobody who wanted a negotiation to succeed would design it like that … conceding such format was an extraordinary mistake by the British'.[30] The best they could do was to create the celebrated 'Irish backstop' which became a constitutional sticking point because it was there *only in case* the 2019–21 trade negotiations to follow could not finally square the circle of the border. But politicians on all sides deeply suspected that 'only in case' would come to mean 'actually in fact' when a problem that had been logically intractable for three years remained just that for the foreseeable future.

The Gordian knots of Britain's Union – its united kingdoms – showed all the signs of tightening around the political parties in the 2020s. There would be many twists and turns to follow. The ultimate impact of Brexit on the Union, however, will revolve around two more basic considerations in the coming years, whatever the immediate political contests. First, is the willingness of pro-EU opinion in Scotland and Northern Ireland to contemplate major constitutional change in order to remain inside the structure of the EU. What this would mean in practice is that a majority of Scots, standing alongside committed Scottish nationalists, might decide that the (considerable) risks of Scottish independence were worth running to remain inside the European single market and to retain the other benefits of EU membership in regional support, common energy, fisheries or policing policies. For the majority Unionist population in Northern Ireland, there is a vigorous argument over whether demographic trends were moving inevitably towards an eventual acceptance of a united Ireland.[31] Some argued that they were; others pointed out that the demographic evidence was contradictory and, in any case, did not lead to a conclusion that even a nominally Roman Catholic majority in the North would favour a united Ireland; or that the Republic would necessarily want it or be able to sustain the economic dislocation involved.[32]

But expansive claims were nevertheless made in the light of the Brexit vote and there was little doubt that public opinion in Northern Ireland felt that the referendum had re-posed the unity question with some urgency. In summer 2018 some 60 per cent of the population in Northern Ireland felt that Brexit made Irish unification 'in the foreseeable future' more likely. Only 40 per cent in the Irish Republic and 25 per cent in the rest of Britain thought the same.[33] By a similar logic of pro-EU Scots, a majority of Unionists in Northern Ireland, it was argued, might decide they would be economically better off inside the EU – that is, in the Republic – and could be prepared to trade in their status in Northern Ireland for the economic benefits. Such arguments were anathema to committed Unionists, of course, but they still swirl around opinion on both sides of the border as the world waits to see what the economic and growth effects of Brexit may turn out to be in the Irish Republic itself.

The second basic consideration is therefore the way the economics of Brexit emerge in Britain during the 2020s; and in this respect, it also applies to the principality of Wales. Any significant decline in British economic growth as a result of Brexit (or as a result of anything else, since it will certainly be ascribed to Brexit) will hit Scotland, Wales and Northern Ireland harder than the south of England. It is built into the current structure of the British economy that the devolved regions are considerably more vulnerable to an economic slowdown, not to mention a recession, than the overheated areas of the south east. And they are, too, the regions which receive significant amounts of EU regional aid and infrastructure support. For example, Northern Ireland has not only received considerable funds from the EU in light of the ending of 'the troubles', but compared to the rest of Britain it is also disproportionately dependent on EU payments under the Common Agricultural Policy. If there is a serious economic downturn, it is unlikely that London could pump enough economic aid into the devolved regions to buy off the anger that would result. The public disillusion in Scotland and Northern Ireland, if not in Wales, might tip majority opinion into judging the constitutional risks worth taking for their economic futures. And where that economic picture would be mirrored elsewhere in England – in the east, the north, the south west – significant segments of the 'England without London' population might not blame them.

So much in the future of the Union, therefore, depends crudely on the economic relationship between Britain and the EU that emerges from the Brexit process – in particular on the relationship with the single market and the customs union – and thence on the performance of the British economy in the first five years or so of the new decade.

Pro-EU observers have fretted since the 2016 referendum that the Brexit process has already left Britain 'diminished' in world politics. The phrase was even deliberately used by the Netherlands prime minister, an avowed friend. Britain was a 'more diminished country compared to what it was two or three years ago', he said.[34] Nothing would confirm that view so dramatically as the breaking up of the UK as an eventual result of the momentum towards Brexit that began in 2016. To emerge from the bruising process of leaving the EU, or even of further protracted negotiations in a new grey zone, only to be plunged into a decade of further constitutional crisis around the Union itself would surely take Britain off that front line of world politics where it has always assumed it naturally belongs. None of this is inevitable, of course, and there are certainly strategic paths to avoid it, as will be explored in Chapter 13. But in a period of domestic and foreign volatility, unprecedented in over a century, the prospect that Britain's political nervous breakdown still has some way to go remains very real. That prospect challenges Britain's geopolitical foundations in some fundamental ways.

The circles and bridges of the Anglosphere

If the English-led British exceptionalism that took Britain out of the EU meant anything in terms of the country's role in world politics, it was surely a return to some deeper faith in the Anglosphere approach to Britain in the world. The prevalent view in 1973 that Britain was now 'a European state with strictly European interests' had been overlaid again by growing interest in the power of the Anglosphere – that belief which energized the Thatcher governments and to which Tony Blair increasingly turned as he faced global challenges.[35] It became permissible to characterize an 'Anglosphere' again in political debate without attracting derision and as the world turned more darkly towards great power competition after the mid-2000s, the notion began to re-emerge as a serious intellectual construct in national politics.[36]

In truth, the notion had never disappeared from British conceptions of its role in the world, though it had been hidden within more convoluted explanations. It was intrinsic to Churchill's famous 'three circles' conception in 1948. Britain, he said, was uniquely placed to play a prominent role in the world since it stood at the confluence of an 'Empire/Commonwealth', a 'united Europe' and an 'English-speaking world' set of circles. These circles were not quite equal, however. It was noticeable that in his conception the Europe circle was 'united', but also that he placed more weight on the other two as he contemplated the future.[37] Margaret Thatcher echoed this thinking from the very beginning of her party leadership in a conscious attempt to point British security back towards Churchillian priorities.[38] Tony Blair thought in rather the same way but turned three circles into an image closer to that of a transatlantic bridge between the United States/Canada on one side and Britain/continental Europe on the other. 'We have a unique role to play', he said, 'call it a bridge, a two-lane motorway, a pivot or call it a damn high wire, which is often how it feels; our job is to keep our sights firmly on both sides of the Atlantic'.[39] This became an underlying assumption in successive iterations of British defence and security policy documents.[40]

Tony Blair initially tried to re-energize Britain's role on both ends of the bridge. His first government tried to be as pro-European Union in its security priorities as it was pro-United States (and thereby also pro-NATO). But British enthusiasm for European defence cooperation ran out of steam after 2001 and the Iraq crisis that followed forced him, however unwillingly, to choose between relations with the White House and those with his European counterparts. His choice to ally with the United States (and Australia which joined in the initial 2003 war on Iraq) was as instinctively Anglosphere as anything that Thatcher or Churchill might have contemplated.

For Brexit supporters, the approach towards the rest of the world would be a confident and unapologetic restatement of all these instincts.[41] British exceptionalism, in this view, was based on history rather than geography. Prime Minister Boris Johnson had already laid out much of his Brexit thinking, at least at a philosophical level, in his first major speech when he became foreign secretary in 2016. Since 1815, he said, Britain and the United States had been intrinsic to building the current international system. More importantly, they represented a different way of approaching the world compared to most European powers.

While continental Europe witnessed the *Zollverein* customs union that drove early German unification and naturally moved European countries towards centralized and federal approaches to law and order, the Anglo-American tradition, by contrast, he said, had concentrated on building global institutions that recognized the strength of diversity. Britain embodied a 'distinctive approach to policy-making as regards China and Asia'; it defended free trade institutions and it contributed to the world, 'in the projection of our values and our priorities' – by implication somehow different from those of other European powers. Brexit was a mission, he said, 'to be more outward-looking and more engaged with the world than ever before'. But it was also, an imperative; 'I know there will be cynics who say we can't afford it. I say we can't afford not to'.[42] Post-Brexit Britain, said another voice, should not merely be mercantilist – though it would certainly be a new version of that – but must connect with 'the nobler traditions of its past'.[43]

In these conceptions Britain's historic and geopolitical commitment towards stability in continental Europe is fully accepted, but that can, and should in this view, be met by NATO, in which Britain still plays a prominent role. NATO, above all, is based on a grand transatlantic bargain which still remains a practical expression of the Anglosphere in action. The intention is to do what is required to defend Western and Central Europe through NATO, without letting defence politics create any momentum for more visionary notions of Europe's future; to know that the European circle is 'safe' while Britain explores the more attractive possibilities of the other two circles. The Commonwealth, it is maintained, much overlooked in recent years as a vehicle for British influence, can play a bigger economic and security role in the world to the benefit of all its fifty-three members, and should be given greater priority as part of the reorientation towards 'global Britain'. This, too, with its ex-Dominions such as Canada, South Africa, Australia or New Zealand, and its great English-speaking democracies, such as India, Ghana or Nigeria, represents a more diffuse version of the Anglosphere that could be beneficial in its own ways. And thirdly – most vague but most important – by using the natural advantages of the Anglosphere, its English language, its traditions and its links to the prosperous and the powerful Britain will get out and about in the world more freely to build new partnerships and so refashion its security and defence in response to the challenges of the 2020s.

The decade to come, however, will impose a severe reality check on this sort of Anglosphere thinking and will certainly market-test Britain's ability to represent it convincingly. Since the 2016 referendum and Boris Johnson's landmark speech that year, the constellation of global forces has moved in directions almost universally unfavourable to Anglosphere thinking. As described in previous chapters, the Western world, within which the Anglosphere had played such an important role, is losing its strategic cohesion. It lacks consensus over the response of different governments to rising great power competition. It is going through a period where it even lacks a level of democratic and moral consensus that would have been regarded as essential twenty years ago. The United States is, of course, the most influential power in the Anglosphere, but it is not at all clear that the United States any longer embodies its traditional Anglosphere roots, as it faces the Asian century amid its own demographic evolution. And in a mood of Jacksonian nationalism, it is anyway not inclined to stray too far beyond some patterns of bilateral relationships – certainly not to offer open-ended support to an imprecise kith and kin network. President Trump's own wish to see Brexit succeed and his evident friendship with Boris Johnson may be welcome to Downing Street, but it does not negate the legal difficulties in the WTO, or the power of America's farming lobby, or congressional opposition, to any quick and highly preferential US trade deal the White House would like to do with Britain.

The European continent is a declining political and economic force in world politics, though this may be partly reversible depending on how the EU, NATO and European national politics are handled over the coming decade. Britain outside the EU will not necessarily be in a better position to exert its influence because Europe is weaker and divided; quite the reverse. A strong London-Berlin-Paris triangle is actually more important with Britain outside the EU than if it stayed in. The reality that Europe needs three leaders, strong at home and strong in their shared convictions, in order to be secure and prosperous, still holds for the same geopolitical reasons that have prevailed since 1945. Outside the EU, Britain may well choose to put more effort and resources into NATO leadership, but the fact remains that, perhaps paradoxically, NATO counts for much less when the continent is troubled and divided.

Regret and sadness at Britain's original Brexit decision among its European partners turned to exasperation and some real anger as the process of disentanglement went forward so divisively. That raises the question of how far the political fallout in EU matters might extend to NATO and to bilateral relations between Britain and its neighbours. How much damage, in other words, will the Brexit process do to Britain's foreign and security policies in general? The prospect is not unprecedented. The Suez debacle in 1956 was a huge failure, a national humiliation, and it effectively ended Britain's pretentions to exercise a global post-war role of any substance. It destroyed Britain's strategic position East of Suez and set the scene for Britain's first application to join the Common Market. But thirty years later Britain had tangibly moved on from that disaster. Major strategic missteps can, in time, be recovered. If Brexit is a major strategic mis-step which causes deep damage to Britain's relations with the most important of its European partners (and that is not certain nor uniformly true throughout Europe), it may nevertheless be quite recoverable, but not in the short term. And not in time to address effectively some of the serious challenges the 2020s are set to pose.

At the turn of the decade the omens were not good. The EU, however haltingly, was determined to move its own vision of defence policy forward after Brexit. It had already excluded Britain from effective discussions on a number of foreign and security issues that mattered to everyone in Europe, and there was an assumption that this would continue until Britain overcame its own domestic political crises. Most revealingly, after long rows over British participation in the future of the EU's Galileo satellite programme, which has fundamental importance to all European defence forces, Britain decided to go it alone to build its own system, duplicating Galileo, possibly with other international partners. This was one of the early, unanticipated, prices of retaining military credibility after Brexit.

Cumulative geopolitical challenges

In the Introduction to this book we expressed the view that the challenges of the 2020s which were anyway becoming more ominous for all European states were likely to become more acute in the circumstances surrounding Brexit. They are easy to enumerate. That Britain finds itself separated from European mainstream politics more deeply than from just the institutions of the EU; that it finds itself more at odds with US policy than it thought possible before 2016; that the United States no longer shares a genuine belief in the organizations and regimes of global governance in which Britain places a great deal of faith; that the Anglosphere is more an emotional grab for the past than a mobilizing force for the future and that Britain is anyway not well placed to use it; and not least, that the UK may splinter in the coming decade and be consumed, not just with a profound constitutional crisis but with a deeper crisis of English identity, the like of which it has not confronted since 1688 – and which would be very unlikely to end in another 'glorious revolution'. It's a cumulative and dystopian vision, which, as we outline in later chapters, is susceptible to prevention or even reversal. But it is certainly plausible. For the more immediate future, Britain's 'tipping point' in the early 2020s promises, as we said, a white-knuckle ride that may oscillate between Britain playing a buccaneering diplomatic role in the globalized world, and the nightmare of straight national isolation – a clearly diminished Britain, caught between disinterested, preoccupied European partners and a Trumpist, disengaged, United States.

Lurking just below the surface of these geopolitical considerations is the matter of the global economy and of Britain's own post-Brexit economic performance. Quite aside from the possibility of a long-term, on/off, trade war between China and the United States, it has been clear for some years that the world economy is moving in more protectionist directions as it steps further away from global governance towards regionally based organizations dominated by the great powers and their close economic partners. This is not an auspicious time to be a single, liberal free-trader in the world. There is some relief for Brexit Britain that, though the world economic recovery has been tepid and fragile since 2015, it has at least been based on roughly synchronous upswings in all sectors. By 2030, on current trends, around 90 per cent of global growth will be outside the European Union, so there is certainly something for a liberal free-trader to play for across the board if it is prepared to pursue every opportunity.[44] But there is also a growing fear among international economists that the 2008 crisis may turn out to be a long-term and more profound crisis – in instalments – that will revisit the world sooner rather than later. Only the banking system is now significantly more regulated than it was then. All the other elements of global indebtedness, sovereign nations, non-financial companies and private finance are actually more indebted than they were in 2008, as we showed in Chapter 2. There is, for instance, a respectable argument to be made that neoliberal economics are now irrevocably broken and that there is a 'rational case for panic'.[45] A Brexit Britain trying to do its own trade deals just as another global economic crisis unfolds in the 2020s, and in a protectionist environment, would be in a very unenviable situation indeed.

It almost goes without saying that Britain's own economic performance after it leaves the EU, or enters into some protracted twilight status with Brussels, will be critical to its ability to achieve any of its geopolitical objectives; however it chooses to define them. A sustained low period of national economic growth, even worse, a recession, would seriously hamper Britain's ability to devote appropriate resources to its future foreign and defence strategies. It would make the British economy much harder to reform, to get away from the imbalances that have created so much social tension in British society. And it would add greatly to any pressures Brexit has already exacerbated, through its own contorted logic, to break up the United Kingdom

If the current 'diminution' of Britain is not to become permanent, and Britain is to meet its own security challenges in the 2020s, both its economy and its political institutions will have to perform a great deal better than they have over the last decade or more.

Chapter 9
Security and foreign policy

In theory, security, defence and foreign policy should be the least challenged areas of British policy as a result of the Brexit controversies. They are, after all, the policy areas in which the EU has been least integrative in practice and where intergovernmental approaches between the members have been most carefully observed. The failure of the nascent European Defence Community in 1954 marked a discouraging false start for the whole European Union concept. The original architects of the 'grand project' had approached the idea of union too directly by impinging at the outset on the sovereign rights of members to defend themselves. Thereafter, in taking the economic path via a Common Market, questions of foreign policy, defence and security were always handled as essentially outside the basic framework of the Rome Treaty. This was anyway reinforced – almost set in stone – in the case of security and defence by the creation of NATO and its central importance during the most dangerous years of the Cold War. Nothing that was done in the EEC that had any bearing on security or defence matters could be allowed to undermine NATO or dilute its collective power. Even thirty years after the Cold War, that sensitivity remains, though Britain's departure from the EU would remove a strong voice that always tried to prevent any EU security or defence initiatives from compromising the NATO alliance in any respect whatsoever.[1]

Those distinctions, however, were easier to make and to uphold in a previous era. The practicalities of security and defence, no less than foreign policy, have created a thickening web of interactions, conventions, deals and treaties that have run in parallel, or augmented, or impinged on EU business and institutions at all levels. Disentangling them is not easy, regardless of any aspirations in the Maastricht or Lisbon Treaties that tried to draw elements into the core of EU business. Though some EU officials might be pleased to think that even security and defence are, in practical terms, increasingly swept into the EU's orbit, the reality is that this is more a consequence of globalization and fifth generation technology than anything set out in treaties or EU directives. And it is very messy for that reason.

The descriptive terms themselves cover a number of policy areas that have increasingly overlapped in recent years. 'Foreign policy' is the most discrete of them. It traditionally covers what governments do, in relation to other governments in the global environment. But it also naturally overlaps with government policy towards companies, businesses, international aid, non-governmental organizations and international institutions from the UN downwards. A great deal of normal EU work therefore impinges on the business of foreign policy. The task of unpicking what is properly a sovereign responsibility and what is a matter for EU coordination through its Common Foreign and Security Policy mechanisms has always required the highest of the mandarin arts that the British Civil Service could produce. Where other countries don't practice these arts as diligently as Britain, their foreign policy on any given issue, by default, effectively becomes whatever is agreed EU policy. In many cases this suits other member countries.

'Defence policy' proper is formally outside the European Union's scope, given the EU's history and the existence of NATO. The organization has no remit to impinge on the way its members choose to make or exercise their own defence policies. They are matters of sovereign responsibility. On the other hand, the EU creates many mechanisms through which the military forces of members can be jointly deployed for EU-designated missions. In 2019 this included seventeen military and policing missions in East Africa, the Sahel, the Mediterranean and the Middle East and in some of the long running trouble spots in the former Soviet Union.[2] They are all contained within the general rubric of being 'conflict prevention and crisis management' operations, so as not to conflict with NATO's superior rationale that it prepares for collective defence as war fighting – if necessary for the last ditch defence of the 'Europe' its twenty-nine members cover. Terminological distinctions, however, are more precise than the reality of military deployments. Many ongoing NATO operations could be described in the same way.[3] The real distinctions are more evident in the participating states involved (since NATO operations might include national contingents that EU operations could not), the willingness to engage (as some states feel more inclined to support one organization over the other) and, significantly, in the size and scale of military deployments and their expectations of the violence that might ensue. In practice, therefore, while defence issues remain firmly in the hands of the governments of NATO and the EU, there is a seventy-year-long tradition of joint collaboration and planning among Europe's military forces, primarily within NATO but latterly, for relatively low-level missions, within the European Union too.

Just as important is the way in which the common understanding of 'defence' overlaps with the more slippery notion of 'security'. By definition, national security is a sovereign concern and it is invested with both a general and a more precise institutional meaning. In popular discussions, 'security' or 'national security' simply refers to the overall security of the state. The government publishes a regular National Security Strategy. In 2018 it undertook a National Security Capability Review. In this general sense, security involves all the instruments of the state, from diplomacy and military power to the emergency services, that have a collective responsibility to keep citizens safe and secure. But there is also the more institutional definition of 'security' which normally refers to national intelligence agencies, police and related services that frequently overlap with defence forces but which are charged with mainly domestic responsibilities. In this usage, if 'defence' means dealing with external challenges, then 'security' complements it by addressing internal challenges. In Britain, the 'Security and Intelligence Agencies' (SIAs) is a collective term to cover MI6, MI5, GCHQ, Defence Intelligence, the National Crime Agency, and some specific policing and government organizations, such as Border Force, that share some responsibilities for counter-espionage, counterterrorism and fighting international crime. In this institutional definition, 'security' is therefore used in a generic sense to cover intelligence and policing. As such, it is part of a series of very thick and sometimes obscure webs of international interaction, some of which have been deeply embedded in the EU for the last two decades – driven particularly by the threat of terrorism and the rapid internationalization of serious crime.

In the five years of what might be described as 'applied Brexit debates' in Britain, where some of the policy realities of the process have been under discussion, the belief endured among both Leavers and Remainers that foreign policy, defence and security would not be major issues – and certainly should not emerge as show-stoppers – in the Brexit process. This belief was based on two premises. First, that the EU has no jurisdiction over foreign or defence policy and was not a serious player in the defence business in any case. It is NATO that 'does' European defence. That would not change with Brexit; indeed, NATO might even be enhanced as it would be so much in Britain's interests to commit more strongly to the alliance. Defence would take care of itself. Secondly, where 'security' has become enmeshed with EU processes, the fact is that British intelligence and policing agencies – the SIAs – give more to their EU counterparts than they receive. Britain is widely acknowledged as the European leader in intelligence-led policing and its principal intelligence agencies, MI6, MI5 and GCHQ, are known as the best in Europe. On this basis, it was anticipated that existing procedures would rapidly be replaced with roll-over agreements or else bilateral deals that maintained essential security relationships, since it was evidently in everyone's interests – especially those of Britain's EU partners. Given the way Brexit diplomacy progressed after 2016, however, the reality for the 2020s will not be so straightforward. In order to understand it properly, it is necessary to distinguish a spectrum of EU/British relations across these sensitive policy areas that extend from coordinated and integrated outputs to determinedly bilateral contacts.

Coordinated relations: Foreign and defence policy

British diplomats have always been philosophical when confronted by the mechanisms of European Union policy on defence and foreign affairs, accepting the need for a fair amount of studied ambiguity when dealing with these matters inside the EU. Any organization with as big a membership and population as that of the EU must necessarily have a way of addressing the external world coherently. Even so, successive EU mechanisms have been stronger on ambition than on delivery of independent policy outputs. The titles and characteristic terms of reference for EU mechanisms to address foreign and defence affairs have been built on tortuous circumlocutions as the organization tried to navigate between the sovereignty of its members, the existence of (transatlantic) NATO and an underlying ambition that any organization the size of the EU should carry more strategic clout in the world. As one EU mechanism for dealing with foreign and defence matters dissolved into another, each with more ambitiously worded titles, so a bureaucracy of coordination, if not so much of direct action, took shape. The Brexit vote gave it more impetus with the anticipation that one of its more sceptically minded members would be leaving the process.

The structure that Britain will be leaving exists at three separate levels. A 'High Representative', who is also a vice-president of the European Commission, is the nearest counterpart to a foreign minister the EU is able to create. The first holder, from 2009–14, was Britain's Catherine Ashton, who set up alongside it the European External Action Service (EEAS) which is as near to a foreign office as the organization can operate. The High Representative oversees the Common Foreign and Security Policy, which works to coordinate the appropriate policy areas of all EU members. Under the auspices of the CFSP, the Common Security and Defence Policy (CSDP), also sometimes known optimistically as the European Defence Union, is charged, among other things, with the 'collective self-defence' of the membership. This is a big rhetorical step, since it duplicates the core role of NATO.[4] Below the level of the CSDP, but more widely focused, is the process of Permanent Structured Cooperation (PESCO) – which is a euphemism for the EU's drive to try at last by all means possible to create a meaningful defence organization. The PESCO initiative of 2017 was a direct response to the Brexit vote. It grew out of the European Union Global Strategy (EUGS) initiative that was launched just a week after the British referendum in a calculated reaction to its outcome. PESCO moved to recognize, in the EU's words, the 'legally binding nature of the commitments' it makes and it launched thirty-four new defence projects in all military spheres under the European Defence Fund.[5] Britain indicated that it certainly would not be joining PESCO but kept the door open to possible third-party participation sometime in the future.

It would be easy to regard all this as a great deal of form without substance – bureaucratic displacement activity to disguise the lack of significant capability or political commitment. It should be recognized, however, that though this system is characteristically bureaucratic, it has also grown to be organically coherent; it has evolved from outlying initiatives to become part of the EU proper and embodies vertical line management with horizontal coverage of its areas of responsibility. It parallels what goes on in most foreign offices and in some ministries of defence. Given the lack of truly sovereign authority in the EU, it is like a modern building with all its inner workings on the outside, since it cannot present a smooth, sovereign exterior to the world. Baroness Catherine Ashton's thankless work up to 2014 in getting the EEAS up and running and making the post of High Representative genuinely significant, amid major crises over Ukraine, Iran, Egypt and the Western Balkans, is recognized more widely in EU history than by many of her contemporaries in Britain.

Does it matter to British foreign policy that it will no longer be participating in these structures? In a strictly operational sense, the answer must be 'no'. They can only be coordinating mechanisms and the incentives for Britain to line up its policies with France, Spain, the Netherlands, Germany or Poland – and vice versa – will be essentially the same in or out of the EU. The ending of US participation in the Iran nuclear agreement in 2018, for example, created a sharp dilemma for Britain, since it had worked hard for the original Iran deal – the JCPoA – and in common with its European partners felt it worth the effort to try to keep it afloat even after the body blow of US withdrawal.[6] For London, this quickly presented itself as a classic 'United States or Europe?' strategic choice over a matter of some international importance. There could be attractions for Britain in following the US lead on this matter, given that Brexit Britain will need influence in Washington. However, stronger instincts to remain consistent over the deal and try to keep it alive in some form led Britain to align itself closely with its European allies and in direct opposition to US policy. This extended to working with Germany and France to implement a scheme actually championed by the EU's High Representative, to create the INSTEX 'special purpose vehicle' in finance, in effect, to circumvent the effects of new US sanctions on Iran so as to continue to implement the terms of the original JCPoA.[7] Washington was not pleased, but this coordinated approach led by the big three in Europe occurred quite outside the Brexit imbroglio and would likely do so in the future. The process of necessary coordination over similar matters, and many less consequential than the Iran deal, would certainly be more bilateral and resource-intensive outside the EU. Britain would be dealing separately with key partners, but policy outcomes may be no worse – and conceivably all the better – for that. The dangers to British foreign policy do not lie in anything it might lose from these structures in relating to the external world, but rather in what it might lose in deeper influence within the core states of the EU itself – in particular with Germany, France and Italy.

The same is largely true in the defence realm proper, where a great deal more money and industrial development are involved and where sovereign sensitivities are at their highest. The 2016 PESCO initiative immediately became the test case of the new 'EU without Britain' status quo. Many critics in Britain interpreted the PESCO project as a naked French attempt to isolate Britain even further in defence matters and diminish its defence industries, to undermine NATO, and even push for the creation of the mythical 'Euro Army' that would spell the beginning of the end of sovereign states in Europe. Grand statements were made at the launch of PESCO, and even a French-led 'E21' initiative was touted as Europe's 'roving strike force'.[8] This is a huge overestimation of the situation. The bogeyman of a Euro Army can be dismissed immediately. Neither the supporters nor the outraged opponents of the idea have thought it through properly. In essence, the idea suffers from all the same political, logical, moral, practical and financial show-stoppers that have prevented the idea of a 'UN Army' ever making it to first base over the last seventy years.[9] In relation to more serious arguments, it is true that PESCO was launched in the hope that the EU could make some substantive progress in defence matters if the British were not part of it. And it is true that, in part, it reflected the desire of the Emmanuel Macron presidency to re-galvanize Europe around a new Franco-German strategic axis. It was also perfectly logical that, in light of NATO's ongoing travails and the equivocal attitude of the United States to European security, the EU should try to strengthen its presence and capabilities in the area of common defence. Supporters of PESCO hope that it will prove the take-off point in eventually giving the EU competence in the one area it has always lacked.

But PESCO's ambitions make little impact on the broader trends of the strategic context in which it exists. The prospect of a revived Franco-German axis cannot be taken for granted in the next few years. Even driven by a sense of exasperation with the British nervous breakdown, there is more going against it than for it, until leaderships in Paris and Berlin are stronger and more settled. Of more structural relevance is the fact that NATO is already having to throw its weight against the trend to *re-nationalize* defence policies among all the European powers. They are becoming more, not less, divergent (paradoxically) as defence spending gets tighter in real terms. The European political consensus on defence priorities has seldom been weaker, notwithstanding the greater awareness of the challenges that revisionist Russia poses to European stability. Since 2007 the EU has had in its armoury thirteen designated battlegroups, drawn from its members' forces, ready to deploy in the interests of the EU on the authority of the European Council. In thirteen subsequent years not once did it obtain that political authority, despite recurrent crises of the sort for which these force arrangements had originally been prepared.[10] Even if political will is present, EU military capabilities without Britain generally are not. A British/German research collaboration in 2018 took the requirements of seven of the smaller ongoing EU military operations and assumed they might all have to ramp up simultaneously. This, the report estimated, corresponded to the EU's highest level of military ambition – a far cry from some of the assertive declarations following Brexit. Its conclusions were unequivocal: 'The EU 28 is out of its depth. There are extensive capability gaps across all domains and often less than one-third of the force requirement would be met.'[11] Improvements could be expected by 2030, but even these would leave EU forces, minus Britain, well short of the (relatively low) levels of military ambition they have specified for themselves. The fact remains that if NATO, with all its long-established procedures and its transatlantic linkages, struggles in the present climate to galvanize European states to up their defence game – to create a genuine step change in European defence capability – the nascent PESCO process can only be a long-term bet.

Even as a French-led aspiration, PESCO also has to be set against President Macron's clear recognition that the bilateral Franco-British defence relationship is now more than ever the practical bedrock of defence among the Europeans if they ever have to act alone. No other national defence forces come anywhere near their hard, military capacities, either together or separately. And President Macron knows as well as anyone that after any British withdrawal from the European Union, the non-EU states of NATO would then constitute a decisive 80 per cent of the alliance's total defence expenditure.[12] Without Britain, the EU as a whole is a minor player in NATO's collective defence game and, notwithstanding France's own military capabilities, is hardly well placed to create its own collective defence club within an EU framework. As part of President Macron's 2019 design to rejuvenate the grand European project, it was significant that he also proposed the creation of a 'European Security Council' on which Britain – outside the EU – would sit. Anything less would simply lack physical credibility.

If the PESCO process results in the creation of more usable and modernized military forces among the states of the EU, that will be to the advantage of European defence as a whole and something that Britain has spent years nagging all its partners about. It should welcome it. If PESCO does not deliver something new and tangible in defence terms, then it will become yet another attempt merely to create duplicate planning and command structures as already exist in NATO. There is only one pool of military forces and military industries in Europe, regardless of how many planners and commanders there are. It would be unhelpful, but not disastrous, to have two structures vying to control Europe's only pool of indigenous military resources. But in a real European military emergency no one would care very much who won that competition. Attention would instead be riveted on whether the right sort of forces existed somewhere on the continent, whether they were ready, and whether they could get to the right place quickly enough. In these tough, practical, respects Britain remains the most important military power among the Europeans whether inside the EU or not.

Integrated relations: Security policy

Security policy, as it relates to the various aspects of national and international policing, is a different matter to defence policy proper. National security policy, as such, is outside the scope of the EU Treaties.[13] There is no question of creating an integrated policing policy inside the EU. Nevertheless, policing *relations*, between the separate police authorities in the member states have in many respects showed a surprising degree of operational integration. The increasingly international character of crime and terrorism, not to mention the legal regulation of financial and commercial enterprises, has created a layer of day-to-day functional cooperation among police and regulatory authorities across the world, and particularly within Europe, that could hardly have been imagined even twenty years ago. In modern, digital economies policing would operate very ineffectually against all but local and petty crime if it did not operate internationally. There are more than forty policing databases and information systems in use across the EU.[14] The EU's joint policing information service, the 'Schengen Information System II' (SIS II), contains almost 80 million records and has been accessed well over 5 billion times by European police forces.[15] It generates around a quarter of a million 'alerts' a year to all EU police forces. By 2018 Britain had posted well over 1.2 million alerts of its own on the system. While there is no such thing as an average year in international crime detection, it is interesting to note that in 2017 there were around 17,000 hits of information from EU partners on British-posted alerts and almost 10,000 hits in Britain on alerts posted by other member states.[16] European police forces are all very different and operate in their own national ways. But they rely on each other for information about almost all types of serious crime.

The practical reality of Britain's policing relations with the EU in the context of Brexit debates revolves around three particular issues. First is Britain's relations with Europol, the EU's police coordination agency, and also with Eurojust, which deals with judicial cooperation in criminal matters. In the long run, whatever happens during even a prolonged transition period, Britain could not stay inside these institutions or, of necessity, be governed by the oversight of the European Court of Justice (ECJ) in their operations, since the ECJ jurisdiction applies to all EU agencies within the treaties. This would not prevent Britain having close relations with Europol as a special sort of third party, however, and it would obviously be in the interests of European policing in general that this should be so. For almost a decade up to 2018 Europol's director was a British civil servant, Robert Wainwright, who was credited with bringing the organization to its current peak of operational utility. On the basis of what seemed to be common sense, London argued for a 'bespoke' model of future cooperation with Europol, given the substantial practical contributions (second only to Germany in most respects) that Britain made to its ongoing operations. Europol, however, has come to be regarded as the jewel in the crown of EU criminal justice policy and the European Commission stuck to a very hard line on Britain's future relations with it, which many observers around Europe thought simply doctrinaire. There are precedents for a close third-party relationship, as has been accommodated in different ways for the United States, Canada, Norway, Switzerland or Australia.[17] Europol became operational in 1999 and only in the last decade has there been some meaningful connection between Europol and its most useful interlocuters in the United States. But by 2019 the FBI had opened offices in eleven European countries and developed close operational third-party relations with Europol, particularly in mutual agreements covering the investigation of international terrorism. The FBI's own operations became intrinsically important to many other sectors of European policing, especially in dealing with corruption, narcotics and paedophilia. There is no reason in principle why Britain should not have at least as close an operational relationship with Europol as the FBI, probably closer.

The second important issue is Britain's future participation in the European Arrest Warrant (EAW) of 2004. It came dramatically into effect for Britain in 2005 when it was used to pick up in Italy one of the '21/7' terrorist group who had attempted more multiple bombings in London and have him face justice in Britain within thirty-five days of his arrest. Before the advent of the EAW Britain arrested and then extradited, to countries everywhere in the world, around fifty foreign nationals a year. During 2016–17, by contrast, Britain arrested over 1,700 foreign nationals for extradition to European countries alone.[18] The EAW has had a huge impact on the efficiency of policing international crime in Britain. Without it, Britain would default to the 1957 Council of Europe Convention on Extradition, which works through diplomatic channels, rather than pre-agreed judicial procedures; it has no time limits, so can last indefinitely; and it does not oblige any country to extradite one of its own citizens to another country to face trial. Not least, most European countries have long stopped using the 1957 Convention so it would be a creaky structure, at best, for Britain to have to revive and use extensively. The Police Federation of England and Wales was in no doubt that the loss of the EAW would create a 'free for all' for foreign criminals in Britain. In 2014 Theresa May, when home secretary, had already put down a marker when she said that without the EAW, Britain could become a 'honeypot' for criminality.[19]

The EAW rapidly became a major piece of the fabric of European policing that would be very hard to replicate elsewhere. But the European Commission took the view that the EAW could not be divorced from the concept of free movement within the EU, the jurisdiction of the ECJ or the observance of the EU Charter of Fundamental Rights. Doctrinaire or not, there was some logic behind this stance, since in matters of criminal arrest the clarity of judicial procedure is of some importance. The EAW is a classic example of a dramatically useful, entirely pragmatic, measure lodged firmly within the institutions of the EU. Withdrawal from it is not easily susceptible to a mere political declaration or a parallel structure to duplicate its effectiveness.

Thirdly, and by far the most important element in the policing relationship between Brexit Britain and the EU, is the question of information exchange. This takes several forms. The SIS II information-sharing arrangement is the most sophisticated of its size in the world and it is the keystone of day-to-day international policing cooperation in Europe. It is backed up by the Europol Information System (EIS), the European Criminal Records Information System (ECRIS), Europol's Secure Information Exchange Network Application (SIENA), the Passenger Name Record system that came into force across the EU in May 2018; and the fourteen-nation Prüm Convention, in operation from 2019, which facilitates the sharing of DNA records, fingerprints and vehicle registrations. Britain's National Crime Agency described the SIS II system as a 'game-changer' for them; and the Prüm decisions, 'something we have been looking for' over a long time, since biometric data are now 'fairly essential' to modern police work. Other British police agencies revealed how locally some of this information is used in Britain when they emphasized 'the importance of ECRIS in assisting custody sergeants with pre-court bail decisions'.[20] It was something of a blow, therefore, to the expectations of the pragmatists among Britain's policing agencies that the European Commission offered only 'streamlining' arrangements to facilitate coordination, rather than any continuance of effective integration between Britain and the EU's data systems. Very few British practitioners thought this would be adequate and hoped that something could be worked out very quickly before existing arrangements lapsed.[21]

It should be remembered that British police and related agencies, including the intelligence services, exchange and derive extensive information from a wide range of sources, outside the continent of Europe and within Europe in both EU and in non-EU arrangements. The situation is described by security chiefs as 'a jigsaw put together from as many different sources as we can get'.[22] So 'EU information' is far from being the totality of available sources. There is now, for instance, a 'Counter Terrorism Group' in Europe that shares information among thirty domestic security services, quite outside the EU framework. Such range and depth of shared information only became available in their current forms in recent years. But there can be little doubt that the very speed with which EU sources have become such a critical piece of the jigsaw also indicates the same speed with which the requirements of intelligence-led policing in digital societies have increased.

In keeping with its pragmatic approach to future relationships, the British repeatedly pressed the EU for bespoke arrangements to deal with all three areas that would keep as much of the present architecture in place as possible. They proposed the creation of an Association Agreement that would provide a broad framework accommodating some legally binding agreements, a 'security partnership' and some oversight and dispute resolution mechanisms, in addition to the possibility that other arrangements could also be made outside any Association Agreement.[23] None of this was acceptable to EU negotiators, however, who insisted that normal third-party arrangements with Britain were the most on offer. But the general approach of concluding some sort of flexible framework agreement is one to which Britain and the EU are likely to return sooner or later in the coming years; unless they are driven politically or ideologically to accept that both must suffer a decline in their own policing capacities for the sake of making any Brexit break-up genuinely painful.

Bilateral relations: Intelligence agencies

Intelligence is widely acknowledged as the second oldest profession. The Old Testament 'contains more references to spies than any history of Britain or of most other countries', says Christopher Andrew.[24] This is another way of saying that intelligence is a natural part of political life and therefore is also an integral element in policing, security, defence and foreign policy. Intelligence, however, is also strongly bilateral. Indeed, it is what might be described as 'sub-governmentally bilateral', where agencies only deal meaningfully with some parts of a foreign governmental machine, even though they may technically have a relationship with the whole of that closely allied foreign government. This is simply because all international (and for that matter, sub-national) intelligence relationships are based fundamentally on trust; and the ability of an agency to protect its sources, its methods and its own information. Trust takes a long time to build and can be quickly undermined or destroyed. It relies a great deal on personal trust and cultural affinity between individuals who operate together and it can be strangely immune from political direction. Agencies may be ordered to work together but no political instructions can make them trust each other.

There are, of course, many multinational intelligence sharing arrangements between countries, and police intelligence is widely shared within the European Union and beyond. Europol's SIENA system, for example, is specifically designed to allow for the rapid exchange of highly sensitive policing data between national forces. But 'intelligence' in this sense is either operational policing details or else exists at a higher level of abstraction than would normally be directly dealt with by national intelligence agencies themselves. In this realm of intelligence, Europol will produce general intelligence briefings for all its members, or for a smaller group of them, but these are more in the way of restricted analyses on trends in crime or locations of recent spikes in incidents, and so on – the sort of material that could be produced by a specialized research contractor. A great deal of 'secret' material that circulates internationally is not classified 'secret' because it contains material that no one else knows, but rather because naming names in an official document would be politically embarrassing if it leaked to the press.

The transfer of genuinely valuable intelligence material – information that is not known, or more usually not *yet* known – arises through a process that might be called 'sequential bilateralism'. That is to say, country A will talk in detail to country B; and country B will similarly talk to country C; and country C to country D. But if the same officials from countries A, B, C and D were all put into a room together, they would say very little to each other. Because with each bilateral exchange, every actor filters what they want from the information, they protect their sources and only tell each other what they think the other needs to know.

National intelligence of this sort lies firmly outside the scope of the Treaties on the European Union as specified in Article 4(2) of the TEU. And so, almost exclusively, do the practical realities of their work. EU security policies deal with intelligence all the time, but it is, necessarily, of the multilateral variety. It is not the stuff of the national intelligence agencies. Such agencies vary greatly from one European power to another. There is no 'one size fits all' model of a bilateral intelligence relationship. British intelligence agencies are believed to have good bilateral relations with French intelligence, who have their own particular areas of expertise and a wide global network. The German intelligence establishment is much smaller than might be expected for a country of its size and still endures a legacy of domestic suspicion after East Germany's *Stasi* years. Relations with the agencies, and also between police forces, in the Netherlands have always been good – so too with Sweden and Norway. But many other national agencies are believed to raise deep suspicion in London when it comes to sharing quality intelligence: Belgian because they are so small and fragmented; Greek because they are thought to be vulnerable to Russian intelligence penetration; and some agencies in the Baltic states for the same reasons. British intelligence agencies tailor their approach to any partner countries very carefully and according to circumstances, whether those partners are inside the EU or not.

There is, however, one unique intelligence sharing arrangement that bucks the trend outlined here. The Five Eyes arrangement (known as the FVEY) between the United States, Britain, Canada, Australia and New Zealand is based on the original UKUSA Agreement of March 1946 between London and Washington to share signals intelligence. That agreement, only published in full in 2010, eventually became the basis for a unique, explicitly Anglosphere, arrangement between the five partners.[25] The FVEY not only share high-quality intelligence, but are believed to help each other with practical monitoring and joint operational assistance and to divide up responsibility for covering certain regions and problem issues in world politics, then sharing the results and information. Anachronistic as the membership is now often accused of being, the Five Eyes remains the premier intelligence club in the world. Everyone wants to join it, but no one else can. It works on the basis of long-established trust between small groups of individuals within their own national cultures. If its membership were bigger or less anachronistic it would simply not work. In the view of its members, they could not successfully expand the FVEY, even if they wanted to.

The principal British intelligence agencies – MI6, MI5, GCHQ and DI – in any case have a high international reputation.[26] As evidenced by the Russian polonium 210 poisoning in the 2006 Litvinenko case and then the novichok poisoning in the 2018 Skripal incident, the world tends to believe British intelligence when it lays out the facts of a case at the highest levels, regardless of what the Kremlin might say to the contrary. This reputation is a considerable plus for Britain in dealing with its European partners on all security matters. GCHQ, in particular, plays a big role across Europe in tracking international crime, terrorism and national espionage threats. No other European country can match its capabilities. For Brexit Britain, however, it may be a source of some frustration that this natural advantage could not realistically be traded against attempts, say, to reach more favourable deals with the EU over the security sphere in general. Bilateral intelligence relationships featuring the sort of high-intensity interactions that the principal agencies deal in could not be traded in any general negotiation without also putting British security at some degree of risk. It would be self-defeating.

Britain's strategic challenge

Since foreign, defence and security policies can be seen to operate at these coordinated, integrated, and bilateral levels, it is evident that security policy – mainly in terms of policing – is the most vulnerable sector to any Brexit-created changes in the status quo. An unfavourable outcome in the early 2020s, such as a failure to move towards some sort of bespoke arrangement that gives Britain a special third-party status in policing cooperation with the EU, would quickly have harmful effects on Britain's ability to deal with international criminal and terror threats. These consequences would not, however, extend to foreign and defence policy in the same way, where coordination can be duplicated relatively easily and existing EU mechanisms are not central to the way British foreign and defence policy works. (This cannot be said of some of the smaller, or even some of the larger, countries in the EU.) And despite the ubiquity of intelligence, as *information*, shared within the EU, the bilateral nature of high-level intelligence collecting and sharing insulates it from most of the disadvantages of an unfavourable Brexit outcome.

A more predictable and unavoidable downside for Britain, however, would be the lack of influence in the management and the future direction of all the EU structures it will be leaving. Though EU ideologues and committed federalists have grumbled for years about British obstructionism in EU forums, many other partners, particularly in Eastern Europe and Scandinavia, have seen that same behaviour as realistic and practical. Three of the most important of these countries, the Netherlands, Sweden and Poland, have worried that without Britain, the EU's foreign policy agenda will slip inexorably towards the concerns and the divisions of Southern Europe. They have valued the convening power of British civil servants to move a forum towards practical and achievable outcomes. Above all, some partners have valued British voices and management objectives as a counterweight to the natural power of German, and sometimes French, diplomacy in EU bodies.

Even if Britain eventually establishes good bespoke arrangements with EU organizations that have minimal impacts on its operational abilities in foreign, defence and security policies, it will be losing its voice in setting priorities for the future of these organizations and procedures. It will not be able to persuade PESCO to avoid duplicating NATO command and planning procedures. It will not be able to press for CFSP resources and priorities to remain focused on European issues where it might hope to have the greatest impacts. It will not be in a position to head off incipient anti-Americanism that hurts NATO when it boils to the surface. It is not clear how such a loss of influence inside the EU might impact on particular issues or how widespread any disadvantages might be. As a senior intelligence insider expressed it in 2019, 'the greatest anxiety for me is how we can continue to influence the management of the EU's sharing structures'.[27] There are already two adverse policy consequences, however, that will follow Britain into the 2020s.

One concerns international sanctions against Russia following the annexation of Crimea in 2014. Britain was always hawkish within the European sanctions regime, in line with its general approach to Russia. But by 2017 the joint US/European sanctions regime was under pressure as European leaders pushed back against tough US sanctions and worried about the effect of them on European energy interests. France and Germany were in the lead in trying to broker a deal with Moscow to resolve the Ukraine problem. Already in 2016, Italy, Hungary and Greece had declared themselves opposed to any automatic renewal of sanctions and were looking for a way out of maintaining them.[28] Some populist governments in Europe take a more relaxed view of Russian policy and its strategic objectives. Britain found itself trying to hold the line against this slippage and it will be all the harder to argue for a tough sanctions policy if it is absent from some (though not all) of the major European forums in which it will be discussed. All economic sanctions are nationally determined and implemented under domestic law. Britain will be able to maintain any anti-Russian sanctions of its own but they will count for far less, and may be domestically damaging, if they are not part of a collective package among key EU states.

A second, very significant, policy area is that of defence procurement and the future of Europe's defence industrial base. It is no secret that the French government, and its defence industries, see Brexit as an opportunity possibly to enhance common defence procurement in Europe, but definitely to steal a march on British defence manufacturers under the PESCO terms of reference. The Eurofighter – now the *Typhoon* aircraft in service among European air forces – will not be replaced by anything so collaborative involving Britain. In 2018 Paris and Berlin declared themselves key bilateral partners for the next generation of European fighter aircraft. Britain has launched its own 'Tempest' project to do the same and is looking for partners, possibly non-European, to join it. This is shaping up to be a zero-sum contest between two very expensive defence projects. But it might also be a lose-lose outcome. If both projects should fail through effective fratricide, the Europeans will buy from the United States or do without a successor aircraft. Disagreements over the Galileo European satellite project soured the prospects that European defence projects could be insulated from the political fallout from Brexit. The next generation European aircraft may take it considerably further.

It is also possible, of course, that Brexit would allow Britain to pursue a more flexible defence procurement policy. While there are strong ties between British and European defence firms that would likely be adversely affected, British defence companies already focus more on non-EU exports and could also benefit in the short term from a devaluation of the pound. In addition, non-EU mechanisms for continued defence industrial collaboration already exist, including the Organisation for Joint Armament Cooperation (OCCAR) or the six-nation 'Letter of Intent' on joint procurement matters. On the other hand, British defence companies also face reduced access to skilled EU labour, the possible relocation of multinational firms in their supply chains and potential disruption to foreign direct investment.[29] Defence industries in Europe are not remotely integrated but they are very collaborative, following a long period of industrial consolidation across the Western economies. Even so, they still respond to national political pressures and are highly vulnerable to protectionism of all kinds. It will be more difficult than usual to keep the politics out of the industry over the coming decade.

In general terms it may be true, as we said above, that foreign policy, defence and security are the least challenged areas of British policy that will emerge as a result of Brexit, though that is a relative judgement in light of other economic, technological and social policy areas that will be heavily affected, whatever the final outcome of withdrawal arrangements and subsequent trade negotiations. Leaving aside the significant issue of policing in an EU context, Britain can look to its foreign, defence and intelligence policies as areas where it will be able to exercise a good deal of national discretion, whatever happens in the EU. They will remain available as policy sectors to counter the image of 'diminution' we noted in the previous chapter – relatively strong cards in the hands of the government if it chooses to play them and is prepared to back them up with resource and political commitment.

The Brexit fallout, however, is not the only challenge that foreign, defence and intelligence policies have to face. In the 2020s it is not even the biggest challenge – just the most immediate and time-consuming. As we have argued in previous chapters, the 2020s will, in any case, test the skill and commitment with which Britain approaches its geopolitical posture and its foreign, defence and security policies. There will assuredly be good opportunities for strategic advantage, but there will – more certainly – be great dangers too. It is impossible to predict precisely in what time frame over the coming decade observable trends that are evident now may present themselves as particular policy issues, whether good or bad. But the effects of Brexit roll up a series of policy choices that Britain might have expected to make over the course of the 2020s into a ball of near-term decisions that will determine very quickly how well-equipped it will be to face the politics of the next decade. It is for this reason that we define the coming three or four years as the 'tipping point'. The concept of 'global Britain' has been promoted as the Brexit vision of the country's future in world politics. Whether deliberately or not, it encapsulates the fundamental challenge of confronting, and managing, the tipping point. There will be no second chance for some time to come, if the challenge of embracing the practicalities of 'global Britain' is not met in the near-term. We turn to this next.

Chapter 10

The meaning of 'global Britain'

The slogan that Brexit would promote 'global Britain' became a cliché after the 2016 referendum. Like all clichés, it conveyed an essential truth but suggested more questions than answers. The British government, locked into tough negotiations with Brussels and even tougher negotiations with its own party and with Parliament, had nothing to say which elaborated usefully on the phrase.[1] Almost two years after the referendum, the Foreign Affairs Committee in Parliament expressed its frustration at the lack of any official definition of the term. 'No minister during our inquiry was able to give the committee a definitive explanation of "Global Britain"', it said.[2] They did no better with the Foreign and Commonwealth Office (FCO), where intellectual responsibility for such thinking should lie. The FCO 'also appeared reluctant to respond to our requests for basic information about the objectives of Global Britain and the resources to be devoted to it'.[3] When pushed into producing something for the committee, the FCO repeated a predictable line that global Britain meant doing all the same as usual but with more focus on the need to be globally effective – 'little more than a continuation of the FCO's current activities' said the committee in disappointment.[4] Apparently stung by this, in June 2018 the FCO 'launched a webpage' which hosted the government's principal documents on global Britain and announced a 'new cross-HMG Global Britain Board, chaired by an FCO Director General' and 'an FCO Global Britain Taskforce'.[5] There was also a 'Global Britain Fund' which, according to the answer to a parliamentary question, was a rebranded version of its departmental policy programme budget.[6] Other than some nods to global Britain in prime ministerial speeches, nothing of any strategic importance on this matter came out of Downing Street for over three years. Since the turn of the century successive British governments had produced glossy brochure 'strategy documents' on any number of security-related subjects – defence policy, counterterrorism, cyber security, international crime, maritime security, new technologies, climate change, to name only the most obvious. But faced with the biggest potential strategic change in over half a century, it produced nothing of any substance on Britain's global future.

The meaning of 'global Britain'

Not for the first time in its history, the British government was reluctant to talk about strategy when it really mattered. This may indicate either that 'global Britain' is genuinely an empty phrase, and the FCO was right to say it will just be doing more of the same, or else that it is such a big potential strategic shift, it defies any characterization unless or until a prime minister provides one. The concept is either too small, or too big, to be officially analysed. In the meantime, parliamentarians tried to derive some content from the public statements made by ministers as they repeated the slogan. Global Britain seemed to mean taking a more determined international outlook, reassuring established international partners that Britain would continue to be proactive and would look to create new global partnerships; that it would remain fully committed to the rules-based international order, and that it was committed to the virtues of free trade. At one point Foreign Secretary Jeremy Hunt offered the Delphic concept that Britain should be part of 'an invisible chain' linking the democracies of the world.[7] Parliamentarians were still left scratching their heads.[8]

None of this connected directly to practical policy. Analysts (and parliamentarians) would not be able to judge whether global Britain was a meaningful phrase for the government unless at least one of two trends were discernible; either, that there were some meaningful shifts of national resources towards a global mission; or that short-term policy trade-offs indicated Britain was prepared to sacrifice something for the sake of a new objective or perhaps a new, or renewed, international partnership. Otherwise, 'global Britain' would remain just a variation on 'business as usual'. As we indicated in the Introduction, Britain crossed a Rubicon in 2016 and whatever the eventual outcome of the Brexit hiatus, a business as usual approach is unlikely to do justice to 2020 challenges.

Outside official circles, however, commentary on the meaning of global Britain was more vigorous. Those sceptical about the lasting value of Brexit stressed the difficulties Britain might face outside the EU and the resource constraints on policy that would arise through the disruptive economic effects Brexit would likely cause, at least for a while. Britain's diplomatic attributes habitually mentioned by the FCO were all strong cards in the government's hand. The list was very well-known and included Britain's status as a nuclear weapons power, a member of the UN's Permanent Five, its role in NATO, in the Commonwealth, in deploying international aid, and playing its role in the G7 and the G20, and with wide networks of regional representation.[9] For the Brexit sceptics, these could not be made any more naturally 'global' than they were already, and Britain would do well to maintain the power of these attributes, or even hang onto them, in the years to come. Most of these commentators thought the concept of global Britain was essentially vacuous and demonstrated what a leap in the dark the whole enterprise had become.[10]

Brexit supporting analysts, on the other hand, were prepared to develop the concept within some classic, and some new, Anglosphere themes.[11] In this respect, the outlines were stated with some consistency. The case rejects a persistent sense of 'declinism' in British debates about the future. Britain, like the other nations of the Western world facing the rise of Asia, shares a condition of absolute decline – but not necessarily of relative decline, as measured against each other. Britain is in a better position than most of its partners and it deserves to be more confident about the future.[12] Moreover, Britain should be more explicitly outward-looking in debates about the country's future in leaving the European Union. Brexit had been portrayed as a self-obsessed and introverted process instead of a new approach to globalism. 'Brexit will be defined by its enemies – and her [Prime Minister May's] blunders', said Fraser Nelson in 2018.[13] That new approach to globalism, said others, would almost certainly involve Britain's own 'pivot to Asia' to make the most of the economic and political opportunities the future would present. Britain should work to reform the World Trade Organisation after Brexit to steer it away from growing protectionism and it should stand up to growing authoritarianism everywhere.[14] For some Brexiteers, it should go even further. Britain outside the EU would deal more bilaterally with the rest of the world – just as the Trump administration preferred to do – and some analysts shared President Trump's scepticism at the utility of international organizations and the ease with which they could be manipulated or even hijacked by the enemies of the democratic, Western powers.[15] If the Jacksonian nationalism of the Trump administration's approach to the world is maintained and then extended into the 2020s, it would mark a serious US campaign to change the way world politics had worked for a long time. 'Global Britain', in this assertive view, should be seen as much more than a survival mechanism outside the EU; more an investment in a US-led attempt to rearrange some of the furniture in the global house. Far from being a throwback to the old Anglosphere, struggling to maintain its own failing international system, this view sees Britain as a proactive member of a new Anglosphere working to re-set the international dial.

There are, therefore, at least three different interpretations of the global Britain concept. There is the view of the Brexit sceptics, many of the them parliamentarians, who suspect that it is no more than a lazy slogan, thrown up by a campaign to leave the EU that was focused almost exclusively on domestic concerns and a retrograde sense of national identity. Then there is the governmental view, that global Britain is a work in progress and reflects a natural evolution towards the accommodation of new realities as and when they arise. Brexit sucked all the air out of other governmental and parliamentary processes. When normal political leadership is resumed, it is maintained, the more precise shape of a global Britain approach will emerge. Finally, there is the committed Brexit view that global Britain will hinge on an old faith, and a renewed commitment, to an Anglosphere approach to world politics. In this interpretation, it is a pity that Brexit debates were so economically focused, as the desire to leave the EU grew out of a more realistic, anti-declinist, British world view in the first place. What Britain needs now, in this view, is the wholehearted embrace of a genuinely alternative strategic perspective.

How can the different views of global Britain be measured against the emerging realities of the 2020s?

Take Brexit out of the equation, and it is clear that any assessment of Britain's future in the world must be set in the context that the 2020s shows all the signs of being a tough decade in any case. This is true for all the 'second rank' powers and will be felt most acutely among the European second rankers, whose influence on world politics has been in absolute decline since the end of the Cold War, even if that fact was largely disguised for about twenty years while the world re-arranged its perceptions of power. As one of the European big three, along with France and Germany, and the one with the most distinctive sense of exceptionalism within continental Europe, Britain is likely to feel the impact of world politics in the 2020s – the good and the bad – quite acutely.

To summarize briefly the argument of previous chapters, the structural challenges of the 2020s begin, first, with the realization that Britain will be operating in a world where great power competition has returned to world politics as a determining force. It is an international environment where the moment of US dominance – the 'uni-polar moment' – was certainly over by 2008. Now the four great powers, the United States, China, Russia and India, increasingly make the political weather for the rest of us. The geopolitical wheels have been turning with increasing speed in the past decade and the competition between the four powers creates pressures that reduce the natural authority of the international structures and institutions on which states had previously relied. It forces other countries into difficult choices and trade-offs. A world of dominant great powers is very different from a multi-polar world where governing institutions are prevalent; or even a uni-polar world where the dominant power had created most of the institutions everyone else was generally content to use. Within this new constellation of global powers, continental Europe is at least a static, and possibly a declining, force. In whatever ways the economic future of the EU unfolds and its development as the 'European grand project' proceeds, it is in no position to express its collective power effectively on the world stage. It lacks the real machinery to do so. More importantly, and despite all EU protestations to the contrary, it lacks the collective political will. In 2018–19 it failed to agree a common policy in dealing with Kosovo, which was in its own neighbourhood and strategically important to it, or even with Venezuela, which was not, on either count. And Europe as a whole, in and outside the EU, cannot summon up a strong political consensus on the most important strategic issues it faces. This is unlikely to change, at least for the near future.

Secondly, world economic developments – always more complex than political constellations – nevertheless also reflect a changing of the guard. Globalization is a fact of international life and it changes the political dynamics within and between societies. But if the push of globalization appears to be inevitable, the actual directions it takes are not, and there is evidence of a – sometimes strong – pushback against its effects within Western societies alongside a determination on the part of autocratic governments to harness only those elements of it that suits them. We are rapidly entering what is characterized as the 'globalization 2.0' era. Wherever globalization is heading, however, there can be no doubt that the world's economic centre of gravity is moving rapidly to Asia – not just to China – and that Asian markets, the economic growth and stability of them, and patterns of Asian investment in the rest of the world, will figure prominently in the strategic policies of all Western countries. It is also clear that after the 'great crisis and the great recession' beginning in 2008, the world economy is not yet out of the woods and a return to structural crises in the early 2020s is entirely possible.

Thirdly, therefore, it is hardly surprising that these developments should be both cause and effect of some disruptive social and economic trends in Britain, most of which are also mirrored in other European countries. Western democratic values are under pressure both at home and abroad. Political populism breaks through conventional politics in many different countries and in their own characteristic national ways, while authoritarian movements and governments are on the rise everywhere. In the 1990s, liberal capitalism appeared to be dominant; now it must justify itself ideologically and fight for the maintenance of its rules and structures – even within the Western world. In the great power world of the 2020s, and notwithstanding the forces of globalization, liberal democracy is in retreat.

Britain must navigate its way through the relationships it has with the great powers, in particular with the United States, China and with Russia. To be secure and maintain the conditions for its prosperity, it must take on the extensive security spectrum of all modern societies, from international crime and terrorism to the territorial defence of the state itself. It must work for its prosperity in a global economy that is dynamic to the point of volatility and which may turn out to be going through the pain of long-term, structural transformation. And it must do so where the 'rules-based international order' to which Britain is naturally committed, is under increasing pressure. Indeed, the rules-based order of world politics may even be shrinking into something closer to the 'jungle rules' of mere coexistence.

Put Brexit back into this equation and it is also clear that the strategic shift it involves superimposes onto this background a number of both *protect* and *project* challenges that are urgent and imperative. It must *protect* as much as possible, the foreign policy and defence collaboration and coordination it already has with European partners in other forums, most notably at the G7 and G20, within the United Nations and through the UN Security Council, in NATO, OCCAR or in any other ad hoc groupings as they arise.[16] It must compensate – bilaterally – for the influence it will lose in the strategic direction and management of EU structures and it must reassure European partners that it will not 'go rogue' on broad European interests, say with India, China or the United States, for the sake of a bilateral trade deal.[17] Early priorities will be the protection of its own research and development infrastructure as it relates to Britain's security and defence and its defence industrial base and the standing of British defence industries in the global marketplace. In particular, it must also protect some key areas of the security apparatus of policing in Britain that could be adversely affected by the loss of integrative arrangements that had proved their practical worth.

Above all, Britain must protect the union of the United Kingdom itself if global Britain – or any sort of Britain – is to tackle the 2020s successfully. A decade of constitutional crisis and reorganization around a new political entity would leave Britain effectively at the mercy of whatever the 2020s bring, even if the UK subsequently survived the challenges of dissolution. Those who might break up the UK can only claim to do so on the argument that a new settlement would equip all parties better to deal with the world as it might emerge in the 2030s and beyond. That may be plausible, but there could be little doubt that the pains of dissolution would hobble all parts of the UK in relation to the external world for the immediate decade to come.

Simultaneously, a global Britain must *project* the strengths it already possesses and make it a reality that any Brexit process has not reduced its ability to defend and promote its national interests. The practical implications of this imperative are less obvious than they might first appear. Britain still enjoys a good international reputation for the practicality and skill of its diplomacy, particularly within international organizations and at multinational negotiations.[18] It is often observed that Britain, among only a few other states in the world, has 'convening power'; that ability to devise and host international initiatives which other states are prepared to take seriously.[19] In other words, and despite the domestic traumas of the Brexit process after 2016, British diplomacy still has some credit in world affairs. The imperative to project it, however, should not be interpreted as a strategy to downgrade the importance of European issues – to be 'global' by somehow being less 'European'. The challenge is to find that happy balance where Britain becomes a more proactive power in the wider world and thereby has more to offer in matters of common interest within continental Europe. It must involve itself not just in dealing with, say, Russian revisionist behaviour, which is a high British priority in European affairs, but with other issues that may be lower British national priorities, such as European energy security and the security problems behind the Nord Stream 2 gas pipeline, or uncontrolled migration across the Mediterranean and south Eastern Europe. Britain's identity of certain interests with EU partners such as Poland, Sweden, the Czech Republic, the three Baltic states, Spain, Portugal or Cyprus, for example, are all points of influence to counteract perceptions of British withdrawal from mainstream European politics.[20] Far from being excluded from significant policy areas by irritated European partners – or worse, excluding itself – Britain's national diplomatic interests are best served by being seen as useful or inventive in such cases, notwithstanding the fact that it has withdrawn from EU policy coordination mechanisms. Britain must look for opportunities to project its strategic and diplomatic utility to European partners *because* it has the freedom to operate more quickly and flexibly (and perhaps more inventively) outside the EU framework, not *in spite* of it. This will be a neat trick if it can be done. The only obvious area in which this might currently apply is in the Western Balkans, where Britain might have more influence as a mediator, acting alone, rather than lining up behind EU policy which is cautious and fragmented in the face of Russian-inspired subversion.

And in the wider world, the projection of British diplomatic power should be perceived as something more than a country operating only in the shadow of the United States. As described in Chapter 5, United States and British policy on a number of key issues are not as coincident as in the past, certainly not in the short term, or possibly even in the long term. More actively promoting broadly Anglosphere interests in world politics would revolve around a group of generic objectives, whatever the immediate attitude of the United States might be. Given the importance of the Anglosphere in the evolution of the current rules-based international order, the maintenance of international regimes to address common problems, bolstering the established rules of the system, putting individual human rights within international law, or promoting the long-term value of free trade are all key parts of an intrinsically Anglosphere approach to world politics. Of course, the way the US interprets these common interests at any time is hugely important, but it is not always the determining factor. The United States stood out of the Ottawa Treaty of 1997 to ban the use of anti-personnel landmines, while Canada, Britain, Australia, New Zealand and most of the countries of West Africa, among 121 original signatories, made it an arms control reality. In 2002 the United States signed up to the foundation of the International Criminal Court but then withdrew from it, while most of West and Central Africa, South Africa, Britain, Canada, Australia and New Zealand all supported and contributed to its work. In 2014, despite outright opposition and strong lobbying from Washington, first Britain, and in short order also India, Australia, New Zealand, South Africa and Canada all joined China's Asian Infrastructure Investment Bank. In 2016 the United States gave notice that it would withdraw from the Paris Climate Change Agreement in 2020, but the other 194 signatories maintained their commitment.

US support for international initiatives is always important, but its indifference or opposition to them is not automatically terminal. With this in mind, Britain will need to be particularly sensitive to the way in which it is generally perceived in the world as it leaves, or diverges from, the EU. Eschewing an automatic 'junior partner' role in US–British relations, still less a sentimental one based on twentieth-century history, in favour of something more hard-nosed and instrumental, may be the best investment Britain can make in projecting its strategic and diplomatic strengths from outside the European Union. The FCO would maintain that this is the case anyway, and that the 'automatic junior partner' image is a straw man.[21] But the Chilcot report on British involvement in Iraq in 2003, which coincidentally also said much about Afghanistan during that decade, gave significant substance to the accusation.[22] It certainly did nothing to diminish a popular view in foreign offices around the world that Britain sacrificed quite a lot of prestige – and some moral leadership – to be a junior partner of the United States in more than one dubious international enterprise after the end of the Cold War.

The compression of strategic choice

As we have stated earlier, the turn of this decade is not a propitious time for a country such as Britain to attempt any significant reorientation of its place in the world and the appropriate roles it might play. International politics, global economics and the ideological zeitgeist, at least for the next few years, all create headwinds blowing against such a course. In the event, perhaps surviving the pressures of the 2020s will be enough, reducing the Brexit imbroglio to the least economically disruptive process possible and ditching any wider ambitions to use it as a springboard to British renewal outside the EU. However much this might be desired by pro-EU campaigners, or those who are simply happy to witness essential continuity in all foreign and security policies, the fact remains that the Brexit vote was a genuine game changer. In the 2016 referendum it was often argued that Britain was only voting about whether to leave an economic pact that many saw as overly constraining on the British economy; alarm about a more fundamental strategic choice was misplaced. But if the significance of the EU in world politics can sometimes be overstated – not least by the EU itself – it is nevertheless clear that the Brexit decision goes much deeper than just Britain's relationship to an economic arrangement. It is 'the biggest thing that we have ever undertaken in peace time' said the head of the FCO in 2018.[23] Certainly, Britain's partners across Europe and the wider world all perceive Brexit as a significant shift of strategic policy.[24]

In superimposing its particular requirements on the existing security outlook for the 2020s, Brexit creates a genuine moment of strategic choice for Britain over the coming two or three years that is unusual in its peacetime history. Such dramatic moments normally only arrive in the shadow of war. But here, a point of strategic inflexion is inescapable. Like the shadow of war, though now for different reasons, Brexit has had the effect of compressing the strategic choices the government might face throughout the next decade down to just a couple of years. We consider how this moment might be faced and the potential resources Britain has to mobilize for it in the final chapters of this book. It is important to understand, however, what it is about Brexit that, in effect, compresses the choices for the 2020s into more immediate and tricky challenges for British policy-makers.

The most obvious compression is that Brexit elevates a *perception* of British isolation in world politics; between a Europe on which it seems to be turning its back, and a United States going in a different strategic direction, both geographically and ideologically. Reality is not as stark as the perception, of course. Official British statements after 2016 repeatedly insisted that Britain would never turn its back on European partners. There would be, Prime Minister May said repeatedly, a 'deep and special' relationship in the future.[25] Britain's relations with other European powers were essentially unaffected. Though this was a deliberate underestimation of the Brexit impact, it contained the essential truth. Britain is still one of the so-called E3 countries – one of the 'big-three' in Europe – and its bilateral relations with twenty-seven other European countries, and its role as an important third party to the EU itself, would remain of considerable importance.[26] 'While we are leaving one organisation, we will still remain a committed, connected member of over 60 others', said Sir Simon McDonald.[27] On the other side of the transatlantic equation, the possibility that some serious, long-term differences had opened between London and Washington has long been a neuralgic issue for British leaders and officials. They try not to speak about it too publicly, or else habitually point to all that the United States still invests in European security and the functional closeness of US–British military and intelligence relations.

It is something of a caricature to portray Brexit Britain as 'isolated' between Europe and the United States; a country diplomatically adrift with an inflated view of its own power in the world.[28] It is more accurate to describe the diplomatic challenge as being to keep as many options open as possible, and keep diplomatic lines of influence readily available throughout the western world, even as Britain reaches out for new partnerships. That is no more than practical continuity. Nevertheless, Brexit makes this continuity equation considerably more difficult to balance, since the world expects Britain to be diminished by it.[29] Some of the issues that trouble the transatlantic community are deep and genuinely divisive. Real choices that have consequences have to be made, and Britain may already have lost some of its natural lines of influence with partners on both sides of the Atlantic. On the European side, it became clear at least from autumn 2017 that at the level of top leadership, the irritation, then the anger, caused by Britain's stance inside the EU had begun to spill over into other diplomatic forums. Britain was regarded as either unhelpful or simply too preoccupied to be a strong European diplomatic player. Britain had, it is true, become diplomatically introspective over the Brexit negotiation period. If it was to avoid the perception – if not the harsh reality – that far from 'punching above its weight' in world politics Britain was not even pulling its weight in European circles, it was clear by 2020 that there was some ground to make up.

On the other side of the transatlantic equation, notwithstanding the personal support of President Trump for the Brexit decision, the United States still waits to see how Britain will emerge on the world stage from the whole process. There is a general expectation – outside the White House – that it will probably be diminished.[30] Certainly, there is no evidence that the US policy community expects Britain to enhance its international power by leaving the EU, or that in the eyes of the United States it is a more useful European interlocutor for being outside EU structures; quite the opposite, in fact.[31] British politicians and commentators habitually confuse the cultural affinity and personal friendships of Washington's leaders and policy insiders with a more hard-nosed American assessment of Britain's practical usefulness to US policy. And none of this lessened a more general international perception of Britain's relative isolation in the transatlantic community; an 'isle of madness' said *Der Spiegel*; 'a Shakespearian tragedy' said *La Tribune*.[32] The first, most immediate and unavoidable imperative occasioned by Brexit – the first strategic compression it creates – is to turn that perception around and ensure it does not become a stark reality.

The second strategic compression – another long-term pressure that must now be dealt with quickly – concerns the resources available for foreign, defence and security policy in the immediate future. This will be examined in more detail in Chapter 13. 'Strategy' is not only a process of defining and then making choices. It is also fundamentally about the allocation of resources. The reason the great powers can pursue meaningful strategies that affect other countries so deeply is because they can transfer considerable resources to back up any strategy. They have a margin of error denied to other countries; a potential to compensate for strategic mistakes or recover from them more quickly because they have bigger resources to allocate. This is not generally the case for second tier, European powers. Britain will not have the power to recover quickly if it loses strategic leverage through lack of resources in the immediate post-EU years. Such resources are not only measured as pure public expenditure, but also measured as personnel and institutional resources, which cannot be manipulated so easily or quickly. Personal skills, institutional learning and information infrastructures are at least as significant as all-important cash, and take longer to create and deploy. The longer-term strategic decisions that will allocate resources to foreign, defence and security policy for the 2020s are a series of political headaches awaiting British policy-makers as they emerge from the Brexit process. The most immediate imperative is to ensure that the existing policy instruments to address Britain's future in world politics are not starved of resources as the result of an even greater public expenditure squeeze occasioned by short-term economic disruption. Depending on Britain's economic circumstances in the early 2020s this may be very hard to do. But another stark fact is that if Britain is seen to be visibly diminished (or for some, yet more diminished) in world politics as an immediate result of leaving the EU, it will not quickly recover its international influence, or its own intrinsic powers of action, in time to deal with the near-term challenges the 2020s seem set to present. If Britain is seen to have spent the years from 2018 until 2023 dealing almost exclusively – and introspectively – with Brexit, it will find that the Chinese economy will have grown by almost a third in that time; an increase almost twice the equivalent of Britain's total GDP. Whatever the special characteristics of Britain's economy, its leverage as a trading nation with China is only going in one direction.[33]

A similar strategic compression challenge extends to the domestic scene in Britain. The polarization of public and political opinion over Brexit, to a degree unprecedented in modern history, was also mirrored in opinions about Britain's subsequent role in the world. In the court of public opinion, they veered between extremes. On one side were assertive Brexiteer pronouncements that there would be a new era in Britain's anglospheric presence in the world. It would not just be a question of compensating for what might be lost, but rather of setting the country on a new course that made the best of the 'globalization 2.0' world. On the pro-remain side there were many, frankly depressive, views that the scale of the strategic error created by Brexit was such that nothing but further decline awaited the country as it was buffeted by the harsh winds of the 2020s.[34] As the vehemently pro-Remain *Economist* fretted, the real worry was that the darker view of Britain's future was turning into a self-fulfilling prophesy. 'The reason Brexit is doing so much damage' it said, 'is not just that it is a mistake. It is a reckoning'.[35] It would take some years to recover from the blow that Brexit might inflict on British foreign and security policy.

The immediate challenge created by this polarization of opinion is that if the government is able to compensate for the reputational damage already done and – more importantly – prevent a lacuna opening in its commitment to external policies in the early years of the coming decade, it still has to sell that fact convincingly to the British public.[36] It is a truism that public confidence in the government's external policies, an acceptance of the commitments it might involve and willingness to have public expenditure allocated to them, is all critical to the success of any strategic decisions or re-evaluations. It is possible that making a visible success of an early strategic shift to non-EU approaches in world politics might help the British public transcend the legacy of bitterness and political division that accompanied Brexit politics after 2015. That could be a tall order. But at the very least, it is imperative – another strategic compression – that in the short term the divisions in public opinion do not simply transfer themselves to Britain's strategic policy choices as they become evident. Nothing would be worse for leaders and policy-makers than to find themselves refighting the Brexit controversy in Parliament, the press and with vocal sections of public opinion whenever they tried to shift the allocation of resources or open up new avenues of policy to address the immediate issues they will face.

A final policy challenge that Brexit compresses is the ability of British government to organize itself to face the external challenges of the 2020s. It will have to do this anyway, since the Brexit process distorted Whitehall to accommodate unique circumstances. In 2016 a 'Brexit department' was created (the Department for Exiting the European Union – DExEU) to handle the negotiations. The DExEU was thereby responsible for trade relations within the EU. A new Department for International Trade (DIT) was formed to deal with all trade relations outside the EU, and the Foreign and Commonwealth Office (FCO), along with the Cabinet Office, and the Department for Business Innovation and Skills (BIS) had some of their functions transferred to it. The new DIT took on the UK Trade and Industry portfolio along with some investment finance responsibilities. The BIS was subsequently repurposed as the Department for Business, Energy and Industrial Strategy – less internationally focused than previously; and the FCO was effectively excluded from the Brexit process altogether to concentrate on wider foreign relations. None of this proved to be a happy bureaucratic arrangement, not least because of fierce political differences between ministers themselves and the role of Downing Street in sucking all Brexit policy-making into the leader's own personal realm – to the point where one commentator labelled Prime Minister May as the 'death star of modern British politics'.[37] Nor was this helped when the role of National Security Adviser was combined with the even more challenging job of Cabinet Secretary in Number 10, under one (very able) civil servant. It was symptomatic of distracted policy when the Cabinet Office produced an overall security review in March 2018 and the Ministry of Defence's contribution to it appeared the following December, clearly struggling to remain consistent.[38] Bureaucratic re-structuring for Brexit and Mrs May's attempts to manage intra-party differences simply added to the policy dislocation and introspection around the whole enterprise.

Unravelling these bureaucratic knots will be an urgent priority for future governments; in particular, to get the management of foreign and security policy across the board back into a more coherent structure, whether traditionally under the FCO working alongside the National Security Council, or else in some other bureaucratic arrangement. The initial instincts of the Johnson government were to centralize even more policy-making in Downing Street and to discuss it primarily within a small group of senior, very committed Brexiteer, ministers. But the problem goes deeper. Whitehall spent more than twenty years trying to create a 'whole of government' approach to policy without making fundamental changes to its own structure. The reasons to reject wholesale reform are quite compelling and were considered carefully in the first Thatcher Administration in 1979. It would take at least one full term of government to achieve anything meaningful and the public would see little benefit in policy outputs – certainly not in time for a subsequent election. Better to concentrate on close coordination within the existing machinery.[39] In 1997 the Blair administration adopted what it termed the 'joined up government approach'. This was subsequently labelled as the 'combined' or 'integrated' approach; then when that proved too ambitious, a less demanding 'coordinated approach' that sought policy integration between a few ministries concerned with a particular issue. In 2010 a 'whole of government' approach was back in vogue and in 2018 the wheel came full circle with the launch of a 'fusion doctrine' across Whitehall that sought again to achieve the joined-up government ambitions of the Blair years.[40]

In truth, 'fusion' is the philosopher's stone of modern government. Whether it is spelt out in a policy initiative or not, it stands as an ideal to which all governments aspire and where achievement can only be a matter of degree. But it will need to be achieved to a high degree, and quickly, within a civil service that is around 30 per cent smaller than it was in 2010. In Chapter 6 we outlined some of the domestic challenges that must now be considered part of British security, including crime fighting, cyber security, or the protection of CNI. They are all intensely cross-departmental as far as Whitehall is concerned, and no less connected to the external world, both governmental and commercial. Britain outside the EU will have to do some of the things it already does reasonably well – such as formal diplomacy or its work for international institutions – but more intensively. And it will have to re-learn some Whitehall skills it had largely given up to EU policy-making in those sectors where Brussels policy is genuinely consequential, such as in trade negotiations, applied research or data management, in market regulation, agriculture, fisheries, energy or environment. British society is not short of expertise in such areas, but Whitehall certainty is.

To pursue a really proactive trade policy in the 2020s, Whitehall needs to draw in specialist and technical trade policy skills in many areas that have previously been handled by the European Union. To deal more bilaterally with its European partners across many sectors of policy, Britain needs to increase the skilled middle management of the Diplomatic Service and have greater access to private sector expertise. In relation both to Europe and the wider world, it needs to upskill the public service quickly in digital management and nearly as quickly in language training. It needs to have people, urgently, in situ in partner countries so they have time to build all-important personal relationships and cultural understanding. In promoting foreign policy in its broadest sense, Whitehall needs better ways of harnessing key private sector activities – in commerce, higher education, research, cultural exchange, entrepreneurship – to serve broad public sector objectives.

If Britain is to be highly agile and opportunistic outside the European Union, it will have to manage independently the highly complex cross-sectoral issues that are expected to be even more prevalent in the 2020s. Britain would certainly have the freedom and flexibility not to be bound by agreed EU policy, but its national policy choices would thereby be all the more exposed. That exposure could include more severe retaliatory action, particularly in the trade sphere, which Britain would confront alone once outside the EU's powerful trade bloc. 'Of all the cauldrons of diplomacy', it has been said, 'few are tougher' than trade negotiations even in 'the brutal world of economic diplomacy'. It will be a tall order for Britain to 'punch above its weight in trade talks as it does in diplomacy, defence, intelligence and finance'.[41]

Brexit has been a bad time for Whitehall. In foreign and security policy, at least, its normal structures were distorted, its policy-making fell prey to inter-ministerial conflict and the political hiatus around Brexit halted substantive policy-making in most other areas. Declarations were made, reviews commissioned, but in truth, practical policy across government had almost ground to a halt by the end of 2017, confronted by the all-consuming problem of giving effect to the 2016 referendum result.[42] Whitehall's Civil Service will, of course, recover from this hiatus. But the strategic compression problem is that it will have to bounce back in a way that re-equips it not only to deal with the extra requirements created by Brexit but also in good shape to confront the more daunting prospects the 2020s were throwing up even before the Brexit decision was taken. It is not in the constitution, or the nature, of the Civil Service to change course in the absence of political direction, still less to operate in any way against it. Only when Britain's political crisis is somehow resolved – when its nervous breakdown is safely in therapy – is it likely that some proper political forward thinking will begin. Thankfully, the system is capable of swinging quickly back into action once it is directed by some conscious strategic leadership, backed by adequate political will.

Britain's security capabilities

Chapter 11

Governmental capabilities – diplomacy, defence, intelligence and security

Foreign policy speeches by government ministers and senior officials, no less than defence and security reviews, normally begin with a catalogue of Britain's relative strengths in world politics. The head of the Foreign and Commonwealth Office (FCO) set it out clearly in 2018.

> We, in the United Kingdom, are a big country. We have a formidable global footprint with an array of assets comparable to any country of similar size. We are a global, free trading nation. The world's fifth largest economy. Fifth biggest exporter. Top destination for inward investment in Europe, and second only to the US globally. Ranked one of the best places to do business in the world. We are the fifth largest diplomatic network in the world. Unique in being a member of the P5, NATO, Commonwealth, G7 and G20. We have 15,000 staff – UK and locally engaged – across 169 countries and territories in 274 posts. We are the only P5 country to spend both 2 percent on defence and 0.7 percent of GNI on development. We are the third largest contributor to development in the world.

'These facts', he said, 'are the essential background' and 'too often they are overlooked. The United Kingdom is a principled, responsible global actor'.[1] It is a reassuring list to those who worry about the effects of Brexit on Britain's security and its role in the world. And, as we describe in the next chapter, Britain's societal capabilities add considerably to any description of these essentially governmental strengths as we assess the range of resources that Britain can mobilize to face the security challenges of the 2020s.

In themselves, however, lists do not record the relative power or longevity of the items on them. Nor do they establish the direction of travel – which items on the list might be strengthening or weakening over time; and how they might be compared against the evolving capacities of other states with similar attributes. A considered judgement requires some attempt to conduct an audit of capabilities – governmental and those that might be classed as societal – that Britain can call upon in the years to come. Not least, as we analyse in Chapter 13, there is also the question of the political will, and skill, to mobilize them effectively sooner rather than later.

Diplomatic networks: Capabilities and confidence

'Diplomacy' as the head of the FCO put it, derives from some perception of national strength. It describes how governments relate to each other in the international world; how they manoeuvre themselves around the other players in the arena of international politics. The term also refers, more technically, to the machinery and skills a state can apply to these manoeuvrings and they represent reputation and continuity, whether or not they are used to greatest effect by political leaders.

British diplomacy is a well acknowledged strength in Britain's relations with the rest of the world. As a governmental capability, 'diplomacy' covers the work principally of the Foreign and Commonwealth Office, but also of other government departments and agencies as they relate to the world abroad, and including the administration of overseas aid through the Department for International Development (DFID). The Ministry of Defence (MoD) operates a network of defence attaches who work from overseas embassies, led by a British ambassador, high commissioner or possibly a head of mission.[2] Other officials covering sectors such as trade, agriculture, environment and so on may be seconded to embassies and missions as the need arises. Intelligence officers may also be part of an embassy team. Some thirty-one different government departments and public bodies were included in the FCO's foreign network in 2018.[3] In essence, the FCO provides the framework for all Whitehall departments in implementing the government's diplomacy. An ambassador or head of mission is ultimately responsible for all official British representation in a foreign country or a mission to an international organization.

The erstwhile exception to this, which drifts in and out of the picture as personalities change, is the temptation for prime ministers and their close advisers (many not even members of the Civil Service) to conduct their own foreign policies, working outside normal FCO channels. Prime Minister Anthony

Eden famously did so in the Suez debacle in 1956. Margaret Thatcher and Tony Blair periodically did so when they trusted in their own personal negotiating skills above those of their diplomats. The Theresa May government, like that of Boris Johnson, not only centralized all its Brexit-related policy inside Downing Street but also, as described in Chapter 10, distorted the normal diplomatic machinery to leave the FCO emasculated across European diplomacy.[4] And though current mandarins would never say it, ex-mandarins were in no doubt that when Boris Johnson was appointed in 2016 to lead the FCO through Brexit as a political manoeuvre by Prime Minister May, he was 'widely regarded as having been a disaster as Foreign Secretary'; and 'the worst Foreign Secretary in living memory' by another with insider access.[5] As prime minister himself in 2019 Boris Johnson appointed a senior team of ministers and advisers that were evidently intended to push Brexit by any means necessary through the political system, as directed from Downing Street. The FCO's formal role and its networks are easily described, but after recent years it faces the future in need of some clarity and drive over how it should best represent government policy in the coming decade.

This, in fact, is largely true across the board in British diplomacy. The Brexit referendum vote was a blow to most of the Civil Service dealing with Britain's overseas relations, if only because it cast a long shadow over how the country would relate to the external world in future and how much of a reorientation in priorities it might involve. As servants of the government, the Brexit process after 2016 was loyally supported in public by policy professionals, but the effect on their organizations was to create much greater uncertainty over how they would operate in future. This was evident in the three main sectors of Britain's diplomatic network; in the broad FCO system, in overseas aid policy and in the Commonwealth.

The FCO has long had a reputation for its expertise in Whitehall and a sense of the international respect its presence across the world has garnered for British diplomacy.[6] Traditionally, Foreign Office elitism was fully embraced. In the 1970s diplomatic training was both language intensive and then highly mentored throughout a well-trodden career path.[7] At the turn of this century a big effort was made through a long-term 'Foresight' programme – what John Dickie called the 'Foresight Saga' – to convert such traditional elitism into high, meritocratic expertise, which most observers regard as having been largely successful.[8] The personnel quality in the FCO and at diplomatic posts remains evidently high. Civil Service traditions still have a strong influence on the way foreign policy is formulated and implemented, and compared to most other countries, policy coordination across Whitehall is generally good. British diplomacy has traditionally been characterized by friends and adversaries alike in the world as 'pragmatic' and 'competent' – good at multilateral diplomacy and able to make positive contributions to any negotiations in which Britain is involved.[9] It is also true that with such an extensive range of posts and missions the FCO runs, at least on paper, the fifth most extensive diplomatic network in the world, consistent with the other members of the UN's P5.[10] This network was even supplemented in 2018 in light of Brexit negotiations through the creation of 150 more diplomatic jobs.

The downside of this favourable picture, however, is that the FCO's extensive diplomatic network is extremely thin compared to the past when British diplomacy was so much admired. Many posts that formerly had significant staffs were severely reduced. More concentration on the biggest posts, such as in Washington, Riyadh, at the UN, or the EU, led to the hollowing out of other posts. The FCO's budget was both reduced and reorganized in light of public spending cuts during the financial crisis. In 2010 its budget was £2 billion; in 2018 its budget for 2020 was projected to be £1.2 billion, amid budgetary transfers with DFID and a responsibility to pay £85 million into the BBC World Service. Not surprising, then, that the FCO was selling up some of its embassy premises, such as the £420 million Bangkok embassy, to fund modernization projects.[11]

The government insisted in 2010 that despite these pressures there would be 'no strategic shrinkage' in Britain's global presence.[12] It was an impossible promise to keep in the circumstances, even – perhaps especially – in the digital age.[13] The long-term effect of cutbacks was that missions struggled along with reduced staffs, there was a big decline in language training, the policy planning staff in the FCO became a shadow of its former, powerful, self and a 'scatter-gun approach' to policy initiatives made it difficult to connect real activity to abstract strategies.[14] Regardless of how extensive the network of posts, or the meritocratic expertise of the younger generation of staff operating them, British diplomacy was not as evident or as proactive in world politics as it once was, and the Brexit process set it further on the back foot through sheer uncertainty. For some observers, the network and 'the Office' in London simply demonstrated 'exhaustion', 'shambles' and 'timidity'.[15]

This should not all be laid at the door of an over-stretched diplomatic service, however. The truth is that Britain had been backing away from the front line of global politics for some years – certainly since the end of the Tony Blair era and the onset of the economic crisis in 2008. Downing Street always makes the near-term running in diplomacy and foreign policy. Some in the FCO thought that the creation of the National Security Council (NSC) in 2010 would be empowering for them, but it empowered the Cabinet Office and Downing Street more. And Downing Street's appetite for proactive foreign policy did not go far beyond the rhetorical, while other leading Whitehall departments were preoccupied with expenditure cuts and then the uncertainties created by the Brexit process.

Everywhere, there were signs of active retreat from the diplomatic front line, regardless of the efforts of leading diplomats. Britain was happy to be excluded from the Minsk II mediation process on Ukraine in 2014, even though it had been a guarantor of Ukraine's security in 1994. It was seen to retreat from responsibilities it had previously assumed at the UN over Somalia and the Chagos Islands; it failed to get a British judge elected to a seat it had long held on the International Court of Justice; and it lost a great deal of its former diplomatic traction across Europe while arguments over withdrawal dominated every agenda.[16] In dealing with the aftermath of the collapse of IS in Syria and Iraq, the government was roundly and publicly criticized, even by Canadian ministers, in seeming to shirk its international responsibilities to deal judicially with surviving jihadists and their families, instead of simply revoking British citizenship in a number of cases on which it would not then comment. The government was not prepared to stand up publicly in defence of the INF Treaty when Russian cheating and President Trump's renunciation of it in 2019 made Europe that bit less secure. It manoeuvred against Parliament specifically to prevent new legislation on financial transparency from becoming official British policy in relation to tax havens, regardless of its stated position on offshore funds. There was, by common consent among observers, a lack of confidence and morale in British foreign policy that demoralized the FCO. This reality does not invalidate the 'essential background' – Britain's inner strengths – the head of the FCO set out in his 2018 speech. It does, however, demonstrate that the formal machinery to mobilize and exploit them fully requires some remedial action as soon as possible. As one ex-diplomat expressed it, 'There has certainly been a loss of confidence in the Diplomatic Service generally, but real confidence depends on the *product* you are promoting. That has been the essence of the problem.'[17]

The administration of British overseas aid is in better shape, and morale among its administrators is visibly higher. Overseas aid was divorced from its role as a part of the FCO and established as a separate department, at cabinet level – as DFID – by the incoming Labour government in 1997. As part of the deal that put the Conservative/Liberal Democrat Coalition government together in 2010, overseas aid was given the statutory guarantee that it would be maintained at the UN-mandated level of 0.7 per cent of Britain's Gross National Income. This amounts to a lot of money, and in 2019 Britain's gross overseas aid totalled over £14 billion – as defined and measured by the OECD.

In the twenty-three years since the establishment of DFID, Britain came to refer to itself as a 'development superpower', in that it is one of the most active and internationally engaged government development organizations in the Western world.[18] USAID, Canada's DFAIT and CIDA, Germany's KfW and GIZ and Sweden's Sida are all notable in the same field but DFID can claim to be second only to USAID in prominence. This is not based on the sums of money different aid organizations control but rather on the effect they have on development in poorer countries and their ability to stimulate self-sufficiency and growth rather than dependence.

The real challenge for DFID has become to justify its development results in terms of British national interests, alongside its ongoing requirement to demonstrate that development aid is spent productively. A relatively high proportion of it (22 per cent) goes to international development organizations, where influence over the outputs is necessarily limited. Significant amounts work through government ministries in the developing world, or foreign national agencies where it may be impossible to prevent corruption. Priorities can be difficult to maintain and there is always an ongoing discussion about the best use of aid funds. The Independent Commission for Aid Impact does not give DFID particularly high marks for maintaining the most effective priorities.[19] Nevertheless, if DFID feels that its budget is effectively ring-fenced under law, the discussions about how it should be directed, how it should be defined as 'aid', as opposed to something else Britain would prefer to give to another country, and how it should contribute to 'global Britain' are all near the top of the political agenda.[20] Other departments in Whitehall, particularly the FCO and the MoD, try to devise ways in which money that would still count as 'aid' might be diverted to some of their projects to offset their own budgetary squeezes.

Nor is overseas aid popular with significant sections of the British public who do not engage much with internationalist arguments about its long-term benefits. Public opinion is volatile on aid questions, depending on how it interprets what is going on abroad. Britain is among only six countries that meet the 0.7 per cent of GNI target, but in 2013 had the most negative public views about it among them. Compared with other significant donor countries, the highest proportion of the British public (66 per cent) wanted to spend less on overseas aid; and the lowest proportion (only 7 per cent) wanted it increased.[21] But by 2016, in light of Europe's immigration crisis, big *Eurobarometer* surveys showed that over two-thirds of the British public was convinced of aid's foreign policy benefits – more than in most other European peoples.[22] Being a 'development superpower' is evidently not seen as a consistent virtue in the eyes of British public opinion.

There is more consistency in the third sector of Britain's diplomatic network, in the shape of the Commonwealth. It is a unique organization. The Commonwealth encompasses fifty-three states across all six continents. Only one former colonial territory (Burma) declined to join the modern Commonwealth at the time of independence, and though some members have left, been expelled and rejoined the organization over the years, it has also attracted membership from states that were never British colonial possessions.[23] The total population of the Commonwealth is 2.4 billion people, fundamentally multi-racial and multi-religious; a rainbow collection of citizens (close to 60 per cent of them under the age of thirty) living in countries rich and poor, post-industrial, industrial and agrarian. Britain is its core member, the Commonwealth Secretariat operates from London, and the British royal family has provided both the constitutional backbone and much of the popular cement that has held the modern version of it, the 'Crown Commonwealth', together for over seventy years.

The royal family appears to be fully committed to this role. And it is not necessarily politically neutral. The Commonwealth represents a fair cross section of global society. The problems of peace and security, economic development, environmental degradation, human rights and governance are all too evident in its fifty-three-nation grouping that covers more than a quarter of the states in the UN and almost a third of the global population. The 2018 Commonwealth Youth Forum – reflecting the 'Common Future' theme of the 2018 Heads of Government meeting – announced that Prince Harry, supported by his wife, Meghan Markle, Duchess of Sussex, would act as Commonwealth Youth Ambassador. This was an important symbolic commitment.[24] After that summit the Prince of Wales undertook an Official Tour to Gambia, Ghana and Nigeria in which he was keen to acknowledge the pains of history. He spoke in Accra of 'the appalling atrocity of the slave trade, and the unimaginable suffering it caused'. He was keen not to seem to dodge national responsibilities for the past but rather to use them as a bridge to a better future for a collective Commonwealth. There is no shortage of high-profile people who value the Commonwealth and want to use its potential more directly in the future.

The age-old puzzle, however, is that the evident strengths of such a diverse group is also its weakness. It may revolve around powerful historical sentiment among its members, and for smaller countries any sort of international representation is welcome, but mobilizing the Commonwealth politically is a different matter. Prime Minister Harold Wilson completely failed to create a Commonwealth initiative to end the Vietnam War in 1965. The organization was deeply troubled during the apartheid years in Southern Africa, though it played a useful role in helping manage post-apartheid politics. Britain's original entry into the EEC was seen as a blow to its Commonwealth policy and Margaret Thatcher was frankly hostile to the Commonwealth when Britain found itself out of step with the general consensus within it.[25] Commonwealth history is littered with positive reinforcement for the ideas behind it but disappointment at both Britain and the collective attitudes of the organization when confronted with significant political decisions. Commonwealth members, for example, have naturally different interests when urged to take action on climate change. And on another difficult political topic, no fewer than forty-two Commonwealth countries (among seventy-eight across the world) criminalize homosexuality while India, as a major player, actively seeks to shift Commonwealth attention away from the human rights issues towards more interstate relationships between members.[26]

Nevertheless, there are regular calls for the British political community to make much greater use of the opportunities the Commonwealth offers. The prospect of leaving the EU and re-orientating to a 'global Britain' role naturally renews this interest. The problem, however, as former Foreign Secretary William Hague pointed out, was that it is 'quite difficult to turn it into something with a united political impetus or trading purpose ... You soon come up against the limits of the political and diplomatic purposes for which you can use such a disparate group from so many continents.'[27] The reality is that what mobilizes most effectively the sympathy of Commonwealth countries for British policy stances are trade, aid and visas. Unless Britain can offer some evident benefits in these political currencies, it will always find it difficult to make it into a policy tool that directly serves its national interests. Keeping the Commonwealth together and deepening its social, sporting and governance links is easier than mobilizing it to a sharp political result. Its fans are dazzled by the size and variety of the Commonwealth. The sceptics shrug and wonder what that really means in practical terms. At best, it is conceded, the Commonwealth is a good vehicle to generate the atmospherics that Britain is a significant country in world politics – a symbol that it punches above its weight. But it does not automatically translate helpful atmospherics into a meaningful political caucus.

It also has to be admitted, however, that the Commonwealth has not been accorded great importance within Britain's foreign policy thinking since it became so deeply enmeshed in the European Union in the 1980s. Indeed, Britain's administration of Commonwealth matters came under intense scrutiny in 2017 when the Secretariat and its leadership under Baroness Scotland was heavily criticized. The high commissioners of Commonwealth countries, it was reported, had 'given up' on the leadership. The Department for International Development even went public with the view that the Secretariat was 'under-performing' and in need of 'urgent reform', threatening to withhold up to £10 million it put into the Technical Cooperation Fund.[28] The FCO and DFID seconded staff to it to underpin the arrangements for the 2018 Heads of Government meeting and to upscale its performance. Accusations rumbled on before and after the 2018 summit.

Remarkable as it is, the Commonwealth does not have a happy recent history. If Britain is to get something of real value from it – for itself and the collective entity – as and when it leaves the European Union it must, at a minimum, reform and reinvigorate the Secretariat functions. It might use an expanded and partly devolved secretariat to encourage intra-Commonwealth political dialogue, centred round some of its regionally powerful members in other continents. It might realign some of its overseas aid priorities to mesh more closely with Commonwealth priorities. Most importantly, the foreign policy establishment would have to review some of its instinctive priorities that previously focused so much on European, transatlantic and Middle East concerns – all outside the normal Commonwealth remit. The political will to mediate some of this concentration in favour of wider Commonwealth concerns is not automatic, whatever the supporters of a new 'global Britain' orientation might suppose.

Defence policy and strategic links

Defence is always regarded as a strong card in Britain's diplomatic hand. Its military forces are demonstrably capable by any international standards. In absolute numerical terms the personnel and equipment of Britain's armed forces are smaller now than at any time since the Napoleonic Wars. But though this is frequently mentioned, it is hardly a meaningful comparison. Even at low numbers, Britain has made extraordinary efforts to maintain 'full spectrum forces' – the ability to perform all major aspects of modern war fighting – which make its military, at least in functional terms, comparable with any of the great powers. That does not, however, make Britain a 'pocket superpower' because in combat, numbers really do matter, as well as an ability to sustain them. But all defence challenges are highly context specific, and British military forces can perform more effectively than most others across a wide range of plausible contexts. As important as the armed forces themselves is the fact that British government and society is better able than many other countries to support them in technological, industrial, personnel, management and political terms, to create an effective national infrastructure backing up the state's military institutions.[29]

The British military is also naturally ambitious, which is not the case in many other military establishments around the world. At the end of 2019 some 37,000 British armed forces personnel were involved in no fewer than thirty-six different operations. It is ambitious to be good at what it does. National conscription has existed in Britain for only 24 of the last 350 years, and the forces take great pride in their historical professionalism as an all-volunteer force. Their characteristic political vice is the conspiracy of optimism over what can be achieved; their characteristic operational vice is tactical 'mission creep' because they are determined to 'make a difference' when they are deployed. British military personnel are not conscripts and they certainly don't join up to have an uneventful life.

Successive governments have laboured international comparisons that with a defence budget rising to almost £40 billion by 2021, Britain remains the fifth biggest military spender in the world.[30] It is the second biggest military spender in NATO, behind only the United States, and the biggest spender among European NATO members. Against the major powers, it spends less than one tenth the level of the United States and between a fifth and a third the level of China; just over three quarters the level of Russia; and just less than India.

At least as significant as defence spending, however, are the relatively high readiness levels of British forces and the fact that they operate command headquarters big enough to go war fighting, and therefore are able to accommodate partner forces which, on their own, cannot. British forces integrate their respective military assets in the space, air, land and maritime domains to a greater degree than almost all other similar military powers (with the singular exception of Israel). They operate top of the range, world-class, weapons systems in all domains and they meld operational effectiveness with some of the most sophisticated command and control networks available to military forces. From operating an independent nuclear deterrent to UN peace-keeping forces, the British military demonstrates competence and effectiveness, albeit at historically low numbers. The forces also have plenty of relevant experience. Between 1991 and 2019 British forces were involved in twelve different combat operations, from Bosnia to Syria, quite apart from Northern Ireland operations that were winding down over these years.[31] Some 800,000 regulars served with the forces during that time – 235,000 of them in at least one of those twelve combat operations.[32]

How does all this compare in global terms? The United States remains far and away the sole *military* superpower in the world. China has almost caught up with the US and has military forces of roughly comparable effectiveness – in China and its immediate neighbourhood – but not yet with the reach to project, support and sustain them overseas at any scale. In this respect, while Britain is ranked a long way behind the United States in overall military capability it is still objectively assessed as the only other genuine 'global military power' in the world with capabilities that still exceed those of China and seven other 'regional military powers' including India, Russia, Japan and Germany.[33] This, it must be stressed, is all based on immediate and deployable forces – not on how they would fare in combat against each other – and it is certain to change soon as investments in power projection pay off for the bigger nations. Nevertheless, judged purely at a technical level, Britain's inherent military capacities at the turn of the decade remain internationally significant.

In continental Europe only France has forces that match these capabilities. Britain and France maintain military establishments of roughly the same size and shape. They are the only two nuclear weapons powers among the European allies, both are permanent members of the UN Security Council, and both have recent (though different) histories of testing operational experience within their forces. They are the only two European powers who are organically capable of deploying their own forces abroad at any scale, or of effectively leading significant multinational operations. Germany's armed forces, by contrast, are only 20 per cent bigger than Britain's but have been cut back more severely since the Cold War. Once NATO's military lynchpin, German forces atrophied to levels that shocked many specialists, though not, apparently, the German public or mainstream politicians. In 2017 it was revealed that less than one-third of Germany's major weapons systems were available for use.[34] The Bundeswehr's crippling lack of mobility had never been remedied since it first became relevant in the early 1990s; its training and readiness levels reached an historic low in 2015.[35] Some other European military forces are large but not well structured, like those of Italy or Turkey; or else quite well structured but small, like those of the Netherlands, Norway or Denmark. The forces of almost all the ex-Warsaw Pact states in Central Europe are notably small and poorly equipped.

More important even than size, however, is the collective inefficiency of most European military forces. That also prevents them from innovating.[36] Between them, the NATO allies field 178 major weapons systems of various types. The United States, with forces almost three times the size, fields around thirty major weapons systems.[37] As a *collective* entity, European forces are not remotely cost effective. It is not surprising, then, that the British defence establishment – which *is* generally cost effective – should account for 43 per cent of all Europe's military research and development spending.[38] It is not just in the troops and the heavy metal that Britain figures so largely in Europe's military persona.

This suggests two inescapable realities. Even a cursory examination of European military forces reveals how completely dependent they would be on the United States in the event of any significant continental conflict – to provide some initial mass and then reinforcement, for transport, engineering, air cover, tactical command and control, intelligence – to name only the most obvious deficiencies. Nothing the European powers are pledged to improve over the next ten years, either within NATO or through rejuvenated EU defence initiatives, will create the step change necessary to alter this simple fact. That does not rule out the Europeans using their own, improved, military forces for other appropriate operations; but it cannot change the truth that they could not defend themselves alone in a war for their own territories or for survival.

The second reality is that Britain cannot logically be excluded from any calculations of European military power. Whatever happens in the 2020s and notwithstanding the outcome of the Brexit process, Britain will remain the most significant military power in Europe. It would still be the second most significant power even if its capabilities declined sharply and were overtaken by improvements in French armed forces. No other European military establishments, not even those of Germany or Italy, will come close to those of France and Britain for some years to come.

And for these reasons Britain's military relationship with the United States remains highly relevant to European defence, despite what may be happening in the broader strategic dialogue between London and Washington. Britain is the '10 per cent ally' of the United States. As an order of magnitude, its defence budget is around a tenth of US defence spending and it gets, roughly, 10 per cent of the equivalent US military capacity for it.[39] The British military establishment works hard to keep its key assets interoperable with those of the US and to structure itself so that it can slot into US military operations at most levels, up to that of full war fighting. In a strategic sense, it intends that its status as the 10 per cent ally – a capable and dependable junior military partner – gives Britain some general political leverage in Washington, but more particularly in campaigns when allied military power is deployed. As described in Chapter 10, this assumption is neither so justified nor so confidently maintained after the last decade of Western military operations, but an ability to be the 10 per cent ally remains the default setting in British military thinking and a long-term political bet on the best way for Britain to face its security future.

In principle, the defence card in Britain's security hand may be of increasing value in the 2020s if its military forces maintain their current and planned levels of capability, irrespective of the way in which Britain departs from European Union members. The value of the card can work both ways. On the one hand, Britain has continued to invest in having global reach for its small forces. The investment in two operational aircraft carriers and the ability to deploy one of them as the core of a powerful carrier battle group – the maximum the Royal Navy could ever offer – is part of a strategic reorientation towards global projection. An enduring (single) warship presence in East Asia effectively became policy after 2015, and investments in bases around the Gulf and in air logistics for all three services made them capable of going 'East of Suez' again in a less ad hoc way than had been required for the Iraq and Afghanistan campaigns. Though China, India, Russia or France may well join the category of effective 'global military powers' fairly soon, it will still remain a rather exclusive club that can offer considerable political opportunities.

On the other hand, Britain cannot sensibly be isolated from Europe's military security equations either, whatever its own pattern of military deployments. It is planning to field a powerful, high-tech army combat division for the 2020s, honed to operate primarily in continental Europe, while the Royal Air Force builds its capability around *Typhoon* and *Lightning II* fast jets and a significant fleet of transport, logistics and command assets. Britain's traditionally solid role within European NATO can be played strongly by example rather than mere exhortation as these systems come on stream in the early 2020s. At the same time, Britain still acts as a natural military and command link between European forces and the indispensable United States.[40] Military relations between Britain and the United States, because of their essentially technical nature and the natural affinity between fellow military professionals, are somewhat shielded from political atmospherics – or at least they build in a natural time-lag before political moods turn into reality. Britain remains in a good position to influence at least the military dimensions of European security, whatever happens more broadly within the EU or through any new Paris–Berlin political axis to rejuvenate the Franco-German relationship. Defence is one of the few areas where Britain cannot be side-lined, against its will, in European circles.

There are, however, three big caveats to such a favourable picture. First, all this military capability and influence has to be scaled against the specific challenges that Russia seems determined to pose across Europe during the coming decade. As discussed in Chapter 5, Moscow has both defensive and offensive motives to pursue the course it does, but for the Western powers the strategic outcomes are largely the same: persistent Russian challenges to the prevailing order, the stability, the borders and the democratic integrity of Western and central European countries; an opportunistic approach to undermining NATO, the EU and the Western consensus wherever possible. Translating this into the military realm, European defence forces have to compete with dramatically improving Russian weapons systems in tactical nuclear forces, submarines, long range missiles, fighter/bomber aircraft, some new armoured forces and some fast, offensive air-mobile ground formations.[41] Russia's armed forces still suffer from many weaknesses, but the areas in which they show most dramatic improvements are those which can most readily hold European forces at risk, create the circumstances for political intimidation, operate quickly around NATO's neighbourhood and even inside its territorial boundaries.[42] They could even be sufficient to deter the United States from acting at all in Europe's defence – so breaking the indispensable transatlantic link, without which Europe cannot defend itself in extremis. Britain's good military example, on its own, cannot be decisive in rebalancing West European forces against Russian military threats in these sectors. And it is up against a weakening, rather than a growing, defence consensus across the twenty-nine NATO members; while autocratic Russia has shown itself willing to use its military forces decisively, and often recklessly, where it sees a strategic advantage. Britain's small, sophisticated military forces, on their own, count for little in European defence unless other partners upscale their own capabilities to ensure that – in or out of NATO – the Europeans have a credible military instrument at their disposal.

The second caveat is that Britain's military strength faces the prospect of becoming more apparent than real under a series of mutually reinforcing pressures, generally characterized as 'overstretch', 'sustainability' and 'credibility'. Overstretch refers to the tendency to work the unprecedently small force structure so relentlessly hard that certain key elements of it simply break. The RAF possessed too few airborne control aircraft to fly every day during the Libya operation in 2011; British warships were unable to go to sea (almost the whole frigate and destroyer fleet at one point in 2017) through shortages of specialist crew members; normal peacetime illness and injuries reduced the army's deployable manpower below acceptable levels in 2018, and so on. Overstretch creates key points of failure that can undermine a whole capability. Building on overstretch, a sustainability crisis is created by the lack of back-up resources. The danger is that Britain's military prowess becomes all shop window and no stock; a force structure that cannot be sustained beyond its first use, cannot tolerate attrition and losses, cannot be kept at fighting tempo for more than a few months. Ground forces, ships and aircraft have to be rotated in and out of combat zones unless they are simply to be sacrificed. For every army battalion on the front line, there normally have to be five *in that specialism* of the army as a whole, to allow for rest and recuperation, re-equipment and normal training, then specialist training for the next deployment to the combat zone. Ships and aircraft have to be repaired and refitted, as do their crews and the back-up support staff on whom they rely. All of the armed services can 'run hot' for some years on operations, but small forces find themselves increasingly hollowed out by lack of sustainability. For some observers, this occurs because the British defence establishment always over-commits itself to forces it knows it cannot really afford; it just cannot help itself. For others, it arises because governments successively 'salami slice' the real value of defence budgets because the careers of politicians are mainly determined by what is in the defence shop window. Either way, British military forces face both an overstretch and a sustainability challenge in the coming decade.

They also face a challenge of credibility. After Iraq and Afghanistan, after the messy operations in Libya, and against IS in Iraq and Syria, the armed forces have to demonstrate to the British public, and to the world, that they are still natural winners. In the twelve combat operations between 1991 and 2019, British forces were often highly successful and they were certainly never defeated. But too often their tactical success was not translated into political or strategic success. There were some big gaps in that fundamental link between the application of force and the political outcomes that create strategic victory.[43] British military forces have to be used carefully in the years to come. They can do a great deal of good in non-combat roles, acting as their own version of British diplomacy and overseas aid. But where they are used for combat, or to threaten combat, their mission has to be linked clearly to achievable political outcomes. Military credibility is like paper money; if it is believed, it has real value. When British forces undertake ceremonial roles at home, they appear magnificent – a golden thread to a powerful past. But if they are not thought to be among the best in the world, and natural winners, they immediately become chocolate soldiers, acting a part for the benefit of tourists.

A third important caveat concerns the new technologies of warfare, some of which are on the verge of maturity and could render much that Britain invested in world-class military equipment from 2010 either ineffective or simply irrelevant. Robotics are on the verge of major breakthroughs in Western civilian societies. Military drones are merely the first ripples of a robotic revolution that will also infuse all defence technology. So too, with the next iteration of computing power that releases revolutionary artificial intelligence. Precise information that aggregates and interprets enormous volumes of detail, and makes it available in real time, promises new levels of military effectiveness. And the ability to find niche vulnerabilities in a targeted society, or the mining and manipulation of its social media may have effects on another country that make military action superfluous. All these possibilities are well appreciated by British defence planners and a certain amount of money – albeit the small change of the total defence budget – is devoted to either exploiting them or else trying to insulate the British military and wider society from their worst effects.[44]

Other breakthrough technologies, however, for which no amount of money from the defence budget will be adequate, hover around the future of defence and war fighting. Biotechnology and genetic engineering, for example, can fundamentally affect agriculture, manufacturing production and people. The negative transformations made possible through an introduction of harmful pathogens into a society goes far beyond any potential of existing, or future, chemical warfare. Nanotechnologies can create miniaturized systems that can be harmful in themselves or else inserted into something else to make them harmful, or perhaps to sabotage them. New materials science, coupled with additive manufacturing in 3D printing technologies, might provide for the cyber transfer of weapons systems and components without any visible manufacture or transport until they were suddenly 'created'. Above all, quantum computing, with sub-atomic particles as processors, already exists in prototype form. If quantum computing genuinely arrives over the coming decade, it will knock big holes in even the best supercomputers presently running. It will be capable of penetrating and operating intensively inside any or all of society's digital systems that conventional military forces were originally designed to protect. British military planners are well aware of these possibilities, though they are not sure what they can do about them.[45] They appreciate, however, that a number of big disruptive technologies are on the edge of breakthroughs, and by most assessments the conventional 'in about thirty years' expectations are now characteristically 'in about a decade'.[46]

No one knows whether, or quite how, such technologies could be weaponized. But they are all close, and some aspects of these technologies could certainly work as weapons. The only certainty is that if they *are* weaponized in any form, it will not be by us, even if Britain is up to date with the science behind them. This will be a game that only great powers – China, the United States and possibly Russia in some sectors – will be able to play. In common with all European second rank powers, Britain may be abruptly confronted with vulnerabilities it can do little or nothing to counter. In that case, European defence questions would revert to 1945 perspectives – in effect, back to square one.

Intelligence: Secrecy among Allies

Britain's intelligence capabilities are regarded as one of the jewels in its security crown. It is the only European power that operates an intelligence arm that is genuinely global in scope. In this respect, it is comparable in effect, if not in size, with United States, Chinese and Russian intelligence operations. Its intelligence agencies – principally, MI6, MI5, GCHQ and Defence Intelligence – constitute an intelligence arm that is 'fearsome to Britain's many enemies, but not much feared by its own citizens'.[47] That is a happy and efficient balance that few other countries enjoy. Between them the agencies handle different aspects of intelligence, as outlined in Chapter 9, covering internal, external, military and cyber fields of operation, though there is increasing overlap in their work.[48] MI6, MI5 and GCHQ are free-standing organizations. The Defence Intelligence organization collates the intelligence products arising from the specialist intelligence units within the armed services, feeding them into the system and in turn sending synthesized assessments back to armed force operations. All intelligence, by its very nature, is fragmentary and diffused. Raw intelligence material is meaningless until it is interpreted and in the interpretation process there is endless scope for inter-agency competition. Britain, however, is noted among its partners for the way in which strategic intelligence is aggregated to a core intelligence assessment through the Cabinet's Joint Intelligence Committee and latterly also through the machinery of the National Security Council. The creation of the NSC in 2010 gave a seat to all the intelligence agencies along with the military and key government departments, presided over, normally weekly, by the prime minister. This integrating system has come to look very like that of Winston Churchill's war cabinet in the 1940s – the British heyday of good intelligence, effectively used. British intelligence assessments are not always right and have been criticized for being blinkered on some of the tectonic shifts in geopolitics.[49] But they are good at detail and never incoherent.

The effectiveness of British intelligence is heavily dependent on its relationship with the United States, whose own agencies were established under the wing of British intelligence operations in the 1940s and quickly came to dwarf them in size and resources. The transatlantic link is organically close in the relationship between GCHQ in Cheltenham and the National Security Agency at Fort Meade in Maryland, in their exchange of information and joint programmes for accessing it. Operating together, the NSA and GCHQ are, by some distance, the best intelligence data hub in the world. MI5 is less naturally orientated towards its US equivalents, since it works closely with policing agencies and depends more on connections throughout continental Europe. Defence Intelligence and MI6, however, have strong working relationships with their US counterparts in many international regions. In the immediate shock of the 9/11 attacks when US airspace was closed to all civilian traffic, the only foreign aircraft allowed into US territory that night was the one carrying British intelligence chiefs to Washington to share their assessments in meetings on 12 September of what had happened.[50]

In the aftermath of the Cold War it seemed that intelligence agencies might have a narrower remit, but the explosion of new security threats to Western countries created the opposite effect. In 1988 MI6 was tasked to operate against international crime that could be considered a security threat. In 1995 MI5 was also tasked to take it on. And the arrival of jihadist international terror in the late 1990s transformed the immediate security agenda for all four principal agencies.

Expenditure on the main agencies increased. In 1995 intelligence spending was just on £900 million when the defence budget was £24 billion – an equivalent of 3.75 per cent. In 2017 the 'single intelligence account' covering the intelligence agencies was £2.2 billion – some 6.1 per cent of the equivalent defence budget of £36 billion.[51] The personnel of the agencies also increased, though rapid upscaling is always difficult for such specialized services. MI5 moved from employing under 3000 people at the beginning of the century, to some 4000 in 2019 – 300 or so seconded from other agencies and departments in Whitehall. In 2010 it also re-opened big operations in Belfast to take over intelligence responsibilities from the Police Service of Northern Ireland.[52] MI6 moved from fewer than 2,500 employees before 2015 to a target of 3,500 in 2020. GCHQ, by far the biggest of the agencies, employed just over 5,000 people in 2010 but is believed now to have over 10,000 employees; around 6,000 in Cheltenham and some 4,000 in other regional centres including Manchester, Harrogate, Scarborough and Bude, and in related organizations such as the NCSC.[53] Since the Cold War, Defence Intelligence has been both run down and then built back up in light of events, and employs a mixture of around 4000 civilian and military personnel at its RAF Wyton base in Cambridgeshire – the biggest concentration of intelligence *analysis* assets in the British system.

These numbers make the British intelligence services bigger and more able than most others in the democratic world, apart from the United States, but considerably smaller than the massive intelligence services run by the autocrats of Russia, China, North Korea or even Iran.[54] Russia is believed to have at least 680,000 performing the roles that Britain's grand total of 21,500 perform. (It may even be 850,000 depending on the shifting role that Russia's military intelligence arm – the GRU – performs.) Iran is believed to have 30,000 doing what MI6's 3,500 do. Chinese numbers, apart from the Ministry of State Security's 100,000 (in the 'MI6 role') are very opaque since so many personnel of the People's Liberation Army and the Chinese Communist Party are used in equivalent roles. On the other hand, the autocrats use their inflated intelligence services principally to enforce conformity on their own populations, which often makes them less effective in the international sphere.

The very existence of Britain's intelligence agencies were state secrets – though almost comically, the worst kept secrets in London – until legislation was introduced in 1989 in the case of MI5, and 1994 for MI6 and GCHQ, to govern their operations more clearly. Avowing, at last, the existence and the work of the intelligence agencies had the effect of putting them on a proper statutory basis so that their operations are covered by a body of law and a series of oversight and accountability mechanisms. These arrangements are constantly, and rightly, challenged by civil society groups and it is fair to say that the laws and oversight arrangements have been continuously updated (some would say nudged by exposure – 'regulation by revelation'[55]) to ensure that British political and security chiefs can honestly claim that the agencies act 'legally', 'proportionately' and only of 'necessity'.[56] It is also a recognition that in the modern era, the agencies need to mobilize the generally high levels of public support for what they do. When operating against serious crime and terrorism, public support and cooperation is vital to success. All the security agencies try to make the best use of public sympathy for their role (something many agencies in partner countries could not rely upon) as they operate to forestall harm as much as they investigate it after it happens.

The question arises as to how robust are these evident advantages embodied in Britain's intelligence community, and how they might best be mobilized against the security issues of the 2020s. In essence those questions will be answered by the ability of British intelligence to address a number of existing and approaching challenges.

The most obvious arises from what the MI6 chief expressed quite starkly in 2016: 'The information revolution fundamentally changes our operating environment', and by 2021, he said, 'there will be two sorts of intelligence services – those that understand this fact and have prospered, and those that don't and haven't'.[57] In the digitally globalized world this sounds like a truism, but it has critical implications for all intelligence services. Intelligence chiefs admit that perhaps 95 per cent of the information they need to collect and interpret is now 'open source intelligence', available for anyone with the right skills to collect it, even excluding what runs on the 'dark net'.[58] The Bellingcat group, for example, who have identified Russian GRU agents and Mexican drug lords by name and passport numbers, have shown how much intelligence can be derived, as they say, 'from open source and social media investigation', and how their skills can be learnt by others.[59] The Wikileaks organization, on the other hand, has become famous for releasing tranches of official documents, obtained secretly or illegally, that embarrass many governments. It has, however, yet to release any documents that embarrass Russia, China, or many of the Central Asian dictatorships. Even what is genuinely 'secret' only becomes gold dust when the turn of events makes it relevant. A great deal of modern intelligence work, therefore, lies in the open source arena. Intelligence success depends on the ability of a system to aggregate mountains of data, interrogate it for the tiny proportions that are relevant and then, crucially, *interpret* those vital snippets in the context of other intelligence inputs. However powerful the information algorithms might be, interpretation will remain an intelligence art, probably of appreciating value as the amount of collectable information – the haystack from which relevant needles must be extracted – grows exponentially. Nevertheless, the agencies no longer own most of the best data, since by clicking 'terms and conditions' that they never read, citizens willingly give much more confidential data to their retailers, service providers, banks and newsfeeds than the intelligence services could ever legally collect – even on the tiny proportion of the population in whom they are genuinely interested.

Sophisticated data analytics, of the sort that GCHQ provides to the rest of the security community, is therefore a key advantage in meeting this challenge. But it also means that the intelligence services have to work closely alongside private sector technology companies who are leading the charge towards data management and the practical applications of AI. The agencies embody great personnel skills in data analytics but they simply do not have the concentrations of expertise, or the time, to replicate the innovation and entrepreneurship of 'the M4 corridor', the 'Cambridge – Milton Keynes – Oxford corridor' or for that matter, 'Silicon Valley'. In the United States, both the NSA and Google ran into real trouble when it became clear they had been working so closely together since 2003, and how much 'the agencies craved the lawlessness that a firm such as Google enjoyed' so that the US government came 'to rely on private enterprise to collect and generate information for it'.[60] It was a sobering lesson in how difficult it is for intelligence organizations to remain abreast of the technology curve, let alone ahead of it. Intelligence organizations have to operate on different protocols compared to other information-based concerns, including the criminal ones. For all their public bravado, most international terrorist groups are not, so far, quite up with the information technology curve; but most international criminal organizations and state-sponsored subversion groups, who are not at all noisy, certainly are.[61] The Snowden revelations of 2013 into the ways US and British intelligence accessed and processed their information did not, in fact, undermine British intelligence workings. But they jolted them through complicity with US intelligence practices that were deemed clearly illegal in the United States and stimulated a degree of public cynicism about the encroachments of the 'surveillance state' into everyone's daily lives.[62] In Britain a 'big brother state' does not, and could not, exist in present circumstances, but recent years have seen a growth of fatalism in the public's belief that it soon will.[63] British intelligence agencies have to retain public trust in their operations even as the private sector leads both on information technology innovation and the raw collection of unprecedented amounts of personal data, inside Britain and across the wider world.

A further challenge is that the sophistication of data management offers the prospects of much greater 'actionable intelligence' where information is collected and analysed in real time, or very close to it, so providing the opportunity – or maybe just the temptation – to act on it immediately. When good intelligence has pinpointed the immediate location of known British terrorists in the Middle East, drone strikes have, controversially, been used to kill them outside a designated British operational zone – raising the spectre of extrajudicial assassination.[64] Thanks to modern data analytics, a great deal of modern intelligence can be regarded as immediately 'actionable' in one way or another. Successful intelligence organizations for the near future will be those that are well integrated with other state instruments so as to take full advantage of actionable intelligence, at home and abroad, but also able to do so without undermining their own objectives or public support for their work.

Ultimately, the effectiveness and reputation of British intelligence services will rest on the continuance of the close relationship with the United States. The Five Eyes intelligence arrangements, outlined in Chapter 9, remain central to the relationship. So, too, do a series of geographical factors – that the south west tip of Britain is the landfall for undersea Atlantic cable traffic; that more High North cable traffic flows near to northern Scottish isles; that Britain has strong bases in the Gulf, another hub of undersea cable traffic between Europe, Africa and Asia; and that it has permanent intelligence hub facilities in Cyprus, Gibraltar and the Indian Ocean.[65] Not least, Britain itself is a good base for some US satellite download stations and listening posts, and in the right geographical zone for phased array early warning radars to protect the US homeland.[66] Australia has similar geographical advantages for US intelligence operations – another reason why the Five Eyes arrangements are impossible to replicate for any other countries.

After the end of the Cold War US agencies concentrated heavily on signals intelligence (SIGINT) – running down many of their personnel-based networks in target countries. Britain maintained many of its human intelligence (HUMINT) assets around the world, however, and was well placed to offer useful HUMINT material to the United States when it suddenly became vital after the 9/11 attacks. But the United States always eventually makes good on its deficiencies, and though Britain can still claim to specialize in good HUMINT, the essence of the US–British relationship in future will really revolve around information, data analytics and, in particular, that GCHQ and the NSA remain 'joined at the hip'.[67] The relationship may also be bolstered, paradoxically, by the return of great power competition in world politics. Western intelligence agencies put a great deal of effort into counterterrorist work from the beginning of this century, but their more traditional state-on-state espionage agenda was not reduced – nor was the attention of Russian or Iranian agents operating in Britain or the United States reduced from previous levels. But China is now in the traditional state-on-state espionage game in a very big way, and Russian espionage against the West has stepped up a gear in the last decade as well as outsourcing many of its traditional functions to sub-state groups. There has been a return to 'Moscow rules' though with new state – and non-state – players. In the past, British and US intelligence insiders would privately pride themselves on their ability to 'walk through' large swathes of Russian and Chinese security systems. But both countries noticeably tightened up their security around 2014 and now present formidable cyber defences.[68] Analysts have warned that Western intelligence is in danger of devoting too much attention to international terrorism and leaving itself under-resourced to handle more old-fashioned challenges.[69] As the spectrum of threats to all Western intelligence agencies grows, the United States may be expected to value its most reliable relationships more highly.

In addition, however, Britain is in a good position to use intelligence assets to strengthen new security partnerships it may aim to make as part of a more 'global Britain' strategy with countries such as Japan or India. The trick is not to create more intelligence structures with new partners, but rather to put more British effort into obtaining useful intelligence that new partners find valuable – something that can be traded and shared. This might be in both SIGINT and HUMINT terms, but HUMINT, in particular, takes years before initial investments normally pay off. At least for the next decade, good intelligence on China is likely to be the most valuable and tradeable currency in the intelligence world. British agencies would have to avoid treading on US toes if they trade in this way, but that should be manageable.

Britain will need all these different attributes if it is to act with agility and effectiveness in security matters over the years to come. Intelligence is the most effective force multiplier, whatever sort of force is under consideration: diplomatic, economic or military. To a small country with a global orientation, it is indispensable and will have to work to its peak in a decade of great power competition that will not naturally favour the 'second rankers'. There is also the prospect that Britain could further leverage its good intelligence reputation to offer more training, mentoring and technical cooperation with other countries where there would be longer-term advantages. MI6 is believed to have working relationships at different levels with around sixty other intelligence organizations around the world – some more savoury than others. It would be a good investment in the rules-based international order to work proactively to convince certain intelligence partners that properly structured, well-connected, and accountable intelligence organizations have been overwhelmingly the more effective in recent history.

Security as risk management

The range of security concerns that impact most strongly within Britain were outlined in Chapter 6. They cover the most diverse of challenges and are conventionally referred to by policy analysts as the 'security' challenges, mainly to distinguish them from 'defence' challenges primarily involving the military. But it has to be understood very much as a spectrum. Intelligence services, for example, serve foreign policy, defence and internal security agendas; one of the roles of the military is to assist the civil power in whatever security needs require it; and the private sector at the forefront of, say, cyber security, certainly assist the military at an international level. The key question, in fact, is not whose policy domain internal security concerns fall under, but rather how much the government can do about any of it. How far do governmental capabilities extend in trying to protect a £2 trillion, 80 per cent service economy of 67 million people that prides itself on being open for business, open to the world, and still in the first rank of technological innovation? The answer defies any unambiguous judgement, since it is matter of risk management. Just as all modern societies live with a significant degree of economic risk that globalization can trigger a collapse as much as great prosperity, or leave them particularly open to health pandemics from abroad, and so on, internal security in a vibrant society is a matter of weighing risks against openness. The remit of a democratic government only extends so far.

As we indicated in Chapter 6, counterterrorism is one of the success stories. The international terrorist threat to Britain is higher than for many other countries and will remain so for some years yet. Britain, however, is widely regarded as a world leader in combating terrorism insofar as it affects domestic society. Whitehall, police, intelligence services and the legal framework are well coordinated. This was not the case in the 1990s but the effectiveness of the transformation has been remarkable. There are aspects of the CONTEST counterterrorism policy that still attract criticism, not least its de-radicalization initiatives. And at least two of the 2017 attacks reflected intelligence failures, in that there were plenty of available dots that were simply not joined up. But the central organization of counterterrorism tightens up every time there is a breach – it has never slipped backwards or simply relaxed even if the general public has. From the top down, counterterrorism in Britain works well. More impressive still is the fact that counterterror awareness has been well ingrained into the public utilities, transport systems, architects, town planners and builders. Through tangible means (like landscaped barriers) and intangible means (like well-exercised procedures) Britain has made itself more resilient against terror attack than any of its partners. Both passive and proactive counterterrorism surrounds the daily lives of most Britons in ways they either don't realize or have stopped thinking about. Nothing can prevent a terrorist incident, of course, even in the most authoritarian societies, and there will doubtless be more. But Britain has proved itself second to none in containing incidents – usually within minutes – neutralizing the danger and getting all the forensics to bring perpetrators to justice if they are still alive.[70]

The same is becoming more true in dealing with serious international crime. At the Whitehall level there are clear strategies and good procedures to bring together all the important players – particularly the National Crime Agency, most of the intelligence agencies, the Home Office, Bank of England, the Inland Revenue, Metropolitan Police and other constabularies as appropriate – to tackle the growing phenomenon whereby (apart from petty criminality) almost all crime is in some respect, international. But international criminal behaviour is a great deal broader than terrorist behaviour, and unlike terrorism or its precursors, the public does not necessarily know it when they see it. Britain's forty-eight police forces are very different in size and shape and not well suited to confront the sheer agility of criminal operations.[71] When drug markets in cities become saturated, or inner-city narcotics policing improves, the criminal 'county lines' open up which pits international narcotics operations against small, rural forces.[72] When better anti-theft technology makes organized car crime more difficult, international gangs switch to people trafficking; as cash becomes more difficult to steal, the gangs switch to cybercrime or child sexual exploitation and so on. Creating a coherent Whitehall response to the agility of criminality is one thing. It is quite another to find the right balance between an FBI-style force with high numbers that would have authority across the country, and the regionalism of British policing that links it so intimately to its own localities.

The same is broadly true in protecting Britain's critical national infrastructure, or in promoting acceptable levels of cyber security. Even in the case of CNI, the government's arm only stretches so far. If it is true that 80 per cent of Britain's CNI resides in the private sector, even the official regulatory bodies cannot ensure that its elements are really safe from systemic breakdown, or from criminal or terrorist attack.[73] This truth is writ large in the case of cyber security in Britain. The first duty of government in this respect is to ensure that its defence-related cyber systems – some of them of the utmost importance – are as safe as they can be. So far, this has generally been achieved and defence, intelligence and key national security cyber systems are constantly updated with some of the best technology available. For an economy that is otherwise so completely cyber-dependent; however, these protections are a tiny sliver of the whole organism to be protected. And aside from the national security sectors, it is impossible to ignore the record of successive British governments in introducing central IT systems which has been quite abysmal.[74] In addition, as we described earlier, the most serious cyber threats to Britain are now state based or else state sponsored; they are created by professionals.

Britain's de facto answer to this range of societal vulnerabilities, in effect, both its strengths and its intrinsic weaknesses, can be summed up in the notion of 'modern deterrence'.[75] All deterrence thinking is based on an acceptance of one's own vulnerability. As a modern, open society Britain is clearly vulnerable to terrorism, international crime, large-scale societal disruption, cyberattacks or whatever. One form of deterrence thinking is 'deterrence by denial'. It is based on the idea that those who would harm Britain can be deterred because it is too difficult to do – or else easier to try against a different country or another group. One reason governments don't talk much about this is because it is intrinsically competitive among allies and friends. If London's financial centre is more secure than its international competitors against terrorism or massive scams, then terrorists and criminal groups may go for the more vulnerable rather than the more valuable. Even small defences might be quite effective, on this logic, if everyone else's defences are even smaller. A more obvious form of deterrence is understood as 'deterrence by retaliation' – something the British government has deliberately extended from its nuclear and conventional defence forces directly to the cyber domain. It has made it clear that in the event of deliberate cyberattack by states or criminal groups, Britain would be prepared to use its own cyber power to cause some real damage to the perpetrators. In a growing, high-tech economy, and one operating in the approaching 'Asian Century', this might be a more potent threat than it first appears. As the Asian tiger economies become more sophisticated, they also become more vulnerable. Western countries have suffered for years though Chinese cyber espionage that attempts to steal very valuable intellectual property. But in recent years Chinese companies have developed valuable intellectual property of their own that would be of great interest to Western governments if they decided to retaliate by hacking into it themselves.

Vulnerability is inevitable in all societies and in a condition of economic globalization it appears, to many observers, to be intense. But it does not have to be debilitating. Britain has many capabilities under direct governmental control both to protect and project itself – from its diplomatic networks, its defence and intelligence forces, policing capacities and the power of government to influence and inform the wider economy and society. There is a lot it can do, and at least from the heights of Whitehall, it strategizes and coordinates better than most of its international partners.

The perennial failure of British government, except in the singularly specific case of terrorist threats, is to be clear (some would say 'just honest') with the public about the limits of its effective, centralized powers. Britain's neoliberal economic consensus goes back to the Thatcher era and stresses how restricted is the government's real ability to influence the markets. It is broadly a 'hands-off' economic approach except where absolutely necessary, and this is interpreted as a positive political virtue. Yet in the wider defence and security sphere, British governments claim and constantly imply they have capabilities far in excess of the reality. Government has real power over intelligence, diplomacy and defence. As it turns the decade, Britain's intelligence sphere is strong, diplomacy is troubled and under-performing and defence is increasingly brittle. But governments talk up these capabilities as if there was little to worry about. They also talk up the coordinating skills of Whitehall in the broader security picture without acknowledging how limited Whitehall's powers are outside the close realms of central government. In confronting Britain's security future, governments have sought to reassure an increasingly sceptical public that they are living in a very safe country, rather than to habituate the public more clearly to the natural hazards of being an open, globalized society in a world in which it is getting tougher, rather than easier, to prosper and stay safe. So much of Britain's potential to face its security future is bound up with its societal strengths and weaknesses. Most of these the government can do very little to direct. But there are some key elements in the societal picture that are capable at least of being emphasized and perhaps mobilized through acts of political will, and we will discuss these in Chapter 12.

Chapter 12

Societal capabilities – economics, finance and soft power

As in all liberal democracies, British society is bigger and broader than anything the government can adequately represent. Britain will be whatever it will be in the coming decade chiefly because of its societal strengths and weaknesses rather than anything the government does. As we have argued in previous chapters, British society is deeply rooted and its economy is powerfully globalized and full of potential. But under those forces of globalization it is also troubled and in a phase of social, economic and political transition as the rapidity of change and the pushback against 'globalization 2.0' takes tangible effect. It is impossible to say how this will pan out in the long run for British society. The more immediate questions concern how Britain's broad, societal attributes play into its security equations for the near-term future.

Even a cursory review of Britain's societal attributes reveals great inner strength and some enduring qualities. Recognizing them and somehow mobilizing them, however – making them count in international political terms – is a different matter.[1] Of course, Britain's societal strengths and weaknesses are critical to its overall economic health, in its ability to grow, innovate, trade, attract international investment and sell its all-important services abroad. And Britain's economic health has an obvious and direct bearing on the government's ability to devote resources to the security policies it can control directly, like defence, intelligence, policing or the diplomatic network.

In a less tangible way, but no less directly, societal attributes also matter in Britain's ability to influence the international environment in its favour, say, to bolster the relevance abroad of a rules-based international order, or to be believed when it calls out Russian assassination squads or Chinese cyberattacks. The international image of a country most certainly provides a general background for effective diplomacy, but it may also constitute an important diplomatic asset at key moments – where it affects issues in those small margins of others' decisions that determine success or failure. An international reputation for business-like honesty, tolerant pragmatism or for fashionable innovation can be a real diplomatic asset at critical points in the decision cycles of other groups and governments. Just as important, societal factors are critical to the collective commitment of the British public to its own security – its willingness to pay for defence, its resilience under terrorist campaigns or cyber-disruption, and the confidence and optimism with which Britons face their future.

Societal attributes – their perceived strengths and weaknesses – are slippery concepts, however, much given to cartoon caricatures and polemical journalism, but they cannot be wished away and they are politically important. In this, we see the essence of any government's task in brigading the most important of those attributes in the service of national security. In the real world there are always embarrassing gaps between image and reality. In the name of international legality Britain protests loudly about foreign political and business corruption, but under the guise of pragmatism it has been very slow to enact 'unexplained wealth orders' against international tycoons who appear to shelter a great deal of illegal money in London. The country's strategic and economic relationship with Saudi Arabia always seems to take precedence over that country's sometimes egregious abuse of human rights and civil liberties. Britain has one of the strictest codes against the use of torture, but has been judged complicit in other states' use of it in counterterror operations. It has a similarly strong code of conduct on international arms sales, but seems prepared to interpret it very liberally, on occasion. Its background role in the war in Yemen, via allies in the Gulf, is hard for government ministers to defend convincingly, and so on. Examples are legion, and where British governments protest their international virtues too loudly, they are frequently left trying to defend the indefensible when a particular story makes Britain, and its government, appear hypocritical. Some revelations are trivial but damaging; others are genuinely serious and have lasting diplomatic consequences.

In response, governments rely on the deep-seated and longer-lasting images created by social institutions and the ingrained trends in societal behaviour to get them off some of the contradictory hooks on which they impale themselves. All governments zigzag under the pressure of events but they hope that the rest of the world, and their own citizens, will believe in an underlying trend – a deeper consistency – that expresses more powerfully the national values they would prefer to project. In this respect, one of the oft-neglected tasks of government is to nurture among key institutions in the wider society a brand image of the country that is credible and meaningful to others. Though governments cannot dictate how their biggest companies, business elites or tourists will behave abroad, they can help to create a 'British brand' among certain organizations and professions to underpin a stronger and more consistent image than immediate policy may be able to support. Crude versions of branding have been tried before. During the Blair years the 'cool Britannia' slogan was prevalent, though the concept was not invented by the government. It was coined by the American journalist Stryker McGuire in 1996, but the government willingly accepted it as a good image of what it wanted to represent.[2] It was, in effect, an updating of the 'swinging sixties London' tag that Labour governments had co-opted to boost export earnings during persistent balance of payments crises. But 'Cool Britannia' attracted a certain amount of ridicule and was declared dead during the economic crisis at the end of the Blair premiership.[3] David Cameron's articulation of a 'big society' approach to Britain's future was too vague and undermined by the austerity caused by the crisis.[4] If anything, Britain's image of itself and to others as a lively and useful country has been replaced only by a return to the 'post-imperial malaise' that the rest of the world now perceives in the Brexit decision. It is not a happy image.[5]

Successful branding must go beyond mere slogans. To be effective, brands must be built over time and express some realities that are unambiguously true; they must be ideas, images and words that sharpen up and give practical expression to what others instinctively, or perhaps only incoherently, feel. In facing the global challenges of the 2020s, therefore, the government could seek to build more proactively on the innate international branding that some of Britain's own institutions have long embodied. There are a number of notable strengths among them that have been many years in the making; certainly, something authentic and positive to work with that would take the image beyond a 'global Britain' slogan that has remained vacuous since the Brexit decision was taken.

The economy, city and society

The world's images of Britain's society and economy and the degree to which they can be leveraged to help influence the international environment are a matter of some uncertainty until it becomes clearer how Brexit might affect Britain during the 2020s. What might be regarded as even the 'immediate impacts' of the Brexit odyssey on British society and economy are not likely to be clear for a decade.

Viewed across the board, Britain's economic future will remain structurally ambiguous in any event. Britain is still likely to be the fifth or sixth biggest economy in the world. With a significant population it is still a big country. Britain's population – less than 1 per cent of the global total – performs well above that proportion in terms of its own wealth, trade, science, education, culture, health, defence, living standards and overall global influence. It remains a country where significant numbers of people from all over the rich and poor world would like to live, and there are a surprisingly small number of countries – maybe 40 out of 200 – of whom that can be said. As British ministers repeatedly pointed out in the Brexit context, the British economy is strong, its full potential is still not yet engaged and it operates within a robust and innovative society. Its labour market is 'flexible', its economy is 'low regulation' and its tax system is designed to 'incentivise'. Its imperial history and multicultural society give it 'links to almost every other nation on earth' – through a series of diasporas that also provide effective inside tracks for trade and investment into new markets.[6] It was one of the first genuinely globalized economies in the world and it rode the initial wave of globalization with evident success.

But if the economy is strong in these respects it is also brittle in others, showing poor comparative performances in production, investment, trade and wage growth.[7] While its main competitors such as the United States, France or Germany have grown at over 2 per cent per annum, Britain will be fortunate to hold onto a 1.6 per cent annual growth in 2020. Its levels of investment are around 5 per cent lower than the OECD average. Productivity was growing at a steady 2 per cent annually before the economic crisis, but more than a decade later had failed to recover. Among the OECD, only Italy's productivity levels were worse.[8] These are not trivial or marginal differences. Britain may have the eighth most flexible workforce according to the World Economic Forum but wages declined in real terms by over 2 per cent while they grew in other OECD states by an average of more than 6 per cent. Real wage growth in Britain increased during 2018–19 but still remained below pre-crisis levels. Almost one in six British workers is self-employed and on average earns less than twenty years ago. A million are on zero-hour contracts. Compared to 1983, a thirty-year-old Briton is worth 20 per cent less; a sixty-year-old is worth twice as much.[9] Britain enjoys close to full employment but still within a low-productivity, 'low pay, insecure labour market'.[10] Its persistent trade deficit with the rest of the world is judged to make the country 'vulnerable to external shocks'.[11]

The services sector, however, accounting close to an astonishing 80 per cent of Britain's GDP, is still 'the real powerhouse of the economy' and 'one of the few parts … to have surpassed its pre-recession peak'.[12] If Britain has an international economic image, it is surely as a service provider and none more so than in its London-centric financial sector.

The city of London is a tangible centrepiece of the British financial brand and a crucial part of its modern economy. The core of 'the City' is built around the banks, the commercial (retail) banks and the investment (the old 'merchant') banks; the investment institutions, such as the pension funds and life insurance companies; and then the various 'exchanges', primarily the London Stock Exchange. These three components actually sit at the centre of a much bigger financial industry, not all of it in London. Nevertheless, the core is extensive and overlapping and undoubtedly remains extremely strong.[13]

The banking and investment core of the City is represented by its sheer concentration of domestic and overseas organizations. Some 250 foreign banks or branches are located in the City, alongside the six or seven significantly large British banks, making this easily the biggest banking centre in Europe and the fourth biggest in the world.[14] More than twice as many dollars are traded in Britain as in the United States; and more than twice as many Euros are traded as in the Eurozone. London accounts for over 33 per cent of the total global turnover in all foreign exchange trading. The third element of the core City is the stock exchange and the international trading that it facilitates. Some 428 foreign companies were listed on the London Stock Exchange in 2018. That represented one in eight of all foreign company listings, sitting alongside listed British companies. Only the globally focused New York Stock Exchange had more; or else the historic Vienna stock exchange, that deals largely with companies in East and South East Europe.[15] London is therefore a major centre of the global equities market – share trading – accounting for almost 3 per cent by value of all global equity trading. And it trades among the biggest companies. The total capitalization of London's own equity market is equivalent to 170 per cent of Britain's own GDP, one of the highest ratios in the rich G7 nations, and worth close on £350 trillion in total market value. Sitting naturally alongside its equity trading is London's investment fund management industry, where it shares the global stage only with the United States and Japan. The whole City was revived in the 1960s as US authorities became restrictive and British authorities more relaxed. The liberalization of services was a key change and by the 1990s London had become one of the three great financial trading centres alongside New York and Tokyo.[16] It had also become a natural home to illicit funds that are now calculated to be worth around £90 billion a year, which both helped and embarrassed British governments who always claimed to take a strong line on such matters.[17]

One of the reasons why this core is so robust, however, and why it will not easily be captured by predatory rivals as Britain leaves the European Union, is because it sits atop a pyramid of other related sectors that all figure strongly in their international performance. Britain's legal services sector is the largest in Europe and the second largest globally. Its insurance sector is the biggest in Europe and the fourth biggest in the world. Its domestic and international accountancy industry is worth £21.1 billion in services.[18] The net export value of the British accountancy industry in 2010 was £600 million. It had risen to £2.6 billion by 2017, something of a vote of confidence when the global economic recession put so many companies into liquidation.

For all these reasons, London is able to lead in the development of new and specialist financial services. It has dominated for years in maritime finance and insurance and has more recently led the field in Islamic and 'Green' finance. And financing new technology enterprises – FinTech – rapidly became a major growth area. In 2018 London was leading the United States in attracting investment into FinTech companies. Taken as a whole, Britain's financial industry and its related professional services had a trading surplus with the rest of the world of £83 billion in 2018. The industry's trade within EU countries accounted for 44 per cent of that surplus; and another 19 per cent of it was with the United States.

Not least, the power of the City and the wider financial services industry is backed up by other less tangible, but important, British soft power assets. The legal order of the UK – in particular, English commercial law – is widely respected and trusted internationally as the basis for secure, and enforceable, contracts. The existence of London as a global air transport hub is important, as – when they arrive – will be improvements in the domestic transport infrastructure and 5G connectivity. The ease with which foreign executives can live and work in an 'open for business' English-speaking country, can appreciate its cultural heritage and take advantage of its educational system for their children, all bolster the attractions of Britain as a global centre of financial services industries.

Nevertheless, it would be foolish to deny that this powerful picture has been clouded by the expectations of Britain operating outside the European Union. With all its underlying strength, the City also had the most to lose from Brexit, given that it served other European countries so intensively and made good profits from doing so. While the attractions of the concentrated British financial services industry were always sufficient to prevent any mass exodus of institutions to other European centres, by 2018 there was a steady drift towards bi-location between Britain and other countries as institutions hedged their bets.[19] There were some significant falls in foreign exchange and derivatives markets as trade moved elsewhere. A failure to negotiate acceptable 'passporting rights' which allow British firms, from insurance to equity investment, to sell their services freely across the EU, would restrict or even end a lucrative business. Over 5,000 British and 8,000 European firms rely on 'passporting'.[20] Depending on the severity of any final deal between Britain and the European Union over financial services, the City, it has been said, could face the prospects of a 'slow puncture'.[21]

Common sense suggests that the British economy will not be structurally reformed in the coming decade, since, if anything, the pressures of Brexit will likely increase incentives to maintain a 'high flexibility, low tax, low regulation' economy in order to compete separately. But neither is there any reason to believe that the British economy will genuinely slip into being the 'sick man of Europe' – many other European economies are already feeling distinctly unwell – any more than it will become Europe's 'buccaneering Singapore'. The realistic expectation is that, in the event of a meaningful Brexit process, the economy will probably move along, performing suboptimally but not disastrously. As we stated above, the economic performance will play out in the absolute resources that can be made available for diplomacy, defence and security. But in more subtle ways it will also play out in the *image* of Britain at home and abroad as an economy and society; the degree to which it has made a positive success of Brexit, or limited the unavoidable damage of it; or else been laid low by a historic strategic error.

Beyond the technical issues of economic performance, there are also the more tangled questions around the general impressions abroad of British society in light of Brexit. In this respect, not much seems to have changed below the levels of elite opinion in other countries. In 2012 the Ipsos MORI organization reviewed global attitudes towards Britain, as well as among Britons themselves, against the backdrop of the global economic crisis, but also in the light of the summer of 2012 that saw the Olympics, the Paralympics and the Queen's Diamond Jubilee.[22] External views of Britain were uniformly positive about its standard of living, its democratic values and institutions, and its culture and arts – all scoring well over 50 per cent approval ratings. Britons were more 'trusted' at the time by other peoples than, say, Americans or Germans. The survey also found that opinion was more positive the further away from Britain it was polled. European neighbourhood admiration for Britain was more grudging, and domestic opinion in Britain – in characteristic self-deprecation – was most sceptical of all.[23] Some 42 per cent of foreigners thought that Britain was a good place in which to invest; only 24 per cent of Britons agreed. And 48 per cent of foreigners thought Britain's economy was strong, whereas only 13 per cent of Britons judged it that way. German opinion, for example, was four times more confident about its own economic performance. British self-deprecation was taken to new levels in the Brexit debates that followed, which produced an evident mood of national fatalism. By 2019, few in Britain, even the majority of committed leavers among the population, expressed any genuine optimism that Brexit would improve living standards, economic growth or even the National Health Service.[24]

Interestingly, while elite opinion in the rest of the world judged Britain to be plainly diminished by Brexit by 2017, general public opinion around the world had not changed very much from its opinion of 2012.[25] The rest of the world still had a distinctly positive view of Britain's impact on world politics, and opinion among Britain's EU neighbours was again more negative than positive and in some cases – in Germany, Belgium and Spain – very negative. Away from Europe, Britain's influence was judged on a par with that of other major EU countries. At least among opinion of peoples outside Europe, if not among policy elites within it, there is something to play for in sustaining positive images of Britain after it leaves the European Union.[26] Much of these general opinion trends revolve around the soft power attributes of the country.

The institutions of soft power

'Soft power' is a valuable but difficult concept, coined and developed around twenty years ago.[27] It is often assumed that 'hard power' describes military or some sort of physical pressure, and 'soft power' is therefore everything else. But the spectrum of hard and soft power does not lie between violence at one end and persuasion at the other. It is better understood as the distinction between a state applying its strength – whether military, economic or political – to achieve an outcome, as opposed to having a natural magnetism and attraction for other reasons, whether or not it applies it directly. So, economics or cultural powers (threatening to cancel cultural exchanges or boycotting Olympic Games, for instance) can be used in a 'hard' way if they are specifically applied to pressurize another actor, just as military prowess (representing sheer credibility as a power in the world) can be a soft power asset if it creates a political magnetism and a desire on the part of others to imitate it. Hard power is applied; soft power exists. The key is to understand how they both work together along a spectrum that encompasses both what governments *do*, and what their societies *represent*. Understanding how hard and soft power interact together is the essence of trying to exercise political power 'smartly'.[28]

In a society as complex as Britain's, therefore, soft power – that power of magnetism and attraction that also encourages imitation – resides in very many institutions.[29] Some of them, like the royal family, are part of the state machinery. Others, like the British Council, the BBC, or the Arts Council are agencies of it, or else public institutions. Most, however, are institutions over which the government has little direct influence. In 2017 the leading international analysis of soft power defined the 'objective categories' of it as 'enterprise, culture, digital presence, government, engagement and education' and the 'subjective categories' as the trends in global public opinion, as conducted by organizations like the Pew Research Center, recording popular images that citizens around the world hold of a particular country.[30] Governments can do what they will to affect the ways institutions and citizens react to the outside world but, in truth, their influence is peripheral at best. In the 2010 survey Britain and France were jointly rated in top place for global soft power with the United States in third place.[31] In 2017 the images created by Brexit and the election of President Trump had pushed both Britain and the United States down the scale a little, leaving France as top rated. Some analysts are rightly sceptical about the veracity of such snapshot rankings.[32] And year on year differences should not matter very much when China and Russia were rated in twenty-fifth and twenty-sixth places out of thirty, with Turkey propping up the ladder.[33] But if they begin to look like a trend over coming years, they may come to matter a great deal in any post-Brexit reckoning.

The unique power of the monarchy

The point is frequently made that the monarchy and its royal family is an obvious instrument of British soft power, but that is not often spelt out in detail. The subject normally merits little more than a reference to the contribution the monarchy makes to earnings from tourism and its role as a potential diplomatic instrument. The institution of the monarchy and the work and life of the royal family, however, rates more prominently in the audit of British soft power.

The net monetary value of the monarchy to the British economy is beyond doubt. An independent valuation consultancy assessed the royal family's capital value – on the same basis it would evaluate any business – to be worth £67.5 billion in 2017; with tangible assets (including palaces and Crown Jewels) of £25.5 billion and cumulative intangible assets within the British economy of £42 billion. That makes it the third biggest brand in the world, by asset value, behind Google and Microsoft.[34] On these calculations, the monarchy put more than £1.7 billion directly into the economy in 2017. In that year even the most avowedly republican pressure group could only find £345.3 million to ascribe to it as the direct and indirect costs to the taxpayer of running the institution.[35] And the most anti-monarchical press in Britain had to accept the net economic logic of this: 'In the end, the question of whether the royal family is worth it, or not, is probably less a financial question than a political, moral and aesthetic one', said the *Independent*, grudgingly.[36]

A soft power assessment, however, is not based primarily on monetary questions. More important, for example, is the fact that, in addition to adding to the government's formal diplomacy, the British royal family can operate across its own international networks among the twenty-six hereditary royal families of the world. It is the most globally recognizable among them all. The royal families of the Netherlands, Spain, Luxembourg, Sweden, Norway, Denmark and Monaco all shared the same ancestor as the British family in King George II. Five of these seven monarchies were invited to, or hosted, a state or official visit after the triggering of Article 50 in the Brexit process. Personal relations with non-reigning royal families, such as those of Greece, Romania or Yugoslavia, are also notable and the older members of the current royal family have grown personally close to some of their counterparts in the Gulf states. None of this directly constitutes a political network, but it creates a background atmosphere in which state-based bilateral politics are conducted.

The monarchy's own royal status is a critical asset, however, in maintaining the existence and the value of the Commonwealth. As described in Chapter 11, the modern multi-racial Commonwealth arose from British decolonization from the 1950s, and Queen Elizabeth II presided over all of the subsequent growth in what is referred to as the 'Crown Commonwealth'. A great deal of its cohesion has been judged to reside in personal loyalty and affection for her. It was critical, therefore, that the 2018 Commonwealth Heads of Government Meeting affirmed that the Prince of Wales should naturally succeed the Queen as Head of the Commonwealth, rather than consider some other, rotating, arrangement that would ease Britain out of the most pivotal role in the organization.[37] That, of course, may be a mixed blessing since it devolves a great deal of personal responsibility onto the next King and the younger royal principals who will be required to support him. But in a Commonwealth of 2.4 billion people, close to 60 per cent of them – 1.4 billion – are under thirty and it will be their attitudes that shape the future of the organization and British leadership within it. Britain is the only country in the world that presides over an international commonwealth of such size and youth potential.

Outside the realms of dynastic linkages, the monarchy plays a subsidiary but sometimes very useful role in conventional British diplomacy. It offers its ceremony and hospitality to foreign leaders; it gives its endorsement to popular global causes; and the royals move across the world, on private trips and royal tours, trailing publicity in their wake. Private trips may only be months in the planning, official royal tours, probably two to three years, but all are subject to change as foreign politics shift. They nevertheless are intended to be consistent with at least medium-term national strategic or economic objectives.[38] It was no accident that in light of Britain's departure from the European Union there were prominent royal tours or visits during 2017 to Poland, Germany, Finland, Denmark and Romania, and in 2018 to Sweden, Norway and Ireland. The Prince of Wales made a big effort to repair strained relations with Greece in 2018 and then undertook a long tour across West Africa – always convening economic envoys in the process.[39]

The value of the royal family as a soft power asset to Britain in the 2020s is at both a generational and a political crossroads. Queen Elizabeth II is the oldest and the longest-reigning living monarch – giving her eldest son, the Prince of Wales, the bittersweet accolade as the longest heir-apparent. Quite soon, 'Project London Bridge' and the media's 'Mrs Robinson' rehearsals will swing into action. Generational change is inherent in the royal succession and the natural evolution of a group of younger royal principals around Princes William and Harry and their immediate families. At all national celebrations, the east front balcony of Buckingham Palace is synonymous with the royal family at any moment in its history. The Golden Jubilee flypast in 2002 featured the extended family; the Diamond Jubilee flypast in 2012 very deliberately featured only the core family and the immediate succession.

The change is more than generational, however. A self-evident core institution of the British state, the monarchy has also increasingly been seen as a 'British brand' of some importance. Its asset value is one thing, but its image in the eyes of the world ranges from soap opera to elite excellence; certainly, on a par with the social prestige of any US president. The royal weddings of Princes William and Harry became global media events in themselves.[40] Moreover, the brand is changing with the deliberate injection of some Hollywood glitter into the mix – latterly also with the 'Markle sparkle' – where younger royal principals help mobilize major celebrities on 'new generation' issues that connect tangibly with citizens – mental health, modern slavery, climate change, wildlife protection and so on.[41] This evolution of the royal brand and a willingness to employ it appear to be part of a strategy, still in development, within the monarchy, to shake it down in preparation for the challenges to come. Royal patronage of charities has been streamlined and domestic and international roles for the new principals discussed. As second in line to succession, Prince William and his family might be expected to concentrate on essentially domestic roles, in preparation for his eventual accession, Prince Harry and family on more international concerns. It is already evident, however, that the younger royal family see their future work intimately bound up with the Commonwealth, and coincidentally also with diplomatic relations across Africa. It was no accident that just after Prince Harry was named as Commonwealth Youth Ambassador, Meghan Markle was appointed vice-president of the Queen's Commonwealth Trust – of which her husband was already president.

Two other major items of reform are likely to feature in any royal family shakedown. If the net value of the monarchy to the British economy is beyond question, it does not automatically follow that the £345 million some claim it really costs is necessarily spent in the most effective ways. It is an open secret that some dysfunctional aspects of the monarchy and its failure to function smoothly as a single branded institution, are driven by its silos of separate, often competing, royal households. It was, and is, ever thus in royal families and dynasties everywhere. But if the British monarchy is to unlock its full potential as a global brand of Britishness, a rich source of soft power – and there is much to play for in the coming decade – it must be streamlined for its foreign roles and able to plan and act coherently in lock-step with government thinking.

Coming full circle, the royal family of the future is also believed to recognize a renewed challenge to its institutional role within a post-Brexit UK. Any monarch is automatically Head of State, but the British monarch also plays a 'Head of Nations' role, officially defined as 'identity, continuity, achievement and service'.[42] It may need all of those elements in a renewed commitment to 'unite the kingdoms' and help hold the British state together if the Brexit imbroglio renews the dissolution dynamic. Princes William and Harry, no less than the Prince of Wales, are believed to be seized of the importance of this upcoming challenge and can be expected to visit all parts of the UK's four nations frequently to help convene disparate stakeholders in a series of 'unity conversations'.[43] In the coming decade it is possible the royal family will find itself attempting to play a national role every bit as historic and important to the British state – to the UK – as that of its seventeenth- and eighteenth-century ancestors.

The hierarchy of 'image institutions'

The monarchy spans Britain's broad societal image and the more particular institutions of soft power like no other. By its very nature, it represents both domains. Other notable institutions can be seen performing their roles in near or more distant orbits from the centre of the state. Some soft power capabilities flow from those institutions whose functions are intimately connected with the creation of an official state image or else those whose reputation for the work they do is highly dependent on the British image they project.

Parliament engages in the generic promotion of its unique British values and practices through its activities in organizations such as the Inter-Parliamentary Union, the NATO Parliamentary Assembly, the Council of Europe and its (now) sophisticated broadcasting and digital access. Similarly, the Commonwealth runs a Parliamentary Association, a Business Council and an Association of Commonwealth Universities, all of which are based on the ideals of unity among the democracies that Britain aims to promote. More uniquely, in Britain's case, is the existence of the British Council, founded in 1834 and with annual revenues in excess of £1 billion. The British Council operates in more than 100 countries, over half the total of the UN membership and it claims that it 'reaches' through its various schemes over half a billion people worldwide. Indeed, its work in Russia led it to estimate that it reached one in seventeen of the population – a good reason why the Russian intelligence services were relieved to have the chance to throw it out of the country altogether in the row over the Skripal poisoning in 2018.[44] It takes pride in working in what it describes as 'high growth countries', 'fragile states' and the most difficult 'marginalized environments' such as Burma or Zimbabwe.[45]

The reach of the BBC is even more impressive, described by some as 'Britain's strongest tool of soft power'.[46] The BBC World Service Group, which includes BBC World Service Radio in forty-two languages, BBC World News television, the BBC news website (plus BBC Monitoring and BBC Media Action), in total reaches some 376 million people weekly. BBC World Service English is the world's biggest radio station; BBC World News television is in 433 million homes worldwide in over 200 countries; and the news website is viewed more than a billion times in most months.[47] More impressive than the figures, however, is the fact that the BBC has a unique British brand in being internationally trusted as a news service. It is particularly highly rated internationally as a reliable source of news at times of crisis. In a world where only one in every six citizens has access to a politically free media, the BBC is more trusted, by more people, than any other international news source. The BBC's separate news services in Pashto, Dari, Persian and Uzbek languages, for example, connect weekly with almost 12 million people in Afghanistan – more than 60 per cent of the adult population.[48] And while the BBC's Persian Service is jammed, banned and abused by the Tehran government, 12 million Iranians – 15 per cent of the population – still listen to it as their window on the world outside.

Such organizations represent the British establishment and depend on government directly or indirectly for their funding, though they nevertheless operate independently – something many foreign leaders and journalists find genuinely difficult to understand. But they represent a brand of British society and values that has much greater longevity than any government.

The same can be said for Britain's intellectual political community – the think tanks, national associations, pressure groups, journalists and civil society watchdogs – the 'influence-seekers' as one analyst calls them.[49] It is surprising how few countries, even among Britain's European partners, have as vibrant and independently minded a policy community as has existed in Britain for many years. Generous government, or political party, funding for think tanks in France, Germany, Switzerland, the Netherlands, Italy or Sweden has not served to pump-prime a much wider, independent policy community in those countries. Only the United States has a richer and more diverse sector than Britain's and many argue that even in the United States it is more introspective and less genuinely international. And London is still the 'NGO-capital of the world'; the easiest and most useful place for NGOs to have offices that put them in easy touch with their networks, though there is evidence of some drift in light of Brexit as some co-locate or move their headquarters to the continent.[50]

British education plays its part in this brand of openness and independence from government. The British Academy and the royal academies and societies representing science, arts, engineering, and so on, have long-standing international reputations that are almost universally favourable and have stood in comparison with the best in the world. Higher education and the private schools sector remain very attractive to foreign nationals. Apart from the United States, no other country has as many higher educational institutions ranked within the top 100 world universities, and over 750,000 foreign students study in Britain in most years.[51] In 2018 no fewer than '55 current world leaders' had studied at British universities; clearly a good investment in long-term influence, if only indirectly.[52] In a similar vein, Britain's private schools have long created an international model that is much imitated. Over 4,000 British schools operate internationally, some of them the famous schools of Britain, and many working along the classic lines of British private schools.[53]

Far more diverse than any of the above, Britain's 'creative industries' have made significant inroads across the world and carry important brands of their own that attract talent and enterprise into the country. From world-class theatre and international orchestras, to architecture, design, film, publishing, advertising, computer gaming and pop music, the creative industries have been a British success story for many years. The British Council has pointed out that the country has 'a tendency … to export its creativity rather than harness it – British ingenuity can be found at the heart of the success of Apple, Marvel and all the other [US] soft power pop culture powerhouses'.[54] But that, in itself, is a measure of the collective creativity within British domestic society. Though creative industries are, by definition, difficult to classify and analyse, the Creative Industries Council calculates that they contribute over £101 billion annually to the British economy. The leading sectors include £41 billion from 'IT, software and games', £17 billion from 'film and TV', £13 billion from advertising and £12 billion from 'publications'.[55] They account for over 3 million jobs in Britain – heavily concentrated in London and the South East and since they are primarily a value-added series of industries, they grow their added value at almost twice the average rate elsewhere in the economy. The creative industries are a serious part of Britain's economic future. They account for about 5 per cent of its GDP and employ at least eight times more people than the 360,000 involved in Britain's defence industries, around four times the 850,000 workers in the automotive industries, and almost three times the 1.1 million in the whole finance and insurance sector. For these reasons alone, and their export of talent abroad, the creative industries are an important source of British soft power and reputational brands of their own that can be expected to have impacts both domestically and internationally.

Not yet included in the general definition of creative industries, the contemporary 'influencers' of social media and their impact on national reputation and image are even more difficult to classify. Social media has had contradictory effects in world politics; helping unify anti-authoritarian protests in many countries even while it accelerates fragmentation in liberal societies by strengthening 'identity groups' who operate in their own 'filter bubbles' and 'echo chambers'.[56] Many observers have pronounced British government 'ill-equipped' to understand the significance of this and deal with it proactively.[57] None of Britain's 'top ten personal influencers' on social media feature in similar United States or Asian lists, though they have over 43 million followers between them.[58] But for good or bad, social media is more developed in Britain than elsewhere in Europe. It is embraced by over 62 per cent of Britain's own population and its total 'penetration', including access via employment is estimated at 85 per cent of the population; the highest among the developed states of Europe.[59] According to the Office for National Statistics, 89 per cent of all adults in Britain accessed the internet regularly in 2019 – up by 40 per cent since 2009.[60] Of more economic relevance, the use of social media for marketing purposes and to establish brand names was judged to make a bigger comparative difference to small and medium enterprises than to the biggest companies. For the future, Britain's SME-heavy economy stands to gain more from the use of social media as a branding and reputational device than many of its competitors if it is used effectively.[61]

Closely connected to the creative industries is also the powerful branding of British sport in the international context. Melvin Bragg judged that the publication in 1863 of the *Rule Book of the Football Association* was one of the seminal volumes of world history since it standardized – according to British thinking – a game and an attitude to playing and watching it, that has become the most popular international sport in history.[62] Not surprising, then, that the English Premier League – with its truly international cast of players and managers –

broadcasts to 212 countries – virtually every country in the world. A billion homes globally have access to Premier League coverage, which makes it available to around one in three of all the individuals on the planet.[63] It earns more every year than the combined incomes of the Bundesliga, La Liga, Ligne 1 and Serie A, and almost three times the combined total of all North American sports.[64] British athletics, cricket, Wimbledon, rugby, the Golf Open, cycling, Formula 1 (where seven of the ten F1 teams are based or co-based in Britain) are all extremely popular international sports in which Britain features prominently. But none of them come close to the sheer power of the English Premier League presenting itself weekly to the global audience. Between them, the monarchy, the BBC and the Premier League are consistently ranked in surveys as 'the most admired British institutions' around the world.[65]

Maintaining soft power and mobilizing societal strength

The problems of evaluating these various societal and soft power strengths for the future are essentially twofold. One is that, though it is hard to disagree that Britain has been correctly referred to by many analysts, not just as a 'development superpower' but now as one of the world's 'cultural superpowers', the new competitors for this accolade are coming up fast.[66] In the last three years, for example, the British film industry has grossed about the same as the Indian film industry in monetary terms. It holds around 7 per cent of global cinema's market share. But the Indian film industry is far and away the biggest producer of films in the world. Its films are multilingual and they have the biggest audiences in the world, which are growing all the time.

British talent in Hollywood, on the other hand, and American use of British film technologies, remains a feature of the industry. But even Hollywood is only the third most prolific producer of modern films.[67] Or again, Britain's strength in offering private school and higher educational opportunities in the world is under intensifying pressure not just from other non-English-speaking competitor countries but through the fashion for countries in the Middle East and Asia to open their own doors to new multinational campuses where the most prestigious university institutions can run satellite operations. Not least, the real revolution in Western higher education is in online and distance learning. None of this negates the competitive edge of elite British institutions, but it may dent their long-term influence around the world; where they are delivering their university courses to the international students, rather than vice versa.

The second problem is that while the government promotes many aspects of Britain's societal and soft powers, through Whitehall's Department for Digital,

Culture, Media and Sport (DCMS), it does so on the back of a decade of austerity that has affected local government, the backbone of so much social activity, more severely than any other public sector. So, DCMS can allocate money from its Cultural Development Fund into regional initiatives, or from the DCMS/Wolfson fund into museum development, or the Arts Council into classical orchestras and touring fine art exhibitions, but none of that can prevent the longer-term effects of the austerity decade diminishing the base on which significant areas of Britain's 'cultural superpower' status have been founded.

British governments have always taken a laissez-faire approach to the promotion of soft power in general, and particularly in relation to the cultural and educational elements of it. There is a good argument that this produces a healthier and more innovative output, but it also leaves the foundations of Britain's cultural strengths to the vagaries of the market – which may increase considerably in another global economic crisis. The implicit model of arts funding in Britain has traditionally relied roughly on a split deriving one-third of funding from audience receipts, one-third from private sponsorship, and one-third from government grants. But government grants have reduced considerably since 2010 while private sponsorship (and prices) have risen accordingly.[68]

Other countries – competitors in soft power terms – have put significant state sponsorship into sports and culture which have not necessarily been the better for it. In recent years the most inventive British approach has been to use the National Lottery – 'a tax on stupidity' as Dr Johnson said of national lotteries in his day – as a source of pseudo-public money for what other countries tend to fund centrally. Otherwise, it has looked to the private sector to sponsor activities and teams and to the international media (not the BBC) to pay market rates to broadcast them. It is an approach that can create vibrant and innovative soft power assets in the upswings of the economic cycle but leave them haemorrhaging talent and fighting for their very existence in the difficult times.

The rise of serious international competitors and the prevailing market approach to Britain's soft power capabilities is likely to be the story of the 2020s in the broad equation of intangible power. The government can only exhort, and to a limited extent shape, the way Britain's societal capabilities will direct themselves in the decade to come. But it can, at least, settle for a better branding exercise than 'cool Britannia', 'swinging London' and certainly 'global Britain' ever provided. Britain's societal strengths are not illusory and its soft power is considerable. It can be realistically branded in a way that could give it purpose in the difficult years to come, both to the external world and to the British themselves. We turn to this in the Conclusion.

Conclusion: Strategic surge for the 2020s

Chapter 13
A strategic surge

In the opening sentence of *Anna Karenina*, Tolstoy famously observed that, 'All happy families are alike; each unhappy family is unhappy in its own way'.[1] Most of the great families that we call countries – like the United States, Russia or China – and those families of countries that we call Europe, the Middle East or South Asia, are all suffering unhappiness at the moment but in their own different ways. There is no global pattern, other than evident change and volatility. Any common causes that might account for this, like global inequality, fragmenting political power or the march of technology, are only discernible at a high level of abstraction, and that is little help to leaders who have to deal with what they see immediately in front of them – however visionary they may be in their own minds.

The British national family has gone through a decade of deepening unhappiness since the onset of the economic crisis in 2008, as we have outlined in this book. Some of the underlying tensions were focused in the Brexit vote of 2016, and others were created by the vote itself and then exacerbated by the way the Brexit process played out over the following years. By the end of the decade the politics of the country were in the grip of a complete nervous breakdown that looked certain to throw the parliamentary jigsaw into the air. Britain embarks on the 2020s in a depressed and confused state of mind.

But in due course this will all pass as a 'new normal' becomes established in national politics. Britain will eventually emerge from the Brexit imbroglio to face its 2020s security future. It will do so in a different relationship with its European partners. Whatever the final outcome of Britain's withdrawal arrangements, even if they are interrupted or effectively rescinded, there can be no going back to the status quo ante of the years before 2015, either with the European Union or with the British public and their politicians. We have all come too far in the last five years for that.

Our international future will assuredly be different to the last decade, let alone to the decade from the end of the Cold War where so many of our expectations were forged. It is our contention that the 2020s will be difficult years for the security of all European countries, and not least for Britain, since all the second rank powers face a global environment where the Big Four are flexing their geopolitical muscles more vigorously and in different ways. At the same time, the Europeans face an economic environment that has still not recovered from the global crisis – and may not even be out of it – and where the United States and China will make most of the economic running in the coming decade. And they live in a world where liberal democracy is in retreat and is not even an exclusive force of natural kinship within their own collective family. All Europe's leaders and their statesmanship will be tested severely in the next few years.

Britain is no exception to these general trends, but it expresses their less than happy implications in its own characteristic ways. The 2020s were always shaping up to be a decade that would highlight Britain's relative weaknesses rather than play to its strengths – less able to be a leader of a strong European security consensus, less easy to stay close to the United States who is thinking more about Asian security, less capacity to 'make a difference' in the wider world where the great power geopolitical wheels were turning again. On the other side of the coin, it was always going to be the case that Britain would have to work harder in the 2020s to make its natural strengths count in security terms – to capitalize on its reputation for strategy that had taken such a beating in Iraq and Afghanistan, to make the most of its excellent but small military forces, its thinly stretched diplomatic network, its robust intelligence capabilities facing new types of challenge, its vibrant and globalized economy still sluggish after the crisis, or its soft power assets, long taken for granted by successive governments. In short, the 2020s was always going to challenge British policy-makers in ways that are generically similar, but specifically different, to its partner countries across the transatlantic community.

But why do we define this security equation of strengths and weaknesses as a 'tipping point' for Britain? What is it about the 2020s that makes the early years of the decade more decisive for Britain than the decade in general? There are many reasons.

There is a good chance that something is going to snap in Britain's own neighbourhood sooner rather than later. European security has come under some acute pressures in the last decade, as described in these chapters. In itself, there is nothing surprising in that. Perceptions of security go up and down with events, and Europe lived through some of its most dangerous years during the Cold War. But if the Cold War was very hazardous it was also relatively predictable and, until the end, it changed only slowly. The decade after the Cold War's end transformed the Europeans' security environment in relatively benign ways that they felt was within their control. But in the last few years the *tempo* of potential strategic change has increased markedly, even as the collective ability of the European powers to deal with it has declined.

When the needle on the European security dial shivers repeatedly, as it has since the Ukraine crisis in 2013, it may then quickly swing a long way around the dial in response to relatively minor crises. That was how the Soviet empire collapsed between 1985 and 1991. In its own unhappy ways, European security may face a similar dynamic. In 2019 Hungary, Romania, Greece and Poland were drifting away from EU policy on different but strategically important issues; large parts of Europe's Mediterranean coast in North Africa became a region of social upheaval; Turkey and Italy were doing separate deals with Russia that would have been unthinkable for two significant NATO members a decade ago; Germany risked energy dependence on Russia with the Nord Stream 2 pipeline; and the US president publicly mused about withdrawing the United States from the alliance altogether. Europe's security needle oscillates ever more erratically on the dial and repeated political reassurances based only on a more predictable past will not calm it. As one senior British defence chief expressed it, European security has self-evidently not broken down, but the risks of it doing so are now considerably higher than in recent years.[2]

The significance of increased European security risks to this country is not only that Britain is the most important military and defence player among the Europeans; no defence response to any structural security crisis would be credible without British military capabilities. But more than that, whether in or out of the European Union, Britain simply has no choice but to be part of Europe's security. As at all times in its modern history, Britain cannot pursue any other role in the world unless its immediate neighbourhood is safe.

Paradoxically enough, Russia's European policy also seems likely to reach a tipping point in the next five years. President Putin has made his revisionist policy in Europe entirely clear and conveys an impression that he has many strategic cards on the table he can play at his leisure – in Northern Europe, Ukraine, the Western Balkans, the Eastern Mediterranean, Libya, and not least in playing European parties and governments off against each other. But the early 2020s will be a difficult time for him and the oligarchs as well. Unless he again amends the constitution, he is due to step down in 2024. But the Russian economy does not enter the decade performing well, and domestic opposition to his oligarchic ruling clique has evidently connected to grass roots support outside Moscow and St Petersburg. In February 2019 Putin responded to growing opposition by announcing a raft of domestic reforms and spending priorities, but even if they are successful, it is unlikely Russia will make up much lost economic ground before 2024. Like all autocrats, President Putin plays the nationalist card against foreign adversaries when he is under pressure. He has gambled and won many times since 1999. There is every chance he will attempt to do so again if domestic opposition builds against him as a failing leader. With so much of the Russian economy in the hands of the few oligarchs who depend on him, a smooth transfer of presidential power in 2024 is one of the less likely outcomes. The immediate danger to Europe is not of outright Russian military action against the European heartland, but rather of miscalculation and reckless gambles around the fringes of the neighbourhood and assertive attempts to achieve showy political goals with barely disguised military intimidation.

China's contribution to Europe's tipping point lies not at all in its military power, which is not yet directly relevant to European security concerns, but rather in the impact of the Belt and Road Initiative, which after six years in gestation can be expected to come to some sort of first stage fruition in the next five. It will be a geopolitical game changer if it meets only some of its evident objectives. This is coupled with rapid and recent increases of Chinese investment in European economies. As China crosses a genuine threshold in becoming a global player – not just a big country – it expands according to international commercial logic, but then tries to use its market power according to its own political logic as a one-party state. From Europe's perspective, China plays the international game along two parallel sets of rules; and the impact of the contradictions in this seems likely to increase in the next few years. Europe needs to attract foreign investment, as do the regions of Asia and Africa that matter to it, but under present circumstances Chinese entrepreneurship and commercial investment shows all the signs of coming with heavy political conditionality decided in Beijing.

For Britain, the dilemma posed by relationships with China's Huawei for the 5G network that will set Britain's digital society up for the coming decade is a good example of one of the new security decisions awaiting all European governments over the next ten years or so. During 2019, the Indian government grappled with the same security issue. In 2019 the United States pressured its most important intelligence allies to expel Huawei from their emerging 5G systems. China was outraged, speaking darkly of retaliation. Yet Britain goes into 5G already as a more successfully digitized society than most of its international partners. It is the only one of the big European countries with a designated 'high' level of digital integration and it stands favourably in comparison with non-European digitization leaders such as the United States, Japan or South Korea. Within the EU, France and Germany, by contrast, are only rated as 'medium', and Italy as 'low' in digital growth and integration.[3] But the benefits of something close to 'full digitization', of the sort the British government says it wants, and which 5G goes a long way to provide, also come at a potential security cost, as the government acknowledges.[4] As we have described in other chapters, the task of 'securing' a modern digitized society, which pays a price in vulnerability for what it gains in economic and commercial benefit, is conceptually complex as well as difficult to do. The security trade-offs may be severe, and compared to the Britain of 2000 or 2010, we are only beginning to understand them properly. There is every chance we will confront some of the specifics in the near future, not so much in the domain of terrorism, but certainly in crime, fraud, political blackmail and maybe also in fundamental 'strategic positioning' between the great powers.

There is also a very domestic perspective on the reason Britain is fast approaching a security tipping point. Quite simply, the cumulative effects of a decade of public expenditure cuts on all its outward-facing attributes, with the exception of intelligence and overseas aid, have left Britain talking a better international game than it plays. The expectation in 2010 was that crisis-driven public spending squeezes could be eased after 2015 with growth in the economy as it emerged from the financial crisis. But the economy came out of crisis straight into recession and emergency cuts could not genuinely be restored. Britain's diplomacy, Commonwealth, defence, security, trade promotion, technology or soft power attributes are not in penury, but they do not have the resources to match the objectives governments set for them. For a decade there has been a structural mismatch between the official aspiration to keep Britain on the front line of world diplomacy and political involvement as against constrained resources – people, money, expertise – that makes it possible to do so. Britain has a credibility problem that is not likely to ease unless aspirations and resources are balanced more consistently.

The government offered an estimate in 2018 (based on generous assumptions) that its total annual spending on security across the board amounted to £58 billion, including defence, aid, intelligence, home security and other particular items. Extrapolating that figure and adding other foreign policy and diplomatic expenditure, a 2020 figure for Britain's external policy instruments would not exceed £60-61 billion. In an economy of just over £2 trillion, that represents 3 per cent of Britain's GDP. This is higher than in France where the figure is about 2.5 per cent and less than the United States where the comparable figure is over 4 per cent.[5] Britain may not be so far out of kilter against these comparisons, but they say nothing about how resources are allocated or how well matched they are to government policy. At the sharp end of diplomacy, defence, trade promotion or societal protection and promotion there is a pervading sense that either Britain's global aspirations are too high or its committed resources are too low. The tipping point is that the cumulative effects of an austerity decade in which ambitious political goals were constantly reiterated cannot be disguised much longer unless the 2020s turn out to be unusually quiet years.

And then there is Brexit. That, in itself, would be a security tipping point for Britain. It is our contention in this book that, for the reasons outlined above, British security is facing serious discontinuities in any case in its broad security environment. That would be the case even if the 2016 referendum had gone in favour of remaining in the EU. The fact that it did not, created its own political fallout among the European allies. Moreover, even if the arrangements for a new relationship between Britain and the EU had gone well between 2016 and 2020, Brexit, on its own, would still be a considerable strategic tipping point. A number of different assumptions prevailed after the 2016 referendum: leaving the EU without a negotiated deal, as Conservative Party maximalists always favoured; getting some sort of deal agreed and ratified; prolonging the negotiation process; or entering a grey zone of 'EU membership limbo' to create more time for further national reflection. All implied very different eventual outcomes, but they also all nevertheless represented a severe strategic jolt for the country. Britain seems, in any case, to be in for its white-knuckle ride, as we outlined in the third section of this book, regardless of what happens next between London and Brussels.

It is not difficult to speculate how the undulating nature of this ride might be experienced. The outcome of Brexit politics in the early 2020s may have the effect of releasing resources and constraints to give Britain more room for political and diplomatic manoeuvre in the world. The country may attract the interest and kudos of being thought to act independently as a capable second rank power, with less of the natural collective cover that other European partners prefer. Brexit might stimulate a national sense of determination to prove that Britain will not be diminished by it either domestically or internationally. Britain might be able to show that it is a *more* useful member of the European and transatlantic security communities outside the EU framework and an enhanced player in global politics. It might be able to prove that its economy can grow vigorously and inventively outside the EU – cashing in on its already successful embrace of globalization and attract even more international talent and investment into it. Britain might, objectively, be *more* secure as a result of the various changes Brexit might itself stimulate in Europe; encouraging the enlarged EU towards a multi-speed, even more 'variable geometry' organization, in which Britain might be an influential power where flexibility and independence of action is valued more highly.

But just as plausibly, it is possible that Britain's absence from the management of EU policing arrangements make it internally less secure; that a sense of diplomatic estrangement in EU circles affects bilateral relations and within NATO so that the overall European security consensus is diminished, regardless of Britain's military capacities. It is possible that Brexit will materially slowdown British economic growth and make it difficult to capitalize on the country's natural strengths and entrepreneurship. If this is the case then public spending for the outward-facing instruments of policy would be hard to sustain at current, let alone higher, levels. On the most unfavourable scenario, the Brexit process could leave British security with the worst of both worlds – living in a dangerous neighbourhood where its contribution to collective security is lessened, and finding itself effectively isolated within a transatlantic community that is being stretched thin between an angry United States and Europeans disengaging from it. And it is also plausible that Britain will not recover from its political nervous breakdown for some years into the 2020s and the mood in the country will be fatalistic, depressive and unambitious – a Britain diminished in the eyes of the world and in its own.

Perhaps the most important Brexit tipping point is even more basic than these dramatic scenarios, however. It is simply the question of whether Britain, as a government and within wider society, recognizes with some clear-sightedness the challenges of the 2020s and engages seriously in its post-Brexit security future. For five years, after the referendum was first called, the sheer domestic drama of the process severely distracted the British government from all but trivial planning for its foreign and security policy implications. It drowned out most attempts to dig beneath the rhetorical flourishes of entrenched political positions and to work out some priorities for the future. That future will not be largely a continuation of the past. Brexit was itself such a big strategic change that it had the effect of overshadowing other big strategic changes in Britain's imminent security situation.

This book has sought to set out the main drivers of Britain's security future for the next decade and to situate the realities of Brexit within them. It makes no attempt to review all the different global themes that will bear on our security for the years to come. The government's Development, Concepts and Doctrine Centre does that, and it lists fifteen broad and important themes, from climate change to the erosion of sovereignty; from automation in the workforce to 'weapons of mass effect'. Our purpose here, rather, has been to focus on the things that leaders and policy planners see in front of them – long-term issues that have short-term impacts; and short-term issues that can explode onto the daily agenda.

Understanding that the early years of the 2020s will present a tipping point – and Britain will tip unfavourably if it does nothing, just as surely as if it does the wrong things – the most important questions for leaders and policy-makers concern what is in their power to influence. What sort of approaches and strategic decisions would make a difference to the way Britain eventually emerges from the Brexit process? How should Britain try to measure up to a moment in its history that, as we said as the beginning of this analysis, ranks in importance with the great free trade debates of the 1840s, the attempts to guide the creation of new world orders after both world wars, and even with the desperate war or peace choices of May 1940?

Britain's strategic policy choices

Successful national strategies are not blueprints or action plans. Such things have their place lower in the pecking order of strategic planning. Successful strategies know that their detail and expectations are unlikely to survive first contact with messy reality and they have to be more flexible than that. Nor is successful strategy something that just exists among a prime minister's inner circle. It might be better summed up as a habit of thinking throughout government that naturally tries to apply ends and means in all things – 'what to do and how to pay for it'. But it must also link the 'ends' to a clear conception of what the country should stand for, what it should be good at, from what it gets best value, and how it maximizes strengths and minimizes weaknesses. A national strategic orientation is not something a government can pursue relentlessly in all circumstances. But the conception of national strategy should be sufficiently clear and strong to indicate those occasions when it really does matter that a line is upheld. And a national strategy should be the natural default option; the line to which the country returns after the zigzags of ambiguous, contradictory or failed policies.

Britain has sometimes been good at operating its foreign and security policy like this – in a strategically literate way. The last occasions were at the beginning of the Cold War in the 1940s and then towards its end in the 1980s. Tony Blair tried to operate according to similar strategic principles and was generally successful, and lucky, for the first five years of his premiership, then unsuccessful and unlucky for the remaining five years. Since then, though Britain has produced any number of strategically worded documents, it is difficult for observers to discern in them a strong or coherent national strategy; or one that balances ends and means. Prime Ministers Brown, Cameron, May and Johnson were all thought to be lacking the strategic instincts to give Britain a clear and positive international orientation. Perversely enough, the most important strategic decision Britain has taken for a very long time, during a period of national strategic drift, was to leave the European Union. And that, as we have described, was essentially an angry ambush by the English shires and the English in the Welsh borders against the Whitehall policy elite who were assumed to be political puppets of anonymous globalization. It was an identity decision; on all sides of the debate, conceptions of national strategy were afterthoughts.

Assessing Britain's general security capabilities, as we have done in this book, suggests that the most appropriate national strategy, and one that also addresses the challenges of the 2020s, might be described as a mixture of 'strategic surge' and 'reorientation'.

There is a good case for a 'strategic surge' for at least the next five years. A strategic surge would brigade together, at least for planning and resource allocation purposes, a broad series of government and private sectors that interact most directly with the country's external security and foreign policies. That means thinking about the synergized power of sectors such as diplomacy, defence, overseas aid, intelligence, governmental research and development, economic hotspots like finance, digital industries or aerospace, alongside a number of influential parts of the soft power spectrum. A strategic surge would aim to strategize across them all, as far as may be possible in a mix of public and private organizations, in order to achieve the most effective impact on those security and foreign policy objectives that will arise in the coming years.[6] The government might claim it already does a lot of this through the existing National Security Council. But the NSC is a liaison mechanism in Whitehall rather than a strategic driver and it does not include the spectrum of hard and soft power assets that a strategic surge could involve. The objective would be to demonstrate British competence and confidence in the world as the country defines a new relationship with its European partners. It is reasonable to suppose that it may take up to ten years to demonstrate to the rest of the world, and to ourselves, that a new version of Britain, on a different European trajectory, can be a genuine success and contribute more to its own, and others' security. It would seek to advance British foreign policy and Western perspectives on international society and contribute to economic prosperity by showing Britain as a healthy actor in world politics. This is unlikely to be achieved unless the present suite of British capabilities is renewed and rededicated to a clearer strategic purpose than has been the case for some years.

A strategic surge would also involve a series of temporary, but significant, uplifts in funding for some of these sectors to restore the depth and sustainability of the capacities that were lost during the decade of austerity. If 'global Britain' thinks it worth increasing its proportion of GDP spent on the outward-facing policy instruments from about 3 per cent to the United States proportion of around 4 per cent, that would imply spending about £20 billion extra, per annum, for a minimum of five years.[7] That amount could have quite a 'surging' effect that could make Britain's diplomatic network sustainable again. It could guarantee that defence would deliver on its planned capabilities for the mid-2020s and, most importantly, make the forces sustainable enough to be credible in significant operations – an important message on both sides of the Atlantic. Within that ceiling it would be easily possible to double or treble the below-par £1.3 billion the government puts into critical R&D each year, and use it to incentivize key industries towards the 'surge objectives'.[8] It could help some of Britain's soft power shop windows to hold off growing competition to their international pre-eminence, particularly in broadcasting, media and arts. There may be a difficulty at the end of a surge period, in tapering off significant amounts of temporary funding after, say, five or seven years; but that is a matter to be managed and well worth the trouble for the benefit of uplifted capacity during a critical period.

These amounts of cash are not implausible; it is a question of strategic judgement over national spending priorities. Whatever the deeper economic impacts Brexit might turn out to have on the British economy, it is apparent that both government and private sector investment, as well as consumer spending, was held back because of prolonged 'Brexit uncertainty'. There is also scope for a future administration to relax austerity planning without breaking the Treasury's own fiscal rules on debt. 'Rarely in recent history', said one economist, 'has quite so much pent up demand sat beneath this economy'. A 'palpable shot in the arm' awaits it from both the Treasury and the private sector once Britain's eventual arrangements with the EU are properly underway.[9] The need for a strategic surge should figure in the government's spending priorities as any immediate or short-term economic upturn materializes.

The second element of a post-Brexit strategy focusses on the objectives a strategic surge might serve. What strategic priorities should Britain demonstrate to the world? Given our analysis of the wide spectrum of modern security challenges, from crime to outright warfare; and our contention that Europe is an increasingly troubled neighbourhood, there is a good case for Britain to concentrate the bulk of its security and defence attention near to home, and make its diplomatic and soft power assets more effective in the wider world. This is less straightforward than it sounds. It is increasingly evident that Britain's Royal Navy, with its new aircraft carrier battle group potential, anticipates operating globally, while the British Army, with a newly capitalized armoured force, anticipates operating in bigger units than for the last two decades, in and around Europe. In effect, they anticipate fighting different sorts of war. Their respective thinking is not a naturally good strategic fit. But stretched armed forces have got to concentrate their political effect somewhere, and for the 2020s there is a powerful logic behind contributing as much as possible to European security.

This view would reject much of the 'Anglosphere' thinking behind the Brexit arguments for Britain's future security role in the world. It would concentrate instead on bolstering Britain's position in European defence, to make the most of its natural relative strength, to offset the loss of influence with other European partners and to help keep the United States committed to transatlantic defence arrangements. Not the least important reason for such a concentration is that beefing up Europe's military and broader security capacities is the best way to insulate the continent from the pressures that Russia will continue to exert on it. If Britain is to concentrate forces anywhere, then for its own sake, it makes sense to prepare them primarily in the service of European security.

It is also in Britain's own economic and social interests to put more relative effort into the wider security spectrum at home. Britain is a more attractive host for foreign investment if it is cyber secure, able to combat crime and fraud, with a secure and reliable national infrastructure. As we have seen, Britain has natural advantages in these respects and it could be more internationally competitive by ensuring that they remain superior to most of the international competition. Modern domestic security and prosperity in the globalized economy are intimately connected.

That does not mean that Britain would be diplomatically absent from regions and issues outside Europe. It would aim to synergize that mixture of hard and soft policy instruments that is defined as 'smart power' to make the most of its opportunities in the wider world. Emerging countries in other regions are not so committed by history or sentiment to the prevailing Western world order of institutions and their associated norms of behaviour. It is not so obvious to many emerging countries that the prevailing order is in their long-term interests. There is everything for the liberal democratic powers to play for in influencing prevailing trends of global opinion. What the liberal democracies are seen to stand for really matters in the darker climate of global politics that now prevails. It is impossible to predict the issues that will occupy British policy-makers of the future. The aim, nevertheless, is that they should show the confidence, and have the diplomatic and soft power capabilities, to involve themselves, for example, with some of the numerous partners along China's BRI – not to frustrate it, but rather to help facilitate its contracts and arrangements; to help habituate Beijing's huge strategic vision into the current international system, rather than creating something more autocratic operating parallel to it. They should have the confidence and facility to be more diplomatically proactive in helping reconcile some of the growing tensions in the Gulf, if only to reduce the moral dilemmas between Western political and economic interests in that region. Or again, Britain may need to show the confidence to differ from US policies on many issues in global politics, playing on hard-nosed transactional assumptions more than past sentiment or automatic 'Anglosphere' identity. A strong transatlantic security relationship between London and Washington should not prevent Britain from differentiating itself clearly from US approaches in other issues and regions if President Trump's 'Jacksonian nationalism' persists and prevails in US approaches to world politics during the 2020s.

A global diplomatic network has to deal with whatever issues arise, but a strategic orientation in the coming years would define where it should concentrate – which issues and relationships matter most in Britain's own interests and its demonstration of Britain, as the 'principled and responsible' actor it sees itself to be.[10] Relations between India and Britain, for example, do not figure greatly in the security realm for the coming decade and are not mentioned much in this analysis. India is the only one of the Big Four powers not to have a structural impact on Britain's security future, though it certainly has some relevance to it. But the opportunities for deeper diplomatic and economic relations between India and Britain are increasingly obvious. The relationship has been fraught and delicate for many years given Anglo-Indian historical legacies and India's Cold War alliance with Moscow. But the Indian diaspora in Britain, the recent flow of investment into British industries and the potential for digital sector collaboration, all suggest that there is great potential for much closer relations between London and New Delhi. A more confident and capable British foreign policy could mine the deep potential of this relationship far more vigorously.

Demonstrating to the world immediately that Britain is determined to be secure at home, and within its own neighbourhood, but also, a proactive and useful member of the international community – a country that is genuinely able to make a difference on some key issues and relationships – is the best way to navigate through its security tipping point within the next three to five years. A 'strategic surge' and a certain amount of 'reorientation' could bring ends and means back into a more natural balance and would give Britain the opportunity to play as good an international game as it talks.

Britain's own unhappy home

For too long, and despite a generation of scholars who have demonstrated to the contrary, security and foreign affairs have been perceived by politicians and public alike as somehow essentially different to domestic matters. Foreign and domestic politics are thought to inhabit different realms, which certainly touch each other at many points, but are not intrinsically integrated; not part of the same set of problems and choices. As our study has shown, however, this is a fundamentally unsustainable assumption in a modern globalized economy. Security and foreign policy deeply affect Britain's economy and society; and domestic politics have determining consequences on the way Britain responds to the external world. The Brexit decision will go down in British history as the *nonpareil* example of this truth.

But it has been an unhappy example, born of deeply rooted discontent and carried forward by a squabbling and unhappy family who threaten to bring the roof down on their new home even as they move into it. We have described some of the evident sources of this national unhappiness. Being 'good' at living in a globalized economy, Britain has paid a social price in seeing a successful economy become lopsided and unbalanced, and prone to short-term fluctuations. It has seen the demographic distribution become similarly unbalanced with a heavily populated and economically overheated southeast, as against regions and coastal communities everywhere else that have not shared equally in globalization's benefits. And the 'hourglass shape' of the economy pulls in foreign labour at its bloated base and from the mid-1990s created a dynamic of rapid demographic change that stoked social unease which found expression right across the British political spectrum.

Not least, and not unrelated, Britain has seen the steady growth of dissolution pressures on the UK's own structure since the 1970s. They have not been satiated by forty years of political devolution. The processes of devolving certain powers to Edinburgh and Cardiff, establishing assemblies and finally creating a new power-sharing executive for Northern Ireland (notwithstanding its suspension by the parties within it), have been constitutionally successful. But they have not corrected the economic asymmetries across Britain, indeed in some respects they have made them worse, and they have not assuaged the demand for more regional autonomy in Scotland and Wales. Devolution has not bought off demands to break up the UK; it has merely focused them. And the Brexit process has refocused them anew, under a different and even more intensive lens.

Domestic revolutions have powerful and lasting effects on any country's foreign affairs and its presence in the world. While Britain has a very conflictual domestic history, it does not much go in for revolutions. But if ever there was a tipping point where Britain's domestic well-being and its external presence in the world were so intimately related, or so urgently exposed, it will surely be in the years after Brexit's course is settled. Britain's domestic security and social cohesion, its economy and the ability to exploit the 'globalization 2.0' period are all directly linked to how it should express its external policies, how much resource it devotes to them and how Britain will be perceived by the rest of the world. Nothing would be so damaging to British security in the next decade as a continuation of the familial unhappiness that brought it to such a political nervous breakdown in 2019.

The structural nature of this national disharmony suggests that it will not pass by itself and will require more than palliative measures. Public trust both in government and the future of the country was at a low ebb in 2019. Only one in seven Britons surveyed in the extensive Edelman Trust Barometer felt that 'the country ... works for them'; six out of seven thought that it was 'increasingly unfair'. Even in 2017, before the Brexit process became so publicly divisive in Parliament, more than six out of ten respondents had thought that the government does not deliver on its commitments, is 'not honest' and is 'not transparent'. The same proportions, though higher among younger people, had felt 'not represented', and from 2016 onwards, a quarter – and then more than a third – expected their standard of living to drop, now and in five years' time. These views were held with only small variations across British regions and social classifications. Fully 60 per cent of the 2019 survey were clear that Brexit had 'harmed social cohesion'.[11] There was a widespread view across Britain's regions that Whitehall and Downing Street had simply ignored the rest of the country outside the southeast. Policy-makers insisted, correctly, that they had initiated any number of regeneration schemes, Business Councils, Regional Development Agencies, the 'northern powerhouse' idea and so on. The problems were partly that such initiatives ran out of political steam after a while, but mainly that they could not reverse the underlying dynamics of the economy or affect the powerful international forces that increasingly shaped it. But they had certainly tried.[12]

The Brexit imbroglio exposed deeper institutional failings in British politics. As Matthew Goodwin pointed out, the evidence suggested that the 60 per cent of Britons who felt 'not represented' (who by fact of demography, means overwhelmingly English voters) wanted something British political parties do not offer – a party that is economically on the left but culturally on the right. They indicate they want a party that would rebalance the economy, tackle inequality, stand up to big international business, but also address the anxieties – and the hopes – that drove the Brexit vote itself.[13] They may, or may not, get a party like this from a post-Brexit political realignment.

But the issue of political realignment is more fundamental. For all its strength and success, there is something structurally wrong with the British economy. And for all its depth and longevity, there is something structurally wrong with the British constitution. This book is not the place to investigate such matters, but we fully recognize the importance of them in Britain's security future. And a failure to address underlying tensions – the unhappy family that is contemporary Britain – in the critical years to come, as we say in previous chapters would hobble any attempt to enhance Britain as a resilient, secure society that can operate successfully in the world when Brexit is at last, somehow, behind us.

There is much to be said for investigating seriously and urgently the prospect of major constitutional reform and even of transforming Britain into a fully federal UK; it may be the only way to preserve it. The UK was largely forged by war and, as Linda Colley says, it is 'periods of protracted peace that have repeatedly presented the most profound threats to union in the UK'.[14] The ultimate domestic price of the 'protracted peace', that is now so much in Britain's interests, might be a genuinely federal UK. If so, a brave and decisive move in that direction may be the best way of retaining some control over a dynamic historical trend. It would require major constitutional change and a written constitution. It would offer Scottish, Welsh and Northern Irish communities a genuinely new constitutional deal, rather than ad hoc concessions on the basis of the old one. It would decentralize government more completely than at any time since the mid-nineteenth century (when it worked rather well in its own era). And it would transfer extensive economic and social powers to the English regions and the four kingdoms of Britain. It would create lots of regional variations, for good and bad; but it might also release the inner dynamism, inventiveness and entrepreneurship of the whole society and not just the 40 per cent of it represented in David Goodhart's 'anywhere generation', who easily fit in with the dynamics of globalization.[15]

Of course, there are major differences of opinion among serious constitutional analysts over the likelihood and feasibility of such big constitutional steps; but not over their desirability. They agree that Britain's constitution has not responded adequately to the economic and social pressures the country has been under over the last half century, and want to address more radically, and with an eye to a more distant horizon, the unhappiness of Britain's current political family.

One group of distinguished constitutional analysts has been quite clear that the success of the UK as a union can only continue if the Union is fundamentally reformed:

> The United Kingdom has been a conspicuously successful multinational and multi-ethnic state for a long time. Recent experience in Europe and elsewhere has shown that carving up multi-national states is rarely a happy process for any of their components; apart from being increasingly impractical as a result of migration flows, it is a difficult and distressing process that impoverishes all who take part in it.

> If we act now, there is no reason why the United Kingdom should be subjected to the same painful dismantling process that has caused so much misery and

national impoverishment elsewhere. But inactivity will have that result: there is sufficiently general discontent with the present situation for it to be clear that if existing constitutional relationships remain unreformed that will invite the dissolution of the UK.[16]

Others take the view that the legal and practical problems of creating a fully federal union may be insoluble, but they agree that other elements of major constitutional reform are nevertheless becoming unavoidable if the UK is to weather the growing dissolution storm.[17] However it is conceived, the belief grows among those in the political elites who have looked beyond the Brexit hiatus that moving decisively towards a more federal UK suggests a route that could simultaneously help rebalance the economy, reconnect political institutions with the majority of citizens, and support British foreign and security policy with a more consensual and vibrant domestic society. In 2016 outlines of a new Act of Union Bill were produced in the House of Lords, and in 2018 Lord Lisvane introduced a full Act of Union Bill into the upper house, providing a detailed blueprint for what might be possible and based on nine fundamental political principles, expressed as 'core purposes' of a new settlement.[18]

It is fully acknowledged that such discussions have been well-aired in academic circles for a long time. There is no shortage of thinking and modelling for British constitutional change that might address some of its current failings.[19] Even if new constitutional thinking became immediately part of the mainstream political agenda, it would still take many years to become a reality.

But during the tipping point of the 2020s it is the journey that is most important. A Constitutional Convention would be an important first step.[20] To embark seriously on such a major political project would, in itself, be an investment in national discussion – perhaps building a nationwide consensus – that would partly compensate, and maybe overcome, the very fracturing of that consensus which Brexit represented and exacerbated. The extent and delicacy of such a big national challenge would partly depend on how it is presented and how it would affect the country's view of itself. Parliamentary discussions in 2019, drowned out at the time by noisy Brexit rows, began to indicate how this might be approached.[21]

The importance of game changing

Branding exercises are much derided in politics, as if they were attempts to disguise a truth or garner support for something that did not deserve it. But most countries and institutions have a brand, whether or not they consciously create it, in the various images that others hold of them. Successful branding works by adopting some attribute of its subject that is both unambiguously true and genuinely important, and it encapsulates in ideas, words and images a method to give it meaning to others, working with the grain of cultural understanding as it does so. Branding packages reputation and even good branding won't compensate for bad reputation.

As we described in Chapters 11 and 12, the different national capabilities that apply to British foreign and security policies all carry their own reputations in the world, some better than others, some more nurtured and self-conscious than others and some clearly used for straight commercial purposes. But the long-term picture has been generally favourable. Governments can choose to be more or less proactive about their country's national image – a brand that helps define them. British governments have never been particularly consistent over whether they should be passive or proactive in promoting the country in this way. Conscious branding can certainly go wrong, and different governments have taken their own views according to immediate priorities. As we point out, however, Britain has a number of attributes and policy instruments that other nations do not and a long history that lends itself to the promotion of international images of Britain. And if in the past they have been largely favourable, there can be little doubt that in the most recent period they have been almost universally unfavourable. The Brexit process has been generally portrayed by the world's press and media – if not always by its readers and scrollers – as anything from British eccentricity to a post-imperial spasm or even a form of xenophobic madness.

There is, in short, a strong case for Britain to work more proactively, and quickly, through all its available channels to press a more positive image of the country as it emerges from Brexit into the 2020s. Waiting until the Brexit process 'sorts itself out' will, in any case, be a protracted and probably unattractive affair and Britain should get ahead of the curve of opinion. If Britain is prepared to engage in a strategic surge and reorientate some aspects of its foreign and security policies it would also have the opportunity to promote a different image to that of an unhappy country, struggling to cope with the pressures of austerity, and backing away from international commitments after getting its fingers burnt in foreign operations. And this is where a fundamental constitutional rethink would also be so important.

What might that image be? There are a number of possibilities. If successful images and 'branding' must be both true and relevant then a British image should embrace Brexit rather than imply that it did not happen, or that it somehow makes no difference. A successful image should also echo the past as well as point to the future. British historical continuity and pragmatic consistency is an element of that. But one of the most potent images that spans the past and looks towards the future is Britain as a game changer. It has done this in the past and is capable of doing it again within the Western world in whose interest it shares so much.

Britain established so many of the rules and new institutions of the international system in the nineteenth and twentieth centuries. It decolonized better than other imperial powers and created a unique Commonwealth. It pioneered new forms of government by consent through five centuries. As Simon Jenkins put it, the hero of the long story of Britain, is Parliament.[22] Britain was important in the 1940s in creating the new Bretton Woods international economic order; it broke with that mould in the 1980s in working with the United States (controversially, as it is now portrayed) in articulating a neoliberal approach to international markets. In this way it opened itself to the forces of globalization earlier than most of its partners. And in 2016 it was a European game changer in voting for Brexit. It would be a real game changer again if it took on constitutional reform as a way of preparing itself for a better, more economically flexible and secure future. Being a game changer is always controversial and certainly does not rule out making costly or deadly mistakes. But it is the image of a country that is prepared to act, and act consequentially; of a country that is not paralysed by its immediate circumstances, or too risk averse to 'make a difference' either within itself or in the world.

Of course, such an image, or any other for that matter, must be true and relevant to what Britain *is*, and what it wants to *become*. But at the turn of the decade there is precious little evidence that such important questions are seriously being addressed. They are repeatedly being asked but only in rhetorical fashion. There have been few answers and certainly no semblance of national discussions about them. The country has been transfixed by its immediate circumstances. The idea that Britain should simply default to 'be the country it always was' in global politics is probably no longer on offer. Brexit really has changed the game for Britain in Europe; and the circumstances of the 2020s seem set to create some new rules and requirements by which to play. It would be better to embrace these realities than be paralysed by them.

Notes

Introduction

1   In this book the name 'Britain' is being used throughout as a more elegant term than 'United Kingdom' or 'UK', neither of which is easy on the reader's eye. United Kingdom is the legally correct term, as it includes England, Wales, Scotland and Northern Ireland, and it is the term used by the government and in official publications. 'Great Britain' is a geographical term, referring to the greater part of the British Isles and excludes the island of Ireland and therefore Northern Ireland. So we use 'Britain' as elegantly synonymous with 'UK'.

2   This had happened twice before in recent Labour Party history, when James Callaghan replaced Harold Wilson on his sudden resignation in 1976 and then in 2007 when Tony Blair finally and reluctantly stood aside for Gordon Brown to assume the prime ministership. Prior to the premiership of Boris Johnson, it happened twice in Conservative circles when John Major replaced Margaret Thatcher in 1990 and when Alec Douglas-Home became prime minister in 1963. In only one of these four cases – John Major – did the successor go on to win a subsequent election.

3   Though Greenland left the EU in 1982, having been part of the organization by virtue of Denmark's membership.

4   HM Government, *The National Security Strategy of the United Kingdom: Security in an Interdependent World*, Cm 7291, March 2008, p. 5.

5   HM Government, *A Strong Britain in an Age of Uncertainty: The National Security Strategy,* Cm 7953, October 2010, p. 27; HM Government, *National Security Strategy and the Strategic Defence and Security Review 2015*, Cm 9161, November 2015, p. 85.

6   Charles Krauthammer, 'The Unipolar Moment', *Foreign Affairs* 70, no. 1 (1990–91).

Chapter 1: The geopolitical wheels

1   In 1960 average life expectancy globally was 53 years; in 2016 it was 72 years. In 1990 global infant mortality stood at 100 per 1000 live births; in 2016 it was 48. In 1800 some 99 per cent of the global population lived in what is now defined as 'extreme poverty' (less than $1.90 per day at PPP rates). In 1980 that figure was 42 per cent globally; in 2014 it stood at 10 per cent. In China the 'extreme poverty'

figure had fallen from 67 per cent in 1990 to 1 per cent in 2014; in India from 45 per cent to 20 per cent over the same period. See also, Steven Pinker, *The Better Angels of Our Nature*, London, Penguin Books, 2011, and *Enlightenment Now*, London, Allen Lane, 2018; also, Hans Rosling, *Factfulness*, London, Sceptre, 2018.

2 See, Michael Mandelbaum, *The Rise and Fall of Peace on Earth*, Oxford, Oxford University Press, 2019.

3 Joseph S. Nye, *Is the American Century Over?*, Cambridge, Polity Press, 2015; Christopher Layne, 'The US-Chinese Power Shift and the End of the Pax Americana', *International Affairs* 94, no. 1 (January 2018), pp. 89–111.

4 Stephen E. Ambrose and Douglas G. Brinkley, *Rise to Globalism: American Foreign Policy Since 1938*, 9th ed., Revised, London, Penguin Books, 2011; Angus Maddison, *Chinese Economic Performance in the Long Run, 960-2030*, 2nd ed., Paris, OECD Development Studies Centre, 2007.

5 Speech to the 19th National Congress of the Communist Party of China, 18 October 2017.

6 Gideon Rachman, 'America, China and the Art of Confrontation', *Financial Times*, 17 December 2018.

7 Graham Allison, *Destined for War: Can America and China Escape the Thucydides Trap?*, Boston and New York, Houghton Mifflin Harcourt, 2017. See also a similar analysis a decade earlier in, Richard E. Bush and Michael E. O'Hanlon, *A War Like No Other: The Truth about China's Challenge to America,* Hoboken, NJ, Wiley, 2007.

8 Niall Ferguson, 'In this Cold War between Trump and China, Beware the Enemy Within', *Sunday Times*, 10 March 2019.

9 Henry Kissinger, *World Order*, London, Allen Lane, 2014.

10 Robert Kaplan, *The Return of Marco Polo's World: War, Strategy and American Interests*, New York, Random House, 2018.

11 Astrid H. M. Nordin and Mikael Weissmann, 'Will Trump Make China Great Again? The Belt and Road Initiative and International Order', *International Affairs* 94, no. 2 (March 2018), pp. 231–249.

12 Dmitri Trenin, *Should We Fear Russia?*, Cambridge, Polity Press, 2014.

13 Having a GDP in 2017 of around $1.6 trillion as opposed to $2.6 trillion in Britain.

14 Michael Burleigh, *The Best of Times, the Worst of Times: A History of Now*, London, Pan Books, 2018, p. 195.

15 Vladimir Putin, Speech to the Duma, Moscow, 18 March 2014, at http://en.kreml in.ru/events/president/news/20603

16 Lawrence Freedman, *Ukraine and the Art of Strategy*, Oxford, Oxford University Press, 2018.

17 United States Government, *US National Security Strategy*, January 2018, and Department of Defense, *US Defense Strategy*, January 2018.

18 Luis Simon, *The Spectre of a Westphalian Europe?,* Whitehall Paper 90, London, Royal United Services Institute, 2018.

19 Shashank Joshi, *Indian Power Projection*, Whitehall Paper 85, London, Royal United Services Institute, 2016.

20   'Full Text of Modi's First Speech After Historic Election Victory', *Business Insider India*, 26 May 2019.

21   Eswaran Sridharan, 'Where Is India Headed? Possible Future Directions in Indian Foreign Policy', *International Affairs* 93, no. 1 (January 2017), pp. 51–68.

22   Martin Wolf, 'India Will Rise, Regardless of Its Politics', *Financial Times*, 5 February 2019.

23   Amrita Narlikar, 'India's Role in Global Governance: A Modi-Fication?' *International Affairs* 93, no. 1 (2017).

24   See, Alyssa Ayres, *Our Time Has Come: How India Is Making Its Place in the World*, Oxford, Oxford University Press, 2018.

25   Peter Frankopan, *The New Silk Roads: The Present and Future of the World*, London, Bloomsbury, 2018, pp. 87–95.

26   Raffaello Pantucci and Sarah Lain, *China's Eurasian Pivot: The Silk Road Economic Belt*, RUSI Whitehall Paper 68, London, Royal United Services Institute, 2017, pp. 30–46.

27   Bruno Macaes, *Belt and Road: A Chinese World Order*, London, Hurst, 2018.

28   Jane's, *Terrorism and Insurgency Monitor*, 14 May 2019.

29   Will Doig, *High Speed Empire: Chinese Expansion and the Future of South East Asia*, Columbia, NY, Columbia University Global Reports, 2018.

30   Patrick Porter, 'Advice for a Dark Age: Managing Great Power Competition', *The Washington Quarterly* 42, no. 1 (2019), pp. 7–12.

31   Michael Kofman and Matthew Rojansky, 'A Closer Look at Russia's "Hybrid War"', *Kennan Cable,* 7, Washington, DC, Wilson Center, April 2015.

32   Thomas Rid, *Cyber War Will Not Take Place*, London, Hurst, 2013.

33   See, for example, the rationale for British planning in, Cabinet Office, *Public Summary of Sector Security and Resilience Plans, 2018*, London, Cabinet Office, 2019, p. 4.

34   P. W. Singer and Allan Friedman, *Cybersecurity and Cyberwar: What Everyone Needs to Know*, Oxford, Oxford University Press, 2014.

35   Ministry of Defence, *Global Strategic Trends*, 6th ed., Shrivenham, Development, Concepts and Doctrine Centre, 2018.

36   There are important debates about the near-term feasibility of this between scientists such as Stephen Hawking in his last work and that of Sir Martin Rees. See their latest works compared in Robert Plomin, *Blueprint: How DNA Makes Us Who We Are*, London, Allen Lane, 2018.

37   David Kay, 'Genetically Engineered Bioweapons', in Albert H. Teich, , et al., eds*., AAAS Science and Technology Policy Yearbook 2003*, New York, American Association for the Advancement of Science, 2003; Jan van Aken and Edward Hammond, 'Genetic Engineering and Biological Weapons', *European Molecular Biology Organisation Reports*, 4, 2003.

38   Michio Kaku, *Physics of the Future: The Inventions That Will Transform Our Lives*, London, Penguin Books, 2011, pp. 192–5.

39   Stanley R. Sloan, *Transatlantic Traumas*, Manchester, Manchester University Press, 2018.

40 The relevant part of Article 5 of the Washington Treaty states: 'The Parties agree that an armed attack against one or more of them in Europe or North America shall be considered an attack against them all and consequently they agree that, if such an armed attack occurs, each of them, in exercise of the right of individual or collective self-defence recognised by Article 51 of the Charter of the United Nations, will assist the Party or Parties so attacked by taking forthwith, individually and in concert with the other Parties, such action as it deems necessary, including the use of armed force, to restore and maintain the security of the North Atlantic area.'

41 EU defence initiatives were limited in size to battlegroup arrangements and maritime task forces. Even if two or more battlegroups were aggregated to the size of a brigade, or maritime task forces aggregated to a maritime battlegroup, the next order of military magnitude – an army division or a battle-fleet – are the basic units with the firepower and numbers required to undertake serious war-fighting operations such as would be required for any conventional defence of European territory.

42 See, for example, the contrast between a sober analysis of EU capacity and ambitions in, Jolyon Howorth, *Security and Defence Policy in the European Union*, 2nd ed., London, Palgrave Macmillan, 2014, pp. 73–97, and the newly ambitious analysis in, Pol Morillas, *Strategy-Making in the EU: From Foreign and Security Policy to External Action*, London, Palgrave Macmillan, 2018.

43 Iver B. Neumann, 'Russia's Europe, 1991–2016: Inferiority to Superiority', *International Affairs* 92, no. 6 (2016).

44 Sloan, *Transatlantic Traumas*.

45 Magnus Petersson and Benjamin Schreer, *NATO and the Crisis in the International Order: The Atlantic Alliance and Its Enemies*, London, Routledge, 2018.

46 Oliver Bouin, 'The End of Europe's Integration as We Knew It: A Political Economic Analysis', in Manuel Castells, ed., *Europe's Crises*, Polity Press, Cambridge, 2018.

47 Niall Ferguson, 'The EU Melting Pot Is Melting Down', *Sunday Times*, 17 June 2018.

48 Annual population growth in sub-saharan Africa is 2.3 per cent against a global average of 1.1 per cent.

49 Burleigh, *The Best of Times, the Worst of Times*, p. 360.

50 Emmanuel Macron, *Revolution*, London, Scribe Books, 2017, Chapter 15; Fabrizio Tassinari, *Variable Geometries: Mapping Ideas, Institutions and Power in the Wider Europe*, London, Centre for European Policy Studies, November 2006.

51 US Government, *US National Security Strategy,* and Department of Defense, *US Defense Strategy*.

52 Richard Haass, 'How the World Order Ends: And What Comes in Its Wake', *Foreign Affairs* 98, no. 1 (2019).

Chapter 2: The global economic turmoil

1 'The Next Recession', *The Economist*, Special Report, 13 October 2018.

2 See, Adam Tooze, *Crashed: How a Decade of Financial Crisis Changed the World*, London, Allen Lane, 2018.

3 Theodore Levitt, 'The Globalisation of Markets', *Harvard Business Review*, May 1983.

4 See, Foreign Affairs, *The Fourth Industrial Revolution: A Davos Reader*, New York, Council on Foreign Relations, 2016.

5 The first industrial revolution was based on steam and water power in the late eighteenth century; the second on electrical power just a century later; the third on communications and internet power another century later again; and the fourth, less than half a century on, is (thought to be) based on the power of information and artificial intelligence that fuses the physical, digital and biological worlds.

6 Joshua C. Ramo, *The Seventh Sense: Power, Fortune, and Survival in the Age of Networks*, New York, Little Brown, 2016, p. 92.

7 See, Niall Ferguson, *The Square and the Tower: Networks, Hierarchies and the Struggle for Global Power*, London, Allen Lane, 2017.

8 See, ibid., pp. 42–3.

9 The EU's General Data Protection Regulation may be regarded as the first international step to create a new multinational framework to deal with the novel economic challenges posed by the internet companies. It remains to be seen to what extent it will provide a model for wider international action.

10 Barry M. Leiner, et al., *Brief History of the Internet 1997*, Internet Society, p. 10.

11 'Apps' is not a precise description and some mobile devices that contained early applications, such as Psion personal organizers or Newton Message Pads, were available in the late 1980s though not using the internet for their essential functionality. 'Apps' in the way they are now commonly understood can be traced to the Palm OS of 1996 and especially the Nokia 6110 mobile phone, launched in 1997, which had the *Snake* game pre-loaded on it. See, AVG Technologies, *A History of Mobile Apps: 1983 and Beyond*, 4 February 2015.

12 Extracted from *Statistica: The Statistical Portal,* at https://www.statista.com/stati stics/276623/number-of-apps-available-in-leading-app-stores/

13 Extracted from *Zephoria: Digital Marketing,* at https://zephoria.com/top-15-valuabl e-facebook-statistics/; https://zephoria.com/twitter-statistics-top-ten/; https:// zephoria.com/top-15-valuable-facebook-statistics/

14 Mark Zuckerberg, speech at Facebook F8 Conference, California, 18 April 2016.

15 Stephen Pappas, 'How Big Is the Internet, Really?', *Live Science*, 18 March 2016; and see, Charles Arthur, 'What's a Zettabyte?', *The Guardian*, 29 June 2011 who says, 'A zettabyte is roughly 1000 exabytes. To place that amount of volume in more practical terms, an exabyte alone has the capacity to hold over 36,000 years' worth of HD quality video … or stream the entire Netflix catalogue more than 3,000 times. A zettabyte is equivalent to about 250 billion DVDs.'

16 'You Ain't Seen Nothing Yet', *The Economist*, 8 June 2019, p. 16.

17 'Facebook Stutters after Series of Scandals', *The Times*, 31 October 2018.

18 In 2000 the top five, by market capitalization, were General Electric, Exxon, Pfizer, Citi and Cisco. Microsoft made its first appearance in this list in 2001, Google and Apple only in 2012. See, Mithi Maniam, 'The Emergence of the GAFA World', LinkedIn, 20 March 2018.

19 Standard Oil N.J. was famously broken up by US anti-trust law in 1911 when it still held 65 per cent of the market. Facebook and Alphabet already control well over half their existing markets, however they are measured.

20 'What Is Populism?', *The Economist*, 19 December 2016.

21 See, Benjamin Moffitt, *The Global Rise of Populism: Performance, Political Style, and Representation*, Stanford, CA, Stanford University Press, 2016.

22 Oliver Bullough, *Moneyland*, London, Profile Books, 2018, p. 23.

23 Note that Western middle-class people are not becoming poorer through this trend; just that incomes are growing more slowly than others, while higher growth rates are evident all round them. And a 3.4 per cent global level of population movement (up from 2.8 per cent in 1990) equates to around 360 million people migrating over a twenty-year period – that is within a single generation.

24 Francis Fukuyama, *Identity: Contemporary Identity Politics and the Struggle for Recognition*, London, Profile Books, 2018, pp. 74–80.

25 Hamish McRae, 'Facebook, Airbnb, Uber and the Unstoppable Rise of the Content Non-generators', *The Independent*, 5 May 2015; Leslie Hook, 'Uber and Airbnb Business Models Come under Scrutiny', *Financial Times*, 30 December 2016.

26 Andrew Hill, et al., 'The Global Hunt to Tax Big Tech', *Financial Times*, 2 November 2018.

27 European Union action through the 2018 General Data Protection Regulation represents the only tangible international pushback to date.

28 See, 'Big Tech Faces Competition and Privacy Concerns in Brussels', Briefing, *The Economist*, 23 March 2019.

29 See, for example, Elias Groll, 'How Washington Helps Tehran Control the Internet', *Foreign Policy*, 4 January 2018; Justin Lynch, 'North Korea Is Using the Internet "Like a Criminal Syndicate"', *Fifth Domain*, 26 October 2018; 'Shifting Patterns of Internet Use Reveal Adaptable and Innovative North Korea Ruling Elite', *Recorded Future: Cyber Threat Analysis*, CTA-2018-1025.

30 In 2015 Freedom House defined 31 per cent of countries as offering 'free' internet access; 23 per cent as 'partly free'; 34 per cent as 'not free' and 12 per cent were not assessed. Freedom House, *Freedom on the Net 2015: Privatising Censorship, Eroding Privacy*, New York, Freedom House, 2015.

31 Julian Nocetti, 'Russia's "Dictatorship of the Law" Approach to Internet Policy', *Internet Policy Review* 4, no. 4, (November 2015).

32 The figure has doubled since 2009. See, *TechinAsia*, 23 January 2017.

33 China is said to employ no fewer than 2 million people monitoring what passes across its www servers. See, Michael Burleigh, *The Best of Times, the Worst of Times: A History of Now*, London, Pan Books, 2018, p. 217.

34 Simon Denyer, 'China's Scary Lesson to the World: Censoring the Internet Works', *Washington Post*, 23 May 2016.

35 'Accounts Show Impact of Repression in Xinjiang', *China Digital Times*, 31 July 2018; 'CAC, Alibaba, Ex-Google Chief on China's Internet', *China Digital Times*, 21 September 2018.

36 'US Adds China's Internet Controls to List of Trade Barriers', *New York Times*, 7 April 2016.

37 'Former Google CEO Predicts the Internet Will Split in Two - And One Part Will Be Led by China', *CNBC*, 20 September 2018; *Daily Telegraph*, 21 September 2018; *Washington Post*, 22 October 2018.

38 See Rob Smith, 'The World's Biggest Economies in 2018', *World Economic Forum*, 18 April 2018, which shows the size of the US economy as $20.4 trillion, China $14.0 trillion, Japan $5.1 trillion, Germany $4.2 trillion, UK $2.9 trillion, France $2.9 trillion, India $2.8 trillion.

39 McKinsey Global Institute, 'By Far the Most Rapid Shift in the World's Economic Center of Gravity Happened in 2000-10', l July 2012, https://globaltrends2030.files .wordpress.com/2012/07/nic-blog-mgi-shifting-economic-center-of-gravity.pdf; see also, 'The World's Shifting Centre of Gravity', *The Economist*, 28 June 2012.

40 Extracted from *Statistica: The Statistics Portal*, at https://www.statista.com/stati stics/267898/gross-domestic-product-gdp-growth-in-eu-and-euro-area/

41 Ibid. https://www.statista.com/statistics/263614/gross-domestic-product-gdp-growth-rate-in-the-united-states/

42 The International Monetary Fund, founded in 1945, the World Bank, founded in 1944, and the World Trade Organisation, founded in 1995.

43 Rana Mitter, 'Under the Iron Rule of Xi Jinping, Anyone Can Disappear', *Sunday Times*, 14 October 2018.

44 Tooze, *Crashed*, pp. 13, 16.

45 *The Economist*, 6–12 October 2018, pp. 18–9.

46 Tooze, *Crashed*, p. 17.

47 Niall Ferguson, 'Many Unhappy Returns to the Crash of 2008', *Sunday Times*, 16 September 2018.

48 On the nature of financial instruments and failures of Britain's regulatory authorities, see, Philip Coggan, *The Money Machine: How the City Works*, 7th ed., London, Penguin Books, 2015.

49 Though, unlike the shorter recession of the early 1930s, it did not then become a depression, mainly because of the application of Keynesian economic solutions that had been devised precisely because of the troubling experience of that decade.

50 Gordon Brown, *My Life, Our Times*, London, Bodley Head, 2017, p. 21.

51 See, ibid., pp. 336–44.

52 Tooze, *Crashed*, p. 438.

53 Ibid., pp. 242–3.

54 'In Davos, Xi Makes Case for Chinese Leadership Role', *Reuters Business News*, 17 January 2017.

55 Collectively, the 'mature economies', whose GDPs can be calculated, make up close to the global total of GDP, which is necessarily a matter of estimation. In 2018 the 'debt mountain' in relation to global GDP was estimated at 320 per cent. See, Ferguson, 'Many Unhappy Returns to the Crash of 2008', 2018.

Chapter 3: The social revolution

1 England was unsuccessfully invaded by French forces who landed in 1216 and again in 1797. It was successfully invaded in 1485 by the usurper who became Henry VII and again in 1689 by the Dutch Prince who became William III. When invasions succeed they are not normally referred to as 'invasions'.

2 Simon Jenkins, *A Short History of England*, London, Profile Books, 2012. Those periods involve the first prolonged British/French conflict commonly called the 'Hundred Years War' (1330–1453); followed immediately by the 'Wars of the Roses' (1453–83) effectively the first *civil* war, as opposed to the overtly *dynastic* wars of the twelfth century; followed by the 'English Civil War' and its authoritarian aftermath (1642–60); and then a second hundred year on/off conflict with France (1701–1815) that began in Europe, was fought across the globe, and then centred back on the Napoleonic Wars for European domination. This latter conflict included an internation civil war (Britain's third) consisting of two Scottish invasions of England (1715 and 1745), supported and supplied by France. The sense of national survival perceived to be at stake in both world wars (1914–18 and 1939–45) speaks for itself.

3 Linda Colley, *Acts of Union and Disunion*, London, Profile Books, 2014, p. 147.

4 Kenneth O. Morgan, 'Editor's Foreword', in The *Oxford History of Britain,* Revised ed., Oxford, Oxford University Press 2010, pp. ix–x.

5 Institute for Government, 'Big Thinkers: Professor Linda Colley on What Keeps Britain Together', 9 January 2014, available at: https://www.instituteforgovernment. org.uk/events/big-thinkers-professor-linda-colley-what-keeps-britain-together

6 John L. Gaddis, *The Long Peace: Inquiries into the History of the Cold War*, Oxford, Oxford University Press, 1987.

7 Interestingly, there has been a recent boom in fictional alternative histories of Britain in the Second World War, such as Robert Harris, *Fatherland*, London, Arrow Books, 2009; C. J. Sansom, *Dominion*, London, Mantle, 2012; Len Deighton, *SS-GB*, London, HarperCollins, 2009; Owen Sheers, *Resistance*, London, Faber and Faber, 2011.

8 See, for example, Ian Bremmer, *Us vs. Them: The Failure of Globalisation*, London, Portfolio/Penguin, 2018.

9 The 'Anglo-American' economic model was built essentially on Keynesian liberal economic thinking after 1945. The 'new right' of the Reagan–Thatcher era created what was frequently referred to as the 'Washington consensus' and more commonly as 'neoliberal' economic thinking.

10 James Meek, *Private Island: Why Britain Belongs to Someone Else*, London, Verso, 2015, pp. 250–1.

11 David Goodhart, *The Road to Somewhere: The New Tribes Shaping British Politics*, London, Penguin Books, 2017, p. 148.

12 Will Hutton and Andrew Adonis, *Saving Britain: How We Must Change to Prosper in Europe*, London, Abacus, 2018, pp. 29–30.

13 'Coastal Britain' should be never be ignored as a significant part of the island nation. Britain has more than 11,000 miles of coastline and thousands of offshore islands.

Its coastal and island heritage were major parts of its national economy and remain a big element in its national consciousness.

14 David Sainsbury, *Progressive Capitalism: How to Achieve Economic Growth, Liberty and Social Justice*, London, Biteback Publishing, 2013, pp. 9–15.

15 The population of England is expected to grow by 5.9 per cent in the 2016–26 decade, Scotland by 3.2 per cent, Wales by 3.1 per cent and Northern Ireland by 4.2 per cent. See, Office of National Statistics, *National Population Projections: 2016=Based Statistical Bulletin,* Office of National Statistics, 26 October 2017.

16 'England's Population Predicted to Reach 60m within a Decade', *The Times*, 10 April 2019.

17 Linda Colley, *Acts of Union and Disunion*, pp. 57–62.

18 Hutton and Adonis, *Saving Britain,* p. 168. Northern Ireland suspended its own joint executive with delegated powers in 2017 when the two governing parties refused to continue to work together, but the resumption of those delegated powers remains available to the province and is constantly urged from London.

19 Stephen King, 'London Is the Driver of the Economy – So Let It Determine Our EU Course', *Evening Standard*, 22 October 2018.

20 They are: Kensington and Chelsea; Westminster; Brent; Newham; Ealing. The North East currently has the lowest immigration rate in Britain at 4 per cent.

21 Hutton and Adonis, *Saving Britain*, p. 15.

22 Goodhart, *The Road to Somewhere*, pp. 136–7.

23 Robert Tombs, *The English and Their History*, London, Penguin Books, 2015, p. 888.

24 Hutton and Adonis, *Saving Britain,* p. 176.

25 Goodhart, *The Road to Somewhere,* pp. 122–3; Douglas Murray, *The Strange Death of Europe: Immigration, Identity, Islam*, London, Bloomsbury, 2018, pp. 11–3.

26 Ibid., p. 12.

27 Ibid. p. 136.

28 Francis Fukuyama, *Identity: Contemporary Identity Politics and the Struggle for Recognition*, London, Profile Books, 2018, pp. 111–23, 134–5.

29 Burleigh, *The Best of Times,* p. 332.

30 Tombs, *The English and Their History*, p. 838.

31 On Britain's relative tolerance, see a survey of surveys in, M. D. R. Evans and Jonathan Kelley, 'Prejudice against Immigrants Symptomizes a Larger Syndrome, Is Strongly Diminished by Socioeconomic Development, and the UK Is Not an Outlier: Insights from WVS, EVS, and EQLS Surveys', *Frontiers in Sociology*, 4(12), February 2019. Also, Goodhart, *The Road to Somewhere,* p. 118; Murray, *The Strange Death of Europe,* pp. 199–200.

32 Mike Savage, *Social Class in the 21st Century,* London, Pelican Books, 2015, pp. 3–20.

33 Goodhart, *The Road to Somewhere,* pp. 4–7, 37–8.

34 Hutton and Adonis, *Saving Britain,* p. 20.

35 Kenneth O. Morgan, 'Epilogue', in Kenneth O. Morgan, ed., *The Oxford History of Britain*, Oxford, Oxford University Press, 2010, p. 692.

36   Colley, *Acts of Union and Disunion*, p. 99, about a third of which, of course, is made up of residents of Northern Ireland.

37   Ibid.

38   See how contrasting analyses nevertheless agree on these points in, Tim Shipman, *All Out War: The Full Story of Brexit,* London, William Collins, 2017; Craig Oliver, *Unleashing Demons: The Inside Story of Brexit*, London, Hodder and Stoughton, 2016.

39   Martin Sandbu, 'Brexit Lays Bare the Extremes of British Society', *Financial Times*, 25 July 2018.

40   Ibid.

41   Peter Kellner, 'The Balance of Power Lies in the Hands of Two Populist Tribes, Not One', *The Times*, 7 September 2019.

Chapter 4: The crisis of liberal democracy

1   Francis Fukuyama, *The End of History and the Last Man*, London, Penguin Books, 1992.

2   'After the 1832 Reform Act, a higher proportion of the male population in Britain … became enfranchised than in almost any other European state. But after 1850, the United Kingdom increasingly lagged behind other parts of Europe, the United States, and even some of its own colonial dominions. … By the start of the twentieth century, the UK franchise was one of the narrowest in Europe.' Colley, *Acts of Union and Disunion,* p. 40.

3   Walter Russell Mead, *God and Gold: Britain, America and the Making of the Modern World,* London, Atlantic Books, 2007; Niall Ferguson*, Empire: How Britain Made the Modern World*, London, Penguin Books, 2004.

4   Jan-Werner Muller, *What Is Populism?*, London, Penguin Books, 2017, pp. 96–9; Niall Ferguson, *The Great Degeneration: How Institutions Decay and Economies Die*, London, Penguin Books, 2014.

5   A. C. Grayling, *Democracy and Its Critics*, London, Oneworld, 2018.

6   See, for example, George Monbiot, *Out of the Wreckage: A New Politics for an Age of Crisis*, London, Verso, 2018; Hutton and Andrew, *Saving Britain*, pp. 152–66; Savage, *Social Class*, pp. 65–92; David Sainsbury, *Progressive Capitalism: How to Achieve Economic Growth, Liberty and Social Justice*, London, Biteback Publishing, 2013, pp. 115–51.

7   Roger Eatwell and Matthew Goodwin, *National Populism: The Revolt against Liberal Democracy*, London, Pelican Books, 2018, pp. 257–62.

8   Ibid., p. 253.

9   Ibid., p. 262.

10   Michael Burleigh, *The Best of Times, the Worst of Times*, London, Pan Books, 2017, pp. 354–60.

11   George Monbiot, *Out of the Wreckage*, pp. 150–1; Grayling, *Democracy and Its Critics*, pp. 189–97.

12 UK Parliament, *Referendums Held in the UK*, https://www.parliament.uk/get-invol ved/elections/referendums-held-in-the-uk

13 Philip Stephens, 'Theresa May Has Lost Control of Brexit', *Financial Times*, 6 December 2018.

14 Markus Wagner and Thomas M. Meyer, 'The Radical Right as Niche Parties? The Ideological Landscape of Party Systems in Western Europe, 1980–2014', *Political Studies* 65, no. 1 (2017), pp. 84–107; Eatwell and Goodwin, *National Populism*, pp. 286–8.

15 Murray, *The Strange Death of Europe*, pp. 11–13.

16 Burleigh, *The Best of Times*, pp. 356–8.

17 Niall Ferguson, *The Great Degeneration*, pp. 119–22. The highest participation rates are for 'sport and recreation' but even here are less than one in three.

18 Matthew D'Ancona, *Post Truth: The New War on Truth and How to Fight Back*, London, Ebury Press, 2017, pp. 19–23.

19 Ghita Ionescu and Ernest Gellner, eds., *Populism: Its Meaning and National Character*, London, Weidenfeld and Nicolson, 1969.

20 Which is why populism can take on left- or right-wing forms, by adapting itself to existing ideologies. See, Eatwell and Goodwin, *National Populism*, pp. 46–8.

21 Muller, *What Is Populism?*, pp. 53–7.

22 George Monbiot, *How Did We Get into This Mess?,* London, Verso Books, 2016.

23 http://www.epicenternetwork.eu/briefings/populism-index-2017-summary/; Matthijs Rooduijn, 'Why Is Populism Suddenly All the Rage?', *The Guardian*, 20 November 2018.

24 UKIP and Sinn Fein.

25 Rooduijn, "Why Is Populism Suddenly All the Rage?'.

26 Hutton and Adonis, *Saving Britain,* pp. 47–81. The authors accuse Conservative Party leaders from John Major onwards of ceding policy leadership in the party to UKIP during the most critical years building to the national referendum of 2016.

27 Joseph Tawney, 'Populism in Latin America', *International Policy Digest*, 12 January 2018.

28 Peter Kovisto, *The Trump Phenomenon: How the Politics of Populism Won in 2016*, Bingley, Emerald Publishing, 2017.

29 See Steven Levitsky and Daniel Ziblatt, *How Democracies Die: What History Reveals About Our Future*, London, Penguin Books, 2019, Chapters 7,8.

30 Michael Kazin, 'Trump and American Populism', *Foreign Affairs* 95, no. 6 (2016).

31 See, Aurel Croissant, et al., eds., *Comparing Autocracies in the Early Twenty-First Century,* Volume 1, London, Routledge, 2014, pp. 20–35.

32 This may work in counter-intuitive ways. Democracies are not necessarily more reliable partners in world politics than autocracies, though the point about the maintenance of international values stands. See, Michaela Mattes and Mariana Rodriguez, 'Autocracies and International Cooperation', *International Studies Quarterly* 58, no. 3 (2013), pp. 527–38.

33 According to its mission statement, Freedom House is 'an independent watchdog organization dedicated to the expansion of freedom and democracy around the

world' – funded partly by the US government though operating as an independent non-governmental organization. See, https://freedomhouse.org/

34   https://freedomhouse.org/report/freedom-world/freedom-world-2018

35   'A decade of declines: dramatic declines in freedom have been observed in every region of the world', https://freedomhouse.org/report/freedom-world/freedom-world-2018

36   Ibid.

37   See, Thomas Hale, David Held and Kevin Young, *Gridlock: Why Global Cooperation Is Failing When We Need It Most*, Cambridge, Polity Press, 2013; Thomas Hale and David Held, et.al., *Beyond Gridlock*, Cambridge, Polity Press, 2017.

38   Jennifer Brown, et al., *Millennials*, House of Commons Briefing Paper Number CBP7946, 11 April 2017.

39   Office of National Statistics, *National Population Projections*.

40   For example, see, William Frey, *The Millennial Generation: A Demographic Bridge to America's Diverse Future*, Brookings Institute, January 2018.

41   Harriet Sherwood, 'Christianity as Default Is Gone': The Rise of a Non-Christian Europe', *The Guardian*, 21 March 2018.

42   Richard Fry, et al, *How Millennials Today Compare with Their Grandparents 50 Years Ago*, Pew Research Centre, 16 March 2018.

43   Joel Stein, 'Millennials: The Me Me Me Generation', *TIME*, 20 May 2013; Tom Eggemeir, 'Why Millenials Want It All and Want It Now', *Digital Marketing Magazine*, 18 November 2015.

44   Kate Samuelson, 'The Millennial Teetotalers: Upending the Stereotype of Boozy Britain', *TIME*, 8 August 2018; Office of National Statistics, *Being 18 in 2018*, Office of National Statistics, 13 September 2018.

45   Sarah O'Connor, 'Millennials Poorer Than Previous Generations, Data Shows', *Financial Times*, 23 February 2018; Jonathan Cribb, et al., *The Decline of Homeownership Among Young Adults,* Briefing Note, Institute for Fiscal Studies, 16 February 2018; Office of National Statistics, *Young People's Career Aspirations Versus Reality,* Office of National Statistics, 27 September 2018.

46   Julie Saussier, *Millennials' Values*, Credit Suisse, 2017.

Chapter 5: Dealing with the great powers

1   The Soviet Union was replaced by fifteen other states, including Russia; East Germany ceased to exist; Czechoslovakia split into two; and former Yugoslavia into seven. One of those seven – Kosovo – is recognized as a new state by the United States and most countries in the EU but not by Russia.

2   See, for example, Mary Kaldor, *New and Old Wars: Organised Violence in a Global Era*, Stanford, CA, Stanford University Press, 1999; Rupert Smith, *The Utility of Force: The Art of War in the Modern World*, London, Penguin Books, 2006; Paul Rogers, *Irregular War: ISIS and the New Threat from the Margins*, London, I.B. Tauris, 2016.

3   Mark Urban, *The Skripal Files: The Life and Near Death of a Russian Spy*, London, Macmillan, 2018, pp. 234–53, 270–85.

4   See, Gov.UK, 'UK Exposes Russian Cyber Attacks', at, https://www.gov.uk/govern ment/news/uk-exposes-russian-cyber-attacks

5   Tessa Berenson, 'Vladimir Putin: Brexit Is Result of "Arrogance" from British Leadership', *TIME*, 24 June 2016; Andrew Roth, 'Putin Tells May to "Fulfil Will of People" on Brexit', *The Guardian*, 20 December 2018.

6   Gov.UK, 'PM Commons Statement on National Security and Russia', 26 March 2018, at https://www.gov.uk/government/speeches/pm-commons-statement-on-national-security-and-russia-26-march-2018; Speech to RUSI by Chief of Defence Staff, *Guardian*, 23 January 2018; Defence Secretary, Statement to Parliament, 22 April 2018, *Daily Telegraph*, 23 April 2018.

7   For example, the 'Rose Revolution' in Georgia, the 'Orange Revolution' in Ukraine, the 'Velvet Revolution' in Armenia or the 'Tulip Revolution' of Kyrgyzstan.

8   A ninth enlargement is anticipated with the accession of North Macedonia to the alliance in 2020, bringing its membership up to thirty states.

9   Rodric Braithwaite, 'Russia, Ukraine and the West', *RUSI Journal* 159, no. 2 (April 2014).

10   'Syria and Russia bomb hospitals in Idlib after they were given coordinates in hope of preventing attacks', *Daily Telegraph*, 30 May 2019.

11   Transnistria has been a breakaway Russian-separatist territory within Moldova since 1992; Abkhazia and South Ossetia are contested Georgian territories conquered by Russian forces in their 2008 war with Georgia.

12   Igor Sutyagin and Justin Bronk, *Russia's New Ground Forces*, RUSI Whitehall paper 89, London, Royal United Services Institute, 2017, pp. 11–12.

13   Adrian A. Basora and Aleksandr Fisher, 'Putin's "Greater Novorossiya" – The Dismemberment of Ukraine', *Foreign Policy Research Institute*, 2 May 2014.

14   Stephen Lewis, 'Russia's Continued Aggression Against Ukraine: Illegal Actions in the Kerch Strait and the Sea of Azov', *RUSI Journal* 164, no. 1 (2019).

15   'Finlandization' is a useful piece of Cold war jargon, referring to the fact that as a small state next door to a very powerful Soviet Union, Finland maintained its independence and freedom by being always sensitive to what would be acceptable in the Kremlin. It was ultimately a (successful) tightrope act.

16   Sutyagin and Bronk, *Russia's New Ground Forces*, pp. 131–3.

17   The Soviet Union certainly had a military plan to launch a massive blitzkrieg attack into Western Europe in the event of all-out war, not because Soviet leaders wanted to conquer Western Europe per se, but because it was the only option that made military sense from their perspective – to defeat NATO and expel US forces from Europe before NATO could decide to 'go nuclear'. The fact that Soviet military leaders increasingly lost faith in this plan's prospects of success didn't prevent it being the only feasible war plan they could devise.

18   Ofer Fridman, 'Hybrid Warfare or Gibridnaya Voyna?: Similar but Different', *RUSI Journal* 162, no. 1, February 2017.

19   Michael Kofman and Matthew Rojansky, 'A Closer Look at Russia's "Hybrid War"', *Kennan Cable* 7, Wilson Center, April 2015.

20   During the Cold War, the Soviet Union was a reliable supplier of gas to the West. But since then Russia has tried to use gas supplies as a political weapon on a number of occasions. The Nord Stream 2 pipeline is planned to pump gas directly from western Russia, across the Baltic Sea into Germany, for further distribution in Western Europe. It will take Germany's dependence on Russian gas to over 50 per cent, and is regarded by many observers as providing unacceptable potential leverage to Russia. Meanwhile, Russia negotiates relatively generous long-term deals to supply Hungary with gas for the mid-2020s.

21   Michael Burleigh, *The Best of Times,* pp. 168–9.

22   Misha Glenny, *McMafia: Seriously Organised Crime*, London, Vintage Books, 2009.

23   Karen Dawisha, *Putin's Kleptocracy: Who Owns Russia?*, New York, Simon and Shuster, 2014; Oliver Bullough, *Moneyland*, London, Profile Books, 2018.

24   Fiona Hamilton, 'Kremlin Is Trying to Undermine Us, Says Cyberdefence Chief', *The Sunday Times*, 15 November 2017.

25   Michelle Obama, *Becoming,* London, Viking, 2018, pp. 403–4.

26   See, for example, Martin Wolf, 'The Looming 100-Year US-China Conflict', *Financial Times*, 4 June 2019.

27   Carla Norrlof, 'Hegemony and Inequality: Trump and the Liberal Playbook', *International Affairs* 94, no. 1, 2018; Arlie Russell Hochschild, *Strangers in Their Own Land*, New York, The New Press, 2016; Katherine J. Cramer, *The Politics of Resentment*, Chicago, Chicago University Press, 2016.

28   See, for example, Donald Trump, *Time to Get Tough*, Washington, DC, Regnery Publishing, 2011, in which he says (p. 2), 'To my mind that's an enemy. If we're going to make America number one again, we've got to have a president who knows how to get tough with China, how to out-negotiate the Chinese, and how to keep them from screwing us at every turn.' See also, Graham Allison, 'The US Is Hunkering Down for a New Cold War with China', *Financial Times*, 12 October 2018.

29   US Government, DoD, USAF, *When the Ice Melts: Developing Proactive American Strategy for the Eurasian Arctic*, Washington DC, US Government, 2015.

30   See, Michael Mandelbaum, *The Ideas that Conquered the World: Peace, Democracy and Free Markets in the Twenty-First Century*, New York, Public Affairs, 2004.

31   Hillary Rodham Clinton, *Hard Choices*, London, Simon and Shuster, 2014, pp. 33–4.

32   Jeffrey Goldberg, 'The Obama Doctrine', *The Atlantic*, April 2016. https://www.the atlantic.com/magazine/archive/2016/04/the-obama-doctrine/471525/

33   Bob Woodward, *Obama's Wars*, New York, Simon and Shuster, 2010, pp. 375–80.

34   See, Adrian Johnson, ed., *Wars in Peace*, London, Royal United Services Institute, 2014.

35   See the main judgements contained in, John Chilcot, et al., *The Report of the Iraq Inquiry,* Vol. 8, section 9.8, paragraph 168. Also, Michael Clarke, 'Planning and Fighting a War', *RUSI Journal* 161, no. 6 (December 2016).

36   Michael Howard, 'What's in a Name? How to Fight Terrorism', *Foreign Affairs* 81, no. 1 (January/February 2002).

37   See, for example, Gov.UK, *2010 to 2015 Government Policy: Counter-Terrorism*, Policy Paper, 8 May 2015.

38 Michael Kaplan, 'Jacksonian Nationalism and American Empire: Review Essay', *The New Jacksonian Blog*, 8 August 2010; Burleigh, T*he Best of Times*, pp. 277–82.

39 Walter Russell Mead, 'The Jacksonian Revolt: American Populism and the Liberal Order', *Foreign Affairs* 96, no. 2 (2017), p. 3.

40 Dan Balz and Griff Witte, 'Europeans Fear Trump May Threaten Not Just the Transatlantic Bond, but the State of Their Union', *Washington Post*, 4 February 2019.

41 Doug Stokes, 'Trump, American Hegemony and the Future of the Liberal International Order', *International Affairs*, 94, no, 1 (2018).

42 See, Gideon Rachman, 'The Trump Era Could Last 30 Years', *Financial Times*, 4 February 2019.

43 In renouncing international agreements, Washington points in all cases to flaws and failings in them that most allies would not dispute. The growing difference in thinking arises over whether failing arrangements are better than no arrangements. See, Richard Haas, *A World in Disarray: American Foreign Policy and the Crisis of the Old Order*, London, Penguin, 2018, pp. 312–20.

44 Eric Lutz, 'Trump Privately Discussed Destroying NATO Alliance', *Vanity Fair*, 15 January 2019. The European allies alone, of course, would be capable of withstanding Russian military pressure if they mobilized their resources properly. But this would take some years while there would be a military power vacuum in the heart of Europe.

45 Balz and Witte, *Washington Post*.

46 See, 'Bipartisan Bill Would Prevent Trump from Exiting NATO', *Washington Post*, 17 January 2019.

47 General James Mattis was appointed from the beginning of the Trump administration and left, upon resignation, on 31 December 2018. General H. R. McMaster was appointed NSA after the early resignation of General Michael Flynn. McMaster served from 20 February 2017 until, upon resignation, 9 April 2018.

48 The White House, *The National Security Strategy of the United States of America*, December 2017; The Pentagon, *Summary of the National Defense Strategy of the United States of America*, 19 January 2018.

49 US European Command and US Department of Defense cited in BBC News, 'Trump: What Does the US Do for the Nato Alliance in Europe?' *BBC*, 10 July 2018.

50 NATO, *The Secretary General's Annual Report 2017,* NATO Public Diplomacy Division, 15 March 2018, p. 32; Heaven Taylor-Wynn, 'Donald Trump Misleads on US Defense Spending, NATO Budget', *PolitiFact*, 12 July 2018.

51 The seven missions involved: Ballistic Missile Defence; the European Reassurance Initiative; Afghanistan; NATO-Russia relations; Kosovo; monitoring the Mediterranean, and counter-piracy off the Horn of Africa.

52 Cheryl Pellerin, '2018 Budget Request for European Reassurance Initiative Grows to $4.7 Billion', US Department of Defense, 1 June 2017.

53 NATO, *The Secretary General's Annual Report 2017,* p. 13; NATO, 'United States and Belgium Safeguard the Airspace of NATO's Baltic Allies', *NATO*, 5 September 2017; NATO, 'United States to Augment Air Policing over Bulgaria, Demonstrating Allied Solidarity', *NATO*, 24 August 2016.

54 Bob Woodward, *Fear: Trump in the White House*, New York, Simon and Shuster, 2018, pp. 219–25, 305–8.

55   Demetri Sevastopulo, 'Why Trump's America Is Re-thinking Engagement with China', *Financial Times*, 15 January 2019.

56   Yuen Yuen Ang, 'Autocracy with Chinese Characteristics: Beijing's Behind-the-Scenes Reforms', *Foreign Affairs* 97, no. 3 (2018).

57   https://tradingeconomics.com/china/gdp-growth-annual

58   Gabriel Wildau, 'China's State-Owned Zombie Economy', *Financial Times*, 29 February 2016.

59   QR coding refers to 'quick reaction' software of the sort used in bar-coding, etc. Bernard Zand, 'A Surveillance State Unlike Any the World Has Ever Seen', *Der Spiegel*, 26 July 2018; Sigal Samuel, 'China treats Islam Like a Mental Illness', *The Atlantic*, 28 August 2018; Human Right Watch, *World Report 2019*, New York, HRW, 2019, p. 142.

60   Kai Strittmatter, *We Have Been Harmonised: Life in China's Surveillance State*, Exeter, Old Street Publishing, 2019.

61   Jonathan Holslag, *The Silk Road Trap: How China's Trade Ambitions Challenge Europe*, London, Polity Press, 2019.

62   European Commission Press Release, 'State of the Union 2017 – Trade Package: European Commission Proposes Framework for Screening of Foreign Direct Investments', 14 September 2017.

63   MI6 employs around 3,000.

64   Chinese Law Translate, *National Intelligence Law of the P.R.C. (2017),* at https://www.chinalawtranslate.com/en/中华人民共和国国家情报法/

65   GCHQ is the parent organization to the National Cyber Security Centre (NCSC) which advises British industry and society on the basis of GCHQ's classified expertise.

66   http://www.world-nuclear-news.org/Articles/CGN-ready-to-ramp-up-UK-ambitions

67   'China has turned Xinjiang into a police state like no other', *The Economist*, 31 May 2018.

68   See, G. John Ikenberry, *After Victory: Institutions, Strategic Restraint, and the Rebuilding of Order after Major Wars*, Princeton, Princeton University Press, 2000.

69   Martin Jacques, *When China Rules the World: The End of the Western World and the Birth of a New Global Order*, 2nd ed., London, Allen Lane, 2009, p. 362.

70   Stephen M. Walt, *The Hell of Good Intentions: America's Foreign Policy Elite and the Decline of US Primacy*, New York, Just World Books, 2018.

71   Ibid., Chapter 13.

72   Lawrence Summers, 'Time US Leadership Woke Up to a New Economic Era', *Financial Times*, 5 April 2015.

73   'BRICs' represents Brazil, Russia, India and China. See, Gabriel Wildau, 'New Brics Bank in Shanghai to Challenge Major Institution', *Financial Times*, 21 July 2015.

74   ASEAN was formed in 1967 and represents Brunei, Indonesia, Malaysia, Philippines, Singapore and Thailand.

Chapter 6: Securing from within

1   See, Kent Aitken, *Governance in the Digital Age*, Ottawa, Public Policy Forum, 2018.

2   See Chapter 2, p. 34; See, Niall Ferguson, *The Square and the Tower: Networks, Hierarchies and the Struggle for Global Power*, London, Allen Lane, 2017.

3   See, for example, Charles E. Lindblom, 'The Science of Muddling Through', *Public Administration Review* 19, no. 2 (1959); *The Policy-Making Process*, Englewood Cliffs, NJ, Prentice Hall, 1982.

4   Steven Rosell, *Renewing Governance: Governing by Learning in the Information Age*, Oxford, Oxford University Press, 1999.

5   David Halpern, *Inside the Nudge Unit: How Small Changes Can Make a Big Difference*, London, W. H Allen, 2015, pp. 50–8.

6   See, for example, Cass R. Sunstein, *Why Nudge? The Politics of Libertarian Paternalism*, New Haven NJ, Yale University Press, 2014; Craig R. Fox and David Tannenbaum, 'The Curious Politics of the "Nudge"', *New York Times*, 26 September 2015.

7   Cabinet Office, *National Risk Register*, London, HM Government, 2008.

8   HM Government, *A Strong Britain in an Age of Uncertainty: The National Security Strategy,* Cm 7953, October 2010, p. 27; HM Government, *The National Security Strategy and the Strategic Defence and Security Review 2015*, Cm 9161, November 2015, p. 85.

9   These included assassinations in Phoenix Park Dublin in 1882, of Airey Neave MP and Lord Mountbatten in separate murders in 1979, Ian Gow MP in 1990; multiple bombs in Whitehall in 1883, in Scotland Yard in 1884, Westminster Hall in 1885 and again in 1974, inside the House of Commons in 1855 and against Downing Street in 1991. Of the other British mainland attacks, the Birmingham pub bombings of 1974 and then three massive bombs in Bishopsgate in 1993, Canary Wharf in 1996 and Manchester's Arndale Centre in 1996, all stand out.

10 Abu Qatada emerged as Al Qaeda's de facto spokesman in Britain after his arrival as an asylum seeker in 1993. His early fatwas mainly concerned the civil war in Algeria but from 1996 his statements and influence came to the attention of the British security services, and by 1998 he had justified and promoted the murder of Jews, British and American nationals on the streets of the UK. See, 'Profile: Abu Qatada', *BBC News,* 26 June 2014; Robin Simcox, 'Abu Qatada's Rap Sheet', *Henry Jackson Society*, 18 January 2012.

11 See, Leela Jacinto, 'Is Londonistan Calling Jihadists Back to the Fold?', *France 24*, 5 June 2017.

12 See, Pool Re, *Terror Threat and Mitigation Report 2018,* 12 November 2018.

13 It would not be accurate to say that jihadism is completely nihilistic, even if some of its adherents make nihilistic statements. And there are many different strands to what is collectively termed 'jihadism'. But in comparison with most previous terrorist movements, apart from outright anarchists, jihadist terror attacks in Western countries have been uniquely indiscriminate and usually unconnected to immediate political campaigns or demands. On the basis of the characteristic statements that accompany them, attacks are designed to 'punish' Western society and polarize it.

14 See, Raffaello Pantucci, *We Love Death as You Love Life: Britain's Suburban Terrorists*, London, Hurst, 2015; The Pool Re, *Terror Threat and Mitigation Report 2018,* ibid., assesses terrorist threats in Britain by methods, in descending order of likelihood as: knives and vehicles, improvised explosive devices, firearms, chemicals, arson, biological agents, hostage-taking, drone attack, radiological, aircraft hijacking, cyberattack and nuclear attack.

15 Vincenzo Oliveti, *Terror's Source: The Ideology of Wahhabi-Salafism and Its Consequences*, Birmingham, Amadeus Books, 2002, pp. 15–20.

16 Originally, the Salafi movement existed in Egypt at the beginning of the twentieth century, but since around 1980 'Wahhabi' refers to beliefs held in Saudi Arabia and 'Salafi' to the same beliefs, and the same people, outside Saudi Arabia. As an international terrorist movement, therefore, jihadists might properly be referred to as 'Salafi-Takfiris' since most are not Saudi or live there. It should also be noted that though Wahhabism/Salafism is exclusively Sunni, a strand of Islamic fundamentalism can also be discerned in 'revolutionary Shi'ism', though this forms no part of jihadism in its present terrorist form.

17 Ed Husain, *The House of Islam: A Global History*, London, Bloomsbury, 2018, pp. 146–8.

18 See, Matthew L. N. Wilkinson, *The Genealogy of Terror: How to Distinguish between Islam, Islamism and Islamist Extremism*, London, Routledge, 2019, pp. 5–6.

19 See, Bernard Lewis, *The Crisis of Islam: Holy War and Unholy Terror*, London, Phoenix, 2003, pp. 101–16. The original Quranic references to the 'people of the book' only mention Christians, Jews and Sabians, on the grounds that they followed monotheistic religions. There were more modern inclusions in this category such as Zoroastrians, Samaritans and Mandeans. There remained unresolved uncertainty, after Muslim conquests in south Asia, whether Hindus might also be included.

20 Marc Sageman, *Understanding Terror Networks*, Philadelphia, University of Pennsylvania Press, 2004, p. 24.

21 The best summaries of all these arguments are to be found in Anthony Richards, eds., *Jihadist Terror: New Threats, New Responses*, London, I.B. Tauris, 2019.

22 From 1992 to 2015 British forces suffered seventy-two deaths and seventy-nine 'seriously wounded' in protection of Muslim communities in the Former Yugoslavia. See, Michael Clarke, *The Challenge of Defending Britain*, Manchester, Manchester University Press, 2019, p. 66. It should also be noted, however, that many early jihadis were effectively radicalized by the plight of Muslims in Bosnia during the 1990s, notwithstanding Britain's attempts to protect them.

23 Pantucci, *We Love Death as You Love Life*, pp. 162–4.

24 On the overwhelming Muslim majority for whom jihadists do not speak, see, Omar Saif Ghobash, *Letters to a Young Muslim*, London, Picador, 2017; John L. Esposito and Dalia Mogahed, *Who Speaks for Islam? What a Billion Muslims Really Think*, New York, Gallup Press, 2007.

25 Damon Perry, *The Global Muslim Brotherhood in Britain: Non-violent Islamist Extremism and the Battle of Ideas*, London, Routledge, 2019, p. 143.

26 Jonathan Powell, *Talking to Terrorists: How to End Armed Conflicts*, London, The Bodley Head, 2014, pp. 15–22. See also, Audrey Kurth Cronin, *How Terrorism*

Ends: Understanding the Decline and Demise of Terrorist Campaigns, Princeton, Princeton University Press, 2009.

27 This stands in interesting contrast to government policy against Irish republican terrorism after 1969, which also sought to contain its effects but was open to the possibilities of political negotiation from at least 1974 onwards.

28 Hannah Stuart, *Islamist Terrorism: Analysis of Offences and Attacks in the UK 1998–2015*, London, Henry Jackson Society, 2017. This report lists 'Islamist related offences' (IROs), which may be arrests and/or known plots, successful or otherwise. The figures it offers range from a total of 269 IROs, of which 135 were 'distinct terrorism offences', that is, connected to a plot. In the four years between 2015 and 2019 around sixty additional IROs might be added to these totals, equally distributed.

29 Ibid., p. vii.

30 Ed Husain, *The House of Islam*, pp. 268–9.

31 See, Tahir Abbas, 'The Impact of Structural Inequalities, Integration, Otherness and Discrimination', pp. 89–91; and Maria Sobolewska, 'Attitudes Towards Muslims from Non-Muslims in the UK', p. 83, in Anthony Richards, *Jihadist Terror: New Threats, New Responses*, London, I.B. Tauris, 2019.

32 Jytte Klausen, 'Neighbourhood Effects – How jihadist Recruitment Really Works', in Anthony Richards, *Jihadist Terror*, p. 147.

33 John Gearson and Hugo Rosemont, 'CONTEST as Strategy: Reassessing Britain's Counterterrorism Approach', *Studies in Conflict and Terrorism* 38, no. 2 (2015). The CONTEST counterterrorism strategy defined its four elements as 'prepare', 'protect', 'pursue' and 'prevent'.

34 Babak Akhgar, et al., eds., *Cyber Crime and Cyber Terrorism*, Amsterdam, Elsevier, 2014, pp. 11–17.

35 Pantucci, *We Love Death as You Love Life*, pp. 278–80, 282–90.

36 Jack Moore, 'Does the Death of Abu Mohammad al-Adnani Spell the End for ISIS?', *Newsweek,* 31 August 2016; Pantucci, *We Love Death as You Love Life*, pp. 280–2.

37 Babak Akhgar, et al., eds., Cyber Crime and Cyber Terrorism, p. 16.

38 Todd South, 'VR, Drones and 3-D Printing Drive Terrorist Innovation', *Marine Corps Times*, 21 September 2017.

39 World News, 'GCHQ's Former Chief Warns Cyber-Attacks Will Soon Cause Death', 6 August 2018.

40 Europol, *European Union, Serious and Organised Crime Threat Assessment (SOCTA) 2017: Crime in the Age of Technology*, Europol, Brussels, 2017, p. 14. Though this may also point to improvements in police intelligence and the evolution of smaller groups.

41 Ibid., p. 14.

42 European Commission, DG Home, *Evidence for Necessity of Data Retention in the EU*, March 2013, p. 2.

43 Europol, European Union, *Serious and Organised Crime Threat Assessment (SOCTA) 2017*, p. 15.

44   More than 730 of them have market capitalization of less than $1 million, though 9 of them have market capitalization of over $1 billion. See, Dan Itkis, 'How Many Cryptocurrencies Does the World Need?' *VB News*, 20 September 2017.

45   Derived from Europol, European Union, *Serious and Organised Crime Threat Assessment (SOCTA) 2017*.

46   European Monitoring Centre for Drugs and Drug Addiction & Europol 2016, *EU Drug Markets Report 2016*, p. 23.

47   Ibid., p. 34.

48   European Monitoring Centre for Drugs and Drug Addiction, *United Kingdom: Country Drug Report 2018.* Available: http://www.emcdda.europa.eu/countries/dr ug-reports/2018/united-kingdom_en

49   Ruth Crocker, et al. *The Impact of Organised Crime on Local Communities.* The Police Foundation, Briefing Paper 4, December 2016.

50   HM Government, Cabinet Office and Government Digital Service, *Digital Efficiency Report*, London, 2012.

51   In December 2018 an official government document acknowledged, for the first time, that the potential cyber vulnerability of the submarine-based nuclear deterrent was an important consideration for the future of the force in the era of artificial intelligence. See, Ministry of Defence, *Mobilising, Modernising and Transforming Defence: A Report on the Modernising Defence Programme*, MoD, London, 2018, pp. 13–15.

52   Halpern, Inside the Nudge Unit, pp. 338–44.

53   House of Lords / House of Commons, Joint Committee on the National Security Strategy, *Cyber Security of the UK's Critical National Infrastructure*, HL 222/HC 1708, p. 39.

54   National Cyber Security Centre (NCSC), *Annual Review 2018*, October 2018, p. 22.

55   Ibid., p. 10.

56   Joint Committee on the National Security Strategy (JCNSS), *Cyber Security of the UK's Critical National Infrastructure*, HC 222 / HL 1708, 19 November 2018, p. 8.

57   Thomas P. Bossert, 'It's Official: North Korea Is Behind WannaCry', *The Wall Street Journal*, 18 December 2017.

58   The scam almost netted $1 billion but was contained at the point of transfer and in the event only $81 million proved immediately unrecoverable. See, 'North Korean "Hacker" Charged over Cyber-Attacks against NHS', *The Guardian*, 6 September 2018; JCNSS, Cyber Security of the UK's Critical National Infrastructure, p. 9.

59   NCSC, Annual Review 2018, p. 10.

60   Foreign and Commonwealth Office, 'UK and allies reveal global scale of Chinese cyber campaign', *Press Release*, 20 December 2018.

61   Ibid.

62   Yuan Yang and Ben Bland, 'Who Is the Chinese Group Blamed for Cyber Attacks on the West?', *Financial Times*, 21 December 2018.

63   UK Parliament, *Intelligence and Security Committee, Foreign Involvement in the Critical National Infrastructure: The Implications for National Security*, Cm 8629, London, June 2013, pp. 11–12.

64 National Cyber Security Centre, *Joint US-UK Statement on Malicious Cyber Activity Carried Out by Russian Government*, 16 April 2018.

65 JCNSS, *Cyber Security of the UK's Critical National Infrastructure*, p. 9 and Question 59 in evidence.

66 'Major Cyber-Attack on UK a Matter of "When, Not If" – Security Chief', *The Guardian*, 23 January 2018.

67 ADS – no longer an acronym – is the trade body representing over 1000 UK registered businesses in the aerospace, defence, security and space sectors.

68 Cambridge Centre for Risk Studies, *Cyber Terrorism: Assessment of the Threat to Insurance*, Cambridge, CCRS, November 2017.

69 Merryn Somerset Webb, 'Cyber Breaches Expose the Limits of the Insurance Market', *Financial Times*, 26 January 2019.

70 In 2019 this was being tested in a class action between Mondelez and insurer Zurich over the losses incurred by Mondelez in the NotPetya attack.

71 Lloyd's of London, *Cyber Security: Critical National infrastructure inquiry. Written evidence from Lloyds,* submitted to JCNSS, *Cyber Security of the UK's Critical National Infrastructure*, op. cit., Paper CNI0034, June 2018.

72 HM Government, *Sector Resilience Plan 2015–2016*, London, April 2016.

73 HM Government, *National Cyber Security Strategy 2016–2021*, London, 2016, p. 40.

74 https://www.euronews.com/2019/08/09/major-power-failure-in-uk-causes-disruption

75 Nationalgrid, *Interconnections: Investor Relations*, Briefing Paper, November 2016.

76 Toby Harris, 'Modern Deterrence and Societal Resilience', *RUSI Commentary*, 10 January 2019.

77 These are, respectively, water regulation, electricity and gas regulation, communications regulation and the Office of Nuclear Regulation. Outside these bodies, the government can only formally direct these industries through legislation. See, National Audit Office, *Regulating to Protect Consumers in Utilities, Communications, and Financial Services Markets*, HC 992, 15 March 2019, p. 7.

78 According to the Department of Work and Pensions, *Press Release*, 2 September 2013, 'The food and grocery industry is the UK's biggest employer – 3.7 million people, 1 in 7 of all jobs'. This total includes jobs in food wholesaling, logistics and manufacturing (all critical to resilience). The number in retailing food selling is only a part of the 2.8 million employees in the retail sales sector as a whole.

79 Cabinet Office, *Cyber Security: Critical National Infrastructure Inquiry*, submitted to JCNSS, *Cyber Security of the UK's Critical National Infrastructure*, CNI0013, paragraphs 6–7.

80 JCNSS, *Cyber Security of the UK's Critical National Infrastructure*, Written Evidence, Q. 28.

81 Ibid., Q. 22.

82 Warwick Ashford, 'Is UK Critical National Infrastructure Properly Protected?' *Computer Weekly*, 3 March 2011.

83 National Audit Office, *Departments' Use of Consultants to Support Preparations for EU Exit*, HC 2105, 7 June 2019, pp. 6–7.

84   In 2019 the five Cabinet posts exercising oversight were Home Secretary, Defence Secretary, Foreign Secretary, Secretary of States for DCMS and Chancellor of the Dutchy of Lancaster. And thirteen CNI sectors were allocated across seven different Whitehall ministries.

Chapter 7: Facing global institutions

1   Malcolm Chalmers, *Which Rules? Why There Is No Single 'Rules-Based International System'*, RUSI Occasional Paper, 10 April 2019.

2   See, for example, Alastair I. Johnston, 'Is China a Status Quo Power?' *International Security* 27, no. 4 (2003); Randall L. Schweller and Xiaoyu Pu, 'After Unipolarity: China's Vision of International Order in an Era of US Decline', *International Security* 36, no. 1 (2011).

3   HM Government, *National Security Strategy and Strategic Defence and Security Review: A Secure and Prosperous United Kingdom*, cm 9161, November 2015, p. 14.

4   The General Agreement on Tariffs and Trade was established in 1947 and was transformed into the World Trade Organisation, on more ambitious principles, in 1995. The Organisation for European Economic Cooperation was created in 1948 and transformed in 1961 to include non-European states as the Organisation for Economic Cooperation and Development.

5   HM Government, *National Security Capability Review*, March 2018, pp. 2, 7; Ministry of Defence, *Mobilising, Modernising and Transforming Defence: A Report on the Modernising Defence Programme*, December 2018, p. 10.

6   See, Dries Lesage and Thijs van de Graaf, eds., *Rising Powers and Multilateral Institutions*, London, Palgrave Macmillan, 2015.

7   See, for example, Foreign Affairs Committee, *China and the Rules-Based International System*, HC 612, 4 April 2019, pp. 9–10.

8   See, Gordon Brown, *My Life, Our Times*, London, The Bodley Head, 2017, pp. 325–44.

9   Ali Burak Guven, 'Defending Supremacy: How the IMF and the World Bank Navigate the Challenge of Rising Powers', *International Affairs* 93, no. 5 (2017).

10 Shahar Hameiri and Lee Jones, 'China Challenges Global Governance? Chinese International Development Finance and the AIIB', *International Affairs* 94, no. 3 (2018).

11 Kristen Hopewell, 'The BRICS – Merely a Fable? Emerging Power Alliances in Global Trade Governance', *International Affairs* 93, no. 6 (2017).

12 Tom Miles, 'World Trade's Top Court Close to Breakdown as US Blocks Another Judge', *Reuters Business News*, 26 September 2018.

13 'Slowbalisation', *The Economist*, 26 January 2019, p. 11.

14 Ibid., pp. 23–4.

15 The EEU includes Russia, Kazakhstan, Kyrgyzstan, Belarus and Armenia.

16 David Lewis, 'Inroads into Eurasia', *The World Today*, October/November 2016.

17 See, Thijs Van de Graaf, 'The IEA, the New Energy Order and the Future of Global Energy Governance', in Dries Lesage and Thijs van de Graaf, ed. *Rising Powers and Multilateral Institutions*, London, Palgrave Macmillan, 2015..

18 Though largely in frustration at the IEA, the International Renewable Energy Agency was formed in Abu Dhabi in 2010, but has not made great progress in governance terms. Otherwise, renewables are overseen by organizations such as the World Energy Council, which is a British registered charity accredited by the UN, or international NGOs such as the World Renewable Energy Congress/Network (WREC/WREN).

19 See, Neil Hurst and Anthony Froggatt, *The Reform of Global Energy Governance*, London, Imperial College / Chatham House, Discussion Paper No. 3, 2012.

20 Joeri Rogelj, et al., 'Paris Agreement Climate Proposals Need a Boost to Keep Warming Well Below 2oC', *Nature*, 534, 2016.

21 John J. Kirton and Ella Kokotsis, *The Global Governance of Climate Change: G7, G20 and UN Leadership*, London, Routledge, 2016.

22 Thomas Hale, 'Climate Change: From Gridlock to Catalyst', in Thomas Hale and David Held, et al., *Beyond Gridlock*, London, Polity Press, 2017, pp. 184–5.

23 Lucas Kello, 'Cyber Security: Gridlock and Innovation', in Thomas Hale and David Held, et al., *Beyond Gridlock*, London, Polity Press, 2017, pp. 205–8.

24 Kieron O'Hara and Wendy Hall, *Four Internets: The Geopolitics of Digital Governance*, Centre for International Governance Innovation Paper Series No. 206, 2018.

25 Tom Parfitt, 'Russia to Shut Out World with Web Firewall', *The Times*, 13 February 2019; Paul Mozur and Karen Weise, 'China Appears to Block Microsoft's Bing as Censorship Intensifies', *New York Times*, 23 January 2019.

26 *Global Commission on Internet Governance*, Centre for International Governance Innovation/Chatham House, Paper Series, No. 8, 2015. See also, Michael Clarke, 'Weapons of Mass Destruction: Incremental Steps', in Thomas Hale and David Held, et al., *Beyond Gridlock*, London, Polity Press, 2017, pp. 239–40.

27 'The future of the four kingdoms of the internet', *Financial Times*, 30 December 2018.

28 House of Commons Defence Committee, *On Thin Ice: UK Defence in the Arctic*, HC 388, 19 July 2018, p. 6.

29 UNCLOS is the United Nations Convention on the Law of the Sea, UNCLCS is the United Nations Commission on the Limits of the Continental Shelf.

30 They are, Canada, the United States, Russia, Norway and Denmark – who are all littoral states in the Arctic – and Finland, Sweden and Iceland, who are not.

31 Stephanie Pezard, et al., *Maintaining Arctic Cooperation with Russia: Planning for Regional Change in the Far North*, Santa Monica, CA, RAND Corporation, 2017, p. 35.

32 Ibid., p. 20.

33 Duncan Depledge, et al., 'The UK's Defence Arctic Strategy: Negotiating the Slippery Geopolitics of the UK and the Arctic', *RUSI Journal* 164, no. 1 (2019).

34 House of Commons Defence Committee, *On Thin Ice: UK Defence in the Arctic*, pp. 17–18. See also, House of Commons Defence Committee, *On Thin Ice:*

Defence in the Arctic: Government Response to the Committee's Twelfth Report, HC 1659, 18 October 2018.

35   Sico van der Meer, 'Not That Bad: Looking back at 65 Years of Nuclear Non-proliferation', *Security and Human Rights* 22, no. 1 (2011), p. 37.

36   See, Michael Clarke, 'Weapons of Mass Destruction', in Thomas Hale and David Hare, eds., *Beyond Gridlock*, London, Polity Press, 2017, pp. 234–8.

37   Jonathan Landay and David Rohde, 'Exclusive: In Call with Putin, Trump Denounced Obama-Era Nuclear Arms Treaty', Reuters, 9 February 2017.

38   Arka Biswas, 'Iran Deal, NPT and the Norms of Nuclear Non-proliferation', *The Diplomat*, 18 February 2016.

39   This failure could not entirely be laid at Russia's door. It signed and ratified the adapted treaty, but the NATO states would not follow suit until Russia had observed previous treaty commitments on which NATO accused it of cheating and restored arms forces numbers to agreed levels.

40   China is a member of the NPT, the CTBT, the CWC and the BWC, though not all have been ratified. None of these agreements constrain a nuclear, chemical or biological weapons programme as effectively as a bilateral or trilateral agreement with other great powers.

41   India had conducted a successful nuclear test in 1974 on the grounds that it was for peaceful purposes, but in 1998 it exploded a military-sized bomb and explicitly joined the 'nuclear club'.

42   Importantly, the ICC is designed to complement national jurisdictions and it can only have ICC jurisdiction in cases where national authorities will not, or cannot, act or where the UN Security Council or individual states refer a case to it.

43   The International Criminal Tribunal for the former Yugoslavia (ICTFY) and also the Special Court for Sierra Leone (SCSL).

44   The 'responsibility to protect' doctrine ('R2P') had been under discussion from the late 1990s in response to the genocidal incidents of that decade. The Canadian government gave it prominence with an influential report in 2001 and the idea was adopted as a (non-binding) resolution at the 2005 high-level UN World Summit meeting as A/Res/60/1.

45   Ingrid Wuerth, 'International Law in the Age of Trump: A Post – Human Rights Agenda', The Lawfare Institute /Brookings Institution, Washington DC, 2016, https ://www.lawfareblog.com/international-law-age-trump-post-human-rights-agenda.

46   See, International Coalition for the Responsibility to Protect, *The Responsibility to Protect: Report of the International Commission on Intervention and State Sovereignty*, Ottawa, International Development Research Centre, 2001.

47   William W. Burke-White, 'Power Shifts in International Law: Structural Realignment and Substantive Pluralism', *Harvard International Law Journal* 56, no. 1 (2015), p. 1.

48   Ibid., p. 76.

49   For example, *sovereignty* is interpreted as an absolute and traditional concept by China and Russia; India and Brazil claim *legitimacy* arises from their processes of democracy rather than the effectiveness of them; and India, Russia and China lead state-centric *economic systems* that frequently clash with international economic law.

50   Burke-White, 'Power Shifts in International Law', p. 1.

51   In Ernest Hemingway's *The Sun also Rises*, Scriber, 2006.

Chapter 8: The geopolitics of Brexit

1   See, Brendan Simms, *Britain's Europe: A Thousand Years of Conflict and Cooperation*, London, Penguin Books, 2016, pp. 242–3.

2   See, Michael Howard, *The Continental Commitment,* London, Pelican Books, 1974; Beatrice Heuser, *Brexit in History: Sovereignty or a European Union?*, London, Hurst, 2019, pp. 241-6.

3   Linda Colley, *Britons: Forging the Nation 1707–1837*, London, Pimlico, 1992, pp. 368–9.

4   Walter Russell Mead, *God and Gold: Britain, America and the Making of the Modern World*, London, Atlantic Books, 2007, p. 5. Mead goes on to say, however, that the Anglo-Americans were also 'dead wrong about what their … victories mean for the world'. Vietnam is sometimes raised as a palpable US defeat, but Max Hastings, for one, is clear that in reality it was not strategically significant. The communists won the war but the capitalists won the peace. In effect, Vietnam's south triumphed over its north. Max Hastings, *Vietnam: An Epic Tragedy*, London, William Collins, 2018, pp. 647–50.

5   Winston Churchill, Speech to Council of Europe, Strasbourg, August 1949.

6   The terminology of the modern EU can be confusing. The Common Market was formally known as the European Economic Community from 1958–65. As its policy areas expanded it became the European Communities from 1965–92. After 1992 it was characterized as the 'three pillars of the European Union' and then, after the Lisbon Treaty of 2007, simply as the 'European Union'.

7   The best recent political and economic account of Britain's history with the EU is: Kevin O'Rourke, *A Short History of Brexit: From Brentry to Backstop,* London, Pelican Books, 2019. See pp. 79–85 on the end of the 'golden age'.

8   F. S. Northedge, *Descent from Power: British Foreign Policy, 1945–1973*, London, George Allen and Unwin, 1974, p. 357.

9   Peter Wilding, *What Next? Britain's Future in Europe*, London, I.B. Tauris, 2017, p. 19.

10 Though Tony Blair subsequently opted into some of the provisions that John Major had previously secured as opt outs.

11 Nick Clegg, *How to Stop Brexit (And Make Britain Great Again)*, London, The Bodley Head, 2017, pp. 11–12.

12 Anthony Barnett, *The Lure of Greatness: England's Brexit and America's Trump*, London, Unbound, 2017, p. 101. Even the Welsh vote was decisively tipped by older English incomers in North Wales and the borders; 'Welsh Brexit vote caused by English retirees', *Nation Cymru*, 22 September 2019.

13 A good summary of the broad argument is, Philip Stephens, 'Brexit Britain's Nervous Breakdown', *Financial Times*, 1 February 2018.

14 Michael Kenny, *The Politics of English Nationhood*, Oxford, Oxford University Press, 2016, pp. 232–4.

15 Richard Wyn Jones, et al., *England and Its Two Unions: The Anatomy of a Nation and Its Discontents*, London, Institute for Public Policy Research, 2013, pp. 6–7, 15–6; See also, Fintan O'Toole, *Heroic Failure: Brexit and the Politics of Pain*, London, Head of Zeus, 2018, pp. 185–8.

16 Wyn Jones, *England and Its Two Unions*, p. 15.

17 O'Toole, *Heroic Failure*, pp. 140–1.

18 Some perceptive analysts had seen this before referendum day but were still surprised that it had such an impact on the result. See, Matthew Goodwin, 'Whether In or Out, Britain Is Divided', *The World Today*, June/July 2016, pp. 38–9.

19 Barnett, *The Lure of Greatness*, p. 123.

20 O'Rourke, *A Short History of Brexit*, pp. 193–9. See also a parallel analysis of French social tensions in, Christophe Guilluy, *Twilight of the Elites: Prosperity, the Periphery and the Future of France*, New Haven, Yale University Press, 2019.

21 O'Toole, *Heroic Failure*, pp. 157–9.

22 Robert Cooper, *The Breaking of Nations: Order and Chaos in the Twenty-First Century*, London, Atlantic books, 2004, pp. 71–2, 78–9.

23 Simms, *Britain's Europe*, p. 246.

24 William Hague, 'Why I Will Be Voting to Stay in Europe', *Daily Telegraph*, 22 December 2015.

25 On the longevity of Scottish nationalist thinking, see, Iain Macwhirter, *Disunited Kingdom: How Westminster Won the Referendum but Lost Scotland*, Glasgow, Cargo Publishing, 2014.

26 See, Andy Philip, 'Indy Ref 2: Poll Says Up to 500,000 No Voters Would Switch Sides in Event of Second Referendum', *Daily Record*, 26 June 2016.

27 Edward Burke, 'Who Will Speak for Northern Ireland? The Looming Danger of an Ulster Brexit', *RUSI Journal* 161, no. 2 (April/May 2016).

28 The UK enacted the Northern Ireland Act of 1998, and, as a result of a referendum in the Republic where over 94 per cent voted yes for the Agreement (on a 56 per cent turnout), the Irish Constitution was amended.

29 Tony Connelly, *Brexit and Ireland: the Dangers, the Opportunities, and the Inside Story of the Irish Response*, London, Penguin Books, 2018, pp. 351–6.

30 Colin Murphy, 'Europe Sees Brexit as Nothing Short of Heresy', *The Sunday Business Post*, 15 October 2017.

31 David McWilliams, 'Why the Idea of a United Ireland Is Back in Play', *Financial Times*, 30 November 2018.

32 Graham Gudgin, 'David McWilliams Is Wrong: Northern Ireland Might Never Get a Catholic Majority', *Newsletter*, 13 December 2018.

33 McWilliams, 'Why the Idea of a United Ireland is Back in Play'.

34 Ben Hall, 'Dutch PM Warns of "Devastating" Impact of No-Deal Brexit on UK', *Financial Times*, 13 February 2019.

35 Northedge, *Descent from Power*, p. 357. See also, Srdjan Vucetic, *The Anglosphere: A Geneology of a Racialized Identity in International Relations*, Stanford CA, Stanford University Press, 2011, Chapters 4 and 5.

36 Michael Kenny and Nick Pearce, *Shadows of Empire: The Anglosphere in British Politics*, Cambridge, Cambridge University Press, 2018, pp. 121–131.

37 Speech to the Conservative Party Conference 1948, Bodleian Library, quoted by Oliver Daddow, 'Britain, the World and Europe', in Bill Jones and Philip Norton, *Politics UK*, 7th ed., London, Longman, 2010, p. 27.

38 Initially in a famous speech on 19 January 1976, available at https://www.margaret thatcher.org/document/102939. See also, Hugo Young, *One of Us*, London, Pan Books, 1990, pp. 170–2.

39 Speech at the Lord Mayor's Banquet, 15 November 2004. www.theguardian.com/politics/2004/nov/16/foreignpolicy.uk. Quoted in Daddow, 'Britain, the World and Europe'. See also, Tony Blair, *A Journey*, London, Arrow Books, 2011, pp. xxxiv–xxxv, 410–1.

40 Compare, for example, Ministry of Defence, *Strategic Defence Review 1998*, Cm 3999, para. 52, with the *Strategic Defence and Security Review 2010*, Cm 7953, p. 10, with HM Government, *National Security Capability Review*, London, The Stationery Office, 2018, p. 33.

41 See, Ben Wellings and Helen Baxendale, 'Euroscepticism and the Anglosphere: Traditions and Dilemmas in Contemporary English Nationalism', *Journal of Common Market Studies 53*, no. 1, 2015.

42 Boris Johnson, 'Beyond Brexit: A Global Britain', Speech at Chatham House, 2 December 2016. https://www.gov.uk/government/speeches/beyond-brexit-a-global-britain

43 See, John Bew and Gabriel Elefteria, *Making Sense of British Foreign Policy after Brexit*, Briefing Paper, London, Policy Exchange, July 2016.

44 See, Liam Fox, 'Road to Brexit', speech to Bloomberg European HQ, London, 27 February 2018.

45 Paul Mason, *Post-Capitalism: A Guide to Our Future*, London, Penguin Books, 2016, pp. 9–30, 261–2; 'Raghuram Rajan Says Capitalism Is "Under Serious Threat"', *BBC News*, 12 March 2019.

Chapter 9: Security and foreign policy

1 See, for example, Jolyon Howorth, *Security and Defence Policy in the European Union*, 2nd ed., London, Palgrave Macmillan, 2014, pp. 14–15.

2 In March 2019 the most current report on these operations was, Council of the European Union, *Common Foreign and Security Policy, Annual Report 2017*, Brussels, 5 July 2017.

3 In March 2019 NATO forces were involved in five big policing and support missions outside their own treaty territories, in Afghanistan, Kosovo, Iraq, the Mediterranean and in supporting the African Union.

4 Though it should be remembered that the now defunct Western European Union (1955–2011) which tried to serve as a Europe-only defence pact also embodied a total commitment to collective defence.

5 EU Information, *Permanent Structured Cooperation – PESCO*, at https://cdn5-eeas.fpfis.tech.ec.europa.eu/cdn/farfuture/wM5QZfoVgVbC4zSzD-u--4o8E9TqY oThT3aNfAC6TQA/mtime:1542983709/sites/eeas/files/pesco_factsheet_novem ber_2018_en_0.pdf

6 For political reasons the Iran nuclear deal was euphemistically named the 'Joint Comprehensive Plan of Action'.

7 Michael Peel, 'Can Europe's New Financial Channel Save the Iran Nuclear Deal?' *Financial Times*, 4 February 2019; Josh Clancy, 'Fury in Washington as Britain Links Up with Brussels to Bypass Iran Sanctions', *The Sunday Times*, 17 February 2019.

8   'The Paper Euro-Army', *The Economist*, 2 February 2019, pp. 31–2.

9   See, among a number of examples, David Chuter, 'Boutros Ghali's Army? Proposals for a United Nations Military Force', in Centre for Defence Studies, *Brassey's Defence Yearbook 1994*, London, Brassey's 1994.

10   See, Anna Barcikowska, 'EU Battlegroups: Ready to Go?' European Union Institute for Security Studies, *Briefing*, November 2013.

11   Douglas Barrie, et al., *Protecting Europe: Meeting the EU's Military Level of Ambition in the Context of Brexit*, London, International Institute for Strategic Studies/ Geselschaft fur Auswartige Politik, November 2018, pp. 2, 35.

12   'Special Report: NATO at 70', *The Economist*, 14 March 2019.

13   Article 4(2) of the Treaties on the European Union (the TEU), states that 'national security remains the sole responsibility of each Member State'.

14   Alexander Babuta, *No Deal, No Data? The Future of UK-EU Law Enforcement Information Sharing*, Briefing Paper, London, RUSI, February 2019, p. 3.

15   European Commission, Migration and Home Affairs, 'Schengen Information System', at https://ec.europa.eu/home-affairs/what-we-do/policies/borders-and -visas/schengen-information-system_en

16   Home Affairs Committee, *UK-EU Security Cooperation after Brexit: Follow-Up Report*, HC 1356, 17 July 2018, p. 12.

17   Babuta, *No Deal, No Data?*, pp. 5–7.

18   In a leaked document. See, 'The Home Office Assessment of Post-Brexit Terror and Crime Risks', *The Times*, 23 August 2017. The 2016–2017 figure is quoted in Home Affairs Committee, *UK-EU Security Cooperation after Brexit: Follow-Up Report*, p. 15.

19   *I- News*, 11 February 2018; Tim Shipman, 'May Warns Tory Rebels Will Make Britain a Honeypot for Criminals', *Sunday Times*, 26 October 2014.

20   Home Affairs Committee, *UK-EU Security Cooperation after Brexit*, HC 635, 21 March 2018, p. 25.

21   Ibid., pp. 28–9.

22   Ibid., p. 26.

23   Home Affairs Committee, UK-EU Security Cooperation after Brexit*: Follow-Up Report*, p. 19.

24   Christopher Andrew, *The Secret World: A History of Intelligence*, London, Allen Lane, 2018, pp. 1–2.

25   Vitor Tossini, 'The Five Eyes: The Intelligence Alliance of the Anglosphere', *UK Defence Journal*, 14 November 2017.

26   'MI' (5 or 6) derives from the 'military intelligence' directorates created in the First World War; MI6 is responsible for foreign intelligence gathering, MI5 for domestic security. GCHQ is the Government Communications Headquarters based in Cheltenham, which handles all aspects of telecommunications and cyberspace. DI is the large Defence Intelligence organization that handles the military intelligence of the three Armed Services, and like the other agencies, passes its material into a central intelligence hub at Cabinet level.

27   Personal interview, March 2019.

28 Tom Keatinge, 'US, Europe and Sanctions against Russia: A Parting of the Ways?' *RUSI Commentary*, 3 August 2017; 'Italy, Hungary Say No to Automatic Renewal of Russia Sanctions', *Reuters*, 14 March 2016.

29 James Black, et al., *Defence and Security after Brexit*, Santa Monica, CA, RAND Europe, 2017, p. 9.

Chapter 10: The meaning of 'global Britain'

1   Bob Seely, 'What is Global Britain?', in George Freeman, ed., *Britain Beyond Brexit: A New Conservative Vision*, London, Centre for Policy Studies, 2019, p. 298.

2   House of Commons Foreign Affairs Committee, *Global Britain*, HC 780, 12 March 2018, p. 7.

3   Ibid., p. 3.

4   Ibid., p. 11. See the Memorandum from the FCO to the Committee at p. 19.

5   House of Commons Library, *Brexit Reading List: Global Britain*, Briefing Paper 8338, 22 August 2018, p. 3.

6   Parliamentary Question No. 159547, 10 July 2018.

7   Jeremy Hunt, 'An Invisible Chain', speech by the foreign secretary to Policy Exchange, 1 November 2018, at https://www.gov.uk/government/speeches/an-invisible-chain-speech-by-the-foreign-secretary

8   In addition to the Foreign Affairs Committee, see, House of Lords, *UK Foreign Policy in a Shifting World Order*, HL 250, 18 December 2018, p. 80.

9   House of Commons Foreign Affairs Committee, *Global Britain*, pp. 19–28.

10 Duncan Bell, 'The Anglosphere: New Enthusiasm for an Old Dream', *Prospect Magazine*, February 2017.

11 Bob Seely and James Rogers, *Global Britain: A Twenty-First Century Vision*, London, Henry Jackson Society, 2019.

12 James Rogers, *Towards 'Global Britain': Challenging the New Narratives of National Decline*, London, Henry Jackson Society, 2017.

13 Fraser Nelson, 'The Wrong Brexit: What Happened to "Global Britain?"' *The Spectator*, 21 April 2018.

14 Seely and Rogers, *Global Britain*.

15 Damon Pool, '"Global Britain" Can Be More Than a Soundbite', *BrexitCentral*, 26 January 2017.

16 OCCAR, in English, is the Organisation for Joint Armaments Cooperation, involving Belgium, France, Germany, Italy, Spain and Britain.

17 'Theresa May Pays the Ultimate Price to Try to Seal Her Brexit Deal', *The Economist*, 30 March 2019.

18 Aniseh Bassiri Tabrizi, 'Informal Groups of States: A Growing Role in EU Foreign Policy after Brexit', *RUSI Journal* 163, no. 4 (2018).

19 In 2018 the Permanent Under Secretary at the FCO picked out, as examples of British 'convening power', the international response to the Salisbury nerve agent attack, global initiatives to prevent sexual violence in conflict, action on modern slavery, the illegal wildlife trade, the education of girls, wider reform agendas at the UN, and smart pledging for UN peace-keeping forces, cyber resilience, the eradication of malaria and action to reduce plastic waste in the oceans. Sir Simon McDonald, Speech to the Royal United Services Institute, 11 May 2018, at: https://rusi.org/event/sir-simon-mcdonald-delivering-uk-foreign-policy.

20 Simon Fraser, 'What Will Britain's Role Be Now?', *The World Today*, December 2017/January 2018, p. 32; Tony Barber, 'Spain and Poland Plan Ties with Post-Brexit UK', *Financial Times*, 7 March 2017.

21 Jonathan Powell, *The New Machiavelli: How to Wield Power in the Modern World*, London, The Bodley Head, 2010, pp. 292–3.

22 John Chilcot, et al., *The Report of the Iraq Inquiry, Volume 8*, London, The Stationery Office, 2016, Section 9.8; Michael Clarke, 'Planning and Fighting a War', *RUSI Journal*, 161(6), 2016.

23 In, 'A Brave New World', TV Documentary, *Inside the Foreign Office*, 2018.

24 See a series of interviews for a research report in, Jess Gifkins, Samuel Jarvis, Jason Ralph, *Global Britain in the United Nations*, London, UNA-UK, 2019, pp. 9–10.

25 Chris Giles, 'The View of Brexit as a "Conscious Uncoupling" Is Fanciful', *Financial Times*, 28 December 2018.

26 The 'big three' should really be the 'big four' to include Italy, as judged by demographic and economic size. But the political reality of the last decade has been that 'European' policy was effectively determined among the 'E3' of France, Germany and, recently to a lesser extent, Britain.

27 Sir Simon McDonald, Speech to the Royal United Services Institute, London, 11 May 2018, at https://rusi.org/event/sir-simon-mcdonald-Dedelivering-uk-foreign-policy.

28 Nevertheless, by 2017, this imagery had become pervasive in press commentary. See, for example, Stephen Castle, 'As "Brexit" Clock Ticks, UK Seems Adrift', *New York Times*, 20 July 2017; Natalie Nougayrede, 'After the G20 Summit, Brexit Britain Looks Increasingly Adrift and Friendless', *Guardian*, 10 July 2017; Paul Taylor, 'Britain Adrift', *Politico*, 28 November 2017.

29 Gifkins, et al. *Global Britain in the United Nations*, p. 10.

30 This was intrinsic from the start, see, Jeffrey Anderson, 'Britain's Decline and Fall', *US News and World Affairs*, 22 June 2016. It was then reinforced by a late realization of how US interests could be affected by Brexit. See, David M. Herszenhorn, et al., 'America Is Woke to Brexit', *Politico*, 1 January 2019.

31 See, Richard Haass, President of the Council on Foreign Relations, New York, speaking to Parliament in House of Lords, *UK Foreign Policy in a Shifting World Order*, HL 250, December 2018, p. 75.

32 Quoted in, 'Bagehot: As Others See Us', *The Economist*, 15 December 2018, p. 34.

33 Fraser, 'What Will Britain's Role Be Now?', p. 33.

34 See, as examples, Kwasi Kwarteng, 'Adieu Europe, Hello the World', *The World Today*, August/September 2016, pp. 18–20; Philip Blond, James Noyes and

Duncan Sim, *Britain's Global Future: Harnessing the Soft Power Capital of UK Institutions*, London, ResPublica, 2017; William James, 'Déjà vu? "Global Britain" Versus the Continental Commitment', *The National Interest*, 1 October 2018.

35 *The Economist*, 15 December 2018, p. 34.

36 See a discussion around this issue in House of Lords, pp. 96–7.

37 Matthew Parris, 'May Is the Death Star of British Politics', *The Times*, 23 February 2019.

38 HM Government, *National Security Capability Review*, London, Cabinet Office, March 2018; Ministry of Defence, *Mobilising, Modernising and Transforming Defence: A Report on the Modernising Defence Programme*, London, MoD, December 2018.

39 Peter Hennessy, *Whitehall*, London, Secker and Warburg, 1989, pp. 635–42.

40 'Fusion doctrine' is set out in HM Government, *National Security Capability Review*, London, The Stationery Office, 2018, p. 10.

41 Ed Conway, 'Size Matters When It Comes to Trading Muscle', *The Times*, 22 February 2019.

42 Nicholas Mairs, 'Brexit Having "Serious Detrimental Effect" on Other Policy Areas, Senior MPs Warn Theresa May', *PoliticsHome*, 16 December 2018.

Chapter 11: Governmental capabilities – diplomacy, defence, intelligence and security

1 Sir Simon McDonald, Speech to the Royal United Services Institute.

2 Ambassadors lead foreign embassies. High Commissioners, with equal status, lead British representation in Commonwealth Countries. Heads of Mission may or may not have ambassadorial status, depending on the Mission in question.

3 House of Lords, International Relations Committee, *UK Foreign Policy in a Shifting World Order*, HL 250, December 2018, p. 82.

4 Henry Mance, 'Foreign Office "Unsustainable" without Funding Boost', *Financial Times*, 28 November 2018.

5 Brian Appleyard, 'Danger Ahead: UK Diplomacy Is Racing Towards a Cliff Edge of Its Own', *Sunday Times*, 3 March 2019; Matthew Parris, 'Johnson Premiership Will Fall Apart in a Year', *The Times*, 8 June 2019.

6 John Dickie, *Inside the Foreign Office*, London, Chapmans, 1992, pp. 11–4.

7 See, Geoffrey Moorhouse, *The Diplomats: The Foreign Office Today*, London, Jonathan Cape, 1977, pp. 74–92.

8 John Dickie, *The New Mandarins: How British Foreign Policy Works*, London, I.B. Tauris, 2004, pp. 4, 19.

9 Robin Renwick, *Not Quite a Diplomat*, London, Biteback, 2019, pp. 274-8.

10 Other audits disagree with this ranking, though not by significant amounts. See, Sam Roggeveen, 'Lowy's Global Diplomatic Index', *The Interpreter*, The Lowy Institute, 15 March 2016.

11 HM Treasury, *Budget 2010*, HC 61, June 2010, p. 43; HM Treasury, *Budget 2018*, HC 1629, October 2018, p. 24; Patrick Wintour, 'Cash-Strapped Foreign Office Sells Bangkok Embassy for £425m', *The Guardian*, 31 January 2018.

12 Speech by Foreign Secretary William Hague, 'Britain's Foreign Policy in a Networked World', London, 1 July 2010; https://www.gov.uk/government/speeches/britain-s-foreign-policy-in-a-networked-world--2

13 Tom Fletcher, *The Naked Diplomat: Understanding Power and Politics in the Digital Age*, London, William Collins, 2017, pp. 78–85.

14 Personal interviews, August–December 2018.

15 Appleyard, 'Danger Ahead'.

16 Jess Gifkins, et al., *Global Britain in the United Nations*, London, UNA-UK, 2019; House of Commons Foreign Affairs Committee, *Global Britain*, HC 780, London, March 2018, p. 13; 'France Hits Nerve with Claim of US Influence', *The Times*, 24 April 2019.

17 Personal interview, 5 December 2018.

18 Gov.UK, 'Penny Mordaunt's Five Pledges for the Future of UK Aid', London, DFID, 15 January 2018.

19 Dominic Kennedy, 'Poorest Countries Miss Out on UK Aid', *The Times*, 26 March 2019.

20 See, 'Developing Countries Warned UK Could Cut Foreign Aid', *BBC News*, 15 January 2018.

21 Luke Charles, 'British Among Least Generous on Oversea Aid', *YouGov*, 9 November 2013, https://yougov.co.uk/topics/politics/articles-reports/2013/11/09/British-amongst-least-generous-overseas-aid

22 Sam Jones, 'Majority of UK Believes Overseas Aid Should Rise, Survey Says', *The Guardian*, 29 February 2016.

23 Cameroon, Mozambique and Rwanda. The United States might be regarded as a state who declined to join on independence, and Ireland formally left the Commonwealth in 1949. But the 'modern Commonwealth' is generally regarded as that which evolved from regular decolonization processes after 1945.

24 http://thecommonwealth.org/fastfacts

25 Ben Pimlott, *Harold Wilson*, London, William Collins, 2016, pp. 389–90; Charles Moore, *Margaret Thatcher: The Authorised Biography*, Vol. 2, London, Penguin Books, 2016, pp. 553–4.

26 Corinne Lennox and Matthew Waites, eds., *Human Rights, Sexual Orientation and Gender Identity in the Commonwealth*, London, Institute of Commonwealth Studies, 2013, p. 5; House of Lords, HL 250, p. 69.

27 House of Lords, HL 250, p. 69.

28 James Landale, 'Concerns Raised over Commonwealth Leadership', *BBC News*, 26 January 2017.

29 John Louth and Trevor Taylor, *British Defence in the 21st Century*, London, Routledge, 2019.

30 HM Government, *National Security Capability Review*, London, Cabinet Office, March 2018, p. 14. In fact, this precise ranking is widely disputed and in 2019 India overtook Britain in most accepted rankings. Nevertheless, few would dispute that Britain remains among the significant defence spenders in the world. See, Michael Clarke, *The Challenge of Defending Britain*, Manchester, Manchester University Press, 2019, pp. 7–9.

31 'Operation Banner' in Northern Ireland was the longest single campaign in British military history and involved some 300,000 armed service personnel over a period of almost forty years.

32 Julia Diehle and Neil Greenberg, *Counting the Costs*, London, King's Centre for Military Health Research, 2016. On the audit of British operations, see, Clarke, *The Challenge of Defending Britain*, pp. 60–8.

33 George Allison, 'Study Finds UK Is Still Second Most Powerful Country in the World', *UK Defence Journal*, 20 November 2017. The assessment rates Britain as, 'A country lacking the heft or comprehensive attributes of a superpower, but still with a wide international footprint and [military] means to reach most geopolitical theatres, particularly the Middle East, South-East Asia, East Asia, Africa and South America.'

34 Andrea Shalal, 'Equipment Shortages Impair German Military Ahead of Key NATO Mission', *Reuters*, 19 February 2018.

35 West Germany's forces in the Cold War were structured to defend their own territory along the inner-German border, falling back, it was assumed, on their own lands. German forces never genuinely addressed the problem of mobilizing anywhere else following the European transformation after 1991. See, Tobias Buck, 'German Military: Combat Ready?', *Financial Times*, 15 February 2018.

36 Munich Security Conference /McKinsey, *More European, More Connected and More Capable: Building the European Armed Forces of the Future*, Munich, 2019, pp. 11–13, 21–6.

37 Ibid., p. 13.

38 Bastian Giegerich and Christian Molling, *The United Kingdom's Contribution to European Security and Defence*, London, IISS/DGAP, 2018, p. 12.

39 Though, in 2020–21 given that President Trump aims to ramp up US military expenditure, that proportion will be closer to 7 per cent on projections that British defence spending will be worth around $51 billion, depending on exchange rates; while US defence spending is likely to be $700–$750 billion, depending on Congressional reactions to the president's budget request.

40 See, House of Commons Defence Committee, *Indispensable Allies: US, NATO and UK Defence Relations*, HC 387, London, June 2018.

41 See, Steven Pifer, 'Pay Attention America: Russia Is Upgrading Its Military', *Brookings Briefings*, 5 February 2016.

42 Dmitry Gorenburg, *Russia's Military Modernisation Plans 2018–2027*, PONARS Policy Memo 495, Elliott School of International Affairs, George Washington University, November 2017.

43 See, Clarke, *The Challenge of Defending Britain*, pp. 60–5.

44 See, Ministry of Defence, *Mobilising, Modernising and Transforming Defence: Report on the Modernising Defence Programme*, London, MoD, 2018, pp. 20–1.

45 See, Development Concepts and Doctrine Centre, *Global Strategic Trends: The Future Starts Today*, 6th ed., London, Ministry of Defence, 2018, pp. 70–2, 101–2, 143–5.

46 Michio Kaku, *Physics of the Future: The Inventions That Will Transform Our Lives*, London, Penguin Books, 2011.

47 Richard J. Aldrich and Rory Cormac, *The Black Door: Spies, Secret Intelligence and British Prime Ministers*, London, William Collins, 2017, p. 486.

48 The best general history of the operations of the agencies since the Second World War is Rory Cormac, *Disrupt and Deny: Spies, Special Forces, and the Secret Pursuit of British Foreign Policy*, Oxford, Oxford University Press, 2018.

49 See, for example, Mark Urban, *UK Eyes Alpha: The Inside Story of British Intelligence*, London, Faber and Faber, 1996, pp. 287–9; Christopher Andrew, *The Secret World: A History of Intelligence*, London, Allen Lane, 2018, p. 702.

50 Gordon Thomas, *Inside British Intelligence: 100 Years of MI5 and MI6*, London, J.R. Books, 2010, pp. 428–9.

51 The Single Intelligence Account covers MI5, MI6 and GCHQ. Defence Intelligence, however, sits within the central defence budget.

52 MI5, *News and Speeches*: https://www.mi5.gov.uk/news/10th-anniversary-of-mi5-hq-in-northern-ireland

53 Lucy Fisher, 'Revealed: GCHQ's Secret Spybase Next to Starbucks', *The Times*, 5 April 2019; 'GCHQ Reveals Secret London Site', GCHQ Press Release, 5 April 2019.

54 On Russian figures, see, Victor Madeira, 'Supplementary Written Evidence Submitted by Dr Victor Madeira', House of Commons Defence Committee, *Russia: Implications for UK Defence and Security*, HC 107, 2016.

55 Cormac, *Disrupt and Deny*, p. 489.

56 These three phrases being the essential tests by which legal warrants are obtained, or other authority granted, for intelligence agency operations.

57 Speech reported in Matt Payton, 'MI6: UK's Secret Service Will Take on an Extra 1000 Personnel by 2020', *The Independent*, 21 September 2016.

58 Private information.

59 See, https://www.bellingcat.com/

60 Shoshana Zuboff, *The Age of Surveillance Capitalism: The Fight for a Human Future at the New Frontier of Power*, London, Profile Books, 2019, pp. 118–9.

61 See an early indication in, Greg Day, *Virtual Criminology and Threat Reports 2007*, McAfee Online, 2007.

62 William Jordan, 'Edward Snowden: Hero?' *YouGov*, 16 June 2013.

63 See, for example, Heather Brooke, *The Silent State: Secrets, Surveillance and the Myth of British Democracy*, London, Windmill Books, 2010; or, 'Britain's Surveillance State', *New York Times*, 23 March 2015.

64 All-Party Parliamentary Group on Drones, *The UK's Use of Armed Drones: Working with Partners*, London, House of Commons APPG, July 2018, pp. 24–5.

65 Over 97 per cent of internet traffic flows via cables, most of them undersea. Less than 3 per cent is via satellite. With appropriate warranty, British agencies are in a good position to delve into a great deal of cable traffic.

66   Louisa Brook-Holland, *US Forces in the UK: Legal Arguments*, House of Commons Library, 8 January 2015.

67   Urban, *UK Eyes Alpha*, p. 298.

68   Private information, January 2019.

69   See, Richard Dearlove, 'Terrorism and National Security: Proportion or Distortion?' Lecture at the Royal United Services Institute, 7 July 2014.

70   The Skripal poisonings in 2018 took longer to contain because of their nature. But no other country had the same speed of forensic capability to contain such a crime; and in identifying the two likely perpetrators, justice has been done as far as possible, since they are subject to international sanctions and unable to travel to most other countries.

71   In 2019 there were forty-five police constabularies covering England and Wales, Police Scotland, the Police Service of Northern Ireland and three Special Police Forces for Transport, the Ministry of Defence and Civil Nuclear policing.

72   National Crime Agency, *NCA Intelligence Assessment: County Lines, Gangs and Safeguarding*, 12 August 2015. http://www.nationalcrimeagency.gov.uk/publica tions/620-NCA-Intelligence-Assessment-County-Lines-Gangs-and-Safeguarding/file

73   Warwick Ashford, 'Is UK Critical National Infrastructure Properly Protected?' *Computer Weekly*, 3 March 2011.

74   Richard J. Aldrich and Rory Cormac, *The Black Door: Spies, Secret Intelligence and British Prime Ministers*, London, William Collins, 2017, pp. 488–9.

75   See, 'modern deterrence', in HM Government, *National Security Capability Review*, London, March 2019, p. 11.

Chapter 12: Societal capabilities – economics, finance and soft power

1   See, Christopher Hill and Sarah Beadle, *The Art of Attraction: Soft Power and the UK's Role in the World*, London, British Academy, 2014, pp. 45–6.

2   Stryker McGuire, 'This Time I've Come to Bury Cool Britannia', *The Observer*, 29 March 2009.

3   See, for example, John Harris, 'Cool Britannia: Where Did It All Go Wrong?', *New Statesman*, 1 May 2017.

4   'David Cameron Launches Tories' "Big Society" Plan', *BBC News*, 19 July 2010.

5   See, Chris Gifford, *The Making of Eurosceptic Britain*, 2nd ed., London, Routledge, 2016, pp. 171–3.

6   See, J. Holden, *Influence and Attraction: Culture and the Race for Soft Power in the 21st Century*, London, British Council/Demos, 2013; National Asian Business Association, Written Evidence to House of Lords, Select Committee on Soft Power and the UK's Influence, *Persuasion and Power in the Modern World*, HL 150, 28 March 2014, pp. 721–5.

7   See, IPPR, *Time for Change: A New Vision for the British Economy*, London, Institute for Public Policy Research, 2017.

8 The 'UK Economy at a Glance', *Financial Times,* website at https://ig.ft.com/sites/ numbers/economies/uk/

9 Stig Abell, *How Britain Really Works: Understanding the Ideas and Institutions of a Nation*, London, John Murray, 2019, p. 316.

10 Grace Blakeley, 'Is the UK Economy Really as Strong as the Government Says It Is?', London School of Economics, *British Politics and Policy*, 14 September 2017.

11 *Financial Times* website, 'UK Economy at a Glance', https://ig.ft.com/sites/ numbers/economies/uk/

12 Ibid.

13 See, Philip Coggan, *The Money Machine: How the City Works*, 7th ed., London, Penguin Books, 2015.

14 See Relbanks data at: https://www.relbanks.com/europe/uk.

15 TheCityUK, *Key Facts About the UK as an International Financial Centre 2018*, London, October 2018, p. 7.

16 Tony Norfield, *The City: London and the Global Power of Finance*, London, Verso, 2017, pp. 185–6.

17 Robert Barrington, 'The City Laundry', *The World Today*, April/May 2018, pp. 14–15.

18 When £37.9 billion of 'in-house' accountancy value is added to this the total jumps to £59 billion. See, Oxford Economics, *The Accountancy Profession in the United Kingdom and Ireland*, Oxford, November 2018, p. 9.

19 Andrew MacAskill, 'London Loses Top Spot to New York in Financial Survey Due to Brexit', *Reuters*, 12 September 2018.

20 Norfield, *The City*, p. 235.

21 Huw Jones, Sinead Cruise and Andrew MacAskill, 'Brexit Britain's Financial Sector Faces "Slow Puncture"', *Reuters,* 11 December 2018.

22 Simon Atkinson, et al., *Britain 2012: Who Do We Think We Are?,* London, Ipsos MORI, 2012.

23 Ben Marshall, 'How Does the Rest of the World View Britain?', *New Statesman*, 19 December 2012.

24 The Policy Institute/Ipsos MORI, *The Public's Brexit Predictions*, London, King's College London, 2018. See also YouGov polling at: https://d25d2506sfb94s.cloudfr ont.net/cumulus_uploads/document/cbirgnop2j/YG%20Trackers%20-%20EU%20T racker%20Questions_W.pdf; and ICM Guardian Polls 1 April 2017; https://www.icm unlimited.com/wp-content/uploads/2017/04/2017_guardian_apr1_poll.pdf

25 Bobby Duffy and Michael Clemence, *Global Influence in a Post-Brexit World: Who Is a Force for Good?* London, Ipsos MORI, 2017; James Blitz, 'Public Opinion Is Being Reshaped by the Costs of Brexit', *Financial Times*, 23 November 2017.

26 Michael Clemence, 'Britain Remains a Positive Global Influence', *Ipsos MORI*, 3 July 2017.

27 See, Joseph Nye, *Soft Power: The Means to Success in World Politics*, New York, Public Affairs, 2005; Joseph Nye, *The Powers to Lead*, Oxford, Oxford University Press, 2008.

28 See, House of Lords, HL 150, pp. 49–51.

29 See, for example, the annual surveys in 'Softly Does It – Global', *Monocle* 11, no. 109 (December 2017/January 2018).

30 Jonathan McClory, *The Soft Power 30: A Global Ranking of Soft Power 2017*, California, Portland/University of Southern California, 2017, pp. 30–1.

31 Jonathan McClory, *The New Persuaders: An International Ranking of Soft Power*, London, Institute for Government, 2010, p. 5.

32 Caitlin Morrison, 'Can Soft Power Really Be Measured?', *The Diplomatist*, 25 October 2012.

33 McClory, *The Soft Power 30*, p. 41.

34 Brand Finance, *Monarchy 2017: The Annual Report on the Value of the British Monarchy*, London, Brand Finance, 2017, pp. 4–9.

35 Republic, *Royal Expenses: Counting the Cost of the Monarchy*, London, Republic, 2017, p. 7.

36 Ben Chu, 'Does the Royal Family Really Make Financial Sense for the UK Economy?' *Independent*, 11 May 2018.

37 https://www.theguardian.com/uk-news/2018/apr/20/prince-charles-next-head-commonwealth-queen.

38 Official Tours are determined by the FCO and approved by the Royal Visits Committee – a Cabinet Office Committee chaired by the permanent under secretary of the FCO and comprising the private secretaries to the Queen, the Prince of Wales, the Duke of Cambridge, the Duke of Sussex and the prime minister, in addition to the keeper of the privy purse, the chief executive of UK trade and investment, the national security adviser and the FCO's director of protocol.

39 https://www.theguardian.com/world/2018/may/09/prince-charles-heads-greece-heal-old-royal-wounds

40 https://www.townandcountrymag.com/society/tradition/a20777122/meghan-markle-prince-harry-royal-wedding-ratings-compared-to-prince-william-kate-middleton/

41 Janice Turner, 'Meghan Shows the Royals How to Survive', *The Times*, 9 March 2019.

42 House of Commons, *The Sovereign Grant and Sovereign Grant Reserve: Annual Report and Accounts 2017–18*, HC 1153, London, House of Commons, 2018, p. 4.

43 Jenny McCartney, 'Can the Royals Patch Up Our Disunited Kingdom?' *Daily Telegraph*, 28 February 2019.

44 'Russia Says 23 British Diplomats Must Leave within a Week', *Reuters*, 17 March 2018.

45 House of Lords, HL 150, p. 115.

46 House of Lords, HL 150, p. 19.

47 Its top three markets are 41 million in Nigeria, 33 million in the United States and 30 million in India. See: https://www.bbc.co.uk/mediacentre/latestnews/2018/bbc-global-audience

48 https://www.bbc.co.uk/mediacentre/latestnews/2018/bbc-news-afghan-adults

49   John Dickie, *The New Mandarins: How British Foreign Policy Works*, London, I.B. Tauris, 2004, p. 176.

50   Simone Rensch, 'The Brexit Effect: NGOs Swapping the UK for the Hague', *Public Finance International*, 1 May 2018; Abby Young-Powell, 'UJ NGOs Head for Europe as Brexit Looms', *Devex*, 21 November 2018.

51   https://assets.publishing.service.gov.uk/government/uploads/system/uploads/attac hment_data/file/739089/Impact_intl_students_report_published_v1.1.pdf

52   Evidence from the British Council to, House of Lords, *UK Foreign Policy in a Shifting World Order*, HL 250, December 2018, p. 90.

53   https://www.independentschoolparent.com/school/international-schools/ ; see also, Hill and Beadle, *The Art of Attraction*, pp. 25–6.

54   House of Lords, HL 150, p. 118.

55   Creative Industries Council, *CIC, UK to the World, 2019*, at http://www.thecreati veindustries.co.uk/uk-creative-overview/facts-and-figures. Other contributors included £9 billion from 'music, arts and culture', £4 billion from 'design and fashion' and £4 billion from 'architecture'.

56   Francis Fukuyama, *Identity: Contemporary Identity Politics and the Struggle for Recognition*, London, Profile Books, 2018, pp. 180–1.

57   House of Lords, HL 250, p. 93.

58   *Cosmopolitan Magazine*, 21 March 2017. Of the ten 'greatest influencers' six were female, and four male.

59   Statistica, https://www.statista.com/statistics/553582/predicted-social-network-us er-penetration-rate-in-the-united-kingdom-uk/; Businessculture.org, 'Passport to Trade', at https://businessculture.org/northern-europe/uk-business-culture/uk-social-media-guide/

60   Office for National Statistics, https://www.ons.gov.uk/peoplepopulationandcom munity/householdcharacteristics/homeinternetandsocialmediausage

61   Businessculture.org, 'Passport to Trade', at https://businessculture.org/northern-eur ope/uk-business-culture/uk-social-media-guide/

62   Melvin Bragg, *12 Books That Changed the World*, London, Hodder and Stoughton, 2006, pp. 89–118.

63   Mark Gregory, *Premier League: Economic and Social Impact*, London, Ernst and Young, 2019, pp. 2–3.

64   Ibid., p. 10.

65   House of Lords, HL 150, p. 125.

66   Hill and Beadle, *The Art of Attraction*, pp. 6, 23; House of Lords, HL 150, p. 115.

67   Nigeria is second to India, and China – a much more restrictive industry – is nevertheless fourth in the rankings.

68   Liz Forgan, Former Director of Arts Council England, interviewed on the *Today Programme*, Radio 4, 25 March 2019. See also, David Sanderson, 'Arts Fundraisers See Rich Pickings in Trouble Firms', *The Times*, 26 March 2019.

Chapter 13: A strategic surge

1 Leo Tolstoy, *Anna Karenina*, London, Penguin Classics, 2006, p. 1.

2 Richard Barrons and Ewan Lawson, 'Warfare in the Information Age', *RUSI Journal* 161, no. 5 (2016); Sam Jones, 'Britain's "Withered" Forces Not Fit to Repel All-Out Attack', *Financial Times*, 17 September 2016.

3 Assessments were collated across thirty-one different digitization indicators. The countries that exceeded Britain were Denmark, Finland, Sweden and the Benelux countries. See, European Commission, Database Factsheet, *Digital Economy and Society Index (DESI) 2017*, 3 March 2017.

4 Department for Digital, Culture, Media and Sport, *UK Digital Strategy: The Next Frontier in Our Digital Revolution, Gov.UK*, 29 December 2015.

5 Authors' calculations.

6 Michael Clarke, *The Challenge of Defending Britain*, Manchester, Manchester University Press, 2019, pp. 102–3.

7 David Richards and Michael Clarke, 'Britain Needs a Strategic Surge Now to Cope with Brexit', *The Times*, 1 March 2018.

8 Britain's private sector spends some £30 billion annually on R&D and the amount has been increasing. But government and private sector spending combined still amounts to less than 1.5 per cent of Britain's GDP; less than the OECD average and far less in absolute and relative terms than most of the states Britain regards as competitors.

9 Ed Conway, 'Long-Term Limbo Risks a Zombie Economy', *The Times*, 15 March 2019.

10 Words of the Head of the Foreign and Commonwealth Office. See Chapter 11.

11 Edelman Trust Barometer 2019, Global Report, at: https://www.edelman.com/s ites/g/files/aatuss191/files/2019-02/2019_Edelman_Trust_Barometer_Global_Re port.pdf; See also, Ed Williams 'Breakdown of trust has turned us into Disunited Kingdom', *The Times,* 28 January 2019.

12 Vernon Bogdanor, *Beyond Brexit: Towards a British Constitution*, London, I.B. Tauris, 2019, p. 204; Philip Collins, 'Truth Behind the Brexit Myth of the "Left Behind"', *The Times*, 2 August 2019.

13 Matthew Goodwin, 'Tigger MPs Will Lose Their Bounce When They Bump into the Voters', *Sunday Times*, 24 February 2019; 'Letters', *The Times*, 20 February 2019.

14 Linda Colley, *Acts of Union and Disunion*, London, Profile Books, 2014, p. 149.

15 David Goodhart, *The Road to Somewhere: The New Tribes Shaping British Politics*, London, Penguin Books, 2017.

16 Constitutional Reform Group, *Towards a New Act of Union: DP01*, September 2015, p. 4.

17 See, Bogdanor, *Beyond Brexit*, pp. 258-61.

18 *Act of Union Bill (HL)*, HL Bill 132, 9 October 2018, p. 2.

19 See, for example, the work of The Constitution Unit at University College London, and its paper by Meg Russell and Jack Sheldon, *Options for an English Parliament*, London, UCL, 2018.

20 See, House of Lords Library, Briefing, *Leaving the European Union: Stability of the United Kingdom's Union Debate 17 January 2019*, 21 December 2018, p. 17.

21 Ibid.

22 Simon Jenkins, *A Short History of England*, London, Profile Books, 2012, p. 290.

Select bibliography

Abell, Stig, *How Britain Really Works: Understanding the Ideas and Institutions of a Nation*, London, John Murray, 2019.

Aitken, Kent, *Governance in the Digital Age*, Ottawa, Public Policy Forum, 2018.

Aken, Jan van and Hammond, Edward, 'Genetic Engineering and Biological Weapons', *European Molecular Biology Organisation Reports* 4 (2003), pp. 557–60

Akhgar, Babak, Staniforth, Andrew and Bosco, Francesca, eds, *Cyber Crime and Cyber Terrorism*, Amsterdam, Elsevier, 2014.

All-Party Parliamentary Group on Drones, *The UK's Use of Armed Drones*: *Working with Partners*, London, House of Commons APPG, July 2018.

Allison, Graham, *Destined for War: Can America and China Escape the Thucydides Trap?* Boston and New York, Houghton Mifflin Harcourt, 2017.

Ambrose, Stephen E. and Brinkley, Douglas G., *Rise to Globalism: American Foreign Policy Since 1938*, 9th edn, Revised, London, Penguin Books, 2011.

Andrew, Christopher, *The Secret World: A History of Intelligence*, London, Allen Lane, 2018.

Ayres, Alyssa, *Our Time Has Come: How India Is Making Its Place in the World*, Oxford, Oxford University Press, 2018.

Barnett, Anthony, *The Lure of Greatness: England's Brexit and America's Trump*, London, Unbound, 2017.

Barrie, Douglas, Barry, Ben, Boyd, Henry, Chagnaud, Marie-Louise, Childs, Nick, Giegerich, Bastian, Mölling, Christian and Schütz, Torben, *Protecting Europe: Meeting the EU's Military Level of Ambition in the Context of Brexit*, London, International Institute for Strategic Studies/Geselschaft fur Auswartige Politik, November 2018.

Bew, John and Elefteria, Gabriel, *Making Sense of British Foreign Policy after Brexit*, Briefing Paper, London, Policy Exchange, July 2016.

Black, James, Hall, Alex, Cox, Kate, Kepe, Marta, and Silfversten, Erik, *Defence and Security after Brexit*, Santa Monica, CA, RAND Europe, 2017.

Blair, Tony, *A Journey*, London, Arrow Books, 2011.

Blond, Philip, Noyes, James and Sim, Duncan, *Britain's Global Future: Harnessing the Soft Power Capital of UK Institutions*, London, ResPublica, 2017.

Bloomfield, Lincoln P., *The Policy-Making Process*, Englewood Cliffs, NJ, Prentice Hall, 1982.

Bogdanor, Vernon, *Beyond Brexit: Towards a British Constitution*, London, I.B. Tauris, 2019.

Braithwaite, Rodric, 'Russia, Ukraine and the West', *RUSI Journal* 159, no. 2 (April 2014).

Bremmer, Ian, *Us vs. Them: The Failure of Globalism*, London, Portfolio/Penguin, 2018.

Brook-Holland, Louisa, *US Forces in the UK: Legal Arguments*, House of Commons Library, 8 January 2015.

Brooke, Heather, *The Silent State: Secrets, Surveillance and the Myth of British Democracy*, London, Windmill Books, 2010.

Brown, Gordon, *My Life, Our Times*, London, The Bodley Head, 2017.

Bullough, Oliver, Moneyland, London, Profile Books, 2018.

Burke, Edward, 'Who Will Speak for Northern Ireland? The Looming Danger of an Ulster Brexit', *RUSI Journal* 161, no. 2 (April/May 2016).

Burke-White, William W., 'Power Shifts in International Law: Structural Realignment and Substantive Pluralism', *Harvard International Law Journal* 56, no. 1 (2015), pp. 1–80

Burleigh, Michael, *The Best of Times, the Worst of Times: A History of How*, London: Pan Books, 2018.

Cabinet Office, *National Risk Register*, London, HM Government, 2008.

Cabinet Office, *Public Summary of Sector Security and Resilience Plans, 2018*, London, Cabinet Office, 2019.

Cambridge Centre for Risk Studies, *Cyber Terrorism: Assessment of the Threat to Insurance*, Cambridge, CCRS, November 2017.

Castells, Manuel, ed., *Europe's Crises*, Cambridge, Polity Press, 2018.

Chalmers, Malcolm, *The Rules-Based International Systems*: *What Are They? And How Do They Relate to Each Other?*, RUSI Briefing Paper, 2019.

Chilcot, John, Freedman, Lawrence, Gilbert, Martin, Lyne, Roderic, and Prashnar, Baroness, *The Report of the Iraq Inquiry, Volume 8*, London, The Stationery Office, 2016, Section 9.8.

Clarke, Michael, 'Planning and Fighting a War', *RUSI Journal* 161, no. 6 (December 2016).

Clarke, Michael, *The Challenge of Defending Britain*, Manchester, Manchester University Press, 2019.

Clegg, Nick, *How to Stop Brexit (and Make Britain Great Again)*, London, The Bodley Head, 2017.

Clinton, Hillary Rodham, *Hard Choices*, London, Simon and Shuster, 2014.

Coggan, Philip, *The Money Machine: How the City works*, 7th edn, London, Penguin Books, 2015.

Colley, Linda, *Acts of Union and Disunion*, London, Profile Books, 2014.

Colley, Linda, *Britons: Forging the Nation 1707–1837*, London, Pimlico, 1992.

Connelly, Tony, *Brexit and Ireland: The Dangers, the Opportunities, and the Inside Story of the Irish Response,* London, Penguin Books, 2018.

Constitutional Reform Group, *Towards a New Act of Union: DP01*, September 2015.

Cooper, Robert, *The Breaking of Nations: Order and Chaos in the Twenty-First Century*, London, Atlantic Books, 2004.

Cormac, Rory, *Disrupt and Deny: Spies, Special Forces, and the Secret Pursuit of British Foreign Policy*, Oxford, Oxford University Press, 2018.

Council of the European Union, *Common Foreign and Security Policy*, Annual Report *2017*, Brussels, 5 July 2017.

Crocker, Ruth, Webb, Sarah, Garner, Sarah and Skidmore, Michael, *The Impact of Organised Crime on Local Communities*, The Police Foundation, Briefing Paper 4, December 2016.

Croissant, Aurel, Kailitz, Steffen, Koellner, Patrick and Wurster, Stefan, eds, *Comparing Autocracies in the Early Twenty-First Century*, Volume 1, London, Routledge, 2014.

Cronin, Audrey Kurth, *How Terrorism Ends: Understanding the Decline and Demise of Terrorist Campaigns*, Princeton, Princeton University Press, 2009.

Dawisha, Karen, *Putin's Kleptocracy: Who Owns Russia?*, New York, Simon and Shuster, 2014.

Day, Greg, *Virtual Criminology and Threat Reports 2007*, McAfee Online, 2007.

Deighton, Len, *SS-GB*, London, HarperCollins, 2009.

Department of Defense, *US Defense Strategy*, January 2018.

Depledge, Duncan, Dodds, Klaus and Kennedy-Pipe, Caroline, 'The UK's Defence Arctic Strategy: Negotiating the Slippery Geopolitics of the UK and the Arctic', *RUSI Journal* 164, no. 1 (2019): 28–39.

Development Concepts and Doctrine Centre, *Global Strategic Trends: The Future Starts Today*, 6th edn, London, Ministry of Defence, 2018.

Doig, Will, *High Speed Empire: Chinese Expansion and the Future of South East Asia*, Columbia, NY, Columbia University Global Reports, 2018.

Duffy, Bobby and Clemence, Michael, *Global Influence in a Post-Brexit World: Who Is a Force for Good?* London, Ipsos MORI, 2017.

D'Ancona, Matthew, *Post Truth: The New War on Truth and How to Fight Back*, London, Ebury Press, 2017.

Eatwell, Roger and Goodwin, Matthew, *National Populism: The Revolt Against Liberal Democracy*, London, Pelican Books, 2018.

Esposito, John L. and Mogahed, Dalia, *Who Speaks for Islam? What a Billion Muslims Really Think*, New York, Gallup Press, 2007.

European Commission, DG Home, *Evidence for Necessity of Data Retention in the EU*, March 2013.

European Monitoring Centre for Drugs and Drug Addiction & Europol 2016, *EU Drug Markets Report 2016*.

Europol, European Union, *Serious and Organised Crime Threat Assessment (SOCTA) 2017: Crime in the Age of Technology*, Europol, Brussels, 2017.

Ferguson, Niall, *Empire: How Britain Made the Modern World*, London, Penguin Books, 2004.

Ferguson, Niall, *The Great Degeneration: How Institutions Decay and Economies Die*, London, Penguin Books, 2014.

Ferguson, Niall, *The Square and the Tower: Networks, Hierarchies and the Struggle for Global Power*, London, Allen Lane, 2017.

Fletcher, Tom, *The Naked Diplomat: Understanding Power and Politics in the Digital Age*, London, William Collins, 2017.

Foreign Affairs, *The Fourth Industrial Revolution: A Davos Reader*, New York, Council on Foreign Relations, 2016.

Foreign Affairs Committee, *China and the Rules-Based International System, HC 612*, 4 April 2019.

Frankopan, Peter, *The New Silk Roads: The Present and Future of the World*, London, Bloomsbury, 2018.

Freedman, Lawrence, *Ukraine and the Art of Strategy*, Oxford, Oxford University Press, 2018.

Freedom House, *Freedom on the Net 2015: Privatising Censorship, Eroding Privacy*, New York, Freedom House, 2015.

Freeman, George, ed., *Britain Beyond Brexit: A New Conservative Vision*, London, Centre for Policy Studies, 2019.

Fridman, Ofer, 'Hybrid Warfare or Gibridnaya Voyna?: Similar but Different', *RUSI Journal* 162, no. 1 (February 2017).

Fukuyama, Francis, *Identity: Contemporary Identity Politics and the Struggle for Recognition*, London, Profile Books, 2018.

Fukuyama, Francis, *The End of History and the Last Man* London, Penguin Books, 1992.

Gaddis, John L., *On Grand Strategy*, London, Penguin Books, 2018.

Gaddis, John L., *The Cold War*, London, Penguin Books, 2007.

Gaddis, John L., *The Long Peace: Inquiries into the History of the Cold War*, Oxford, Oxford University Press, 1987.

Ghobash, Omar Saif, *Letters to a Young Muslim*, London, Picador, 2017.

Giegerich, Bastian and Molling, Christian, *The United Kingdom's Contribution to European Security and Defence*, London, IISS/DGAP, 2018.

Gifkins, Jess, Jarvis, Samuel and Ralph, Jason, *Global Britain in the United Nations*, London, UNA-UK, 2019.

Glenny, Misha, *McMafia: Seriously Organised Crime*, London, Vintage Books, 2009.

Global Commission on Internet Governance, Centre for International Governance Innovation / Chatham House, Paper Series, No. 8, 2015.

Goodhart, David, *The Road to Somewhere: The New Tribes Shaping British Politics*, London, Penguin Books, 2017.

Gorenburg, Dmitry, *Russia's Military Modernisation Plans 2018–2027*, PONARS Policy Memo 495, Elliott School of International Affairs, George Washington University, November 2017.

Grayling, A. C., *Democracy and Its Critics*, London, Oneworld, 2018.

Gregory, Mark, *Premier League: Economic and Social Impact*, London, Ernst and Young, 2019.

Guilluy, Christophe, *Twilight of the Elites: Prosperity, the Periphery and the Future of France*, New Haven, Yale University Press, 2019.

Guven, Ali Burak, 'Defending Supremacy: How the IMF and the World Bank Navigate the Challenge of Rising Powers', *International Affairs* 93, no. 5 (2017), pp. 1149–66.

Haass, Richard, *A World in Disarray: American Foreign Policy and the Crisis of the Old Order*, London, Penguin, 2018.

Haass, Richard, 'How the World Order Ends: and What Comes in Its Wake', *Foreign Affairs* 98, no. 1 (2019).

Hale, Thomas, Held, David and Young, Kevin, *Gridlock: Why Global Cooperation Is Failing When We Need It Most*, Cambridge, Polity Press, 2013.

Hale, Thomas and Held, David, et al., *Beyond Gridlock*, Cambridge, Polity Press, 2017.

Halpern, David, *Inside the Nudge Unit: How Small Changes Can Make a Big Difference*, London, WH Allen, 2015.

Hameiri, Shahar and Jones, Lee, 'China Challenges Global Governance? Chinese International Development finance and the AIIB', *International Affairs* 94, no. 3 (2018).

Harris, Robert, *Fatherland*, London, Arrow Books, 2009.

Hennessy, Peter, *Whitehall*, London, Secker and Warburg, 1989.

Heuser, Beatrice, *Brexit in History: Sovereignty or a European Union?*, London, Hurst, 2019.

HM Government, *A Strong Britain in an Age of Uncertainty*: *The National Security Strategy*, Cm 7953, October 2010.

HM Government, Cabinet Office and Government Digital Service, *Digital Efficiency Report*, London, 2012.

HM Government, *National Cyber Security Strategy 2016–2021*, London, 2016.
HM Government, *National Security Capability Review*, London, Cabinet Office, March 2018.
HM Government, *National Security Strategy and Strategic Defence and Security Review: A Secure and Prosperous United Kingdom*, cm 9161, November 2015.
HM Government, *Sector Resilience Plan 2015–2016*, London, April 2016.
HM Government, *The National Security Strategy of the United Kingdom: Security in an Interdependent World*, Cm 7291, March 2008.
Hochschild, Arlie Russell, *Strangers in Their Own Land*, New York, The New Press, 2016.
Holslag, Jonathan, *The Silk Road Trap: How China's Trade Ambitions Challenge Europe*, London, Polity Press, 2019.
Home Affairs Committee, *UK-EU Security Cooperation after Brexit: Follow-Up Report HC 1356*, 17 July 2018.
Home Affairs Committee, *UK-EU Security Cooperation after Brexit HC 635*, 21 March 2018.
Hopewell, Kristen, 'The BRICS – Merely a Fable? Emerging Power Alliances in Global Trade Governance', *International Affairs* 93, no. 6 (2017).
House of Commons Defence Committee, *Indispensable Allies: US, NATO and UK Defence Relations*, HC 387, London, June 2018.
House of Commons Defence Committee, *On Thin Ice: UK Defence in the Arctic*, HC 388, 19 July 2018.
House of Commons Defence Committee, *On Thin Ice: Defence in the Arctic: Government Response to the Committee's Twelfth Report*, HC 1659, 18 October 2018.
House of Commons Foreign Affairs Committee, *Global Britain*, HC 780, 12 March 2018.
House of Commons Library, *Brexit Reading List: Global Britain*, Briefing Paper 8338, 22 August 2018.
House of Commons Library, *Leaving the European Union: Stability of the United Kingdom's Union Debate 17 January 2019*, Briefing Paper, 21 December 2018.
House of Lords, *UK Foreign Policy in a Shifting World Order*, HL 250, 18 December 2018.
Howard, Michael, *The Continental Commitment*, London, Pelican Books, 1974.
Howard, Michael, 'What's in a Name? How to Fight Terrorism', *Foreign Affairs* 81, no. 1 (January/February 2002).
Howorth, Jolyon, *Security and Defence Policy in the European Union*, 2nd edn, London, Palgrave Macmillan, 2014.
Human Right Watch, *World Report 2019*, New York, HRW, 2019.
Hurst, Neil and Froggatt, Anthony, *The Reform of Global Energy Governance*, London, Imperial College/Chatham House, Discussion Paper No. 3, 2012.
Husain, Ed, *The House of Islam: A Global History*, London, Bloomsbury, 2018.
Hutton, Will and Adonis, Andrew, *Saving Britain: How We Must Change to Prosper in Europe*, London, Abacus, 2018.
Ikenberry, G. John, *After Victory: Institutions, Strategic Restraint, and the Rebuilding of Order after Major Wars*, Princeton, Princeton University Press, 2000.
International Coalition for the Responsibility to Protect, *The Responsibility to Protect: Report of the International Commission on Intervention and State Sovereignty*, Ottawa, International Development Research Centre, 2001.
International Institute of Strategic Studies, *The Military Balance*, London, IISS, 2017.

Ionescu, Ghita and Gellner, Ernest, eds, *Populism: Its Meaning and National Character*, London, Weidenfeld and Nicolson, 1969.

Jacques, Martin, *When China Rules the World: The End of the Western World and the Birth of a New Global Order*, 2nd edn, London, Allen Lane, 2009.

Jenkins, Simon, *A Short History of England*, London, Profile Books, 2012.

Jenkins, Simon, *A Short History of Europe: From Pericles to Putin*, London, Penguin Books, 2018.

Johnson, Adrian, ed., *Wars in Peace*, London, Royal United Services Institute, 2014.

Johnston, Alastair I., 'Is China a Status Quo Power?' *International Security*, 27, no. 4 (2003), pp. 5–56.

Joint Committee on the National Security Strategy (JCNSS), *Cyber Security of the UK's Critical National Infrastructure*, HC 222 / HL 1708, 19 November 2018.

Jones, Bill and Norton, Philip, *Politics UK*, 7th edn, London, Longman, 2010.

Jones, Richard Wyn, Lodge, Guy, Jeffery, Charlie, Gottfried, Glenn, Scully, Roger, Henderson, Ailsa and Wincott, Daniel, *England and Its Two Unions: The Anatomy of a Nation and Its Discontents*, London, Institute for Public Policy Research, 2013.

Joshi, Shashank, *Indian Power Projection*, Whitehall Paper 85, London, Royal United Services Institute, 2016.

Kaku, Michio, *Physics of the Future: The Inventions That Will Transform Our Lives*, London, Penguin Books, 2011.

Kaldor, Mary, *New and Old Wars: Organised Violence in a Global Era*, Stanford, CA, Stanford University Press, 1999.

Kaplan, Robert, *The Return of Marco Polo's World: War, Strategy and American Interests*, New York, Random House, 2018.

Kazin, Michael, 'Trump and American Populism', *Foreign Affairs*, 95, no. 6 (2016), pp. 17–24.

Kellner, Peter, 'The Balance of Power Lies in the Hands of Two Populist Tribes, Not One', *The Times*, 7 September 2019.

Kennedy, Hugh, *The Caliphate*, London, Pelican Books, 2016.

Kenny, Michael, *The Politics of English Nationhood*, Oxford, Oxford University Press, 2016.

Kenny, Michael and Pearce, Nick, *Shadows of Empire: The Anglosphere in British Politics*, Cambridge, Cambridge University Press, 2018.

Kirton, John J. and Kokotsis, Ella, *The Global Governance of Climate Change: G7, G20 and UN Leadership*, London, Routledge, 2016.

Kissinger, Henry, *World Order*, London, Allen Lane, 2014.

Kofman, Michael and Rojansky, Matthew, 'A Closer Look at Russia's "Hybrid War"', *Kennan Cable* 7, Wilson Center, April 2015.

Kogan, David, *Protest and Power: The Battle for the Labour Party*, London, Bloomsbury, 2019.

Kovisto, Peter, *The Trump Phenomenon: How the Politics of Populism Won in 2016*, Bingley, Emerald Publishing, 2017.

Layne, Christopher, 'The US-Chinese Power Shift and the End of the Pax Americana', *International Affairs* 94, no. 1 (January 2018).

Leiner, Barry M., Cerf, Vinton G., Clark, David D. and Kahn, Robert E., *Brief History of the Internet*, Reston, VA, Internet Society, 1997.

Lesage, D. and Graaf, T. van de, eds, *Rising Powers and Multilateral Institutions*, London, Palgrave Macmillan, 2015.

Levitsky, Steven and Ziblatt, Daniel, *How Democracies Die: What History Reveals About Our Future,* London, Penguin Books, 2019.

Levitt, Theodore, 'The Globalisation of Markets', *Harvard Business Review*, May 1983.

Lewis, Bernard, *The Crisis of Islam: Holy War and Unholy Terror*, London, Phoenix, 2003.

Lewis, David, 'Inroads into Eurasia', *The World Today*, October/November 2016.

Lewis, Stephen, 'Russia's Continued Aggression Against Ukraine: Illegal Actions in the Kerch Strait and Sea of Azov', *RUSI Journal* 164, no. 1 (2019), pp. 18–26.

Lindblom, Charles E., 'The Science of Muddling Through', *Public Administration Review* 19, no. 2 (1959).

Louth, John and Taylor, Trevor, *British Defence in the 21st Century*, London, Routledge, 2019.

Macaes, Bruno, *Belt and Road: A Chinese World Order*, London, Hurst, 2018.

Macron, Emmanuel, *Revolution*, London, Scribe Books, 2017.

Macwhirter, Iain, *Disunited Kingdom: How Westminster Won the Referendum but Lost Scotland*, Glasgow, Cargo Publishing, 2014.

Maddison, Angus, *Chinese Economic Performance in the Long Run, 960–2030*, 2nd edn, Paris, OECD Development Studies Centre, 2007.

Mandelbaum, Michael, *The Ideas That Conquered the World: Peace, Democracy, and Free Markets in the Twenty-First Century*, New York, Public Affairs, 2004.

Mandelbaum, Michael, *The Rise and Fall of Peace on Earth*, Oxford, Oxford University Press, 2019.

Mason, Paul, *Post-Capitalism: A Guide to Our Future*, London, Penguin Books, 2016.

Mattes, M. and Rodriguez, M., 'Autocracies and International Cooperation', *International Studies Quarterly* 58, no. 3 (2013), pp. 527–38.

Mead, Walter Russell, *God and Gold: Britain, America and the Making of the Modern World*, London, Atlantic Books, 2007.

Mead, Walter Russell, 'The Jacksonian Revolt: American Populism and the Liberal Order', *Foreign Affairs* 96, no. 2 (2017), pp. 2–7.

Meek, James, *Private Island: Why Britain Belongs to Someone Else*, London, Verso, 2015.

Meer, S. van der, 'Not That Bad: Looking Back at 65 Years of Nuclear Non-proliferation', *Security and Human Rights* 22, no. 1 (2011).

Ministry of Defence, *Global Strategic Trends*, 6th edn, Shrivenham, Development, Concepts and Doctrine Centre, 2018.

Ministry of Defence, *Mobilising, Modernising and Transforming Defence*: A R*eport on the Modernising Defence Programme*, London, MoD, December 2018.

Moffitt, Benjamin, *The Global Rise of Populism: Performance, Political Style, and Representation*, Stanford, CA, Stanford University Press, 2016.

Monbiot, George, *How Did We Get into This Mess?*, London, Verso Books, 2016.

Monbiot, George, *Out of the Wreckage: A New Politics for an Age of Crisis*, London, Verso, 2018.

Moore, Charles, *Margaret Thatcher: The Authorised Biography*, Vol. 2, London, Penguin Books, 2016.

Morgan, Kenneth O., ed., *The Oxford History of Britain*, Oxford, Oxford University Press, 2010.

Morillas, Pol, *Strategy-Making in the EU: From Foreign and Security Policy to External Action*, London, Palgrave Macmillan, 2018.

Muller, Jan-Werner, *What Is Populism?*, London, Penguin Books, 2017.

Munich Security Conference/McKinsey, *More European, More Connected and More Capable: Building the European Armed Forces of the Future*, Munich, 2019.

Murray, Douglas, *The Strange Death of Europe: Immigration, Identity, Islam*, London, Bloomsbury, 2018.

Narlikar, Amrita, 'India's Role in Global Governance: A Modi-fication?' *International Affairs* 93, no. 1 (2017).

National Audit Office, *Departments' Use of Consultants to Support Preparations for EU Exit*, HC 2105, 7 June 2019.

National Audit Office, *Regulating to Protect Consumers in Utilities, Communications and Financial Services Markets*, HC 992, 15 March 2019.

National Cyber Security Centre, *Annual Review 2018*, October 2018.

National Cyber Security Centre, *Joint US-UK Statement on Malicious Cyber Activity Carried Out by Russian Government*, 16 April 2018.

NATO, *The Secretary General's Annual Report 2017*, NATO Public Diplomacy Division, 15 March 2018.

Neumann, Iver B., 'Russia's Europe, 1991–2016: Inferiority to Superiority', *International Affairs* 92, no. 6 (2016).

Nocetti, Julian, 'Russia's "Dictatorship of the Law" Approach to Internet Policy', *Internet Policy Review* 4, no. 4 (November 2015).

Nordin, Astrid H. M. and Weissmann, Mikael, 'Will Trump Make China Great Again? The Belt and Road Initiative and International Order', *International Affairs* 94, no. 2 (March 2018).

Norrlof, Carla, 'Hegemony and Inequality: Trump and the Liberal Playbook', *International Affairs* 94, no. 1 (2018).

Northedge, F. S., *Descent from Power: British Foreign Policy, 1945–1973*, London, George Allen and Unwin, 1974.

Nye, Joseph S., *Is the American Century Over?*, Cambridge, Polity Press, 2015.

O'Hara, Kieron and Hall, Wendy, *Four Internets: The Geopolitics of Digital Governance*, Centre for International Governance Innovation Paper Series No. 206, 2018.

O'Rourke, Kevin, *A Short History of Brexit: From Brentry to Backstop*, London, Pelican Books, 2019.

O'Toole, Fintan, *Heroic Failure: Brexit and the Politics of Pain*, London, Head of Zeus, 2018.

Obama, Michelle, *Becoming*, London, Viking, 2018.

Oliver, Craig, *Unleasing Demons: The Inside Story of Brexit*, London, Hodder and Stoughton, 2016.

Oliveti, Vincenzo, *Terror's Source: The Ideology of Wahhabi-Salafism and Its Consequences*, Birmingham, Amadeus Books, 2002.

Pantucci, Raffaello, *We Love Death as You Love Life: Britain's Suburban Terrorists*, London, Hurst, 2015.

Pantucci, Raffaello and Lain, Sarah, *China's Eurasian Pivot: The Silk Road Economic Belt*, RUSI Whitehall Paper 68, London, Royal United Services Institute, 2017.

Perry, Damon, *The Global Muslim Brotherhood in Britain: Non-violent Islamist Extremism and the Battle of Ideas*, London, Routledge, 2019.

Petersson, Magnus and Schreer, Benjamin, *NATO and the Crisis in the International Order: The Atlantic Alliance and Its Enemies*, London, Routledge, 2018.

Pezard, Stephanie, Tingstad, Abbie, Van Abel, Kristin and Stephenson, Scott, *Maintaining Arctic Cooperation with Russia: Planning for Regional Change in the Far North*, Santa Monica, CA, RAND Corporation, 2017.

Pifer, Steven, 'Pay Attention America: Russia Is Upgrading Its Military', *Brookings Briefings*, 5 February 2016.

Pimlott, Ben, *Harold Wilson*, London, William Collins, 2016.

Pinker, Steven, *Enlightenment* Now, London, Allen Lane, 2018.

Pinker, Steven, *The Better Angels of Our* Nature, London, Penguin Books, 2011.

Plomin, Robert, *Blueprint: How DNA Makes Us Who We Are*, London, Allen Lane, 2018.

Pool Re, *Terror Threat and Mitigation Report 2018*, 12 November 2018.

Porter, Patrick, 'Advice for a Dark Age: Managing Great Power Competition', *The Washington Quarterly* 42, no. 1 (2019), pp. 7–25.

Powell, Jonathan, *Talking to Terrorists: How to End Armed Conflicts*, London, The Bodley Head, 2014.

Powell, Jonathan, *The New Machiavelli: How to Wield Power in the Modern World*, London, The Bodley Head, 2010.

Ramo, Joshua C., *The Seventh Sense: Power, Fortune, and Survival in the Age of Networks*, New York, Little Brown, 2016.

Richards, Anthony, Margolin, Devorah and Scremin, Nicolo, eds, *Jihadist Terror: New Threats, New Responses*, London, I.B. Tauris, 2019.

Rid, Thomas, *Cyber War Will Not Take* Place, London, Hurst, 2013.

Rogelj, Joeri, Elzen, Michel den, Höhne, Niklas, Fransen, Taryn, Fekete, Hanna, Winkler, Harald, Schaeffer, Rodríguez, Sha, Fu, Riahi, Keywan and Meinshausen, Malte, 'Paris Agreement Climate Proposals Need a Boost to Keep Warming Well Below 2°C', *Nature*, 534, 2016.

Rogers, James, *Towards "Global Britain": Challenging the New Narratives of National Decline*, London, Henry Jackson Society, 2017.

Rogers, Paul, *Irregular War: ISIS and the New Threat from the Margins*, London, I.B. Tauris, 2016.

Rosell, Steven, *Renewing Governance: Governing by Learning in the Information Age*, Oxford, Oxford University Press, 1999.

Rosling, Hans, *Factfulness*, London, Sceptre, 2018.

Russell Hochschild, Arlie, *Strangers in Their Own Land*, New York, The New Press, 2016.

Russell, Meg and Sheldon, Jack, *Options for an English Parliament*, London, UCL, 2018.

Sageman, Marc, *Understanding Terror Networks*, Philadelphia, University of Pennsylvania Press, 2004.

Sainsbury, David, *Progressive Capitalism: How to Achieve Economic Growth, Liberty and Social Justice*, London, Biteback Publishing, 2013.

Sansom, C. J., *Dominion*, London, Mantle, 2012.

Savage, Mike, *Social Class in the 21st Century*, London, Pelican Books, 2015.

Schweller, Randall L. and Pu, Xiaoyu, 'After Unipolarity: China's Vision of International Order in an Era of US Decline', *International Security* 36, no. 1 (2011), pp. 41–72.

Seely, Bob and Rogers, James, *Global Britain: A Twenty-First Century* Vision, London, Henry Jackson Society, 2019.

Sheers, Owen, *Resistance*, London, Faber and Faber, 2011.

Shipman, Tim, *All Out War: The Full Story of Brexit*, London, William Collins, 2017.

Shipman, Tim, *Fall Out: A Year of Political Mayhem*, London, William Collins, 2018.

Simcox, Robin, 'Abu Qatada's Rap Sheet', Henry Jackson Society, 18 January 2012.

Simms, Brendan, *Britain's Europe: A Thousand Years of Conflict and Cooperation*, London, Penguin Books, 2016.

Simon, Luis, *The Spectre of a Westphalian Europe?*, Whitehall Paper 90, London, Royal United Services Institute, 2018.

Singer, P. W. and Friedman, Allan, *Cybersecurity and Cyberwar: What Everyone Needs to Know*, Oxford, Oxford University Press, 2014.

Sloan, Stanley R., *Transatlantic Traumas*, Manchester, Manchester University Press, 2018.

Smith, Rupert, *The Utility of Force: The Art of War in the Modern World*, London, Penguin Books, 2006.

Sridharan, Eswaran, 'Where Is India Headed? Possible Future Directions in Indian Foreign Policy', *International Affairs* 93, no. 1 (January 2017).

Stockholm International Peace Research Institute, *Yearbook*, Stockholm, SIPRI/Oxford University Press, 2017.

Stokes, Doug, 'Trump, American Hegemony and the Future of the Liberal International Order', *International Affairs* 94, no. 1 (2018), pp. 133–50.

Strittmatter, Kai, *We Have Been Harmonised: Life in China's Surveillance State*, Exeter, Old Street Publishing, 2019.

Stuart, Hannah, *Islamist Terrorism: Analysis of Offences and Attacks in the UK 1998–2015*, London, Henry Jackson Society, 2017.

Sunstein, Cass R., *Why Nudge? The Politics of Libertarian Paternalism*, New Haven, NJ, Yale University Press, 2014.

Sutyagin, Igor and Bronk, Justin, Russia's *New Ground Forces*, RUSI Whitehall Paper 89, London, Royal United Services Institute, 2017.

Tassinari, Fabrizio, *Variable Geometries: Mapping Ideas, Institutions and Power in the Wider Europe*, London, Centre for European Policy Studies, November 2006.

Teich, Albert H., et al., eds, *AAAS Science and Technology Policy Yearbook 2003*, New York, American Association for the Advancement of Science, 2003.

The Pentagon, *Summary of the National Defense Strategy of the United States of America*, 19 January 2018.

The White House, *The National Security Strategy of the United States of America*, December 2017.

Tolstoy, Leo, *Anna Karenina*, London, Penguin Classics, 2006.

Tombs, Robert, *The English and Their History*, London, Allen Lane, 2014.

Tooze, Adam, *Crashed: How a Decade of Financial Crisis Changed the World*, London, Allen Lane, 2018.

Tossini, Vitor, 'The Five Eyes: The Intelligence Alliance of the Anglosphere', *UK Defence Journal*, 14 November 2017.

Trenin, Dmitri, *Should We Fear Russia?*, Cambridge, Polity Press, 2014.

Trump, Donald, *Time to Get Tough*, Washington, DC, Regnery Publishing, 2011.

UK Parliament, Intelligence and Security Committee, *Foreign Involvement in the Critical National Infrastructure: The Implications for National Security*, Cm 8629, London, June 2013.

United States Government, DoD, USAF, *When the Ice Melts: Developing Proactive American Strategy for the Eurasian Arctic*, Washington, DC, US Government, 2015.

United States Government, *US National Security Strategy*, January 2018.

Urban, Mark, *The Skripal Files: The Life and Near Death of a Russian Spy*, London, Macmillan, 2018.

Vucetic, Srdjan, *The Anglosphere: A Geneology of a Racialized Identity in International Relations*, Stanford, CA, Stanford University Press, 2011.

Wagner, Markus and Meyer, Thomas M., 'The Radical Right as Niche Parties? The Ideological Landscape of Party Systems in Western Europe, 1980–2014', *Political Studies* 65, no. 1 (2017), pp. 84–107.

Walt, Stephen M., *The Hell of Good Intentions: America's Foreign Policy Elite and the Decline of US Primacy*, New York, Just World Books, 2018.

Wellings, Ben and Baxendale, Helen, 'Euroscepticism and the Anglosphere: Traditions and Dilemmas in Contemporary English Nationalism', *Journal of Common Market Studies*, 53, no. 1 (2015), pp. 123–39.

Wilding, Peter, *What Next? Britain's Future in Europe*, London, I.B. Tauris, 2017.

Wilkinson, Matthew L. N., *The Genealogy of Terror: How to Distinguish between Islam, Islamism and Islamist Extremism*, London, Routledge, 2019.

Woodward, Bob, *Fear: Trump in the White House*, New York, Simon and Shuster, 2018.

Woodward, Bob, *Obama's Wars*, New York, Simon and Shuster, 2010.

Wuerth, Ingrid, *International Law in the Age of Trump: A Post – Human Rights Agenda*, Washington DC, The Lawfare Institute/Brookings Institution, 2016.

Young, Hugo, *One of Us*, London, Pan Books, 1990.

Index